1987
The Supreme Court Review

198
Th

"Judges as persons, or courts as institutions, are entitled to
no greater immunity from criticism than other persons
or institutions . . . [J]udges must be kept mindful of their limitations and
of their ultimate public responsibility by a vigorous
stream of criticism expressed with candor however blunt."
—*Felix Frankfurter*

". . . while it is proper that people should find fault when
their judges fail, it is only reasonable that they should recognize the
difficulties. . . . Let them be severely brought to book,
when they go wrong, but by those who will take the trouble
to understand them."
—*Learned Hand*

THE LAW SCHOOL

THE UNIVERSITY OF CHICAGO

upreme Court Review

EDITED BY

PHILIP B. KURLAND

GERHARD CASPER

AND DENNIS J. HUTCHINSON

 THE UNIVERSITY OF CHICAGO PRESS

CHICAGO AND LONDON

INTERNATIONAL STANDARD BOOK NUMBER: 0-226-46440-7

LIBRARY OF CONGRESS CATALOG CARD NUMBER: 60-14353

THE UNIVERSITY OF CHICAGO PRESS, CHICAGO 60637

THE UNIVERSITY OF CHICAGO PRESS, LTD., LONDON

© 1988 BY THE UNIVERSITY OF CHICAGO, ALL RIGHTS RESERVED, PUBLISHED 1988

PRINTED IN THE UNITED STATES OF AMERICA

TO
PAUL A. FREUND

Who embodies law's mission
"to impose a measure of order
on the disorder of experience
without
stifling the underlying
diversity, spontaneity and disarray."

CONTENTS

RICHARD A. EPSTEIN

TAKINGS: DESCENT
AND RESURRECTION

Private property is one of our oldest legal institutions, and it is one
toward which a profound ambivalence has persisted from ancient
until modern times. In this paper I shall concentrate on the ambivalence to property as it relates to the Supreme Court decisions
during the 1986 Term. But in order to analyze these decisions
correctly it is necessary, however briefly, to place them in the context of the larger philosophical debates over the social function of
private property.

The two sides of the general debate are well marked. On the one
hand, private property has often been praised as the bulwark of
individual liberty, to be held sacred and inviolate against any and
all intrusions. On this view, its protection becomes, as it was for
Locke, the *raison d'etre* for the state. On the other hand, private
property has been attacked as the mark of special privilege—indeed
theft—that allows the lucky few to dominate the unfortunate many.
It becomes the social institution that marks mankind's fall from
grace. Neither of these extreme positions can be maintained. But
quickly having ruled out the extremes, there remains open the
difficult and vexing task of marking the intermediate path.

Today there are many who are openly hostile to private property,
and who would gravitate toward the pole that sharply limits its role
in social, economic, or political affairs.[1] This skeptical attitude to-

Richard A. Epstein is James Parker Hall Professor of Law, University of Chicago.

AUTHOR'S NOTE: I should like to thank William Fischel for his astute comments on an
earlier draft of this paper.

[1]See, e.g., Fiss, Why the State?, 100 Harv. L. Rev. 781 (1987).

ward property has been reflected by the sharply reduced protection that private property has received in modern American constitutional law. If property serves no sensible social function, then why should judges strain to protect it? It was not always so. The Framers gravitated toward the other pole. For, while property was to be held sacred and inviolate, the Framers always shrunk from the logical implications of that position. Lest it fall prey to the same institutional infirmities that undermined the old Articles of Confederation,[2] the Constitution gave the federal government extensive powers to tax, but only for the limited purposes "of the common defence and the general welfare of the United States."[3]

This ambivalence toward private property is reflected as well in the eminent domain clause of the Fifth Amendment: "nor shall private property be taken for public use, without just compensation." If the Framers intended to protect property from all state incursions, then the clause was singularly ill-fitted for its intended purpose.[4] Takings should have been forbidden without individual consent of each owner, except in those cases where the property-holder was guilty of the commission of a tort.[5] No longer may any

---

[2]Articles of Confederation, Article VIII. Federalist No. 30 (Hamilton).

[3]Art. I, §8, cl. 1: "The Congress shall have Power To Lay and collect Taxes, Duties, Imposts and Excises, to pay the Debts and provide for the common Defence and general Welfare of the United States; but all Duties, Imposts and Excises shall be uniform throughout the United States." There is some quarrel over whether the phrase "provide for the common Defence and the general Welfare of the United States" was an independent power unhinged from the rest of the clause. While the punctuation could be improved, I think that the structure of Article I, §8 precludes so extravagant a reading because it renders nugatory the entire structure of enumerated powers.

[4]Here the contrast with the language of the Fourth Amendment is instructive: "The right of the people to be secure in their persons, house, papers, and effects, against unreasonable searches and seizures, shall not be violated. . . ." There is no just compensation provision found here, and the effort to import one, as Judge Posner has suggested, Posner, Rethinking the Fourth Amendment, 1981 Supreme Court Review 49, is highly strained. One way to justify the exclusionary rule under the text of the Fourth Amendment is to note that exclusion of evidence is the next best thing to injunctive relief, given that rights mentioned in the Fourth Amendment should not be "violated"—period.

[5]It also shows that the Framers of the Constitution, while influenced heavily by the Lockean conception that the legislature should not take property without consent—"The *supreme power cannot take* from any man any part of his *property* without his own consent" John Locke, Of Civil Government, Second Treatise §138—deviated from his formulation of the privilege by allowing the taking upon payment of just compensation. It therefore follows that the takings clause should be read as being inspired by Locke's treatise but not as following its language, or its logic, to the end. Such was the attitude that I have taken in Epstein, Takings: Private Property and the Power of Eminent Domain (1985) (hereinafter cited as Epstein,

property owner routinely block the state when it wants to take property for the public use. In most cases, all-out resistance becomes hopeless and the individual owner is allowed only to have damages equal, one would hope, to the loss sustained by the taking in question. Under this grand compromise, the state can use its powers to make the public at large (including the original property owner) better off, but state officials are disciplined in their behavior by the requirement that it pay compensation to the individual property owner, who is thereby not made to shoulder more than his fair share of the public debt. There is therefore a close match between the traditional principles of natural justice on the one hand, and the more consequentialist accounts of social welfare on the other.[6] The same compensation requirement serves the twin goals of equity in the individual case and of imposing sensible restraint on government power—to improve the odds that this power will be exercised only to advance the public welfare generally.

The Takings Clause then stakes out in principle the right middle ground between the absolute protection of private property on the one hand, and its total constitutional disregard on the other. But it does so only in the most general terms, and leaves the details of the constitutional compromise to be worked out by interpretation. That task is more formidable than it might at first appear. Thus it is highly misleading to think that the overall possibilities are exhausted by three discrete choices: full protection, no protection, or partial protection. While the two end points do represent single unambiguous (and unacceptable) positions, the intermediate position of partial protection of property is not a unique point, but a large set that contains a vast array of different approaches that share in common only their rejection of the two extremes. No matter how hard or often it tries the Supreme Court seems unable to develop any coherent principles that mark either right or stable choices in that large middle ground.

Takings). The point was misunderstood in Note, Richard Epstein on the Foundations of Takings Jurisprudence, 99 Harv. L. Rev. 796 (1986), which, among its many weaknesses, failed to note the significance of the textual differences between Locke's formulation and that contained in the Takings Clause itself. It is also instructive to note that Locke had no place for judicial review in his scheme of governance, which again sets his vision apart from that of our Constitution.

[6]For further elaboration, see Epstein, A Last Word on Eminent Domain, 41 Miami L. Rev. 253 (1986).

The results in three very important takings cases last term confirm anew that the Court's vacillations and indecisions have yet to run their course. The reason for the confused, and often contradictory, results is that the Supreme Court has never been prepared to give the Takings Clause the natural reading that its text suggests. Instead it has contented itself with the general observation that there is no "set formula" for takings cases and that "essentially ad hoc, factual inquiries" are the best that it can do in so complex an area[7]—usually as a prelude for denying the constitutional claim.[8] The cases continue to mount up, and the pressures to distinguish and to reconcile them increase, until this array of ad hoc decisions becomes wholly incomprehensible to legal and lay observer alike.[9]

In the past one could say with some confidence that the intellectual disarray was in the service of a political balancing act of the first order: to reconcile the explicit constitutional protection of private property with the massive social and economic regulation of the activist and welfare state that started before the New Deal, and that was fully legitimated by it. But during this past Term, the confusion has deepened because the philosophical agenda of the Court has lost much of its original purity. There are now some clear hints that the Court is prepared to recognize that the Takings Clause places barriers in the way of unbounded social planning, just as the first amendment places barriers in how Congress and the states may regulate religion or speech.

The 1986 Term brought forth three major takings cases, each of them a surprise in its own right. But these cases did not generate any consistent world view, as one might expect given the shifting composition of the Court.[10] The first case, *Keystone Bituminous Coal Ass'n v. DeBenedictis*,[11] shatters any easy illusion about the unity of the law, for it marks yet another step in the apparently remorseless expansion of state power, gutting, although not explicitly overrul-

---

[7]The theme is reasserted again in Keystone Bituminous Coal Ass'n v. DeBenedictis, 107 S.Ct. 1232, 1247 (hereinafter cited as *Keystone*).

[8]See, *e.g.*, Penn Central Transp. Co. v. New York City, 438 U.S. 104 (1978).

[9]See, *e.g.*, Ackerman, Private Property and the Constitution (1977).

[10]See Easterbrook, Ways of Criticizing the Court, 95 Harv. L. Rev. 802 (1982), for an account of the difficulties in aggregating individual preferences into consistent institutional choices. But the conflicts here are surely greater, going as well to matters of first principles on the function of both government and property.

[11]107 S.Ct. 1232.

ing, the celebrated decision of *Pennsylvania Coal Co. v. Mahon*.[12] The next two cases, however, saw the Supreme Court take a far more protective stance toward private property, with revised majorities. In *First English Evangelical Lutheran Church of Glendale v. County of Los Angeles*,[13] the Court by a six to three vote imposed important limitations upon the ability of the state to impose temporary restrictions on land use, without paying compensation. In the last case, *Nollan v. California Coastal Commission*,[14] the Court by a narrow five to four majority took refuge in the difficult doctrine of unconstitutional conditions to hold that the Takings Clause does place some limitations upon the power of the state to regulate the use and development of private real estate.

A unified conceptual framework is necessary to analyze these decisions. In past work I have identified four general questions, which taken together exhaust the relevant issues in takings cases.[15]

First, has there been a taking of private property?

Second, if so, has it been justified under the police power so that no compensation need be paid?

Third, if not, has the taking been for a public use? and

Fourth, if so, has just compensation, be it in cash or kind, been provided?

The remainder of this paper uses this framework as a guide for general discussion, and in order to show how the answer to particular cases, however prosaic they appear, quickly drives us back toward general theory.

I. KEYSTONE BITUMINOUS COAL V. DEBENEDICTIS

The first of these three cases, *Keystone Bituminous Coal Ass'n v. DeBenedictis*, was in a sense a replay of the Supreme Court's 1922 decision of *Pennsylvania Coal Co. v. Mahon*, with only one substantial difference—the outcome. The social and economic background of both cases is identical. Pennsylvania is a state with extensive coal

---

[12]260 U.S. 393 (1922).

[13]107 S.Ct. 2378 (1987) (hereinafter cited as *First English*).

[14]107 S.Ct. 3141 (1987) (hereinafter cited as *Nollan*).

[15]See Epstein, Takings; I have also used this framework in the earlier paper I wrote on eminent domain, Epstein, Doctrine, Not Deference: The Eminent Domain Cases, 1982 Supreme Court Review 351, 353–55.

resources located under its land, and the question, which should delight any economic analyst, is how does the owner of the land maximize the joint value of two inconsistent uses, that of the surface and the mineral rights below. The Pennsylvania landowners did not await the growth of economic theory in order to reach their own conclusion on the question. In the years between 1890 and 1920, a large number of landowners sold the mineral rights to coal companies in standard transactions whereby the surface owners expressly took the risk of cave-ins and subsidence from mining operations. The sales of the mineral rights made perfectly good sense because the companies had far greater expertise in mining coal than did the surface owners. It was therefore possible to find some price greater than the value of the coal to landowners, but less than its value to the coal companies. The transfer of the mineral rights therefore left both sides better off than they were before the deal took place.

Yet, it may be asked, why did the original owners retain the surface rights? If these had been transferred, then the coal owners would not have had to worry about the danger of lawsuit from cave-in or subsidence, and they surely could have drawn up simpler deeds without the divided ownership of the land. Yet there are drawbacks to this solution as well. The coal companies would have had to increase the purchase price paid to the original owners, when there is no reason to think that the surface rights were worth more to the coal companies than to the people already using them. Unlike the purchase of the mineral rights, the purchase of the surface rights only would move resources from higher to lower value uses.

Once the original landowners retained the surface rights, it became necessary to anticipate conflicts that might arise from the inconsistent use of surface and mining rights. The most evident conflict concerns that over cave-in and subsidence. If this question had been left unmentioned in the original conveyances, then the courts would have to fill in the gaps as best they could. This gap-filling exercise is often chancy and uncertain, given the weaknesses in the available theories as to what the parties "would have intended." Yet for these conveyances of mineral rights, the uncertainty had been resolved in favor of the surface owner by the 1917 Pennsylvania case of *Penman v. Jones*,[16] which held that unless the rights

---

[16]100 A.2d 1042 (1917). It is worth mentioning that the question of contract construction was not authoritatively resolved until long after some important grants had been made. The clarity of *Penman's* default rule is all to the good. It is less clear whether it is the best rule.

of support had been clearly waived by the owner of the surface estate, they were retained by him notwithstanding any sale of the mineral rights.

Pennsylvania Coal and *Keystone* did not, however, turn on the vagaries of the implied term. The risk of subsidence of surface lands is neither remote nor improbable. It is the ordinary stuff of coal mining. The parties therefore did direct their attention to this question, and by explicit terms agreed that the risk of subsidence should fall on the surface owner, The logic behind this choice must have been as follows. It makes no sense to avoid the conflict of interest by having the coal companies acquire the surface as well as the mineral rights, for then the interim use value of the land before subsidence (which itself need never come) is lost to both sides. Since by their joint subjective evaluations the right to mine is more valuable to the companies than the right to the fully protected surface is to the landowner, then the surface owner should take the risk of failure, while retaining the benefit of the use of the land until the subsidence occurred. This result was achieved by having the surface owner sign over the support rights, the so-called "third" or support estate, to the mineral company. The full deal is thus what one would expect from the ordinary economics of property rights, and the Coase theorem.[17] The transaction costs between the parties were low, so that rights and duties, including the risk of loss, were allocated to maximize the joint value of the whole. Whatever the surface owner lost in the value of the support rights, he gained by an appropriate upward adjustment of the sale price of the mineral rights to the coal company. There were too many transactions on identical terms for everyone to have gotten the economics wrong.

As a case of private bargaining, then, the transaction between the coal companies and the surface owners proved to be quite stable. At any relevant time, individual surface owners could have reacquired by purchase the support rights for their land from the coal companies. The paperwork was simple enough, but undoing the original deal did not make economic sense, if only because the coal companies rightly would demand a very high price to surrender support rights under one piece of land which could well limit their capacity to work large tracts of coal under adjacent parcels. Once acquired, therefore, the title to the mineral and the support rights

---

[17]Coase, The Problem of Social Cost, 3 J. Law & Econ. 1 (1960).

tended to remain in place—at least insofar as private markets were concerned.

The account does not, however, mean that the value of the support rights was worth little or nothing to the surface owner. Quite the opposite, a priori it makes perfectly good sense to assume that these support rights were worth a great deal to the surface owners— even if they were worth more to the coal companies. What owner wants to have houses and fields fall into large holes in the ground? This assignment of property rights, while stable in private economic markets, need not prove stable in political markets, however, where very different decision rules operate, especially when there are no constitutional constraints on legislative behavior. While no surface owner may be prepared to pay the coal companies what it takes to recover the support rights, many surface owners may well be quite willing to invest the smaller sums needed to persuade the legislatures to pass laws that will prevent the coal companies from mining in ways that cause damage or subsidence to coal properties. These opportunities are always present because the distribution of votes and political influence is not the same as the distribution of property rights, if only because the coal companies do not vote, and their shareholders may well reside out of state. Coal companies (or for that matter, their unions) are never without their political clout, but clout is not the same as invincibility. In principle there is no reason to think that the landowners must necessarily fail. Their relative political power could be, and indeed has proved, quite sufficient to get the legislature to move to upset the distribution of property rights between coal companies and surface owners that the contracts between them had mandated. Pennsylvania offers two powerful illustrations of the political process at work, and both ended up in the Supreme Court, where they received strikingly different treatment.

The first manifestation of the political power of landowners was the Kohler Act, passed by Pennsylvania in 1921, which provided that it shall be unlawful "so to conduct the operation of mining anthracite coal as to cause the caving-in, collapse, or subsidence" of a wide class of both public and private structures including public buildings, bridges, churches, schools, hospitals, hotels, and the like in addition to "any dwelling used as a human habitation, or any factory, store or other industrial or mercantile establishment."[18] The

---

[18]Penn. Pub. L. 1921, p. 1198, which is set out in *Pennsylvania Coal*, 260 U.S. 393 n. 1.

effect of these restrictions was to undermine the covenant that was contained in the original sale of the mineral rights, and to do so without providing any monetary compensation, let alone any just compensation, for the surface owners. Justice Holmes wrote a short and powerful opinion about the case, which reversed the decision below,[19] and found that the statute worked a taking of property which was not justified by the operation of the police power. In so reaching his decision, Holmes was quite concerned to distinguish these cases from the rent control statutes, whose constitutionality he had sustained just a year before in *Block v. Hirsh*.[20]

Holmes noted that the Kohler Act imposed permanent restrictions upon the owner of the mineral rights, for which no compensation at all was paid. The rent control statutes were another matter. "The late decisions upon law dealing with the congestion of Washington and New York, caused by the war, dealt with laws intended to meet a temporary emergency and provided for compensation determined to be reasonable by an impartial board. They went to the verge of the law but fell far short of the present act."[21] These statutes were quite another tradition, even if it were assumed that their operation provided some large public benefit. "We are in danger of forgetting that a strong public desire to improve the public condition is not enough to warrant achieving the desire by a shorter cut than the constitutional way of paying for the change."[22] And earlier in the same vein he had written:[23]

> The protection of private property in the Fifth Amendment presupposes that it is wanted for public use, but provides that it shall not be taken for such use without compensation. A similar assumption is made in the decisions upon the Fourteenth Amendment. When this seemingly absolute protection is qualified by the police power, the natural tendency of human nature is to extend the qualification more and more until at last private

---

[19]274 Pa. St. 489 (1921).

[20]256 U.S. 135 (1921). See also the companion cases, Marcus Brown Holding Co. v. Feldman, 256 U.S. 170 (1921); Levy Leasing Co. v. Siegel, 258 U.S. 242 (1922).

[21]*Pennsylvania Coal*, 260 U.S. at 416. In so writing he followed the lead of the Pennsylvania Coal's counsel. *Id.* at 402–03. (Though he did not argue the case, John W. Davis was listed first on the brief.) Holmes was a bad prophet on rent control. The statutes have proved to be permanent, the compensation provided inadequate, and the boards the subject of rampant political squabbling.

[22]*Id.* at 416.

[23]*Id.* at 415.

property disappears. But this cannot be accomplished in this way under the Constitution of the United States.

The position that Holmes announced in *Pennsylvania Coal* can be instructively analyzed in terms of the four questions set out above. First, it is clear that private property has been taken by the state. The support estate is a valuable interest in real property recognized and protected under Pennsylvania law. "[The statute] purports to abolish what is recognized in Pennsylvania as an estate in land—a very valuable estate—and what is declared by the Court below to be a contract hitherto binding on the plaintiffs."[24] Indeed the result could hardly be otherwise under any system which recognized the rights of owner to dispose of some portion of his property while retaining the rest.

By the same token the taking is not justified (without compensation) under the police power. Here Holmes does not give the clean account of the police power that would make this conclusion plausible, but only notes that the power could not be expanded indefinitely if the institution of private property is to survive. The reason for his indecision rests no doubt upon his earlier opinion concluding that the rent control acts do lie within the scope of the police power. It is here that his intellectual difficulties really begin. The ordinary apartment lease is a contract between landlord and tenant, which allocates the risk of price movements between the parties, as clearly as the sale the mineral estate allocates the risk of cave-in and subsidence. The sensible line for the police power is the line between harms inflicted upon strangers to the contract and harms inflicted upon persons who have consented to the risk.[25] It is in effect the line which prevents ownership of private property to be a cloak for aggression or fraud against others.

Now that Holmes already has crossed that fatal line, he does not have any coherent position that explains why the state may override the expression of consent in one case but not in the next. Yet he understands well enough that private property cannot survive if consent, when obtained without force and fraud, may be routinely disregarded as a source of obligation and right. He therefore reaches the right conclusion, relying on intermediate grounds—the use of

---

[24]*Id.* at 414.

[25]For an elaboration, see Epstein, Takings, chs. 9 & 10.

an impartial board, the payment of some rent—to distinguish away the rent control cases. But these factors only show that there was a taking with partial compensation; they do not show that there was either justification for no compensation, or the payment of full compensation. Having gotten round the difficulties of the moment, Holmes does not give any theoretical account of what the limitations of the police power are. The weakness was to be of great importance in *Keystone*—where it was effectively exploited by Justice Stevens.

Turn next to public use. Here Holmes's position is emphatic: the public use requirement is quite distinct from the police power limitation. While there are some substantive limitations on the police power, the public use requirement, it appears, is satisfied, almost routinely, as the subsequent cases have held.[26] But the issue is in fact far more vexed in principle, given that these cases all involve a transfer of property rights from A, the coal companies, to B, the surface owners, under circumstances where voluntary transactions do not seem to be particularly difficult to consummate. One could therefore argue that the transfer is for "private use," or take, as I have done elsewhere, the position that the transaction would meet the public use requirement if the surface owners could be made to divide the gains from the forced condemnation with the coal companies, so that both sides are left better off than before.[27]

Holmes was correct not to trouble himself deeply about public use, because the statute in any event flunked the just compensation requirement. Of cash payments there were certainly none, so the statute survives only if a sufficient implicit in-kind benefit from the regulation enures to the benefit of the burdened mineowner.[28] Just such a benefit was identified by Holmes in the earlier case of *Plymouth Coal Co v. Pennsylvania*,[29] where the mineowners were all required to leave a pillar of coal by the edge of the property line, for their mutual safety and security. In cases like this compensation that one mineowner receives is from his neighbor's discharge of the parallel obligation of support. It is just this idea that led Holmes

---

[26]Berman v. Parker, 348 U.S. 26 (1954); Hawaiian Housing Authority v. Midkiff, 467 U.S. 229 (1984).

[27]See, Epstein, Takings, ch. 12.

[28]For a discussion of implicit in-kind compensation, see generally Epstein, Takings, ch. 14.

[29]232 U.S. 531 (1914) (per Pitney, J.).

to formulate his famous rule that the "regulation secured the average reciprocity of advantage that has been recognized as a justification of various laws."[30] Nothing of the sort is present in the instant case, however. Far from having regulations that work for the reciprocal benefit and burden of all mineowners as a class, the statute imposes regulations that hurt mineowners as a class and help surface owners as a class. As there is no compensation explicit or implicit, Holmes reached the right conclusion that the statute was unconstitutional.

Pennsylvania Coal has long been regarded as perhaps the single most important decision in the takings literature.[31] Its clear insistence that the just compensation requirement bites in at least some instances of general regulation has been the major reason why takings law has not been wholly swallowed up by an expansive construction of the twin exceptions to the takings clause—the police power and implicit in-kind compensation—that are necessarily part of the overall development of takings doctrine.

The issue that was settled in uneasy fashion by *Pennsylvania Coal* was undone in *Keystone*. The statute challenged in *Keystone* was the 1966 Bituminous Mine Subsidence and Land Conservation Act,[32] which, as its title suggests, was concerned with bituminous instead of anthracite coal. That distinction to one side, the parallel between the 1921 Kohler Act and the 1966 Preservation Act was almost eerie, as the key provisions of the later statute were carbon copies of the earlier one. In substance the 1966 statute provided that "in order to protect the health, safety and general welfare of the public," no one was allowed to mine in ways that caused subsidence to a wide variety of public structures and to any dwelling used for

---

[30]*Pennsylvania Coal*, 260 U.S. at 415. Here Holmes takes a little liberty with Justice Pitney's opinion in *Plymouth Coal*. Pitney did not stress the implicit in-kind compensation arguments between neighboring landowners. Rather he held that these regulations were justified under the police power for the protection of the employees in the mine. 232 U.S. at 540. In so doing Pitney reflected the general understanding of his time that the police power trumped private contracts on matters of employee health and safety. Indeed, *Plymouth Coal* conceded the basic validity of the regulation, but raised a limited due process challenge to the indefinite administrative procedures used for determining pillar size.

[31]See, *e.g.*, Ackerman, Private Property and the Constitution 156—analyzing "what is both the most important and the most mysterious writing in takings law—Mr. Justice Holmes's opinion, for the Supreme Court, in Pennsylvania Coal Co. v. Mahon." See also, Rose, Why the Takings Issue Is Still a Muddle, 57 So. Cal. L. Rev. 561 (1984).

[32]Pa. Stat. ann., Title 52, §1406.1 et seq. (Purdon Supp. 1986).

human habitation, unless they had first obtained the consent of the surface owner and fully repaired or compensated the resulting damage.[33] Pursuant to the statute, the Pennsylvania Department of Environmental Resources promulgated regulations that required the coal companies to keep in place some 50 percent of the coal located below or near the stated structures in order to provide surface support. It was taken as given that some 27 million tons of coal, or about 2 percent of the total, had to be left in place in order to comply with the statute. No findings were made as to the increased costs that the regulations imposed upon the companies with respect to the coal that they were allowed to remove, quite possibly by more expensive methods.

Given the virtual identity of the two statutes, the plaintiff's strategy was to argue that the holding in *Pennsylvania Coal* dictated the outcome in the instant case. At first blush the strategy seems sensible—but it failed. It is instructive to note how Justice Stevens was able to evade the force of a precedent which appears to be on all fours with the present case.

The initial foray against Holmes in *Pennsylvania Coal* was procedural. The challenge to the Kohler Act arose when a surface

---

[33]The full text reads:

Section 4. Protection of surface structures against damage from cave-in collapse, or subsidence.

In order to guard the health, safety and general welfare of the public, no owner, operator, lessor, lessee, or general manager, superintendent or other person in charge of or having supervision over any bituminous coal mine shall mine bituminous coal so as to cause damage as a result of the caving-in, collapse or subsidence of the following surface structures in place on April 27, 1966, overlying or in the proximity of the mine

(1) Any public building or any noncommercial structure customarily used by the public, including but not being limited to churches, schools, hospitals, and municipal utilities or municipal public dwelling service operations.

(2) Any dwelling used for human habitation; and

(3) Any cemetery or public burial ground; unless the current owner of the structure consents and the resulting damage is fully repaired or compensated.

The 1966 Act applied to all structures, while the earlier Kohler Act was largely limited to structures located in towns and villages. This difference in scope reflects the fact that anthracite coal is concentrated around Scranton, while bituminous deposits are widely spread out in the western portions of the state. If city lands are worth more than country lands, then ironically it seems that the state may make greater use of its police power to protect lands of relatively little value than it can to protect lands of greater value.

owner filed an action to stop the mining that threatened to undermine his house. In a sense therefore the case did involve, as Justice
Holmes noted in his opinion, "a single house."[34] The question of
principle, of course, transcended this isolated case, because what
was at issue was the facial validity of the statute whose operation
had vast consequences throughout the state. Holmes duly noted
the point:[35]

> But the case has been treated as one in which the general validity
> of the statute should be discussed. The Attorney General of
> the State, the City of Scranton, and the representatives of other
> extensive interests were allowed to take part in the argument
> below and have submitted their contentions here. It seems,
> therefore, to be our duty to go farther in the statement of our
> opinion, in order that it may be known at once, and that further
> suits should not be brought in vain.

In essence Holmes had the good sense to conclude that so long
as the challenge was to the statute on its face, it was best to have
all interested parties brief the case in order to reach the soundest
possible decision once and for all. Stevens, however, turns Holmes's
declaration about "our duty" into the incredible observation that
"uncharacteristically—Justice Holmes provided the parties with an
advisory opinion discussing the general validity of the Act,"[36] an
observation that eluded Justice Brandeis, who cared about such
things, in his lone dissent in *Pennsylvania Coal*.[37] Stevens's assertion
that Holmes issued an advisory opinion would only make sense if
the statute could not be declared unconstitutional on its face.[38] But
Mahon was argued and written on the ground that the plaintiff's
challenge was facial, as indeed it was. Any variation between cases
might concern such factual details as whether this mining operation
will result in subsidence to that house. But the basic structure of
the statute is invariant across all these cases, because the statute

---

[34]*Pennsylvania Coal*, 260 U.S. at 413.

[35]*Id*. at 414–15.

[36]*Keystone*, 107 S.Ct. at 1241.

[37]260 U.S. at 416. See, *e.g.*, his opinion in Ashwander v. Tennessee Valley Authority,
297 U.S. 288, 341 (1936).

[38]Such was the position wrongly reached by the Supreme Court when it ducked the facial
challenge to Hodel v. Virginia Surface Mining and Reclamation Ass'n, 452 U.S. 264 (1981),
on which Stevens heavily relied. See *Keystone*, 107 S.Ct. at 1247. I have criticized *Hodel* in
Epstein, Takings, at 124–25.

never provides any compensation for any coal owner whose rights
to remove coal from the earth have been abrogated. Far from issuing
an advisory opinion, Holmes rightly concluded that the defect of
the Kohler Act was so grave that it had to be struck down on its
face. To say that this opinion should be confined to a single house,
or as Stevens elsewhere suggested, to its "particular facts," is like
saying that *Erie Railroad v. Tompkins*[39] was a railroad trespass case,
or *Marbury v. Madison*[40] a case about a disappointed officeholder
asking for a commission.

There was cunning in Stevens's procedural declamations. Once
he had demoted the authority of Holmes's observations essentially
to gratuitous dicta, he was free to start afresh with the substantive
analysis, which rested heavily upon precedents that had been decided after *Pennsylvania Coal.* In his opinion Stevens organizes his
discussion around the categories that have become fashionable in
modern takings law—that is the ad hoc inquiries into such factors
as "the economic impact of the regulation, its interference with
reasonable investment backed expectations, and the character of the
government action."[41] The effect of this reformulation of the problem is, of course, to distance the analysis of the takings question
from the original constitutional text which it is supposed to expli-
cate. The fluidity of the analysis is well shown by Stevens's treatment, for he predictably decides that the interference with private
rights is small and the government justification for that interference
is large. Nonetheless it is, I believe, more instructive to reorient
his analysis so that it is directed toward the same set of four questions raised by the Clause itself, and addressed in Holmes's opinion
in *Pennsylvania Coal.* The rerun of the script hardly produces a
duplicate of the original play.

On the first question, it is clear first that Stevens works from the
modern view that there are strong distinctions between regulations,
including "mere restrictions" upon use, and takings of property.
He also accepts the basic position that the ownership of the thing
is not lost so long as the owner is able to make some productive
use of it. Within his framework, the question then turns on the
identification of the whole "thing" which is owned by the mineown-

---

[39]304 U.S. 64 (1938).

[40]1 Cranch. 137 (1803).

[41]107 S.Ct. at 1247, citing Kaiser Aetna v. United States, 444 U.S. 164, 175 (1979).

ers, and the part of it that is taken by the state. Here if the support estate and the mineral estate are treated as separate entities, then the mineowners have lost all of one bit of property, even if the state regulation has left some second piece of property untouched. The consequence that follows under current law is that we have crossed the line between permitted regulation and improper taking, so that compensation is now in order. On the other hand, however, if the support estate is treated as incident to the larger mineral estate, then the Pennsylvania statute only has a small effect upon the entire holdings of the mineowner. Stevens makes the sensible argument that the economic use of the support estate is so closely tied to the mineral interest; there is one large estate, only a small fraction of which is taken over by the regulation. His conclusion therefore is that the owner retains enough of the property he started with so that no compensation is in order. Given his premises, the conclusion is hardly indubitable, but depending upon one's taste in abstract metaphysics, it might well be correct.

The problem with his analysis is that his distinction between regulations and takings is itself incoherent. The difficulty itself has long been recognized in the literature, and the problem has been raised with just this example by Professor Michelman in his classic article on the subject.[42] Stevens dutifully cites Michelman when he writes: "Because our test for regulatory taking requires us to compare the value that has been taken from the property with the value that remains in the property, one of the critical questions is determining how to define the unit of property 'whose value is to furnish the denominator of the fraction.' "[43] In so doing Stevens distorts what Michelman wrote and understood. The quoted language is from the first section of Michelman's article, written in an overtly skeptical and critical fashion. Thus Michelman wrote of that section: "The purpose is the limited one of showing that none of the standard criteria yields a sound and self-sufficient rule of decision—that each of them, when attempts are made to erect it into a general principle, is either seriously misguided, ruinously incomplete, or

---

[42]Michelman, Property, Utility, and Fairness: Comments on the Ethical Foundations of "Just Compensation" Law, 80 Harv. L. Rev. 1165 (1967) (hereinafter cited as Michelman).

[43]107 S.Ct. at 1248. The portion in the quoted brackets is from Michelman, note 42 *supra*, at 1192.

uselessly overbroad."[44] His discussion of the numerator and denominator is designed to show the weakness of that test which asks
"whether the claimant's loss is or is not outweighed by the public's
concomitant gain."[45] Nonetheless, Stevens then proceeds to undertake in sober fashion the very inquiry that Michelman regards as
ruinous or worse—reaching ironically the view opposite to that
which Michelman probably endorsed on the question.[46]

To be sure, Stevens is able today to assemble a good bit of case
law on his side, including *Penn Central Transportation v. New York
City.*[47] But no amount of precedent can render coherent a position
that is not. The general principle of eminent domain law has always
been, and logically must be, this: What has the state taken, and
not what has the owner retained.[48] It is clear that Supreme Court
doctrine recognizes that partial takings are covered as much by the
eminent domain clause as total takings are. The state cannot simply
take an acre from a large estate so long as it leaves the owner a
handsome residue. All this is not to say, however, that there are
no differences between a taking of the whole and a taking of the
part.

Where takings are partial and limited, it is more likely that they
will be justifiable under some limited account of the police power.
The antinuisance justification under the police power, for example,

---

[44]*Id.* at 1184.

[45]*Ibid.*

[46]Thus Michelman wrote:

> Inasmuch as mining rights are well recognized, divisible interests in land, and
> inasmuch as "rights" to particular surface uses have come to be recognized as
> species of "property" under the label of "easement" or "servitude," why not say
> that my land consists of two "things"—mining rights and surface rights, or
> foundry rights and residue—and that the relevant denominator in testing a
> regulation which impinges only on mining rights or foundry rights is the value
> of *those* rights—which the regulation totally destroys.

Id. at 1193.

[47]438 U.S. 104 (1978). "In deciding whether a particular governmental action has effected
a taking, this Court focuses rather both on the character of the action and on the nature of
the interference with rights *in the parcel as a whole*—here the city tax block designated as the
'landmark site.' " *Id.* at 130–31 (italics in both *Keystone* and *Penn Central*).

[48]See, Epstein, Takings, at 62. Similarly the rule on damages follows the same lead. "It
is the owner's loss, not the takers gain, which is the measure of the value of the property
taken." United States v. Causby, 328 U.S. 256, 261 (1946).

might well excuse the state from having to pay compensation when it shuts down a landowner's pig farm, so long as it allows him other uses of his property. It will not excuse the state from paying compensation if it both shuts down the pig farm and takes possession of the land for itself. Similarly, where the imposed limitations are small, and the benefits thereby created are diffuse, then partial taking may well be one for which the state regulation has simultaneously supplied implicit-in-kind compensation to the regulated landowner. This was clearly the point to which Holmes had directed his remarks about the average reciprocity of advantage.[49]

Yet once these various differences are taken into account, it never follows that the eminent domain clause does not reach the case at all simply because only small amount of property—whether in percentage or absolute terms—has been taken. If the state takes the life estate or the term, it cannot avoid compensation because the original owner keeps the reversion.[50] When the state took the overflight easement in *United States v. Causby*,[51] compensation was owed to the owner of the soil, whether he had retained the full title in fee, or had separated his mineral estate. There is no obvious explanation as to why the restrictions upon use at issue here should be treated any differently. So long as the use in question is part of the original bundle of property rights, then its loss is a partial taking of part of the property in question, one which presumptively requires compensation.[52] This view allows one to give a consistent and coherent answer to all takings questions, without having to identify first what constitutes "the" property in question. Whether we speak of the entire taking of the small whole, or of the partial taking of the large whole, the constitutional constraints are the same, and the outcome invariant. Holmes himself understood the point when he wrote:[53]

---

[49]See Epstein, Takings, ch. 14, for a further explication.

[50]The point is important in *First English*. See also Kimball Laundry Co. v. United States, 338 U.S. 1 (1949); United States v. Petty Motor Co., 327 U.S. 372 (1946); United States v. General Motors Corp., 323 U.S. 373 (1945), all involving leasehold interests of indefinite terms.

[51]328 U.S. 256 (1947).

[52]I defend this position at length in Takings, chs. 5–8.

[53]*Pennsylvania Coal*, 260 U.S. at 414. It is just this sentiment that Michelman seems to echo in the passage quoted supra.

It is our opinion that the act cannot be sustained as an exercise
of the police power so far as it affects the mining of coal under
streets or cities in places where the right to mine such coal has
been reserved. As said in a Pennsylvania case, "For practical
purposes, the right to coal consists in the right to mine it."
Commonwealth v. Clearview Coal Co., 256 Pa. St. 328, 331. What
makes the right to mine coal valuable is that it can be exercised
with profit. To make it commercially impracticable to mine
certain coal has very nearly the same effect for constitutional
purposes as appropriating or destroying it.

The effort by Stevens to distinguish this language reads as follows: "We do not consider Justice Holmes' statement that the Kohler
Act made mining of 'certain coal' commercially impracticable as
requiring us to focus on the individual pillars of coal that must be
left in place. That statement is best understood as referring to the
Pennsylvania Coal Company's assertion that it could not undertake
profitable anthracite mining in light of the Kohler Act."[54]

In reaching this conclusion, Stevens in effect has read into the
earlier Holmes opinion the entire diffuse structure of regulatory
takings law. And it is a forced and contrived performance at best,
given the overall tenor of Holmes's opinion. Holmes said that the
coal which had to be left in place in order to provide support for
the surface owner had been taken. He did not mean to say that the
taking occurred because there was somewhere in the record[55]—on
a preliminary motion no less—evidence that the loss of this coal
disrupted the operations of a given mine or threatened to drive the

---

[54]107 S.Ct. at 1249.

[55]The Court in *Keystone, ibid.*, observes that the coal company claimed that one company
was "unable to operate six large collieries in the city of Scranton, employing more than five
thousand men. Motion to Advance for Argument in Pennsylvania Coal Co. v. Mahon. O.T.
1922, No. 549, p. 2" The citation here is something of a giveaway. The argument was made
in a preliminary motion where it appeared after a sentence which read in full: "It is of
paramount importance that an early decision of this can be had for the following reasons."
Motion, *ibid.* The point was hardly relevant to the coal company's view of the case on the
merits, which in that same motion was stated to be that "the Kohler Act effected a revolu-
tionary change in the law. It deprived the coal owner, without compensation, of his right
to mine any coal which might cause damage to structures on the surface, notwithstanding
the fact that, in his deed, he had expressly been given this right. . . ." The Coal Company's
argument before the court on the merits pursued *only* the theme that the deprivation of its
support estate was confiscation. 260 U.S. at 394–404. "The Kohler Act, however, is a
permanent provision. It transfers for all time the Third Estate—right to the perpetual use
of this coal—in the Mahon lot from the Coal Company to private individuals, and that
without any compensation whatsoever." *Id.* at 403.

coal companies into bankruptcy. It was just for this reason that Holmes was prepared to support the facial invalidation of the statute:[56] the particular facts did not matter. It is only the modern takings law that treats general land use regulation as a form of general rate-of-return regulation, subject to a very lax standard of judicial review. The purpose of the eminent domain clause is surely to restrict government behavior, to prevent the form of interest group politics outlined above.[57] The legislature cannot avoid the imperatives of the takings clause by calling its mass transfer of the support estate a "regulation."

Similarly, Stevens is wholly misguided in his analysis of the relationship between police power justification and the public use requirement. Here his tactic is to note the progression of decisions which have expanded its scope since *Pennsylvania Coal*.[58] In so doing, Stevens does not provide any independent account of the police power of his own, but contents himself with endorsing the expansion. He rightly accepts the idea that the state can regulate nuisances, but then continues by noting:[59]

> "The nuisance exception to the taking guarantee is not coterminous with the police power itself." This is certainly the case in light of our recent decisions holding that the "scope of the 'public use' requirement of the Takings Clause is 'coterminous with the scope of a sovereign's police powers.' "

The purpose of the police power limitation is to justify state takings without compensation. The modern reading of the public use lim-

---

[56]See *supra* at 14–15.

[57]See *supra* at 8.

[58]See, *e.g.*, Miller v. Schoene 276 U.S. 272 (1928) (cutting down cedar trees to protect apple trees not a compensable taking); Euclid v. Ambler Realty Co, 272 U.S. 365 (1926) (zoning proper exercise of police power); Goldblatt v. Hempstead 369 U.S. 590 (1962) (restriction of gravel removal, proper use of police power). Note that none of these cases involves the relationship between consenting parties.

[59]*Keystone*, 107 S.Ct. at 1245 n. 20, quoting from the Rehnquist dissent in *Penn Central*, 438 U.S. at 145, and from Ruckelhaus v. Monsanto Co. 467 U.S. 986 (1984), which in turn quoted from *Midkiff* at 467 U.S. 229. The footnote also cites my book Takings in support of this astonishing proposition at 108–12. In fact, the passages quoted stand for exactly the opposite proposition: "Meeting the public use limitation does not allow the state to take property without just compensation. Satisfying the police power limitation, in contrast, does allow the state to take without compensation." *Id.* at 109. It is, I think, an author's privilege to say that he would rather be wholly ignored by the Supreme Court than be cited in support of propositions against which he has devoted large portions of his professional energy.

itation is so expansive that private parties may never resist a taking so long as the state is prepared to pay compensation. To argue that the two limitations are identical must mean therefore that since the state may take property whenever it wishes, it need never pay for the property that it has taken. Even Stevens would shrink from that implication, but he gives us no way to escape it. The proper line is the one which Holmes had abandoned before *Mahon* in the rent-control cases. There can be no claim that the police power governs where the injured party has assumed the risk in question,[60] for no court knows how to decide which contracts it likes and which it does not.[61]

The transformation of takings law carries over to Stevens's treatment of the just compensation requirement. Holmes tried to do that by invoking the idea of average reciprocity of advantage, in a case where each mineowner benefited from the support columns left in place by the other. The theory which is involved here is essentially that of disproportionate impact. Thus where the statute in question provides parallel benefits and burdens to all interested parties, there is good reason to think that the benefits for each will equal or exceed the costs in question. If the restrictions on each person are the taking, and the benefits received are the required compensation, then the average reciprocity of advantage really means that a taking is compensated (implicitly and in-kind) even in the absence of a cash transfer from the state to the individual citizen.[62]

---

[60]See Takings, ch. 11.

[61]It should come as no surprise that Stevens rejected any argument that the state regulation impaired the obligation of contracts (see Art. I. §8, cl. 10). He first noted that the clause could not be read "literally," 107 S.Ct. at 1251, and then proceeded to import that same broad police power exception into it that he had read into the Takings Clause. His disapproval toward the coal companies is captured in the following outburst: "In any event, it is petitioners' position that, because they contract with some previous owners of property generations ago, they have a constitutionally protected legal right to conduct their mining operations in a way that would make shambles of all those building and cemeteries." *Id.* at 152.

But that is not the company's position. It only asserts that if the state wishes to alter the contractual balance it must compensate for the losses that it imposes. The just compensation limitation was rightly read into the Contracts Clause in West River Bridge Co. v. Dix, 6 How. 507 (1848), so that contract rights were not inviolate before this case. After *Keystone* they are not protected at all. For an analysis of the police power and just compensation limitations on the Contracts Clause, see Epstein, Toward a Revitalization of the Contract Clause, 51 U. Chi. L. Rev. 703, 730–47 (1984).

[62]See, for a fuller explication, Epstein, Takings, ch. 14.

Stevens is not a man to cast aside the use of a good phrase, so he invokes this phrase in support of his own very different position.[63]

> The Court's hesitance to find a taking when the state merely restrains uses of property that are tantamount to public nuisances is consistent with the notion of the "reciprocity of advantage" that Justice Holmes referred to in *Pennsylvania Coal*. Under our system of government, one of the state's primary ways of preserving the public weal is restricting the uses individuals can make of their property. While each of us is burdened somewhat by such restrictions, we, in turn, benefit greatly from the restrictions that are placed on others.

The shift in the use of the average reciprocity of advantage should be manifest. Holmes found that the test was flunked by the Kohler Act precisely because all the benefits went to the surface owners and all the costs were borne by the mineowners. Stevens for his part changes the total focus of the test to make it into a grand declaration of the benefits of citizenship generally. For Holmes the test of average reciprocity of advantage was really a way of asking whether the parties whose property was taken received compensation in-kind for the loss in question in the same transaction. For Stevens the test is transformed into a conclusive presumption that such compensation has been provided, wholly without regard to the operation and effect of the particular statute. There is no way in which he, or anyone else, can find the benefits which from this statute give compensation for the losses that were inflicted under the 1966 Bituminous Coal Act. Indeed under Stevens's misdirected rendering of Holmes's test, no restrictions on use ever could be unconstitutional because the state might also right the balance on some future occasion. The same logic could be pressed into service to justify the outright confiscation of land, "Don't worry, we did it to you today, but we shall do it to someone else tomorrow. Be happy you share in the benefits of citizenship." But if it is said that the confiscation of land is a rare event, so that tomorrow may never come, then the same observation applies to the holders of the mineral interests in *Keystone*.

There are powerful allocative consequences that depend on the way in which a court chooses to apply the test of "average reciprocity of advantage." Under Holmes's view each statute has to stand on its own bottom. The average reciprocity of advantage is

---

[63]107 S.Ct. at 1245.

therefore strong evidence that there are social gains from the legislation that are sufficient to offset the costs the statutes imposed.
That condition is not satisfied when separate statutes are placed
into the same capacious barrel, for now interest group politics can
force the passage of statutes that cause enormous losses for losers
without generating compensating gains to winners. Only the need
to compensate when property is taken can discipline the legislature.

Keystone showed not the slightest understanding of why we have
an eminent domain clause at all. Because the Court could not understand its function, it twisted its language. It collapsed the police
power limitation into the public use limitation, and it removed the
just compensation restriction from the clause. It is perhaps too much
to ask a court to understand the intellectual foundations of the
eminent domain clause, but surely it is not too much to ask that it
be careful and honest with constitutional language, and the relevant
precedents and scholarship. Given the low quality of Keystone, there
was really no place to go but up. The amazing thing is how fast
the transformation took place in the next two cases.

II. FIRST ENGLISH EVANGELICAL LUTHERAN CHURCH V. LOS ANGELES

In *First English Evangelical Lutheran Church v. Los Angeles
County*, the Lutheran Church had operated a campsite, called
"Lutherglen," which consisted of a retreat center and recreational
area for handicapped children. The complex contained bunkhouses,
a church, and an outdoor chapel. The campsite was located on a
twelve-acre plot along the Middle Fork of Mill Creek. The creek
was the natural drainage area for a watershed area maintained by
the National Forest Service. In 1977 a forest fire denuded the hill-
sides above the campsite, exposing it to serious risk of flood. That
risk became a reality in 1978, when the runoff from an eleven-inch
rainstorm destroyed all the buildings in the camp complex. In 1979
in response to the situation, the County passed an Interim Ordinance which provided that "[a] person shall not construct, recon-
struct, place or enlarge any building or structure, any portion of
which is, or will be, located within the outer boundary lines of the
interim flood protection area located in Mill Creek Canyon."[64] The

---

[64]*First English*, 107 S.Ct. at 2382.

reasons given for the ordinance were the familiar ones of health and safety. The effect of the ordinance was to prohibit any reconstruction of the Lutherglen complex.

The Church brought suit against the County on several distinct grounds. Two torts claims against the County, not relevant to the case when it was argued in the Supreme Court, were for creating dangerous conditions that resulted in the initial flooding, and for seeding the clouds during the rainstorm.[65] The second half of its complaint challenged the ordinance of the County as a "taking" of its property without just compensation when it denied the Church "all use" of its property so long as the ordinance was in effect. The California Court of Appeals, following the precedent of its own Supreme Court, held that the Church was not in a position to ask for any monetary relief against the ordinance until the ordinance was found to work an unconstitutional taking.[66] Even then the only remedy open to the plaintiff was an action for declaratory judgment or mandamus, asking that the restrictions in question be removed. Thus under the view of the California Supreme Court,[67] compensation becomes payable only if the state decides to keep its ordinance in effect after it has been held to be a taking. The California Supreme Court did not hear the case, but the United States Supreme Court did.

The decision itself involved two separate issues, one substantive and one procedural.[68] I shall consider only the takings question here. On that question the United States Supreme Court found that the California Courts had wrongly concluded that mandamus or declaratory judgment was the only remedy for an interim taking. Damages had to be paid for the loss of use in the interim period,

---

[65]The Los Angeles County Flood Control District was joined as a defendant in the tort counts, but not for the taking issue.

[66]The decision in the intermediate California Court does not appear to be reported.

[67]See Agins v. Tiburon, 24 Cal.3d 266, 598 P.2d 25 (1979), 157 Cal.Rptr. 372, aff'd on other grounds, 447 U.S. 255 (1980).

[68]The procedural question was whether the judgment of the Court below was "final" so that the case was properly before the Supreme Court. The question of interim takings had arisen before on at least three separate occasions, MacDonald, Sommer & Frates v. Yolo County, 106 S.Ct. 2561 (1986); Williamson Country Regional Planning Comm'n v. Hamilton, 473 U.S. 172 (1985); and San Diego Gas & Electric Co. v. San Diego, 450 U.S. 621 (1981). In each case the Supreme Court held that the same procedural defect, want of finality, precluded a decision on the merits. Here Rehnquist, C.J., thought it sufficient that the trial court had struck the Church's claim for relief as "entirely immaterial and irrelevant [, with] no bearing upon any conceivable cause of action herein." First English, 107 S.Ct. at 2382.

at least where the landowner was denied all use of its property. When the issue is considered in light of the four questions set out above, it is hard to see how the Court could have reached any other conclusion on this point of law, once it decided to take it up. But the issues raised by the case, and the implications of the Court's decisions, are both more subtle and profound than might appear at first glance.

Turning to the four questions, the first issue, again, is whether there is any taking of private property. A similar question has arisen frequently with respect to "temporary takings" when the government moved into possession of leased property for a term of years. These cases make it crystal clear to everyone that the government has to pay for the rental value of the property, and that its obligation remains undiminished whether the original lease is for a definite term, or for such duration as suits the purposes of the government, as with a lease renewable from year to year.[69] As a matter of principle, how could it be otherwise, for surely the state cannot avoid paying for the fee simply by renewing one-year leases in perpetuity. There are to be sure some subtle questions of damages in calculating whether the landowner is entitled to various expenditures, including those for the loss of good will or consequential damages.[70] Yet no matter how these questions are resolved, the existence of some obligation to compensate remains secure.

The critical question is whether the same analysis should apply where the state stops short of temporary occupation, that is, in the case of regulatory takings. Justice Stevens, writing in dissent, argues that the gap between occupation and takings is one that cannot be spanned under the takings clause. He writes: "The diminution of value inquiry is unique to regulatory takings. Unlike physical invasions, which are relatively rare and easily identifiable without making any economic analysis, regulatory programs constantly affect property values in countless ways, and only the most extreme regulations can constitute takings."[71]

[69]See, e.g., Kimball Laundry Co. v United States, 338 U.S. 1 (1949); United States v. Petty Motor. Co., 327 U.S. 372 (1946); United States v. General Motors Corp. 323 U.S. 373 (1945).

[70]For the record, I generally think that he is. See, Epstein, Takings, at 51–56 (consequential damages) and 80–88 (loss of good will).

[71]First English, 107 S.Ct. at 2393. There is a haunting resemblance to Holmes in Pennsylvania Coal: "Government hardly could go on if to some extent values incident to property could not be diminished without paying for every such change in the general law." 260 U.S. at 413.

Yet there is surely no textual warrant for the difference between two classes of takings, both guaranteed by the same clause. A restriction of use on the fee is a partial taking of property, which prima facie calls for compensation. Similarly, the restriction on use for some shorter period of time is also a partial taking, albeit of a smaller part, of the property interest in question. The difference in degree may have effects on damages, police power justifications, or implicit in-kind compensation, as they did in *Pennsylvania Coal*.[72] But they do not take the case outside the takings clause altogether. Let the government reduce rental value by 25 percent, then it can make up the difference as long as the restriction is in effect. Justice Stevens is therefore wrong to insist that only "extreme" forms of government misconduct are reached by the clause. Any taking will do. There is no occasion to have two domains within the takings law, one for occupation and the other for cases of regulation. The principles applicable to occupation are fully applicable to regulation, and so the decision in *First English* rightly holds.[73]

The police power question raises interesting complications of its own, which the Supreme Court did not reach because the County conceded that the interim taking had occurred and then argued that the only remedy was lifting the restrictions imposed by the ordinance. Once, however, the County's argument has been rejected, then the police power question surges to the fore: does the police power extend only to protect third parties from injuries, or may it be used to protect individuals from the ill consequences of their own conduct—in a word, for reasons of paternalism. If one were to adopt the broad accounts of the police power so congenial to Justice Stevens, then the plaintiff is doomed because health and safety are clearly implicated as the County has urged. Indeed even the *Lochner* court[74] had an attitude of deference toward matters of health and safety. But in principle both these attitudes are suspect. The key line, urged above, was that the police power should be construed to prevent the use of force or fraud against strangers. Based upon the Supreme Court decision, the facts here seem tolerably clear: the restrictions were not imposed upon the Church to protect downstream persons from its wrongful activities. They were imposed to protect the Church from building its own structures, which pre-

---

[72]See text at notes 48–52 *supra*.

[73]See 107 S.Ct. at 2388.

[74]198 U.S. 45 (1905).

sumably it could do at its own risk: if the buildings go down, then they have to bear the loss in question. The risk of injury to persons on the premises with permission expands the state interest, for surely there would be presumptive tort liability in the event that a flood occurred. Limiting occupancy or requiring insurance is thus an appropriate function of the state, especially since the handicapped are the persons for whom paternalism seems almost by definition to be appropriate. But even if occupancy and use may be limited on these grounds, there is no reason for a total ban on construction, which removes all alternative uses of the property as well.

Putting the uncertainties of the police power to one side, then all that remains is public use and just compensation. Since the temporary taking has already been completed, it follows that some interim damages have to be awarded to make good the loss. On the facts of this case, the compensation required seems trivial. Thus initially, it must be recognized that any diminution in the value of the land attributable to the fire and the flooding must be absorbed by the Lutheran Church and not by the state. The question therefore is what value would the Church (or the market) attach to land that was in fact largely unusable because it had been destroyed by one flood and could be destroyed by another. In all likelihood, the damages, if not nonexistent, were small relative to the value of the land prior to the forest fire. One can picture the tort actions that handicapped children could bring against the Church for personal injuries, should the old complex be rebuilt. It is of course possible that there are complications that I have missed. The flood could have been a very rare event, and reforestation might have taken place quickly. These questions of valuation can only be answered on a fuller record. But from what little appears here, the Church may have established the right constitutional principle, but it is hard to see why it should be able to take much advantage of it.

The case then seems to be pretty straightforward. What arguments could be raised against the result? Los Angeles County essentially raised two points. First, in line with the California *Agins* decision, the County insisted that an award of monetary damages would, as Justice Rehnquist paraphrased it, "force the legislature to exercise its power of eminent domain,"[75] even after it decides to

---

[75]107 S.Ct. at 2382. The point was renewed by the Solicitor General who suggested that the decision for the Church would "permit a court, at the behest of a private person, to require the . . . Government to exercise its power of eminent domain. . . ." *Id.* at 2389.

desist. This point, at least, is clearly incorrect. The state simply need not impose the ordinance in the first place. The taking therefore occurs not at the time of the final judicial determination, but at the earlier moment when the regulation was first placed into effect. The courts hardly force the state to take in the *future* when it demands damages for losses inflicted in the *past*. The state need not keep the ordinance in place any more than it has to renew short-term leases.

The second point is far more difficult and controversial. As stated by the California Supreme Court in *Agins*, the argument goes as follows:[76]

> In combination, the need for preserving a degree of freedom in the land-use planning function, and the inhibiting financial force which inheres in the inverse condemnation remedy, persuade us that on balance mandamus or declaratory relief rather than inverse condemnation is the appropriate relief under the circumstances.

Rehnquist's response to the point was simply to say that matters of convenience do not justify the abrogation of the constitutional command.[77] But a more complete assessment of the point is in order, given the weightiness of the challenge. The critical inquiry is whether the need for government discretion in planning offers some principled reason to suspend the obligation of the state to compensate.

At one level it might appear that the appeal to convenience made by the California Supreme Court in *Agins* has no textual source in the Constitution, and thus may be dismissed as a policy option that the Constitution precludes. But unwittingly perhaps, the California Supreme Court does make an important contention, once the implicit-in-kind compensation doctrine is brought to the fore.[78] The question is whether all state citizens are left better off ex ante if the state or local government adopts a uniform rule which holds that the state is not liable for any interim losses of property brought on by regulatory planning. The point here is that every property owner has property taken when he cannot recover for his interim

---

[76]Agins v. Tiburon, 24 Cal.3d, at 276–77, 157 Cal. Rptr., at 378, 598 P.2d at 31.

[77]"We, of course, are not unmindful of these considerations, but they must be evaluated in light of the command of the Just Compensation Clause of the Fifth Amendment." 107 S.Ct. at 2387.

[78]See, for a fuller treatment, Epstein, Takings, ch. 14.

losses, but (from the ex ante perspective) is compensated for the loss in that he can no longer be called to fund through taxation the similar losses that are sustained by others. Stated otherwise, a general rule of no compensation for interim losses seems a bona fide average reciprocity of advantage for all citizens.

The argument is in fact more complicated than this because the absence of a disproportionate impact does not guarantee that adequate compensation has been provided. There are other ways to approach the same question, including a substantive evaluation of the likely social consequences that follow from the adoption of this universal "no liability" rule. To take a torts analogy, the choice between negligence and strict liability for physical injuries seems to be sufficiently close that either rule could be adopted by the legislature, without raising serious constitutional questions.[79] The result would be different, however, if the state simply decided (broadly and proportionately) to repeal all tort law, including that which allowed property owners to eject willful trespassers from their premises, without providing any alternative remedial structure. This massive departure from the common law inaugurates a legal regime of lawlessness so manifestly inadequate to the needs of people in general, that the benefits received will never equal losses suffered for virtually everyone. Typically, the courts will not have to face the problem because the statute will not be enacted.

This same distinction between large and small deviations from the basic takings prohibition is relevant here. The California rule in *Agins* does not provide that local governments should be exempt from liability only where they have made honest, reasonable, and good faith interpretations of the law, which just have turned out wrongly to work a temporary taking. It provides in effect that there should never be any compensation for interim losses, even where state officials have acted in a partisan, provincial, and perverse fashion to deny landowners their ordinary rights of use and development. In effect the California rule in *Agins* sets up a domain where state officials may use their coercive powers at will. If the incentive structure is such that local politicians can satisfy local voters by excluding outside developers,[80] then they will surely ex-

---

[79]See the discussion in Takings at 238–42.

[80]See, *e.g.*, Haas v. City and County of San Francisco, 605 F.2d 1117 (9th Cir. 1979), discussed in Takings at 269–72.

ploit it. One outlandish set of restrictions after another may be erected. When the first set of controls is struck down—of course, only for the future—then a second scheme, different in its details but equally oppressive in its consequences, can quickly be enacted in its place. Then a third.

The California Supreme Court well understood that some discretion is necessary for decisionmaking. But it wholly ignored the other, uglier, side of the coin. The increase in discretion leads to massive opportunities for its abuse, which the electoral process often inflames instead of restrains. There are limits to the deference accorded government under any constitutional regime. While the implicit, ex ante compensation test with difficulty might be extended to reach a reasonable, good faith standard, it cannot be tortured to allow any group of government officials to act wholly without constraint, which is just what the California Supreme Court *Agins* decision accepts. Rehnquist need not have resorted simply to a wooden literalism to defend his view on this point, for a sensible mode of constitutional construction which allows all the so-called issues of convenience to be taken into account on the question of ex ante, implicit in kind compensation.[81] But this expanded analysis does not support the rule announced by the California Supreme Court.

There is a second source of uncertainty that is also left unresolved by *First English*. Justice Rehnquist was careful to circumscribe the rule he announced to the facts that were before the Court: the obligation to pay for interim loss therefore only arose where the ordinances had "denied appellant all use of its property for a considerable period of years."[82] Here the stress is on the phrase "all use." If confined to this class of cases the rule itself marks only a tiny extension beyond the cases of temporary leasehold occupation. More concretely, if so limited, the decision will have absolutely no effect in the complex array of zoning cases where the strategy of the government is to allow the landowner some limited class of uses

---

[81] This discussion reveals yet another cost of the unfathomable substantive rules on regulatory takings. Whether we adopt a negligence, or as I prefer, a strict liability standard for government takings, the residual loss will lie somewhere. Only a relatively clear set of rules will minimize the total loss to both property owners and the public at large. And once the rules are made clearer, then blunders by either government or citizen are more easily charged against their own personal accounts.

[82] 107 S.Ct. at 2389.

while denying him the rest. In essence local planners will be able to deflect the decision by allowing some modicum of residual use, relying all the while on administrative stratagems to prevent growth and development. *First English* may become an inconsequential sport, a part of the law of flood plains and not of the law of eminent domain generally.

Yet there is no reason in principle to consign the decision to the remote corners of our jurisprudence. Interim damages should be required for any interim loss of damages not justified under the police power. Matters of valuation, so critical in zoning cases, have to be answered. But these are hardly so small as to escape judicial notice. A real estate developer forced to wait ten years to build apartment houses on land which the local government wishes to reserve for luxury homes on ten-acre plots has suffered very substantial losses, equal to the present discounted value of the difference between the regulated and unregulated land for a ten-year period. What sense is there to insist upon compensation for the puny damages in *First English* and to ignore them for the massive losses caused by local zoning? Once *First English* is rightly extended to zoning cases, then it is no longer of interest only to the owners of remote campsites. Regardless of context, any time the local government starts the meter running, then presumptively it will have to pay interim damages should its restrictions be adjudged a compensable taking under the constitution.[83] If this development takes place, then the question whether local government officials are judged by strict or reasonableness standard will become critical. But no matter how that question is decided, *First English* will be a permanent fixture in every land use battle in the United States.

III. NOLLAN V. CALIFORNIA COASTAL COMMISSION

Nollan v. California Coastal Commission presents the counterpart to *First English*. *First English* skirted the question of what counts as a taking; *Nollan* presents that issue head on. Yet again the decision

---

[83]The measure of damages will deserve some mention. Landowners may urge that the damages for interim zoning be determined by the difference in the interim period between the present discounted rental value of the unregulated land and the discounted rental value of the land under regulation. In fact the correct measure would seem to be the present discounted value of the land subject to the most extensive *permissible* regulation and its present discounted value under the interim system in place.

is as important for the issues that it leaves unresolved, as for those which it authoritatively decides. Simply deciding any land use case against the state and in favor of the owner is news enough in itself. Identifying a change in direction, however, does not speak to its permanence and magnitude. *Nollan* marks a bend in the road, but, as with *First English*, only time and the Court will tell whether it also marks a fundamental change in judicial orientation.

The California Coastal Commission is charged with the general supervision and management of the extensive coastal resources within the state,[84] and in discharge of that function has been charged with maintaining the delicate balance between the interests of the public in the shoreline, and its access to it, and the interests of adjacent property owners. As a matter of traditional law, the normal division between the public and the private domain has been set at the mean high water mark. Toward the beach side of the mark, the public (which includes all adjacent landowners) has free access to come and go as it pleases, usually under some variant of the public trust doctrine.[85] On the other side of the line, the property owner is normally entitled to exclusive rights of occupation and use under the ordinary principles of private ownership. There is no question that the state may change the appropriate balance of entitlements by the exercise of its eminent domain power. Thus it can take lands along the beach for a public park, it can acquire easements over adjacent private lands that will give the public access to the beach, and it can acquire various easements and restrictive covenants over beachfront property—all with a view to enhancing the general level of public enjoyment of the land and waters that are already in the public domain. The only catch, of course, is that the state must pay the private owner for the lost value, which could be great when beach front property is both scarce and desirable.

The core of the debate in *Nollan* was over the familiar issue: the extent to which the state could use its general police powers to circumvent its need to resort to its eminent domain power. The particular government initiative challenged in *Nollan* involved the linkage of two separate elements of property together in part of a

---

[84]See generally California Coastal Act of 1976, Cal. Pub. Res. Code Ann. §30000.

[85]See generally, Rose, The Comedy of the Commons: Custom, Commerce, and Inherently Public Property, 53 U. Chi. L. Rev. 711, 713 (1986). For my views on the subject, see Epstein, The Public Trust Doctrine, 7 Cato J. (1987) (forthcoming).

single overall scheme. First, there are the development rights that each beachfront property owner has in his own parcel. As a matter of general law it has been long settled that Coastal Commission can limit private construction. Second, there are potential easements, parallel to the beach, which enable members of the public at large to move from point to point along the beach in easy and comfortable fashion. These must normally be purchased.

The strategy adopted by the Coastal Commission was simplicity itself. Any landowner who wished to increase the size of existing structures on his land by more than 10 percent could obtain permission to do so only if he first agreed to deed the public at large a lateral easement, parallel to the beach.[86] No easement, no approval. If forced to make the trade, property owners value building rights more than they fear beachfront easements. Indeed, some forty-three landowners had each deeded the easement in order to obtain the property rights.[87]

The Nollans resisted this Hobson's choice. They had acquired a lease with an option to purchase land graced by a decrepit 504 square foot bungalow. While proceedings dragged on before the California Coastal Commission and in the courts, the Nollans simply ripped the bungalow down and erected a three-bedroom house in keeping with the neighborhood, and completed the purchase, without notifying the Commission of their actions.[88] Once back in court, the Nollans rested their case on the ground that the Coastal Commission's program constituted a taking of their land without just compensation. They won by a five-four decision in the Supreme Court, featuring an opinion by Justice Scalia and a dissent by Justice Brennan.[89]

Why should the Nollans win? The simplest way to put the challenge to the majority is to pose anew the most probing inquiry in the Brennan dissent.[90]

> In this case, California has employed its police power in order to condition development upon preservation of public access to

---

[86]*Nollan*, 107 S.Ct. at 3144.

[87]*Id.* 107 S.Ct. at 3158 n.9 (Brennan, J., dissenting).

[88]*Id.* at 3143–44.

[89]Marshall, J., joined the Brennan dissent. There were short separate dissents by both Justices Blackmun and Stevens that do not require separate attention.

[90]107 S.Ct. at 3152.

the ocean and the tidelands. The Coastal Commission, if it had so chosen, could have denied the Nollans' request for a development permit, since the property would have remained economically viable without the requested new development. Instead, the State sought to accommodate the Nollans' desire for new development, on the condition that the development not diminish the overall amount of public access to the coastline. Appellants' proposed development would reduce public access by restricting visual access to the beach, by contributing to an increased need for community facilities, and by moving private development closer to beach property. The Commission sought to offset this diminution in access, and thereby preserve the overall balance of access, by requesting a deed restriction that would ensure "lateral" access: the right of the public to pass and repass along the dry sand parallel to the shoreline in order to reach the tidelands and the ocean. In the expert opinion of the Coastal Commission, development conditioned on such a restriction would fairly attend to both the public and private interests.

Justice Brennan treats the Coastal Commission as the fountain of public generosity. If it could have prevented all development, then it did the Nollans and their fellow landowners a favor by allowing them to obtain development rights for the relatively small cost of the lateral easement ceded to the public at large.

Justice Scalia's opinion devotes an unusual amount of space to refute the Brennan dissent, but it is a close question whether he has met the challenge. As one would expect, Scalia begins first with the proposition that the lateral easement over the Nollans' land is a property right, which normally could be taken only through the exercise of the eminent domain power. This issue hardly seems controversial even under the modern law, given that members of the public have sought to make use of private land, thereby undercutting the owner's right of exclusive possession. Scalia then rightly puts the question of the case as follows: "Given, then, that requiring uncompensated conveyance of the easement outright would violate the Fourteenth Amendment, the question becomes whether requiring it to be conveyed as a condition for issuing a land use permit alters the outcome."[91]

The Scalia opinion thus introduces, perhaps for a first time, the vexed doctrine of unconstitutional conditions into the law of emi-

---

[91]*Id.* at 3146.

nent domain.[92] That principle, which holds that "a state is without power to impose an unconstitutional requirement as a condition for granting a privilege,"[93] has been applied in a wide range of cases that govern such issues as access to public highways,[94] or the privilege of doing business in other states.[95] There is thus ample authority on the record which says that the truism of Justice Brennan, that the greater includes the lesser power, is not necessarily true. But the doctrine of unconstitutional conditions does not mean that no conditions can ever be attached to the doing of business or the exercise of a constitutional right. A corporation may not, for example, be subject to discriminatory taxes as a condition for doing business in a foreign state, but it is quite plausible to require that it agree to service of process in a state in which it wishes to do business. The task of an adequate theory of unconstitutional conditions is to figure out which conditions may be attached to what privileges and why. Justice Scalia sensed that he was on treacherous ground, so he tried to avoid the hardest analytical questions by resort to what can best be described as a form of constitutional estoppel.[96]

> The Commission argues that among these permissible purposes [*i.e.* under the police power] are protecting the public's ability to see the beach, assisting the public in overcoming the "psychological barrier" to using the beach created by a developed shorefront, and preventing congestion on the public beaches. We assume, without deciding, that this is so—in which case the Commission would be able to deny the Nollans their permit outright if their new house (alone, or by reason of the cumulative impact produced in conjunction with other construction) would substantially impede these purposes, unless the denial would

---

[92]For the most exhaustive and useful account of the subject, see Kreimer, Allocational Sanctions: The Problem of Negative Rights in a Positive State, 132 Penn. L. Rev. 1293 (1984).

[93]Frost Trucking Co. v. Railroad Commission of California, 271 U.S. 583, 598 (1926) (per Sutherland, J.).

[94]In *Frost, ibid.*, it was held that the state might be able to exclude private business traffic from public highways absolutely, but it could not condition their use of the highways upon the willingness to be regulated as a common carrier by the Railroad Commission.

[95]Western Union Tel. Co. v. Kansas, 216 U.S. 1 (1910). The state could not condition the entry of Western Union to do business upon its willingness to pay a graduated tax upon the value of its capital stock.

[96]107 S.Ct. at 3147.

interfere so drastically with the Nollans' use of their property
as to constitute a taking.

Nonetheless, he parted company with the Coastal Commission
by insisting that there must be some kind of strong fit between the
general condition imposed and the type of end that it is designed
to serve. Scalia would, for example, allow the state to condition
land development upon conformity with a height restriction, which
would better enable persons from the highway to gain a view of
the beach.[97] And he would go so far as to allow the state to condition
the construction upon their meeting "a requirement that the Nollans
provide a viewing spot on their property for passersby with whose
sighting of the ocean their new house would interfere."[98] Nonetheless, on the facts of this case the Nollans still prevail: "The evident
constitutional propriety of the distinction disappears, however, if
the condition substituted for the prohibition utterly fails to further
the end advanced as the justification for the prohibition."[99] In Scalia's view, any insistence that the public be allowed a lateral easement
is "unrelated" to the purposes which the state may choose to advance, and hence fails. Scalia then offers an analogy from the free
speech area.[100] The state may impose an absolute ban upon shouting
fire in a crowded theater, but it cannot condition the right to so
shout upon payment of $100 into the public treasury. "In short,
unless the permit condition serves the same governmental purpose
as the development ban, the building restriction is not a valid regulation of land use, but 'an out-and-out plan of extortion.' "[101]

Does Scalia make good his use of unconstitutional conditions as
it applies to this case? Here initially one could challenge him on
the ground that it is simply too difficult to decide whether one
condition is "related" to some legitimate government end. "Related," to be sure, is not a term without a fair degree of vagueness
at the margins, and Scalia's opinion will at the very least usher in
a new round of litigation to determine the sense of its contours.
Nonetheless, it is hard to dismiss the concept as simply being

[97]Id. at 3147–48.

[98]Id. at 3148.

[99]Ibid.

[100]Ibid.

[101]Ibid.

without any content at all. Suppose, for example, the state were to say that it would not allow owners of beachfront property to install new toilets, or to patch their roofs unless they first deeded a lateral easement (or 10 percent of the land outright) to the state. It does not seem too much to say that there is something amiss here, even if the state had the power to exclude new toilets or roof repairs under the police power. While there may be some, even many, messy cases at the margins, there are surely many cases of "unrelatedness" that do seem clear. To attack Scalia on this point is therefore to fall into an unattractive dilemma. Either the critic decides to abandon the doctrine of unconstitutional conditions altogether, or, to preserve the doctrine, he must find some term that has more clarity than the term "unrelated" in order to distinguish between those conditions that are rightly imposed (e.g., agreement to service of process as a condition for doing business within the state) and those which are "unrelated" (the payment of an extortionate tax).

Brennan does not attack Scalia's use of unconstitutional conditions, not even to contest its applicability in the context of eminent domain. Instead he takes on Scalia's proposed test from a more functional point of view. Once forewarned by *Nollan* itself, he believes that the Commission should have little difficulty in satisfying Scalia's legal standard. "With respect to the permit condition program in general, the Commission should have little difficulty in the future in utilizing its expertise to demonstrate a specific connection between provisions for access and burdens on access produced by new development."[102] But is it business as usual for the Coastal Commission? Brennan, for example, never indicates what the connection between lateral access and development restriction really is, but he only assures us that once "alerted to the Court's apparently more demanding requirement, it need only make clear that a provision for public access directly responds to a particular type of burden on access created by a new development." How, we are not told.

Scalia for his part will not tolerate any obvious sleight of hand, for he makes it abundantly clear that more must be shown. "We view the Fifth Amendment's property clause to be more than a

---

[102]107 S.Ct. at 3161.

pleading requirement, and compliance with it to be more than an exercise in cleverness and imagination."[103] How much more is an open question. But one way to read this passage is to say that in land use cases Scalia has abandoned the "rational basis" test of prior land use cases from *Euclid* to *Agins* in favor of a standard demanding intermediate scrutiny of government restrictions, at least in cases where unconstitutional conditions are lurking in the background. Thus Scalia pointedly notes that all the citations to the rational basis standard in the Brennan dissent are equal protection cases.[104] The Takings Clause with its own explicit substantive requirement now calls for a heightened level of scrutiny. Scalia wrote:[105]

> But there is no reason to believe (and the language of our cases gives some reason to disbelieve) that so long as the regulation of property is at issue, the standards for takings challenges, due process challenges, and equal protection challenges are identical, any more than there is any reason to believe that so long as the regulation of speech is at issue the standards for due process challenges, equal protection challenges, and First Amendment challenges are identical.

Not quite the stuff to rehabilitate property rights after *Carolene Products'* footnote 4,[106] but close.[107]

It is, moreover, not difficult to see why Scalia is so concerned with this particular use of government power. To be sure, we do not have the easy case here where one landowner has been singled out for special attention. As Scalia urges, it would be quite intolerable if the Coastal Commission demanded the lateral easement from some landowners but not others, operating under standards

---

[103]*Id.* at 3150.

[104]Minnesota v. Clover Leaf Creamery Co., 449 U.S. 456 (1981); Williamson v. Lee Optical of Oklahoma, 348 U.S. 483 (1955); and Day-Brite Lighting, Inc. v. Missouri 342 U.S. 421 (1952), discussed by Scalia, J., in *Nollan*, 107 S.Ct. at 3147 n. 3, and by Brennan, J., *id.* at 3151 & n. 1.

[105]107 S.Ct. at 3147 n. 3.

[106]United States v. Carolene Products, 304 U.S. 144 (1938), on which see Miller, The True Story of Carolene Products, *infra* at 397.

[107]I believe that Scalia is wrong to assume that there are differences in the level of review as one moves from clause to clause in property cases. So long as the right to dispose of property is part of property itself, then every equal protection case raises what are rightly understood as property cases. On this view *CloverLeaf*, note 104 *supra*, is ripe for invalidation on any intermediate standard of scrutiny, see Epstein, Takings, 143–45.

no one could understand.[108] But again it cannot be assumed that, simply because disproportionate impacts and arbitrary behavior are intolerable, the uniform rule is necessarily acceptable. Thus it is instructive to expand the vista just a small bit, and to assume, as is doubtless the case, that some landowners have already been able to erect new and large structures before the California Coastal Commission implemented its new policies. The net effect of the systematic policy is to create an automatic cleavage between the two classes of landowners. One group, owners of already improved land, can support the new restrictions on the ground that they benefit from both the improved access to other points along the beach, and from the slowdown in development to which they (having built) attach high value. The source of political competition is not difficult to see; in a perfectly natural sense, there is a disproportionate impact once one considers the different initial positions of the various landowners within the Coastal Commission's jurisdiction. The doctrine of unconstitutional conditions seems sensibly to play a role here, precisely because it tempers the domination of factions in the making of public decisions.[109]

Indeed my major concern with the Scalia opinion is that it did not go far enough. Why invoke the troublesome doctrine of unconstitutional conditions at all? For Scalia, the point seemed clear enough. The power of the state to restrict development under the name of the police power has been so well established that he could

---

[108]See 107 S.Ct. at 3147 n. 4, noting that singling out the Nollans "even if otherwise valid, might violate either the incorporated Takings Clause or the Equal Protection Clause." One of the principle purposes of the Takings Clause is "to bar Government from forcing some people alone to bear public burdens which, in all fairness and justice, should be borne by the public as a whole." Armstrong v. United States, 364 U.S. 40 (1960). There is here no waffling about the basic principle, as is found for example in Brennan's opinion in Penn Central Transportation Co. v. New York City, 438 U.S. 104, 123–24 (1978), where it is buried in the longer sentence that continues with the ominous words, "this Court, quite simply, has been unable to develop any 'set formula' to determine when 'justice and fairness' require that economic injuries caused by public action be compensated by the government, rather than remain disproportionately concentrated on a few persons." The difference in emphasis between Scalia in *Nollan* and Brennan in *Penn Central* is palpable.

[109]The same point was evident, moreover, in Sutherland's opinion in Frost v. California Railroad Comm'n, 271 U.S. at 591, where he noted that the ability of the state to convert all private carriers into public carriers by the imposition of restrictions on entry has clear effects on market structure: "Its primary purpose evidently is to protect the business of those who are common carriers in fact by controlling competitive conditions. Protection or conservation of the highways is not involved."

not undertake, even if he wanted to, a frontal assault upon the doctrine. The creative marriage between the law of unconstitutional conditions and eminent domain thus constitutes a perfectly respectable and imaginative intermediate strategy to cut back upon an adverse line of authority. But as a matter of first principle, the real question is what gives the state the untrammeled power to restrict development? As I have already urged in connection with both *Keystone* and *First English*,[110] the police power limitation within a system of constitutional law cannot be regarded as an open sesame to government power. It must be restricted to the protection of external harms, namely, the use of force and misrepresentation. If this is correct, then it follows that whenever the state wants to secure "visual access" over private lands for the public at large, it must purchase the restrictive covenant that will provide that access by limiting height or bulk as the case may be. Scalia therefore is wrong when he argues that height and view restrictions are simply within the scope of the police power as a matter of course.

Once it is recognized that the police power is limited with respect to the ends that it serves, there is really no need to resort to the doctrine of unconstitutional conditions at all. Instead what we have here is a public analogy to the private law doctrine of the duress of goods.[111] Suppose that a robber comes to his victim and says, "I will allow you to keep your wrist watch on condition that you give me your money." This is a clear case of robbery because the victim owns both watch and wallet and is required to choose between them. He has a "choice," but it is not the kind of choice that a merchant, contemplating sale, gives his customer when he says, "If you want my wrist watch, then you must give me your money." In the first case both initial entitlements are in the victim; in the second, there is one entitlement each in the merchant and the customer. The first case is coercion and the second case is trade.

Rightly understood, *Nollan* is a case of coercion and not of trade. I take it that no one would think that the doctrine of unconstitutional conditions was needed where the state said to a citizen, "you may keep your First Amendment rights of speech, so long as you abandon your First Amendment rights to the free exercise of religion."

---

[110]See supra at 000, 000.

[111]See generally, Epstein, Unconscionability: A Critical Reappraisal, 18 J. Law & Econ. 293, 295–98 (1975).

If he can have both, then he need not choose between them. *Nollan* involves that type of choice. As there is (given its proper explication) no police power right to have the overview of the Nollans' land without compensation, the choice that the state gave was really: "surrender either a restrictive covenant or a lateral easement over your land."[112] There is no justification for putting the landowner to this choice, even if the covenant costs the landowner ten times the easement. Scalia renders a judgment of what constitutes a taking without first developing any substantive theory of property rights, which once developed supports a stronger set of limitations on state power that the court now accepts. He has sacrificed intellectual clarity for judicial moderation, and has fashioned a doctrine which still permits some rampant public abuse (total limitation of development without compensation) by invoking the elusive doctrine of unconstitutional conditions, which never quite escapes Brennan's forceful challenge. Could someone argue tomorrow that Scalia's use of unconstitutional conditions only applies where the state has sought to obtain some possessory interest over the landowner's property? Sooner or later someone will have to confront the police power justifications head-on.

While the police power question dominates the case, *Nollan* is also relevant to the question of implicit-in-kind compensation. Justice Brennan suggests, for example, that the Nollans[113]

> gain an additional benefit from the Commission's permit program. They are able to walk along the beach beyond the confines of their own property only because the Commission has re-

---

[112]Restrictive covenants are property interests that normally are acquired by grant, and whose condemnation requires payment by the state. See, *e.g.*, Southern California Edison Co. v. Bourgerie, 9 Cal.3d 169, 107 Ca. Rptr. 76, 507 P.2d 964, (1973), which involved a covenant by a private party over land condemned by the state (actually Southern California Edison) and is hence distinguishable because the covenant was not created by the state when it imposed restrictions on land previously unencumbered. But so long as any restriction on use is a partial taking, then compensation is required in order to impose the covenant. It is instructive that Scalia himself recognizes the point when he rightly criticizes Brennan's narrow view of property interests: "To say that the appropriation of a public easement across a landowner's premises does not constitute the taking of a property interest but rather, (as Justice Brennan contends) 'a mere restriction on its use,' *post*, at 3154 n.3, is to use words in a manner that deprives them of all their ordinary meaning." *Nollan*, 107 S.Ct. at 3145. Amen. What is true of easements is true of restrictive covenants as well, for they, too, restrict use. See Epstein, Takings, at 103–04, 267–68.

[113]107 S.Ct. at 3158.

quired deed restrictions as a condition of approving other new beach developments. Thus, appellants benefit both as private landowners and as members of the public from the fact that [other] new development permit requests are conditioned on preservation of public access.

Brennan's argument only proves that there is some benefit given in return, but it does nothing to measure its value. Here explicit evidence should of course be taken, but there are telltale signs that the landowner's gain may not equal his loss. First, the evidence of motive cuts against the Commission, which desired to benefit the public at large, and not the neighbors. Why else did the Commission oppose new construction because it would increase the use of the beach by adjacent property owners? Second, the neighbors could have negotiated limited rights of passage, valid only among themselves, if they desired increased access. Third, Brennan's argument ignores the reduction in value in the retained lands associated with the anticipated use of the easement. But there is no reason to be dogmatic on any of these questions, for evidence on valuation can be taken at trial. If the benefits from parallel use did exceed the costs to the Nollans, then they are not entitled to compensation even if the Coastal Commission gave them no original choice. But if the benefits from parallel use were small in relation to the additional burdens so imposed, then the benefits provided function as a set off but against, but not a discharge of, the state's obligation to compensate. Brennan's mistake here repeats his error in *Penn Central:* the existence of an in-kind benefit does not guarantee its adequacy.[114] The correct disposition of *Nollan* turns on an issue of valuation, not of law.

Enough has been said to show that the gulf between Brennan and Scalia remains very large. In effect Brennan is prepared to continue with business as usual—to allow the police power and indirect compensation arguments routinely to defeat the claim for compensation in any regulatory takings case. Should he ultimately prevail, *Nollan* will be an aberrant footnote concerned with some tricky point of lateral easements. But what if Scalia—even the Scalia

---

[114]See Penn Central Transportation v. City of New York, 438 U.S. 104, 137 (1978), noting that transferable development rights over other property were compensation for the development rights lost, without evaluating their worth to the owner. See Epstein, Takings, at 188–90.

of unconstitutional conditions—continues to command a majority of the court? Then it is conceivable that a substantial number of zoning practices may well be found wanting. The government says to a landowner, we will allow you to construct your new house only if you make a special contribution to the support of schools or local hospitals. Here there is no conflict of land uses between landowners and the public at large. Instead we have a case in which an owner, who is entitled both to keep his property free of the tax lien and to develop it fully, is forced to choose between them. It follows therefore that the common practice of subdivision exactions[115] is constitutionally infirm under *Nollan's* view of unconstitutional conditions. The state must use general revenue taxes to support public projects, and cannot load off their costs upon latecomers to development.

The ambiguities in both *First English* and *Nollan* hint of the enormous swings that could take place in future years. If both cases are read narrowly, then essentially no change has occurred. *First English* will not apply to any regulatory taking which allows the landowner some interim use of his property; *Nollan* will not apply where the only property rights at stake are the public's right to possessory interests in or over private property. Ordinary zoning and land use control will carry on as before.

Yet if both cases are given their broader—and sounder—reading, then together they will mark a major shift in the power of government in land use cases. Under the combined influence of these two cases, local governments will find themselves under very heavy restraints when they seek to prevent new development. *First English* now holds that they are no longer given the costless right to stymie development by a succession of invalid regulations, and *Nollan* for its part holds that the scope of regulatory takings is far greater in the land use area than previously understood.

The effects of a broad reading of these two rules is, moreover, likely to be synergistic. Thus any developer who is considering the possibility of suit against a local government will generally have to balance three factors: the cost of litigation, the likelihood of success,

---

[115]On which see generally, Ellickson & Tarlock, Land Use Controls, Cases and Materials 737–60 (1981). Note there is an obvious exception where the special charges are designed to provide special benefits to the developed land. See on special assessments, Epstein, Takings, at 286–90.

and the gains if success occurs. For the sake of simplicity we can assume that the first set of costs are not likely to vary much in consequence of the recent Supreme Court decisions. But the benefit side of the developer's calculation shifts on both variables. If applied to ordinary zoning cases, *First English* could increase the rate of return from suit by promising interim damages, which prior law had generally denied. *Nollan* then expands the class of regulatory takings by limiting the scope of the police power, subjecting it to some higher level of scrutiny, and by importing the doctrine of unconstitutional conditions into the law of eminent domain. The cost-benefit calculations have shifted, and it will now pay to challenge many administrative actions that in the past would have been routinely accepted.

IV. Conclusion

If takings litigation had been unsettled before the recent Term, it is surely unsettled now. One could seek to reconcile *Keystone* with *First English* and *Nollan* on the ground that the first involves mineral rights, while the last two are special kinds of land use cases. But this effort must ignore the manifest inconsistency in judicial philosophy at work in these three cases. The issue of takings and the police power will return to the Supreme Court frequently, perhaps with a vengeance. Once it gets there the Court may not be able to skirt the issues that have been left unresolved by the earlier cases. In my view the course that it should follow is clear: move along the general path that it has set for itself in both *First English* and *Nollan*.

The reasons are substantive. The Takings Clause is best understood, not as some useless constitutional relic, but as part of a comprehensive effort to discipline the excesses of government by demanding that it pay when it takes private property for general public purposes.[116] In so doing, the Clause forces the government officials to put their money where their mouth is when they assert that certain social gains are worth the private costs that they impose. If one believed that government officials were always virtuous, and

---

[116]For a short statement of the overall position, as it links the Bill of Rights federalism and the separation of powers, see Epstein, Self-Interest and the Constitution, 37 J. Legal Ed. 153 (1987).

private landowners always corrupt, then this added form of external discipline would be quite unnecessary. But our entire constitutional system, both in its structural features and its protection of individual rights, takes the opposite view of government behavior. People do not shed their self-interest when they assume positions of public trust and power. The judicial efforts to eviscerate the takings clause, of which *Keystone* is perhaps the most regrettable illustration, rest on the failure of the Supreme Court to appreciate the social function that private property serves as a constraint against centralized power in a system of limited government. That is the great vice of *Keystone*, which should quickly die, if it is not dead already.[117] The decisions in *First English* and *Nollan*, for all their internal equivocations, start from the opposite premise, for, as Scalia has said, some government actions are nothing more than "out-and-out extortion." It is the Court's job to see that the political branches treat public office as a public trust. And a demanding task it is.

---

[117]It seems no accident that Justice Rehnquist has begun the rehabilitation of *Pennsylvania Coal*, which he quoted with evident approval in *First English*, *e.g.*, 107 S.Ct. at 2386, 2389.

DANIEL R. FISCHEL

FROM MITE TO CTS: STATE ANTI-TAKEOVER STATUTES, THE WILLIAMS ACT, THE COMMERCE CLAUSE, AND INSIDER TRADING

I. INTRODUCTION

On March 10, 1986, Dynamics Corporation of America, a New York Corporation with its principal place of business in Connecticut, was the beneficial owner of approximately 9.6 percent of the common stock of CTS Corporation, an Indiana corporation with its principal place of business and substantial assets in Indiana. On the same date, Dynamics initiated a cash tender offer for another one million shares of CTS stock for $43 per share. The common stock of CTS was selling for approximately $36 prior to the offer. If successful, the offer, coupled with the shares already owned, would give Dynamics approximately 27.5 percent of the common stock of CTS.

Daniel R. Fischel is Professor of Law and Professor in the Graduate School of Business, The University of Chicago.

AUTHOR'S NOTE: I should like to thank Michael Bradley, Frank Easterbrook, David Haddock, William Landes, John Langbein, Fred McChesney, Roberta Romano, and participants in faculty workshops at McGill University and the University of Chicago for their helpful comments. The John M. Olin and Sarah Scaife Foundations provided helpful financial support.

The success of Dynamics' tender offer was imperiled, however, by the passage of an anti-takeover statute by the state of Indiana. Less than a week before the commencement of the takeover bid, the Governor of Indiana had signed into law a revised Business Corporation Law. The revised statute includes a so-called "Control Share Acquisitions Chapter"[1] which provides, in essence, that shares of Indiana corporations acquired in a hostile tender offer are stripped of all voting rights. The Chapter further provides that voting rights can be restored by a shareholder vote in which "interested shares" cannot be voted.[2] The vote must be held within fifty days after the prospective acquirer requests a special shareholders meeting and complies with certain other conditions including paying the expenses of the meeting. If the acquirer fails to comply with the statute, or if the "disinterested" shareholders fail to restore voting rights to the control shares, the acquirer's shares may be redeemed by the target company at "fair market value."[3]

Rather than comply with the Control Shares Acquisitions Chapter, Dynamics filed suit in federal court seeking injunctive relief and a declaration that the Chapter was preempted by the Williams Act and imposed an unconstitutional burden on interstate commerce in violation of the Commerce Clause. Dynamics' arguments were premised on the Supreme Court's decision in *Edgar v. MITE Corp.*[4]

In *MITE*, the Court held that an Illinois anti-takeover statute was unconstitutional under the Commerce Clause because it placed a substantial burden on interstate commerce that outweighed any local benefits. A four-Justice plurality of the Court further concluded that the statute constituted a "direct" restraint on interstate commerce because it regulated interstate transactions wholly outside of Illinois. For this reason, the plurality asserted that the statute violated the Commerce Clause without any inquiry into the state

---

[1]Ind. Code §23-1-17-1 *et seq.* (Supp. 1986). Under the Act, an entity acquires "control shares" whenever it acquires shares that, but for the operation of the Act, would bring its voting power in the corporation to or above any of three thresholds: 20 percent, 33⅓ percent, or 50 percent. §23-1-42-1.

[2]"Interested shares" are shares that are beneficially owned by the acquirer, an officer, or an inside director of the corporation. §23-1-42-3.

[3]§23-1-42-10(b).

[4]457 U.S. 624 (1982).

interests involved. Finally, three Justices also concluded that the Illinois Act was invalid under the Supremacy Clause.

After *MITE*, state anti-takeover statutes were routinely declared unconstitutional by lower courts.[5] The Indiana Control Shares Acquisition Chapter was no exception. The district court held that the Chapter violated the Supremacy Clause and also impermissibly burdened interstate commerce.[6] The Seventh Circuit Court of Appeals, in an opinion by Judge Richard A. Posner, affirmed on both grounds.[7]

The Supreme Court, however, in a decision described as a "landmark"[8] and "the most important takeover decision in years,"[9] reversed.[10] The opinion of the Court, written by Justice Powell and joined by Justices Brennan, Marshall, Rehnquist, and O'Connor, emphasized that the Control Share Acquisitions Chapter was compatible with the investor protection goals of the Williams Act and thus was not invalid under the Supremacy Clause. The Chapter, the Court further held, did not violate the Commerce Clause because it did not discriminate against interstate commerce and did not subject interstate activities to inconsistent regulations. Justice Scalia concurred in parts of the opinions and in the judgment. Justice White, joined by Justices Blackmun and Stevens, dissented on the Commerce Clause issue. Justice White dissented alone on the preemption issue.

Dynamics Corp. of America v. CTS Corp. raises a host of important issues which transcend the holding of the case itself: What is the effect of takeovers and state anti-takeover statutes designed to minimize their occurrence? What is the relationship between state anti-takeover statutes and the Williams Act? What are the implications of the Court's decision on a state's ability to regulate takeovers and securities markets generally? Does *CTS* overrule *MITE*? What does

---

[5]See, *e.g.*, Fleet Aerospace Corp. v. Holderman, 796 F.2d 135 (6th Cir. 1986); Mesa Petroleum Co. v. Cities Service Co., 715 F.2d 1425 (10th Cir. 1983); Telvest Inc. v. Bradshaw, 697 F.2d 576 (4th Cir. 1983); Martin-Marietta Corp. v. Bendix Corp., 690 F.2d 558 (6th Cir. 1982); National City Lines, Inc. v. LLC Corp., 687 F.2d 1122 (8th Cir. 1982); Icahn v. Blunt, 612 F. Supp. 1400 (W.D. Mo. 1985).

[6]637 F. Supp. 389 (N.D. Ill. 1986).

[7]794 F.2d 250 (7th Cir. 1986).

[8]New York Times, April 21, 1987, p. 1, col. 4.

[9]Wall Street J., April 22, 1987, p. 3, col. 1.

[10]107 S.Ct. 1637 (1987).

the decision signify about the Court's attitude toward the Commerce Clause? And, finally, does the decision signal a changed attitude toward takeovers in light of the widely publicized insider trading controversy?

II. The Opinion of the Court of Appeals

The Seventh Circuit, following the reasoning of the Supreme Court in *MITE* and other prior cases, began its analysis with the premise that the Williams Act was not designed to favor either of the contestants in takeovers.[11] The Court recognized that this predicated Congressional neutrality was not dispositive of the preemption issue, because the critical issue was whether the states must be neutral as well. Nevertheless, the Seventh Circuit reasoned that any doubts of the Williams' Act preemptive intent were "stilled by the weight of precedent,"[12] and[13]

> Of course it is a big leap from saying that the Williams Act does not itself exhibit much hostility to tender offers to saying that it implicitly forbids states to adopt more hostile regulations, but this leap was taken by the Supreme Court plurality and us in *MITE* and by every court to consider the question since.

Having established this framework for the preemption issue, the Seventh Circuit found its application to the Indiana statute "straightforward" because the statute "upsets the balance struck by the Williams Act."[14]

The balance was upset in two ways. First, the Williams Act requires that tender offers remain open for twenty business days. The Indiana statute, by contrast, requires that offers remain open for fifty days. Second, the Indiana statute, unlike the Williams Act, strips the voting rights from acquired shares unless restored by a vote of "disinterested" shareholders. Together, the delay and uncertainty whether voting rights will be restored constitute a "lethal dose . . . very few tender offers could run the gauntlet that Indiana

---

[11] 794 F.2d 250, 261 (7th Cir. 1986). See also Edgar v. MITE Corp., 457 U.S. 624, 633 (1982); Piper v. Chris-Craft Industries, Inc., 430 U.S. 1, 24 (1977); Rondeau v. Mosinee Paper Corp., 422 U.S. 49, 58 (1975).

[12] 794 F.2d at 262.

[13] *Ibid.*

[14] *Ibid.*

has set up."[15] Any differences between the Indiana statute and the Illinois statute that the Supreme Court plurality in *MITE* found to be preempted by the Williams Act were deemed by the Seventh Circuit to be of "no practical significance."[16]

After having declared the Indiana statute unenforceable by reason of the Supremacy Clause, the Seventh Circuit then turned to its validity under the Commerce Clause. Again following *MITE*, the Court applied the well known test of *Pike v. Bruce Church, Inc.*[17] and held the Indiana statute unconstitutional:[18]

> In this case, as in *Edgar v. MITE Corp.*, where a majority of the Supreme Court held that Illinois' anti-takeover statute violated the Commerce Clause, the balance inclines heavily against the out-of-staters . . .
>
> Unlike a state's blue sky law the Indiana statute is calculated to impede transactions between residents of other states. For the sake of trivial or even negative benefits to its residents Indiana is depriving nonresidents of the valued opportunity to accept tender offers from other nonresidents.
>
> . . . Even if a corporation's tangible assets are immovable, the efficiency with which they are employed and the proportions in which the earnings they generate are divided between management and shareholders depends on the market for corporate control—an interstate, indeed international, market that the state of Indiana is not authorized to opt out of, as in effect it has done in this statute.

Finally, the Court attempted to distinguish the Indiana statute from other actions a state might take in regulating the internal affairs of corporations that would make takeovers more difficult. Unlike a law requiring cumulative voting, which would make it more difficult to oust an incumbent board of directors, the Court stated, the Indiana statute's "effect on the interstate market in securities and corporate control is direct, intended and substantial."[19] To allow states to regulate interstate tender offers by "jiggering with voting

---

[15]*Id.* at 262–63.

[16]*Id.* at 263.

[17]397 U.S. 137 (1970).

[18]794 F.2d at 263–64.

[19]*Id.* at 264.

rights," the Court concluded, "would invite facile evasions of the [commerce] clause."[20]

III. The Supreme Court's Opinions

A. JUSTICE POWELL'S MAJORITY OPINION

1. *The preemption issue.* The Supreme Court, like the Seventh Circuit, began its analysis of the Supremacy Clause[21] issue with the reasoning of *MITE*. Unlike the Seventh Circuit, however, the Supreme Court concluded that *MITE* did not compel invalidation of the Indiana statute.

The Court first emphasized that the plurality opinion on preemption in *MITE* did not represent the views of a majority, and therefore was not controlling.[22] But the Court found no need to question the reasoning of the plurality opinion because of the differences between the Illinois statute in *MITE* and the Indiana statute at issue in *CTS*. The defect of the Illinois statute emphasized by the plurality in *MITE* was that it "operated to favor management against offerors, to the detriment of shareholders."[23] The Indiana statute, by contrast, "protects the independent shareholder against both of the contending parties."[24] For this reason, the Court concluded, the Indiana statute was completely consistent with a "basic purpose of the Williams Act" since it placed "investors on an equal footing with the takeover bidder."[25]

The Court then elaborated on how the Indiana statute placed investors on an "equal footing" with a potential acquirer. Independent shareholders faced with a tender offer, in the Court's view, "often are at a disadvantage."[26] The Court stated that a takeover bid can be structured to induce individual shareholders to tender even if, acting as a group, they would prefer not to sell. "If share-

---

[20]*Ibid.*

[21]U.S. Constitution, Art. VI, Cl. 2.

[22]107 S.Ct. 1637, 1645 (1987).

[23]*Ibid.*

[24]*Ibid.*

[25]*Id.* at 1645–46 (quoting Piper v. Chris-Craft Industries, Inc., note 11 *supra*, at 30, and the legislative history of the Williams Act).

[26]107 S.Ct at 1646.

holders believe that a successful tender offer will be followed by a purchase of nontendering shares at a depressed price," the Court stated, "individual shareholders may tender their shares—even if they doubt the tender offer is in the corporation's best interest—to protect themselves from being forced to sell their shares at a depressed price."[27]

By allowing these pre-existing shareholders to vote as a group, the Court claimed, the Indiana statute protects shareholders from this "coercive" effect of tender offers. And, the Court continued, protecting shareholders from coercion not only does not conflict with the Williams Act, but rather "furthers the federal policy of investor protection."[28]

The Court then rejected the argument that the Indiana statute administered a "lethal dose" to acquirers by delaying tender offers for fifty days. The Court first questioned whether the Indiana statute imposes an absolute fifty-day delay. Offerors, the Court stated, are free under the Williams Act to accept shares within the normal twenty-day period conditional on having voting rights restored within a certain period of time.[29] Second, assuming the Indiana statute does impose some delay, the Court stressed that "nothing in *MITE* suggested that any delay imposed by state regulation, however short, would create a conflict with the Williams Act."[30] Rather, the test was whether the state regulation imposed "unreasonable delay."[31] Because fifty days was less than the sixty-day maximum period that Congress has established for tender offers,[32] the Court concluded that the Indiana statute did not impose unreasonable delay. Finally, the Court emphasized that if limiting an acquirer's free exercise of choice after a successful tender offer were sufficient for a state regulation to be invalid under the Supremacy Clause, a variety of state regulations whose validity had never been questioned (such as cumulative voting and other provisions limiting the ability to remove directors) would also be invalid.[33] Thus the

---

[27] *Ibid.*

[28] *Ibid.*

[29] *Id.* at 1647.

[30] *Ibid.*

[31] *Ibid.*

[32] 15 U.S.C. §78n(d)(5) (1982 ed. and Supp. III).

[33] 107 S.Ct. at 1647–48.

Court concluded that "the possibility that the Indiana Act will delay some tender offers is insufficient to require a conclusion that the Williams Act preempts the Act."[34]

2. *The Commerce Clause issue.* The Commerce Clause, Article I, §8 of the Federal Constitution, grants to Congress the power "[t]o regulate Commerce . . . among the several States." The Clause says nothing about limitations on the authority of states to regulate interstate commerce. For at least 135 years, however, it has been settled that the Clause prohibits states from taking certain actions respecting interstate commerce absent congressional authorization.[35] As the Court recognized, however, its prior decisions attempting to delineate precisely what actions are prohibited to states have "not always been easy to follow."[36] Rather, a "variety of tests" have been proposed "to describe the difference between those regulations that the Commerce Clause permits and those regulations that it prohibits."[37]

In yet another attempt at defining the permissible scope of state regulation, the Court began with the premise that "[t]he principal objects of the dormant Commerce Clause scrutiny are statutes that discriminate against interstate commerce."[38] From this premise, the Court concluded that the Indiana Act "is not such a statute" because "it has the same effect on tender offers whether or not the offeror is a domiciliary or resident of Indiana."[39]

Alternatively, the Court stated, state statutes may be invalid under the Commerce Clause if they "affect interstate commerce by subjecting activities to inconsistent regulations."[40] The Indiana statute, however, "poses no such problem," the Court stated, because offerors will not have to comply with any other law "[s]o long as each state regulates voting rights only in the corporations it has created."[41] Thus "the Indiana Act does not create an impermissible risk of inconsistent regulation by different states."[42]

---

[34]*Id.* at 1648.

[35]*See* Cooley v. Board of Wardens, 12 How. 298 (1851); *cf.* Gibbons v. Ogden, 9 Wheat 1 (1824).

[36]107 S.Ct. at 1648.

[37]*Ibid.*

[38]*Ibid.*

[39]*Id.* at 1648–49.

[40]*Id.* at 1649.

[41]*Ibid.*

[42]*Ibid.*

The error of the Court of Appeals, the Court stressed, was to ignore these "threshold" issues and focus instead on the Indiana Act's "potential to hinder tender offers."[43] The Court dismissed this concern. Virtually all corporations, the Court stated, are created and regulated by the law of their incorporating state. It is inevitable that such laws, by prohibiting certain transactions, and regulating others, will "affect certain aspects of interstate commerce."[44] Moreover, "[t]his necessarily is true with respect to corporations with shareholders in states other than the state of incorporation."[45] State laws regulating large corporations, such as those listed on national organized exchanges, routinely affect residents of other states.

Thus state laws such as the Indiana Act that may hinder tender offers are no different from state laws that regulate mergers. Several states, for example, require supermajority votes to approve mergers. "By requiring a greater vote for mergers than is required for other transactions," the Court stated, "these laws make it more difficult for corporations to merge."[46] The Court also cited other state laws that may inhibit corporations with shareholders in multiple states from engaging in certain transactions.[47]

The Court also emphasized Indiana's legitimate state interest "in promoting stable relationships among parties involved in the corporations it charters."[48] Echoing its earlier analysis of the preemption issue, the Court emphasized that the "primary purpose" of the Indiana Act was to "protect the shareholders of Indiana corporations" from "the possibility of coercion in some takeover bids."[49]

Finally, the Court stressed that *MITE* does not stand for the proposition that a state has no legitimate interest in protecting nonresident shareholders. *MITE*, the Court stated, involved an Illinois statute that "applied as well to out-of-state corporations as to in-state corporations."[50] The Indiana Act, by contrast, was different:[51]

---

[43]*Ibid.*

[44]*Id.* at 1650.

[45]*Ibid.*

[46]*Ibid.*

[47]*Ibid.*, discussing appraisal remedy statutes, and provisions authorizing staggered boards of directors, cumulative voting, and dual class common stock.

[48]*Id.* at 1651.

[49]*Ibid.*

[50]*Ibid.*

[51]*Id.* at 1651–52.

> We agree that Indiana has no interest in protecting nonresident shareholders of *nonresident corporations*. But this Act applies only to corporations incorporated in Indiana. . . . Moreover, unlike the Illinois statute invalidated in *MITE*, the Indiana Act applies only to corporations that have a substantial number of shareholders in Indiana. See Ind. Code §23-1-42-4(a)(3) (Supp. 1986). Thus, every application of the Indiana Act will affect a substantial number of Indiana residents, whom Indiana indisputably has an interest in protecting.

Accordingly, the Court rejected the contention that the Indiana Act is unconstitutional because it "will limit the number of successful tender offers."[52] Although the Court stated that "[t]here is little evidence that this will occur,"[53] it stressed that the issue was not relevant to its analysis. "[E]ven if the Act should decrease the number of successful tender offers for Indiana corporations," the Court concluded, "this would not offend the Commerce Clause."[54]

B. JUSTICE SCALIA'S CONCURRING OPINION

Justice Scalia agreed with the majority that the Indiana Act neither discriminates against interstate commerce nor creates an impermissible risk of subjecting offerors to inconsistent regulations. For these reasons, he concluded "without further analysis that [the Indiana Act] is not invalid under the Commerce Clause."[55]

Justice Scalia questioned, however, both the necessity and the accuracy of the Court's analysis of the purpose of the Indiana Act. Not only did he "not share the Court's apparent high estimation of the beneficence of the state statute at issue here,"[56] but he expressed doubt whether the inquiry was an appropriate judicial function:[57]

> While is has become standard practice at least since *Pike v. Bruce Church* to consider . . . whether the burden on commerce imposed by a state statute "is clearly excessive in relation to the putative local benefits," such an inquiry is ill suited to the ju-

---

[52]*Id.* at 1652.

[53]*Ibid.*

[54]*Ibid.*

[55]*Ibid.*

[56]*Id.* at 1653.

[57]*Id.* at 1652–53.

dicial function and should be undertaken rarely if at all. This case is a good illustration of the point. Whether the control shares stature "protects shareholders of Indiana corporations . . . or protects incumbent management" seems to me to be a highly debatable question, but it is extraordinary to think that the constitutionality of the Act should depend on the answer. Nothing in the Constitution says that the protection of entrenched management is any less important a "putative local benefit" than the protection of entrenched shareholders, and I do not know what qualifies us to make that judgment. . . .

As long as a state's corporation law governs only its own corporations and does not discriminate against out-of-state interests, it should survive this Court's scrutiny under the Commerce Clause, whether it promotes shareholder welfare or industrial stagnation.

On the Supremacy Clause issue, Justice Scalia agreed with the Court that the Williams Act did not preempt the Indiana Act, but unlike the Court, reached this result without reference to the purpose of the Act. Justice Scalia asserted that the express anti-preemption provision of the Securities Exchange Act, coupled with a state's traditional role in regulating the voting rights of domestic corporations, establishes that no conflict exists between the Indiana Act and the Williams Act.[58]

C. JUSTICE WHITE'S DISSENTING OPINION

Justice White dissented. Although Justice White did not dispute the majority's characterization of the Indiana Act as protecting shareholders of Indiana corporations, he concluded nevertheless that the Act was invalid under the Supremacy Clause. The purpose of the Williams Act, Justice White asserted, was to provide investors with sufficient information to make an informed decision whether or not to sell.[59] The Indiana Act, by contrast, prevents minority shareholders in certain circumstances from selling their stock and thus does not further the federal policy of investor protection.[60]

Further, Justice White, joined by Justices Blackmun and Stevens, concluded that the Indiana Act violates the Commerce Clause because its effect is to preclude out-of-state purchasers from acquiring

---

[58]*Id.* at 1653.

[59]*Id.* at 1654.

[60]*Ibid.*

shares of Indiana corporations.[61] Moreover, the dissenters emphasized that the purpose of the Act as admitted by Indiana itself in
contrast with how it is labeled, is to allow shareholders, who may
be Indiana residents, to determine whether a company should be
liquidated or its assets removed from the state.[62] A law with such
a protectionist purpose, the dissenters asserted, "is the archetype
of the kind of state law that the Commerce Clause forbids."[63]

IV. State Anti-Takeover Statutes and the Williams Act

The Court in *CTS* reasoned that the Indiana Act furthered
the federal policy of investor protection embodied in the Williams
Act by protecting shareholders from the coercive aspects of tender
offers. This line of argument is troublesome on two grounds. First,
it suggests incorrectly that the issue of preemption turns on whether
the Indiana Act in fact protects shareholders. Second, the Court's
reasoning reflects a fundamental misunderstanding of the effects of
tender offers, state anti-takeover statutes, and the Williams Act.

A. ARE TAKEOVERS COERCIVE?

There is now extensive evidence on the economic effects of takeover bids for the shareholders of target companies.[64] Takeover bids
offer shareholders of target companies a premium of approximately
50 percent on average over the pre-offer price. Those shareholders
who sell receive this premium; those that remain as shareholders
after a transfer of control occurs also experience a substantial capital
gain. If a takeover bid is defeated and the target is not acquired by
another firm, the price of the target's shares returns to the pre-offer
level.

Thus the shareholders of target companies are beneficiaries when
a takeover bid is made. This point has been documented in every
serious study on the issue and was explicitly recognized by the

---

[61]*Id.* at 1655.

[62]*Ibid.*

[63]*Id.* at 1656.

[64]The evidence is summarized in Jensen & Ruback, The Market for Corporate Control:
The Scientific Evidence, 11 J. Fin. Econ. 5 (1983). The more recent evidence is summarized
in Jarrell, Brickley & Netter, The Market for Corporate Control: The Empirical Evidence
Since 1980, J. Econ. Perspectives (forthcoming 1987).

Court in *MITE*.[65] In *CTS*, however, the same Court that decided *MITE* just five years earlier had a very different view of tender offers. The Court in *CTS* reasoned that tender offers, particularly two-tier tender offers where the price offered in the first step is higher than in the second, place "independent shareholders" at a "disadvantage." This concern that takeovers may victimize shareholders of target corporations has been articulated more frequently in recent years. It has been advanced in the academic literature[66] and has been adopted by the Delaware Supreme Court in another context.[67]

Precisely what is meant by the term "coercion"? One definition is the pressure that exists to sell to obtain the premium. Coercion in this sense, however, always exists whenever a good offer is presented that is open for a limited period. If Smith offers Jones $100,000 more for Jones's house than it is worth, but tells Jones he must decide immediately, Jones will feel tremendous pressure to sell. But so long as Jones retains the ability to refuse to sell and be in the same position he was before, it is hard to see how he is disadvantaged by having the option to sell to Smith. If the term is to have any meaning, therefore, the opportunity to sell on advantageous terms cannot by itself be deemed coercive.

There is another definition of coercion, however, which focuses on a perceived collective action problem faced by shareholders when a hostile tender offer is made. Consider the following hypothetical situation. The shares of Target Corp. are selling at $50 a share. Bidder Corp. makes an offer to purchase 51 percent of Target Corp.'s shares at $60 and simultaneously announces that the remaining 49 percent will be acquired at $30 in a second-step merger. If shareholders could act collectively, they would reject the offer because the pre-offer price of $50 is higher than the blended price of approximately $45 offered by Bidder Corp (51% × $60 + 49% × $30). Acting individually, however, shareholders of Target Corp. might decide to tender at $60 to avoid having to sell all of their shares at $30 as would occur if 51 percent of Target's shareholders decided to tender.

[65]457 U.S. at 643–44.

[66]See, *e.g.*, Bebchuk, Toward Undistorted Choice and Equal Treatment in Corporate Takeovers, 98 Harv. L. Rev. 1693 (1985).

[67]Unocal v. Mesa Petroleum Co., 493 A.2d 946 (Del. 1985).

Thus the collective action problem faced by a target's shareholders may, at least in theory, result in shareholders being induced to sell for less than their shares are worth.[68] What makes the matter complicated is that the same collective action that may lead to this result may also cause the defeat of a value increasing transaction.

Let us modify the preceding example. Target Corp.'s shares are again selling at $50 when Bidder Corp. announces a tender offer to purchase any and all of the Target's shares at $70. Suppose Target's shareholders believe that the unpurchased shares will be worth $80 if the offer is successful and Bidder Corp. acquires control but only $50, the pre-offer price, if the offer is unsuccessful. If Target Corp.'s shareholders could act collectively, they would tender at $70 to avoid having to settle for $50 since, by definition, the $80 value can only be realized if the offer is successful. Acting individually, however, Target's shareholders may decide not to tender, thinking that if enough shareholders decide to sell at $70, they will be able to have all of their shares worth $80. If enough shareholders attempt to free ride in this manner by not tendering, of course, the offer will be defeated and all shares will again be worth $50.[69]

The preceding discussion illustrates an important general point—to be successful all tender offers must be front-end loaded. Unless shareholders believe that they are better off by tendering than by not tendering, they have no incentive to tender. Thus, what the Supreme Court deemed coercive—a front-end loaded offer where the payment is higher at the first step than at the second—is actually a precondition to having a successful offer. Such front-end loading, either explicitly in a two-tier offer or implicitly in other types of offers, is necessary for the free-rider problem to be overcome.

Resolution of the question whether a two-tier (or other type of) offer is coercive in an economic sense, therefore, requires a determination whether the offer is designed to exploit or to overcome a

---

[68]I ignore here the (minor) complication that arises if certain shareholders place a value on their shares in excess of the market price. The evidence demonstrates that the supply of shares in publicly held corporations is highly, if not perfectly, elastic. See Schleifer, Do Demand Curves for Stocks Slope Down? 41 J. Fin. 579 (1986); Scholes, The Market for Securities: Substitutions versus Price Pressure Effects and the Effects of Information on Share Prices, 41 J. Bus. 179 (1973).

[69]For a discussion of the free-rider problem in the context of takeovers, see Grossman & Hart, Takeover Bids, the Free-Rider Problem, and the Theory of the Corporation, 11 Bell J. Econ. 42 (1980).

collective action problem. What the Supreme Court did was to emphasize the first possibility but to ignore the second. This error in analysis is more serious because the evidence provides no support for the proposition that two-tier offers facilitate the appropriation of wealth from shareholders of target corporations. On the contrary, the evidence demonstrates that the Supreme Court's concern about two-tier tender offers reducing shareholders' welfare is entirely misplaced.

In reality, a variety of market and legal mechanisms exist that eliminate the possibility of a welfare reducing transaction effectuated by a two-tier bid. Let us return to the hypothetical discussed above where a target's shares are selling at $50 and a bidder attempts to acquire them for $45 by paying $60 in a first step and $30 in the second. This attempt can always be defeated by a bid at current value by raising the price in the first tier (to $70 in the hypothetical example). The bid at current value can be made by either a competing third party bidder[70] or by incumbent management in a self-tender offer.[71] More generally, the highest valuing acquirer can always devise an offer that will dominate any offer, no matter how constructed, by the second highest valuing acquirer.[72] Alternatively, large blocs of shares can be purchased by arbitragers to overcome the collective action problem.[73]

In addition, the shareholders of any firm can avoid the possibility of a two-tier offer altogether by any number of charter amendments.[74] Fair price amendments, for example, require that a bidder

---

[70]See Bradley, Desai & Kim, The Rationale Behind Interfirm Tender Offers, 11 J. Fin. Econ. 183 (1983).

[71]See Bradley & Rosenzweig, The Law and Economics of Defensive Stock Repurchases and Defensive Self-Tender Offers, 99 Harv. L. Rev. (1986).

[72]See Bradley, Desai & Kim, Synergistic Gains from Corporate Acquisitions and Their Division Between the Stockholders of Target and Acquiring Firms, J. Fin. Econ. (forthcoming). Alternatively, the highest valuing acquirer can purchase the shares from the first bidder if the first bidder has been successful.

[73]Schwartz, Search Theory and The Tender Offer Auction, 2 Yale J. Law, Econ. & Org. 229 (1986). On the role of large shareholders in facilitating beneficial transfers of control, see Schleifer & Vishny, Large Shareholders and Corporate Control, 94 J. Pol. Econ. 461 (1986).

[74]See Carney, Shareholder Coordination Costs, Shark Repellents, and Takeout Mergers: The Case Against Fiduciary Duties, 1983 Am. Bar Foundation Res. J. 341. See also Romano, The Political Economy of Takeover Statutes, 73 Va. L. Rev. 111, 145–80 (1987); Baysinger & Butler, Anti-Takeover Amendments, Managerial Entrenchment, and the Contractual Theory of the Corporation, 71 Va. L. Rev. 1257 (1985).

pay the same nominal amount in the second step as in the first (but less in real terms because of the time use value of money). Similarly, super-majority requirements ensure that shareholders overwhelmingly approve the terms of a proposed second-step merger before it can be consummated. Other devices that do not need shareholder approval, such as poison pills, also effectively preclude the possibility of a two-tier bid.

Finally, if all else fails, the appraisal remedy is an additional safeguard against two-tier bids being used to facilitate a value decreasing transaction.[75] The ability of the bidder in the above hypothetical to succeed was dependent on the bidder's ability to pay the remaining target shareholders $30 in the second step when they were previously selling for $50. The appraisal remedy, which requires that dissenting shareholders be paid "fair value" for their shares, makes this impossible.

That two-tier bids are not used to effectuate welfare reducing transactions is confirmed by the evidence. Premiums paid to targets' shareholders when two-tier bids are made are positive, large, and virtually identical to the level of premiums paid in other types of corporate acquisitions.[76] Moreover, the overwhelming majority of two-tier bids are made in negotiated transactions where the target's shareholders are represented by its management.[77] The use of two-tier bids in negotiated transactions demonstrates that this acquisition technique is used to overcome the free-rider problem discussed above rather than to exploit the inability of shareholders to coordinate.

The evidence on the economic effects of charter amendments and poison pills further demonstrates the weakness of the coercion argument. Charter amendments and poison pills are typically justified as protection against the coercive effects of two-tier tender offers. If this claim were accurate, stock prices should rise when charter amendment and poison pill are adopted. Instead, depending on exactly what type of charter amendment or poison pill is adopted,

---

[75]See Fischel, The Appraisal Remedy in Corporate Law, 1983 Am. Bar Foundation Res. J. 875.

[76]See Comment & Jarrell, Two-Tier and Negotiated Tender Offers: The Imprisonment of the Free-Riding Shareholder, J. Fin. Econ. (forthcoming).

[77]Ibid.

stock prices either remain the same or go down.[78] Thus shareholders
do not appear to value the "protection" they are receiving from
coercive tender offers. Rather, they appear to be more concerned
about the reduced probability of receiving a takeover bid in the first
instance.

Moreover, not all firms adopt charter amendments or poison pills.
The shareholders of these firms are likely to value protection from
the alleged coercive effects of tender offers even less. The conclusion
is inescapable that the alleged coercive effect of tender offers is not
a problem.

B. WHY ARE STATE ANTI-TAKEOVER STATUTES ADOPTED?

In *MITE*, the Supreme Court characterized the Illinois anti-
takeover statute at issue as operating to favor incumbent management against offerors, to the detriment of shareholders. In *CTS*,
by contrast, the Court characterized the Indiana statute as protecting independent shareholders from coercive tender offers.

The Court suggested that the effects of the two statutes were
different. The Illinois statute at issue in *MITE* provided for a twenty-
day precommencement period before an offer could be effective
and allowed the Illinois Secretary of State to hold a hearing to
review the "fairness" of a tender offer. No deadline was set by
which time the hearing had to be held. The Indiana statute, by
contrast, required a shareholder vote within fifty days and did not
allow for administrative review. Moreover, bidders could make their
offer conditional on having voting rights restored by shareholder
vote. For these reasons, the Court concluded that the Indiana statute, unlike the Illinois statute at issue in *MITE*, did not impose
unreasonable delay and was not enacted for the purpose of protecting incumbent management.

As the Seventh Circuit recognized, however, these differences
are only ones of degree. Both statutes share the common charac-

---

[78]See Jarrell & Poulsen, Shark Repellents and Stock Prices: The Effects of Anti-Takeover
Amendments Since 1980, Office of the Chief Economist, Securities and Exchange Commission (1986) (summarizing earlier studies and finding that non–fair price amendments have
a statistically significant negative effect on share prices, while fair price amendments have
an insignificant effect); Reingart, The Economics of Poison Pills, Univ. of Chicago Working
Paper (1987) (finding that poison pills have a statistically significant negative effect on share
prices).

teristic of delay (and impose additional disclosure obligations as well). Bidders and investors suffer because delay reduces the probability of a successful offer. The additional time can be used by incumbent management to engage in defensive tactics that reduce the value of the firm (and thus make it unattractive to a bidder) or search for a white knight. A bidder's ability to make a conditional offer, which the Court stressed in *CTS*, does protect bidders from the possibility of obtaining control with no voting rights. But a conditional offer does not protect bidders from a target's management using the fifty-day period to engage in defensive tactics (such as selling a valuable division) or seeking a white knight. In either case, the returns to bidders from acquisition activity are reduced.

Why do states enact statutes that delay takeover bids? The question is important because state anti-takeover statutes are a pervasive phenomenon. Prior to *MITE*, thirty-seven states had enacted anti-takeover statutes.[79] Many of these same states adopted so-called "second generation" statutes after the Illinois statute was struck down by the Court in *MITE*.[80] The Court's decision upholding the Indiana statute in *CTS* will no doubt spur even more states to adopt similar statutes.

There are three plausible, and sometimes overlapping, reasons why states might adopt anti-takeover statutes. The first is that the statutes are enacted to provide target firms' managements more bargaining power. By making it more difficult for a bidder to succeed in a non-negotiated transaction, state statutes induce bidders to negotiate directly with targets' management. This in turn has the effect of allowing targets' management to negotiate on behalf of their shareholders to obtain a greater share of the gains created by the transfer of control than if no negotiation occurred.

It is important to recognize that the increased bargaining power hypothesis is related to, but different from, the coercion hypothesis discussed in the preceding subsection. The two are related in that they both are premised on bidders' ability to exploit collective action problems faced by target shareholders. They are different in that

---

[79]See Warren, Developments in State Takeover Regulation: MITE and Its Aftermath, 40 Bus. Law. 671 n.2 & 3 (1985), for a list of the thirty-seven state anti-takeover enacted prior to *MITE*.

[80]For a discussion of the second-generation state anti-takeover statutes, see Sargent, Do the Second-Generation State Takeover Statutes Violate the Commerce Clause?, 8 Corp. L. Rev. 3, 5–6, 8–12 (1985); Warren, note 8 *supra*, at 694–700.

the coercion hypothesis focuses on protecting target shareholders from being induced to sell their shares for less than they are worth absent a change in control while the increased bargaining power hypothesis focuses on allowing target shareholders to capture more of the gains from a value increasing transfer of control.

A second explanation can be labeled the management entrenchment hypothesis. This hypothesis is premised on the conflict of interest that typically exists between management and shareholders once a takeover is made. Under this interpretation, managers use the additional delay to defeat an outstanding offer (or deter the offer from being made at all) to the detriment of shareholders.

The third and final explanation for state anti-takeover statutes is that these statutes are an attempt to prevent firms from exiting the state with the resulting loss of jobs. Transfers of control frequently result in a change of management. The new management team may take certain actions such as changing firm location, closing plants, or firing workers. State anti-takeover statutes which make transfers of control more difficult decrease the probability that these events will occur.

It is difficult to distinguish among these three explanations. Roberta Romano has studied the politics behind state anti-takeover statutes and has concluded that the laws are passed in response to lobbying pressures of large firms within the state that may be takeover targets.[81] Other groups such as labor groups, community organizations, and the organized bar (with the exception of Delaware), she found, play little role in the support for the laws and their passage. Professor Romano's study was not exhaustive—it considered the passage of anti-takeover laws in only a few states and focused intensively on only one (Connecticut). Nevertheless, her results cast doubt on the validity of the prevention of firm exit and job loss explanation of state anti-takeover statutes.

In distinguishing between the increased bargaining power and management entrenchment hypotheses, her finding that state statutes are typically passed in response to lobbying pressure of a large firm likely to be subject to a takeover attempt is ambiguous. Management seeking the law may be attempting to get increased bargaining power to negotiate on behalf of their shareholders more effectively or, alternatively, to defeat the offer altogether.

---

[81]See Romano, note 74 *supra*.

There is a fine line between negotiating hard to get the best possible price and negotiating harder than shareholders would like so as to prevent the offer from succeeding. That offers sometimes are defeated does not distinguish between these situations because managers, even if they are acting as perfect agents, may misjudge what the bidder is willing to pay and bargain too hard. Similarly, the fact that the enactment of a state anti-takeover statute typically results in shareholders of target corporations receiving higher premiums is also inconclusive because some offers may succeed, albeit at higher cost, despite the opposition of target management.

It is important to emphasize, however, that state anti-takeover statutes may not be in shareholders' interests even if the increased bargaining power hypothesis is correct. Any gains obtained by shareholders of target corporations are paid for by shareholders of bidder corporations.[82] Of course, this may not be of concern to a particular state if the target but not the bidder is located there. Indeed, the absence of bidder firms in a state appears to be one of the main determinants of whether that state will adopt an anti-takeover statute.[83]

Even for shareholders of target firms, however, the effect of increasing the bargaining power of management is unclear. While the increased bargaining power may result in higher premiums, it will also result in fewer offers and less monitoring. Whether the expected gains from higher premiums outweigh the expected losses from fewer offers (and hence fewer opportunities to sell at a premium) and reduced monitoring is an empirical question.

The existing evidence on this question is too meager to provide an unambiguous answer. But there are reasons to believe that state anti-takeover statutes do not improve, and may reduce, shareholders' welfare. The additional delay resulting from state anti-takeover statutes such as Indiana's could be created by contract. Firms, for example, could include provisions creating delay in their corporate charter when they go public or amend their charters in this manner.

---

[82]For a general discussion of this point, see Easterbrook & Fischel, Auctions and Sunk Costs in Tender Offers, 35 Stan. L. Rev. 1 (1982); Easterbrook & Fischel, Corporate Control Transactions, 91 Yale L. J. 698 (1982).

[83]Romano, note 74 *supra*, at 142–45. This result is somewhat surprising, however, since bidders in any particular state (except perhaps Delaware) will typically be interested in acquiring corporations incorporated in other states.

Either of these mechanisms, however, would require shareholder approval (by their willingness to pay in the first situation or their vote in the second). Firms rarely pursue either of these alternatives. It is possible that firms lobby for anti-takeover statutes in those situations where shareholders would refuse to approve a charter amendment with the same effect.

Moreover, as discussed above, researchers who have studied the stock price effects of defensive tactics that are sometimes justified as attempts to increase bargaining power (*i.e.*, charter amendments and poison pills) have concluded that these attempts do not increase, and may decrease, stock prices.[84] If private attempts to increase bargaining power are not valued by the shareholders of firms that make the attempt, it is unlikely shareholders of other firms will be benefitted by a law that applies to firms that do not make the attempt.

Finally, three studies have tried to measure directly the effect of passage of state anti-takeover statutes on shareholders of firms incorporated in that state. Such studies face severe methodological problems because of the difficulty of identifying discrete days when new information becomes available.[85] The day of passage will not even satisfy this requirement if passage was anticipated. Nevertheless, the results of the studies are interesting. One found that state anti-takeover statutes in Connecticut, Missouri, and Pennsylvania had no effect on share prices;[86] a second that the New York statute had a negative but statistically insignificant effect;[87] the third that the Ohio statute had a large negative and statistically significant effect on the share prices of the Ohio firm that lobbied for the law and a smaller, but still statistically significant negative effect on the share prices of other Ohio corporations.[88] This latter study provides at least preliminary support for the management entrenchment ex-

---

[84]See studies cited in note 78 *supra*.

[85]See Binder, Measuring the Effects of Regulation with Stock Price Data, 11 Bell J. Econ. 167 (1985) for a discussion of the difficulty of isolating the effects of legislation with stock price data.

[86]Romano, note 74 *supra*, at 180–87.

[87]Schumann, State Regulation of Takeovers and Shareholder Wealth: The Effects of New York's 1985 Takeover Statutes, Bureau of Economics Staff Report to the Federal Trade Commission, March 1987.

[88]Office of the Chief Economist, Securities and Exchange Commission, Shareholder Wealth Effects of Ohio Legislation Affecting Takeovers, May 1987.

planation for this particular state anti-takeover statute. The studies taken together perhaps are too equivocal to support this interpretation of the statutes.[89] But what is clear is that the evidence provides no support for the proposition that investors are "protected" or otherwise benefitted by state anti-takeover statutes.

C.   STATE ANTI-TAKEOVER STATUTES AND THE
   ### INCORPORATION DEBATE

Academics have long debated the pros and cons of our system of corporate law in which fifty states compete with each other to attract incorporations. The traditional view espoused by William Cary is that this competition for the franchise taxes and other revenues resulting from incorporation leads to a "race for the bottom" to the detriment of investors.[90] Cary's argument was that since managers choose the state of incorporation, states have incentives to choose legal rules that allow managers to exploit investors. Delaware, the state which in Cary's view allowed the most exploitation, was therefore the most successful in raising revenues from incorporations.

This traditional view was forcefully attacked by Ralph Winter and others.[91] The fundamental defect in Cary's argument, these scholars pointed out, was that it was premised on an assumption of investor irrationality. Why would rational investors, with virtually an infinite number of investment substitutes, place their money in firms incorporated in states with rules that operated to their detriment? To attract investment dollars, therefore, entrepreneurs choosing a state of incorporation will search for legal rules that maximize investors' welfare. Thus states, to compete for the revenue produced by incorporations, must adopt rules that are in the

---

[89]On the other hand, the studies may underestimate the adverse effect of state anti-takeover statutes on share prices. Prior to *CTS*, these statutes were routinely declared unconstitutional. See note 5 *supra*. As a result, the effect of these statutes was in all probability less than if their validity was not in doubt.

[90]See Cary, Federalism and Corporate Law: Reflections upon Delaware, 83 Yale L. J. 663 (1974).

[91]See Winter, State Law, Shareholder Protection, and the Theory of the Corporation, 6 J. Legal Stud. 251 (1977); Fischel, The "Race to the Bottom" Revisited: Reflections on Recent Developments in Delaware's Corporation Law, 76 Nw. U. L. Rev. 913 (1982); Easterbrook, Manager's Discretion and Investor's Welfare: Theories and Evidence, 9 Del. J. Corp. L. 540 (1984).

interest of investors. The success of Delaware, under this view, results from its having provided investors with a package of legal rules that operates to the benefit of managers and investors alike. Winter's thesis has been supported by several empirical studies[92] and has dominated the theoretical debate.

The proposition that state anti-takeover statutes reduce share-holders' welfare, however, presents a conundrum for the Winter thesis. Thirty-seven states enacted state anti-takeover statutes prior to *MITE*. After the Illinois statute at issue was invalidated, most of these states (and some others) enacted new anti-takeover statutes. If competition among states is optimal for investors, how could so many states pass laws which harm these same investors?

This question is a difficult one—Winter's thesis appears to be contradicted by the passage of state anti-takeover statutes by so many states. In fact, the state anti-takeover statute experience suggests two complexities in the incorporation debate not fully appreciated by Winter and those who adopted his thesis. First, Winter (like Cary) focused on states' incentive to attract incorporations to raise revenue from franchise taxes. This is probably an oversimplification of the state legislative process. From the perspective of individual state legislators, increased revenue from franchise taxes is something of a public good. No individual state legislator can capture the benefits of increased revenue at the state level. Thus the prospect of increased revenues at the state level does not provide a strong incentive to act. But individual legislators can capture the benefits from other types of more direct payments such as campaign contributions. Such direct payments can motivate individual legislators to act even if the long-run economic vitality of the state is reduced. Managers of target firms facing a takeover benefit from the law; their relatively small number makes it possible to mobilize in support of the law. The (greater) losses imposed by the law are borne by dispersed shareholders and future entrepreneurs who want to raise capital for firms incorporated in the state.

The second and related complexity not fully appreciated by Winter and his followers in the incorporation debate is the possibility

---

[92]See Dodd & Leftwich, The Market for Corporate Charters: "Unhealthy Competition" Versus Federal Regulation, 53 J. Bus. 59 (1980); Romano, Law as a Product: Some Pieces of the Incorporation Puzzle, 1 J. L. Econ. & Org. 225, 273 (1985). See also Baysinger & Butler, Race for the Bottom v. Climb to the Top: The ALI Project and Uniformity in Corporate Law, 10 J. Corp. Law 431 (1985).

of ex post opportunistic behavior by a firm's managers.[93] If state anti-takeover statutes reduce investors' wealth, investors will discount the price they are willing to pay for shares accordingly. Thus entrepreneurs who want to raise funds for new ventures bear the loss if they decide to incorporate in a state with an anti-takeover statute. Entrepreneurs can avoid this loss, however, if the firm goes public in a state without an anti-takeover statute and later pressures the state to adopt such a law or switches its state of incorporation to a state where such a law exists. In this event, managers benefit from entrenchment but shareholders (and future entrepreneurs) bear the loss.[94] The combination of managers behaving opportunistically coupled with the receptivity of state legislators to campaign contributions and other direct payments provides the most plausible explanation for the prevalence of state anti-takeover statutes.

Does the Winter thesis survive the widespread adoption of state anti-takeover statutes? The answer depends on how the thesis is characterized. If the thesis is that the competition among states for incorporations always produces the optimal result in every state, the answer is no. But if the thesis is that this competition creates a powerful tendency for states to enact laws that operate to the benefit of investors (the opposite of the Cary view), then there is no inconsistency.

Significantly, Delaware, the most important state for purposes of the development of corporate law and the state where most large firms are incorporated, has been among the least willing to enact an anti-takeover statute.[95] Even after *CTS* was decided, the Delaware legislature considered but refused to adopt an anti-takeover

---

[93]Jonathan Macey and Geoffrey Miller have argued that opportunistic behavior by the Delaware organized bar has influenced the development of Delaware's corporation law. See Macey & Miller, Toward an Interest-Group Theory of Delaware Corporation Law, 65 Tex. L. Rev. 469 (1987).

[94]This is something of an oversimplification because shareholders will anticipate the possibility that managers will attempt to entrench themselves. Because the phenomenon of state anti-takeover statutes is so recent, however, it is probably safe to assume that shareholders did not fully anticipate the proliferation of these statutes when the firms they invested in went public. One recent study found that only 17 percent of a random sample of 360 publicly traded firms sold common stock at least once in an eleven-year period. See Mikkelson & Partch, Valuation Effects of Security Offerings and the Issuance Process, 15 J. Fin. Econ. 31 (1986).

[95]Precisely why Delaware has been reluctant to enact an anti-takeover statute is less clear. One possibility is that the diverse interests of firms (bidders and targets) incorporated in Delaware make it impossible for any particular firm to dominate the legislative process. A second possibility is that any anti-takeover statute enacted would be constitutionally suspect

statute modeled after the Indiana statute that the Court upheld. Thus the number of states that have enacted anti-takeover statutes is a misleading indicator of the importance of such statutes. Moreover, the more states that adopt anti-takeover statutes, the greater the opportunity for other states to attract investment capital by not following this approach. It is probably no coincidence that California, the state with perhaps the largest number of new firms going public, has never had an anti-takeover statute. Finally, it must be remembered that state anti-takeover statutes are a relatively recent phenomenon. When the Williams Act was enacted in 1968, just one state (Virginia) had such a statute and even there only for one year. It is still too early to know what the long-term equilibrium will be.

One evolutionary development which has already occurred is the addition of opt-out provisions to most state anti-takeover statutes. The Indiana statute upheld in *CTS*, for example, contains such a provision.[96] This provision allows a firm to decide whether or not it is to be subject to a state anti-takeover statute. These opt-out provisions may not be perfect. They do not require a shareholder vote for management to elect to be governed by the statute. Thus they do not prevent a firm's management from opting out of a statute's coverage and then opting back in when a takeover bid appears imminent. A strong argument could be made that a shareholder vote, costly and time consuming though it may be, should be required as a check on this type of opportunistic behavior.[97] Perhaps this or some other modification will be adopted by contract or legal rule in the future. The relevant point, however, is that the form of anti-takeover statutes is evolving, making the situation in the future uncertain.

D. DOES THE WILLIAMS ACT PREEMPT THE INDIANA ANTI-TAKEOVER STATUTE?

In *MITE*, a plurality of the Court examined the structure and legislative history of the Williams Act, the federal statute regulating

---

even after *CTS*. The Court in *CTS* stressed that the Indiana anti-takeover statute only applied to corporations incorporated in Indiana and which had a substantial number of resident shareholders. 107 S.Ct. at 1651–52. Very few Delaware corporations have a substantial number of shareholders residing within the state.

[96] Ind. Code §23-1-42-5 (Supp. 1986).

[97] As proposed by Romano, note 74 *supra*, at 186.

tender offers. The plurality concluded that the Act was designed to protect investors and adopted a position of "neutrality" between bidders and targets. The Illinois anti-takeover statute, the plurality found, was unlike the Williams Act in that it operated to entrench management to the detriment of shareholders. Because the Illinois statute violated the federal policy of neutrality and upset the balance struck between bidders and targets, the plurality concluded that the statute was preempted by the Williams Act.

The Court in *CTS* adopted the *MITE* plurality's characterization of the Williams Act as an investor protection statute which struck a careful balance between bidders and targets. Where the Court in *CTS* differed from the plurality was in its characterization of the state anti-takeover statute at issue. The Court in *CTS* concluded that the Indiana statute was, like the Williams Act but unlike the Illinois statute in *MITE*, designed to protect investors and not favor either bidders or targets.

Neither the analysis of the Court in *CTS* nor the plurality in *MITE* is convincing. The Court's analysis in *CTS* is unconvincing because, as discussed above, the Indiana and Illinois statutes have more similarities than differences. But the *MITE* plurality's analysis is also unconvincing. There is no fundamental difference between the Williams Act and state anti-takeover statutes. Whatever differences do exist, like the differences between the Illinois and Indiana anti-takeover statutes, are only ones of degree.

The notion that the Williams Act is "neutral" between bidders and targets, stressed by the plurality in *MITE* and in several other Supreme Court opinions, is a myth.[98] The Williams Act was passed in 1968 in reaction to the growing popularity of hostile tender offers. The Act imposed disclosure obligations on bidders, established waiting periods during which offers had to remain open, required that bidders accept shares tendered pro-rata (rather than first come, first served), and provided target shareholders with withdrawal rights. In each of these areas, no comparable federal regulation previously existed and none was placed on targets. The Williams

---

[98]For a critical discussion of the Williams Act, see Fischel, Efficient Capital Market Theory, the Market for Corporate Control, and the Regulation of Cash Tender Offers, 57 Tex. L. Rev. 1 (1978). See also Jarrell & Bradley, The Economic Effects of Federal and State Regulations of Cash Tender Offers, 23 J. Law & Econ. 371 (1980); Jarrell, State Anti-Takeover Laws and the Efficient Allocation of Corporate Control: An Economic Analysis of Edgar v. MITE Corp., 1 Sup. Ct. Econ. Rev. 1 (1983).

Act, in short, imposes the same types of disclose and delay burdens on bidders as do state anti-takeover statutes. It is in no way "neutral." Thus the non-neutrality of state anti-takeover statutes cannot be the basis for their preemption.

It is still conceivable that state anti-takeover statutes might be preempted if the Williams Act meant to strike a particular balance between the contending factions and not have this balance undone by the states. This argument based on the particular balance struck by Congress in the Williams Act is frequently equated with the neutrality argument discussed above, but the two are completely different. Even though the Williams Act is not "neutral" in any meaningful sense, it is still possible that Congress did not want the states to place even more onerous burdens on bidders than does federal law. This appears to have been the reasoning of the Seventh Circuit in *CTS*, although Judge Posner did not appear to be completely persuaded by this reasoning and ultimately relied on the precedential authority of *MITE* and other Supreme Court cases interpreting the Williams Act.

The Seventh Circuit was correct to be skeptical. The "particular balance" argument, without more, has no meaning. Every statute strikes a "particular balance" in that Congress could have gone farther or less far. Unless all state laws are preempted whenever a federal law exists in a given area, an obvious impossibility, the recognition that Congress struck a "particular balance" is irrelevant in determining whether a state law is invalid under the Supremacy Clause.

A state law is preempted only if Congress not only struck its own balance but also precluded the states from striking any other. In the area of takeover regulation, Congress has provided no such indication. The Williams Act contains no express provision preempting state law. On the contrary, the securities laws contain an express savings clause designed to save state statutes from preemption.[99]

Moreover, parallel state and federal regulation exists throughout the securities area. State and federal laws exist that regulate the

---

[99] 15 U.S.C. §7866(a) provides in pertinent part: "Nothing in this title shall affect the jurisdiction of the securities commission . . . of any state over any security or any person insofar as it does not conflict with the provisions of this title or the rules and regulations thereunder."

sale of securities, the voting process, and trading while in possession of valuable information.

State law frequently strikes a different "balance" than federal law in these areas. For example, the federal securities laws which govern the sale of securities are disclosure statutes.[100] Provided disclosure obligations are met, the federal regulatory requirements are met. Many state blue sky laws which also govern the sale of securities, however, are merit regulation statutes. Under a merit regulation statute, it is not enough that full disclosure is made. The offeror must also satisfy the state securities commissioner of the underlying merit of the securities being sold. Despite the different balance struck by state and federal law, the federal securities laws do not preempt state blue sky laws.

As Justice Scalia emphasized, the pervasive parallel state and federal regulation of securities markets coupled with the absence of any indication that Congress in the Williams Act meant to preempt state law is dispositive of the Supremacy Clause claim. There was no need for the Court to laud the Indiana statute to reach this result. Preemption should not depend on whether the Justices like the state law at issue.

Justice White, in his dissenting opinion on the preemption issue, took the position opposite from the majority but committed the same mistake. Justice White stressed how takeovers can be beneficial and how the Indiana statute, unlike the Williams Act, effectively prevents shareholders in some circumstances from selling their stock at a premium to a willing tender offer. Justice White is surely correct that the Indiana Act goes farther than the Williams Act in deterring takeover bids. But this proves nothing. The relevant question is whether the Williams Act denies states that option, and Justice White offered no reason to believe that it did.

V. The Indiana Anti-Takeover Statute and the Dormant Commerce Clause

A. COMPETITION AMONG STATES AND THE COMMERCE CLAUSE

The fifty states compete with each other in a multiplicity of ways. One means of effecting this competition is by lawmaking. The

---

[100] See Easterbrook & Fischel, The Mandatory Disclosure System and the Protection of Investors, 70 Va. L. Rev. 669 (1984), for an analysis of the philosophy underlying the securities laws.

Commerce Clause, as it has been read, however, restricts the states' ability to compete in this area by limiting the ambit of the laws that states may enact. Whether this restriction is desirable depends on an understanding of the effects of such competition among the states.

The literature on the economics of federalism emphasizes that competition among jurisdictions will be desirable provided that the effects of any laws enacted will be felt within the enacting jurisdiction and that certain other assumptions are satisfied.[101] Conversely, the probability that welfare-reducing regulation will be adopted is considered to be a function of whether its effects can be exported to other states. Thus a law that produces a benefit of ten within the state and a cost of twenty outside the state will be enacted even though it is welfare reducing. The greater the ability of a jurisdiction to export costs to another jurisdiction, the argument runs, the weaker the incentive of the jurisdiction to balance costs and benefits when enacting regulation.[102]

One justification for the grant to the federal government of the power to regulate interstate commerce in the Commerce Clause was this problem of externality. Under this view, the framers contemplated that states would be free to act provided they did not use this power to export costs to other states. In this event, the other states were likely to respond in kind. The result, the framers may have feared—indeed, as they had seen under the Articles of Confederation—would be retaliatory trade barriers, tariffs, and taxes. To minimize this possibility, the argument runs, the framers included the Commerce Clause in the Constitution. By exercising its authority to regulate interstate commerce granted by the Commerce Clause, the federal government can nullify or preempt welfare-reducing state legislation and thus improve total social welfare. This view of the Commerce Clause has been suggested by some who see a coherent economic rationale to much, if not all, of the Constitution.[103]

---

[101]The classic statement is Tiebout, A Pure Theory of Local Expenditures, 64 J. Pol. Econ. 416 (1956).

[102]This point is emphasized in different contexts by Easterbrook, Antitrust and The Economics of Federalism, 26 J. Law & Econ. 23 (1983), and Levmore, Interstate Exploitation and Judicial Intervention, 69 Va. L. Rev. 563 (1983). See also Posner, Economic Analysis of Law 602–07 (3d ed. 1986).

[103]See Posner, The Constitution as an Economic Document, 55 Geo. Wash. L. Rev. (forthcoming) (1987).

There are serious problems, however, with this interpretation of the Commerce Clause. The validity of its premise—that competition among states will be more likely to produce optimal legislation so long as the costs and benefits of the legislation are internalized within the enacting state—is far less clear than has been commonly assumed. Even if gains and losses are internalized, laws that impose net costs may still be enacted if the gains are captured by an organized entity while the (greater) losses are spread across a more dispersed group that is unable to mobilize to prevent the law's passage.

Conversely, mechanisms exist which limit states' ability to enact welfare-decreasing legislation where costs are exported to other states. The individuals adversely affected by such laws may attempt to seek redress, for example, by making campaign contributions to legislators within the enacting state. Moreover, states, like nations, have strong incentives to reach voluntary agreements designed to prevent exploitation. Varying the earlier example slightly, if two states can each enact a law which creates benefits of ten within the state and costs of twenty to another state, both will be better off by agreeing with each other not to pass the laws.[104] (A formal agreement, of course, would require the acquiescence of Congress.)

Thus the issue whether laws that export costs are more likely to be welfare reducing than those that do not depends on an assessment of comparative transactions costs. Laws may be welfare decreasing (or increasing) whether or not their effects are fully felt within the state. The rationale for a special provision like the Commerce Clause which only applies to situations where the effects of a regulation are not fully felt within the enacting state, by contrast, is based on the assumption that there is a sharp difference between the two situations.

Perhaps some differences do exist that suggest laws which export costs are more likely to be welfare reducing for the nation as a whole than laws that do not. One is that all affected citizens have the right to vote if the effects of a law are fully felt within the enacting state. Because of pervasive free rider and collective action problems in the voting process, however, this difference is likely to be unim-

---

[104]This is a simple application of the Coase Theorem. See Coase, The Problem of Social Cost, 3 J. Law & Econ. 1 (1960).

portant. More significant is that the exporting of costs expands the pool of victims. The population of the other fofty-nine states will always be greater than the population in any one state. And the greater the number of adversely affected individuals at any given total cost, the smaller the harm incurred by any individual and the more difficult the resulting coordination problems. Thus exporting costs may make it easier for a state to enact welfare-decreasing legislation by spreading the costs over a larger number of individuals. This increase in the target area may provide some basis for the distinction implicit in the Commerce Clause between laws that export costs and those that do not.

But even if the Commerce Clause can be justified as a matter of theory as a solution to problems of externality, the reality may be far different. Indeed, the economic theory of regulation posits that a model of governmental action, federal or otherwise, that assumes the government acts to cure market failures such as externalities is inconsistent with reality.[105] Few would argue, for example, that the pervasive economic regulation of capital, product, and labor markets at the national level is all a response to market failures. Rather, a large and growing literature demonstrates that much, perhaps most, of these regulatory schemes are products of interest-group politics where the result is the displacement of competition, not the correction of market failures.[106]

Thus the Commerce Clause is a mixed blessing at best. The Clause may have provided some benefits by deterring welfare-reducing regulation by the states. But these benefits must be balanced against the costs of additional rent seeking behavior made possible by the jurisdictional grant to the federal government to displace competition among the states.[107] This jurisdictional grant

---

[105]Peltzman, Towards a More General Theory of Regulation, 19 J. Law & Econ. 211 (1976); Stigler, The Theory of Economic Regulation, 3 Bell J. Econ. & Mgt. Sci. 3 (1971). See also Becker, A Theory of Competition among Pressure Groups for Political Influence, 98 Q. J. Econ. 371 (1983).

[106]See, *e.g.*, Jarrell, Change at the Exchange: The Causes and Effects of Deregulation, 27 J. Law & Econ. 273 (1984); Maloney & McCormick, A Positive Theory of Environmental Quality Regulation, 25 J. Law & Econ. 99 (1982); Moore, The Beneficiaries of Trucking Regulation, 21 J. Law & Econ. 327 (1978).

[107]See Kitch, Regulation and the American Common Market, in Tarlock, ed., Regulation, Federalism and Interstate Commerce (1981), for a related argument that the jurisdictional grant in the Commerce Clause to Congress should not be equated with a commitment to free trade.

has enabled interest groups in many cases to reverse the results of competition in the marketplace and among states. Under this view, what is welfare reducing will frequently be the regulation produced by this interest group battle, not the competition among states that is displaced.

B. COMPETITION AMONG STATES AND THE DORMANT COMMERCE CLAUSE

Why is the dormant Commerce Clause needed in addition to the Commerce Clause itself?[108] One possibility is that the dormant Commerce Clause is needed because the legislative process is costly and complex. It is difficult to enact legislation at the national level. Because of this difficulty, it is unrealistic to assume that the federal government will be able to act whenever a state attempts to export costs to other states. Thus the Commerce Clause will act to deter only the most egregious cases of welfare-reducing state regulation. The dormant Commerce Clause, under this view, fills this gap by providing a mechanism whereby welfare-reducing state legislation can be invalidated.

A second possibility is that the dormant Commerce Clause acts as an implied contractual term that deters opportunistic behavior by states. If states could contract with each other costlessly, laws which imposed net costs across states would not exist. Because such contracts cannot be written and enforced costlessly, the dormant Commerce Clause fills this gap.

The purpose of the dormant Commerce Clause, then, is to accomplish what the Clause itself was supposed to accomplish but has not because of interest group politics. The dormant Commerce Clauses entrusts the decision of which state laws unduly interfere with interstate commerce to federal judges rather than to Congress. Because federal judges are appointed for life with the emoluments of office guaranteed, they are less susceptible to special interest pressures than legislators who are dependent on interest groups for

---

[108]Since Cooley v. Board of Wardens, 12 How. 299 (1852), the Supreme Court has held that the Commerce Clause, by its own force, prohibits states from regulating interstate commerce in discriminatory or unduly burdensome ways. The legitimacy of this doctrine is open to question, notwithstanding its veneration. No other clause in the Constitution granting power has ever been construed to be self-enforcing, certainly not by the courts. Nor does the Constitution explicitly make control of interstate commerce an exclusively national power. For a critique of the doctrine, see Currie, The Constitution in the Supreme Court: The First Hundred Years 1789–1888 230–36 (1985).

support. Thus the judicial process is more likely to produce results that are consistent with the economic rationale of the Commerce Clause—the prevention of legislation that is welfare increasing for a particular state but welfare decreasing for the nation as a whole.

But the dormant Commerce Clause also imposes costs in the form of overdeterrence. There are benefits in having a competition among states where states can experiment with different types of regulatory regimes. The federal government also benefits from this competition (assuming government officials act to maximize the public interest) because it can watch the development of different state regulatory regimes and choose among them. Under the Commerce Clause, states are free to experiment until a contrary consensus exists in both Houses of Congress and Congress acts. Under the dormant Commerce Clause, by contrast, experimentation by states can be halted by a single judge (subject to appellate review) as a result of a suit brought by a single litigant.

Of course, the greater ease of invalidation of state laws under the dormant Commerce Clause might be a benefit if only welfare-reducing laws were invalidated. But there is no assurance that this will be the case. The prior discussion has assumed that it is a simple exercise to determine what the costs and benefits of a particular state law are, and how these costs and benefits are distributed across states. Obviously, this assumption is simplistic. Frequently, the costs and benefits of a particular law may be observable, even dimly, only after an extended period of time. The dormant Commerce Clause, by making invalidation easier, increases the probability that premature judgments will be made in assessing the effects of a particular law. Moreover, the judicial process is not well suited to sifting through massive amounts of messy economic data on the effects of a state law in a given state and in other states.

Liberal application of the dormant Commerce Clause, in sum, may decrease the incidence of welfare-decreasing legislation but may also decrease the incidence of valuable experimentation by states. Thus dual effect makes it impossible to resolve at an abstract level whether the dormant Commerce Clause has been a valuable judicial innovation.

C. THE DISCRIMINATION REQUIREMENT

For a state law to be invalid under the dormant Commerce Clause, it must discriminate against interstate commerce. But what does discrimination mean? The definition adopted here is the exporting of costs to other states which exceed the benefits obtained by the enacting state.[109] Note that discrimination in this sense, as discussed above, exists only because of positive transactions costs. If states could costlessly contract with each other, discriminatory state laws as the term is used here would not exist.

It is important to emphasize that this definition is different from the conventional understanding which equates the dormant Commerce Clause with the prevention of protectionism—a state policy of preferring local to foreign firms in one way or another.[110] The reason why exporting costs is not equivalent to protectionism is that states can favor local firms without exporting costs to other states.[111] The relevant question under the dormant Commerce Clause is not whether a state follows a policy of protectionism but rather who pays for it.

Recognizing that state laws that discriminate against interstate commerce are those that export costs to other states in excess of benefits received, however, is only the first step of the inquiry. The second, and more difficult step is identifying which state laws satisfy the discrimination requirement. There are three overlapping possibilities: (1) laws that discriminate on their face; (2) laws that have a discriminatory purpose; and (3) laws that have a discriminatory effect. The Supreme Court has not been consistent in its treatment of which of these types of state laws satisfy the discrimination requirement. Before elaborating on this point, however, it is worth discussing whether there is a fourth category of state laws that can trigger judicial scrutiny under the dormant Commerce Clause.

---

[109]The Supreme Court has itself suggested this definition of discrimination. See, *e.g.*, South Carolina Highway Dept. v. Barnwell Bros., 303 U.S. 177, 186 (1938) (Commerce Clause forbids regulations that are "a means of gaining a local benefit by throwing the attendant burdens on those without the state").

[110]See, *e.g.*, Regan, The Supreme Court and State Protectionism: Making Sense of the Dormant Commerce Clause, 84 Mich. L. Rev. 1091 (1986).

[111]The Court, for example, has consistently subjected taxes to stricter scrutiny than subsidies. See, *e.g.*, Reeves Inc. v. Stake, 447 U.S. 429 (1980); Hughes v. Alexandria Scrap Corp., 426 U.S. 794 (1976). While there is substantial doubt as a matter of economic theory whether any difference exists between subsidies and taxes, the distinction is based, at least implicitly, on the notion that a state can favor local firms if it bears the cost. See also Levmore, note 102 *supra*, for a more extended discussion of the distinction between subsidies and taxes.

The rhetoric used by the Supreme Court in its decisions certainly suggests that there is. At least since *Pike v. Bruce Church*,[112] perhaps the best known modern decision interpreting the dormant Commerce Clause, it has been understood that nondiscriminatory statutes are invalid if the burden on interstate commerce outweighs the local benefits received. As Justice Stewart stated for the Court:[113]

> Where a statute regulates evenhandedly to effectuate a legitimate local public interest, and its effects on interstate commerce are only incidental, it will be upheld unless the burden imposed on such commerce (i.e., the protectionist effect) is clearly excessive in relation to the putative local benefits.

The Court appears to draw a distinction between discriminatory statutes and statutes that regulate "evenhandedly" but impose burdens on interstate commerce that are "clearly excessive" to the local benefits received. But if discrimination, as suggested here, is interpreted to mean the exporting of costs to other states in excess of the benefits received by the enacting state, this distinction makes no sense. Any state law that imposes burdens on interstate commerce that clearly exceed the putative local benefits is discriminatory, at least in effect. Thus the famous balancing test of *Pike v. Bruce Church* that is supposed to be applied to nondiscriminatory statutes is more accurately characterized as a test for determining whether a statute is discriminatory.

It is now possible to return to the issue of what types of state laws satisfy the discrimination requirement and thus are invalid under the dormant Commerce Clause. The Court has consistently held that state laws that discriminate on their face against out-of-state firms are virtually *per se* invalid.[114] What is far less clear is whether the converse of this proposition is also true—that state laws that are facially nondiscriminatory are virtually *per se* valid. Some of the Court's decisions appear to support this proposition.[115] Others

---

[112]397 U.S. 137 (1970).

[113]*Id.* at 142.

[114]See, *e.g.*, Lewis v. BT Investment Managers, Inc., 447 U.S. 27 (1980); Hughes v. Oklahoma, 441 U.S. 322 (1979); City of Philadelphia v. New Jersey, 437 U.S. 617 (1978).

[115]See, *e.g.*, Commonwealth Edison Co. v. Montana, 453 U.S. 609 (1981); Minnesota v. Clover Leaf Creamery Co., 449 U.S. 456 (1981); Exxon Corp. v. Governor of Maryland, 437 U.S. 177 (1978).

suggest that state laws that have a discriminatory effect or purpose are invalid.[116]

The Court in *CTS* emphasized the facial neutrality of the Indiana anti-takeover statute and its evenhanded application to all acquirors including those from Indiana. Moreover, the conspicuous absence in the Court's opinion of any discussion of the *Pike* balancing test that was relied upon by the Court of Appeals and the Court itself in *MITE* suggests that it did not consider the existence or non-existence of discriminatory effect or purpose to be particularly relevant. On the other hand, the Court may have viewed these questions as irrelevant given its conclusion that the Indiana statute was a garden variety state corporate law provision enacted to protect investors. *CTS*, in other words, does not unambiguously settle the issue whether a facially neutral statute can be invalid under the dormant Commerce Clause if the law has a discriminatory effect or purpose.

Justice Scalia's concurring opinion, however, is much clearer on this issue. He stated that the absence of facial discrimination ends the inquiry under the dormant Commerce Clause (at least if the law does not create inconsistent regulations across states). For this reason, Justice Scalia advocated that the *Pike* balancing test be overruled. The dissenters in *CTS*, however, like the Court of Appeals and the Court itself in *MITE*, did not equate absence of facial discrimination with validity under the dormant Commerce Clause. Rather, they were willing to consider whether the state anti-takeover law at issue had a discriminatory effect and concluded that it did.

Why should facial discrimination be treated differently from discriminatory effect and purpose? In one sense, this differential treatment is incongruous. What matters under the dormant Commerce Clause is the effect of discriminatorily exporting costs. The language of a statute or the purpose of the statute is relevant only because a facially discriminatory statute or one enacted with a discriminatory purpose has a higher probability of having a discriminatory effect.

In another sense, however, the primacy of facial discrimination relative to effect and purpose is eminently reasonable. Whether a statute is facially discriminatory can be determined with a high

---

[116]See, *e.g.*, Hunt v. Washington Apple Advertising Commission, 432 U.S. 333 (1977).

degree of accuracy at low cost. And there is a high probability that a statute that discriminates on its fact against out-of-state firms is likely to have the effect of exporting costs. In contrast, it frequently will not be possible to determine at low cost or with a high degree of accuracy whether a statute has a discriminatory effect or was enacted with a discriminatory purpose. Analyzing the incidence of costs and benefits of a particular statute, as discussed above, is a messy and difficult undertaking.

Moreover, an important distinction exists between the incidence of costs and benefits in the short run versus the long run. Suppose state A wants to attract a particular industry located in state B and state B passes a law preventing the move. In the short run, state B may be able to impose costs on state A. In the long run, however, the harm to state A will be dissipated by entry and the development of substitutes. The incidence of the law will shift to state B as the barrier to exit will cause firms in the future to be less willing to locate there in the first instance. This distinction between the short versus long run is one of many complications courts face in determining the incidence of a law. The ascertainment of legislative intent or purpose—what state legislators thought they were accomplishing by enacting the particular statute—can also be a daunting and ultimately futile exercise.

In contrast, a focus on facial discrimination has the benefit of easy administration. It also minimizes the risk that the dormant Commerce Clause will be used to discourage valuable experimentation by states. The problem with the focus on facial discrimination is that it facilitates evasion of the purpose underlying the dormant Commerce Clause. If only facial discrimination matters, states are free to enact laws that export costs to other states provided that they take the cosmetic step of ensuring that the language of the statute is nondiscriminatory.

Ultimately, the choice between limiting judicial review to the issue of facial discrimination, as advocated by Justice Scalia and perhaps the majority in *CTS*, or having more expansive judicial review on the existence of discriminatory effect, as advocated by the dissenters in *CTS*, the Seventh Circuit, and the Court itself in *MITE*, is impossible to resolve. The facial discrimination test is easy to apply, allows states discretion to experiment, but also allows states much greater ability to export costs to other states. Inquiry into discriminatory effect and purpose has the opposite effects. The indeterminacy of these trade-offs no doubt helps to explain why the Court has been so inconsistent in this area.

D. DOES THE INDIANA ANTI-TAKEOVER STATUTE DISCRIMINATE AGAINST INTERSTATE COMMERCE?

Corporate law has long been based on the principle that a corporation is governed by the law of its state of incorporation. Corporations of any size, such as publicly held firms, have investors throughout the country. Thus it is routine for the laws of a state where a corporation is incorporated to govern transactions between investors in other states.

At first blush, this system of corporate governance where the laws of individual states regulate transactions between individuals in other states might itself seem suspect under the dormant Commerce Clause. Whether a tension in fact exists between corporate governance and the dormant Commerce Clause depends again on the distinction between short and long run incidence of a law. In the short run, states can enact welfare-decreasing legislation that imposes costs on residents of other states. State anti-takeover statutes, as discussed above, may be paradigm examples of cost-exporting legislation that is enacted in response to lobbying pressure by in-state constituents. In the long run, however, states have no ability to export costs to non-resident investors. When entrepreneurs want to raise capital for a corporate venture, they must decide where to incorporate. The choice of where to incorporate in turn affects the price investors are willing to pay for shares. And because shares of stock have many perfect substitutes which offer the same risk-return combinations, it is impossible for the entrepreneur to pass on the effects of the law to investors.[117] Thus it is the entrepreneur who makes the decision where to incorporate, and not the purchasing shareholders even if non-residents, who bear the costs of the decision where to incorporate. Nor can a state export costs to the founding entrepreneur since corporations can be incorporated anywhere, regardless of the firm's physical location. States that enact laws that are harmful to investors will cause entrepreneurs to incorporate elsewhere.

---

[117]See Jensen & Meckling, Theory of the Firm: Managerial Behavior, Agency Costs and Ownership Structure, 3 J. Fin. Econ. 305 (1976).

Thus states can impose costs on non-resident investors in the short run but not the long run. The same is true, as discussed above, with most state laws. There is, however, one difference between laws that affect capital markets as opposed to product, labor, or other markets. Because of the extreme mobility of capital, the long-run adjustment in response to any state law will be extremely rapid. It is much easier to move investment dollars than to relocate a factory or a workforce. For this reason, there is less need for legal intervention to protect non-residents in their capacity as investors. Perhaps this explains why state corporation laws are rarely thought to be in tension with the dormant Commerce Clause.

What then is different about state anti-takeover statutes? The Indiana statute, like most corporate laws, is facially non-discriminatory and applies only to corporations incorporated in the enacting state. The statute governs transactions among non-residents, but so do all state corporation laws. Blue sky laws which only apply to transactions with resident investors are the exception and not the rule.

One possible basis for a distinction between the Indiana statute and corporation laws in general is the effect of the Indiana statute on the market for corporate control. Both the Seventh Circuit and the dissenters in *CTS* appear to take this position. As Judge Posner stated:[118]

> Even if a corporation's tangible assets are immovable, the efficiency with which they are employed and the proportions in which the earnings they generate are divided between management and shareholders depends on the market for corporate control—an interstate, indeed international, market that the state of Indiana is not authorized to opt out of, as it in effect has done in this statute.

That a market is national or international in scope does not necessarily mean, however, that the effects of a law are not felt within the enacting state. If Indiana passes a law that causes a less advantageous division of earnings from the perspective of investors, these investors may simply pay less for shares of Indiana corporations.

There is an argument that can be made, however, at least on a theoretical level, that corporate statutes in general are unlike those that affect corporate control. Corporate shares, as discussed above,

---

[118]794 F.2d at 264.

have many close substitutes, and thus states have little ability to export costs to investors of other states, except perhaps in the very short run. The same is not necessarily true of a controlling interest of shares in a corporation. Control is valuable because it gives the purchaser the ability to determine the use of the corporation's assets. Fewer substitutes are likely to exist for the assets owned by a corporation than for individual shares of the corporation. Many investments are indistinguishable from a single share of IBM, but few if any have the identical physical assets, technology, goodwill, and so forth. This uniqueness of bundles of assets, as contrasted with marginal shares, may give states what is in effect some market power. This market power enables states to force bidders to pay more to acquire bundles of assets within the state.

This argument, even if theoretically correct, is fraught with practical difficulties. How is a court to determine whether close substitutes exist for a particular bundle of assets? In addition, there are difficult line-drawing problems with this argument. Many provisions of state corporation laws affect corporate control transactions. Most state laws in this area can be understood as attempting to facilitate corporate control transactions.[119] But no doubt exceptions exist that, like the Indiana statute, impede corporate control transactions. Are these exceptions unconstitutional under the dormant Commerce Clause?

On a more fundamental level, there is no basis for the Seventh Circuit's assertion that there is a constitutional bar to a state opting out of the market for corporate control. Suppose a state adopted a corporation law that provided shareholder voting would be governed by the rule of one person, one vote rather than one share, one vote; or that only shares held for a year could be voted; or that mergers had to be approved by unanimous consent regardless of the number of shareholders. Each of these hypothetical laws would have a far greater deterrent effect on corporate control transactions than the Indiana statute whose effect is limited to delay. Moreover, any of these hypothetical laws would be just as much of, in the language of the Seventh Circuit, a "direct," "intended," and "substantial" regulation of the "international" market for corporate control. But it is extremely unlikely that any of these provisions would

---

[119]See Easterbrook & Fischel, Corporate Control Transactions, 91 Yale L. J. 698 (1982).

be unconstitutional under the dormant Commerce Clause. Rather, the presumption would be that the competition among states would be a sufficient deterrent to the enactment of such value-decreasing legislation.

Even if there is no constitutional bar to a state opting out of the market for corporate control, however, a problem may arise if the method used is a legislative change that applies to current investors who are primarily non-residents. Such investors are not protected by the pricing mechanism as they are when the firm initially goes public. Moreover, non-resident investors are not represented in the political process when the state decides to amend its law. Thus they are particularly vulnerable to exploitation by the legislature acting at the behest of incumbent management in the amendment process. Indeed, this description may well capture what actually happened in *CTS* fairly well.

The difficulty with this analysis is that it assumes what needs to be proved—that the Indiana anti-takeover statute was enacted to benefit resident management to the (greater) detriment of non-resident investors. The rhetoric used was the opposite. The stated statutory purpose is to protect shareholders, not victimize them.

In the final analysis, *CTS* is a hard case because it squarely presents the dilemma of what the proper scope of judicial review should be under the dormant Commerce Clause. One approach, that of Justice Scalia, is to treat the facially neutral character of the Indiana anti-takeover statute as dispositive regardless of the effect on investors. An alternative approach is to go beyond the facially neutral character of the statute and inquire into its purpose and effect. As with many laws, however, ascertaining the effect and purpose of the Indiana anti-takeover statute is no easy task.

While some evidence does exist that anti-takeover statutes are harmful to investors, this evidence, as discussed above, is meager. No evidence was presented on the effect of the Indiana anti-takeover statute specifically. The "real purpose" of the law is also elusive. The statute was clearly intended for the purpose of making it more difficult to acquire corporations incorporated in Indiana. But such a statutory purpose is not the same as an intent to export costs to non-resident investors. State legislators may have been willing to enact the law even if the effects were felt solely by dispersed residents within the state. And, let us not forget, Indiana claimed investors were benefitted, not harmed, by the anti-takeover statute.

In light of the tenuous nature of the evidence, the Court in *CTS* was probably correct to hold that the Indiana anti-takeover statute did not violate the dormant Commerce Clause. But it did so for the wrong reasons. The Court, as with its preemption analysis, mistakenly believed that it had to defend the economic wisdom of the statute to find it constitutional. It would have been enough to find that the statute is facially nondiscriminatory and it did not have an obvious discriminatory effect or purpose, assuming effect and purpose are relevant. The Seventh Circuit and the three dissenters also mistakenly equated the economic wisdom of the statute with its constitutionality. Only Justice Scalia recognized that the welfare effects of a statute is a different issue from whether it is constitutional.

E. STATE ANTI-TAKEOVER STATUTES AND THE PROBLEM OF INCONSISTENT REGULATIONS

The Court stated in *CTS* that statutes may be invalid under the dormant Commerce Clause if they "affect interstate commerce by subjecting activities to inconsistent regulations."[120] This "inconsistent regulations" test appears to be distinct from the discrimination test. The Court's opinion suggests that a statute that is facially nondiscriminatory may still be invalid under the dormant Commerce Clause if it violates this separate requirement.

The application of this test in the *CTS* case was straightforward. Because the Indiana statute is limited to corporations incorporated there, it does not affect corporations incorporated in other states. So long as all other states limit their anti-takeover laws to firms incorporated within the state, no corporation is subject to the anti-takeover law of more than one state. Thus no firm will be subject to inconsistent regulation by multiple states.

In other situations, however, the inconsistent regulations test could prove difficult to apply. Suppose a state after the *CTS* decision enacts an anti-takeover law that applies to corporations that either are incorporated or have their principal place of business within the state. Such a law creates the possibility that the same firm will be subject to the anti-takeover laws of two different states, the state of incorporation and the state of principal place of business. And

---

[120]107 S.Ct. at 1649.

if states pass anti-takeover laws that apply to firms that have substantial assets within the state, large corporations might be subject
to the laws of multiple states.

The implication of *CTS* is that state statutes that subjected firms
to inconsistent regulations in this manner might be invalid under
the dormant Commerce Clause. But there are problems with this
result. Which state statutes are invalid? Are any statutes inconsistent with the law of the state of incorporation invalid, or does the
test depend on which state law comes first? And what constitutes
inconsistency? Is it sufficient that the statutes are different or is it
necessary that it be impossible to comply with each of the statutes
simultaneously?

Something more than being subjected to different regulations
must be required for a statute to be invalid under the dormant
Commerce Clause. Firms that engage in interstate commerce are
subjected to differing state regulations routinely. Firms that sell
products in several states, for example, are subject to different tort
rules in each state. Some states have a negligence rule, others have
strict liability; some have liberal rules concerning the awarding of
punitive damages, others do not. Numerous other differences exist
in other areas of law as well. Even in the area of corporate law,
firms under the blue sky laws are regularly subjected to different
state regulatory schemes. A firm that issues securities must comply
with the blue sky laws of the fifty states as well as the federal
securities laws. These blue sky laws may be very different from
each other. Some states have a system of merit review by the state
securities commissioner, for example, while others do not. The
Supreme Court over half a century ago in a series of decisions held
that blue sky laws do not offend the dormant Commerce Clause
because their effect is confined to residents within the state.[121] Presumably the Court in *CTS* did not mean to overturn these decisions
or, for that matter, state tort law either. Precisely what the Court
did intend with its inconsistent regulations test, however, is not at
all clear.

One possibility suggested by the Court's opinion is that the "inconsistent regulations" test is applicable only when states regulate
in areas which "are in their nature national, or admit of one uniform

---

[121]See Hall v. Geiger-Jones Co., 242 U.S. 539 (1917); Caldwell v. Sioux Falls Stock Yards
Co., 242 U.S. 559 (1917); Merrick v. N.W. Halsey & Co., 242 U.S. 568 (1917).

system, or plan of regulation."[122] But what does this mean? The capital market and the market for corporate control, as the Court of Appeals in *CTS* correctly pointed out, are international in scope, yet states routinely regulate these markets. Moreover, the test for whether an activity is "inherently national" cannot be whether it has been traditionally regulated by the states. Such a test would be completely circular: Whether states could regulate would be a function of whether the activity is inherently national; whether an activity is inherently national would be a function of whether it is traditionally regulated by the states.

An approach that avoids this circularity would frame the question in terms whether costs are being exported in excess of local benefits. Under this interpretation, the inconsistent regulations test is no different from the discrimination test. Indeed, no separate test is necessary. But the inquiry still is very complicated because, as discussed above, it is no simple matter to determine whether or not the effects of a state regulation are felt primarily within the enacting state.

F. DOES CTS OVERRULE MITE?

After *CTS*, the continuing vitality of *MITE* is in doubt. *MITE* involved the constitutionality of an Illinois anti-takeover statute which applied to tender offers for any corporation for which 10 percent of the outstanding shares were held by Illinois residents whether or not the corporation was incorporated or had its principal place of business in Illinois. In the one part of *MITE* that represented an opinion of the Court, the statute was held to be invalid under the dormant Commerce Clause. The Court reached this result by application of the *Pike v. Bruce Church* balancing test.

The Illinois statute, the Court reasoned, had a substantial effect on interstate commerce since, by deterring tender offers, it hindered the reallocation of economic resources to their highest valued use.[123] Balanced against this burden on interstate commerce, the Court found no legitimate local interest such as shareholder protection furthered by the statute.[124] For Illinois residents, the Court stated,

---

[122]107 S.Ct. at 1649, quoting from Cooley v. Board of Wardens, 12 How. at 319.

[123]457 U.S. at 643–44.

[124]*Id.* at 644.

the statute provided no protections not already provided by the Williams Act.[125] Moreover, the Court concluded that the shareholder protection justification for the statute was "somewhat incredible" because the statute applied to corporations that were neither incorporated nor had their principal places of business in Illinois.[126]

In *CTS*, by contrast, the Court viewed tender offers as a coercive device rather than a mechanism for improving economic efficiency. Moreover, the *Pike* balancing test was ignored by the Court in *CTS*, and Justice Scalia in his concurring opinion argued that the whole exercise is an improper judicial function. Thus it is unlikely that state anti-takeover statutes in the future will be found unconstitutional under the reasoning of *MITE* and *Pike*.

It is interesting to speculate whether a statute like the Illinois anti-takeover statute in *MITE* would be constitutional after *CTS*. Under a literal reading of *CTS*, such a statute would not discriminate against interstate commerce. The Court in *CTS* reasoned that the Indiana statute was facially neutral because "[i]t has the same effects on tender offers whether or not the offeror is a domiciliary or resident of Indiana."[127] Exactly the same could be said about the Illinois anti-takeover statute at issue in *MITE*.

It is possible, indeed likely, that this is an overly narrow reading of *CTS*. The Court in *CTS* limited its discussion of discrimination to the effects of a statute on offerers, but the concept of discrimination, even facial discrimination, need not be so limited. No reason exists why the concept is not equally relevant to the effect of a statute on targets. Indeed the Court in *CTS* repeatedly emphasized the difference between the extraterritorial reach of the Illinois statute in *MITE* as compared with the Indiana statute which only applies to firms incorporated in Indiana.[128] Thus an Illinois-type statute might be held to discriminate against interstate commerce, even under the analysis in *CTS*. The reason is that the statute would by its terms apply to corporations that are incorporated and have their principal place of business in other states. Thus the statute would be invalid because it facially discriminates against interstate

---

[125]*Id.* at 645.

[126]*Ibid.*

[127]107 S.Ct. at 1648–49.

[128]*Id.* at 1651–52.

commerce by attempting to regulate tender offers for out-of-state corporations.

Economic theory also suggests that the Illinois anti-takeover statute in *MITE* should be declared unconstitutional. The extraterritorial reach of the Illinois statute makes it much more difficult for entrepreneurs and investors to opt out of the statute's coverage by their incorporation and investment decisions. Thus the incidence of the law on non-residents will be more pronounced and last for a longer period than a law limited to corporations incorporated within the state.

The extraterritorial reach of the Illinois-type statute would also cause it to be suspect under the inconsistent regulations test. If percentage of share ownership within a state is a sufficient basis to regulate tender offers, then so too must percentage of assets within a state. Multiple states, as discussed above, would be able to regulate tender offers for certain corporations, and the possibility exists that these regulatory schemes would be inconsistent. Indeed, it is this possibility of inconsistent regulations created by the Illinois statute in *MITE* that the Court in *CTS* appears to have found problematic.[129]

There are problems with invalidation of a state anti-takeover statute because of the possibility of inconsistent regulations. Large corporations, as discussed above, face inconsistent regulations under state blue sky and other laws on a routine basis. Moreover, regulation of corporations is not inherently national but rather traditionally has been the province of the states. Until the Supreme Court provides some content to the inconsistent regulations test, therefore, it is unclear whether this test will provide a separate basis for invalidation of state anti-takeover statutes with an extraterritorial reach.

While *CTS* gutted *MITE*, it is doubtful whether *MITE* has been overruled. The Court's continual emphasis in *CTS* on the importance of a state regulating only the corporations incorporated within that state suggests that a statute like the Illinois anti-takeover statute in *MITE* would still be unconstitutional. Even after *CTS*, such a statute could be found to be facially discriminatory and thus unconstitutional under the dormant Commerce Clause.

---

[129]*Id.* at 1649.

VI. Postscript: The Relation Between Takeovers and Insider Trading

One profound difference between *MITE* and *CTS* is the attitude of the Court toward takeovers. In *MITE*, the Court viewed takeovers as benefitting shareholders and increasing economic efficiency; in *CTS*, by contrast, the Court's view appeared to be the opposite. This change in position is, in one sense, surprising. The consensus among economists is that takeovers perform a valuable monitoring function and provide a mechanism for the transfer of assets to higher valued uses.[130] This consensus existed at the time of *MITE* and still exists. What, then, explains the Court's change of position?

Several commentators suggested that the widely publicized criminal indictments of persons alleged to have engaged in unlawful insider trading in connection with takeover activity convinced the Court in *CTS* that the time had come to put the brakes on takeover activity.[131] Indeed, *CTS* Corporation made sure in its brief to refer to the insider trading "scandal," thus suggesting a link between the constitutionality of its anti-takeover statute and the criminal indictments.[132] Some members of Congress also apparently see a connection between takeovers and insider trading. Legislation has been introduced in Congress to extend the Williams Act by requiring faster disclosure and longer waiting periods. One of the stated rationales of this proposed legislation is to deter illegal insider trading.

The perception that it is necessary to extend the regulation of takeovers as a way of preventing improper use of valuable information is unfortunate for several reasons. First, we do not yet know what really happened. The criminal indictments thus far have been resolved by guilty pleas to charges such as the filing of false statements that are unrelated to insider trading. Little factual record has been developed. In particular, it is unclear whether the use of valuable information by investment bankers and arbitragers was

---

[130]See note 64 *supra*.

[131]See, *e.g.*, Wall Street J., July 1, 1987, p. : The *CTS* "decision came on the heels of Wall Street's insider-trading scandals and amid a national uproar against takeovers. While the justices didn't directly acknowledge that background, their tone indicated that they, too, believed the merger game had gone too far."

[132]Brief for Appellant CTS Corp., pp. 9, 26.

consensual or appropriated from clients. The extent to which what has occurred is a real scandal depends critically on this issue.[133] Even as a purely legal matter, considerable uncertainty exists. The Supreme Court has thus far refused to decide whether the misappropriation of information constitutes a violation of the federal securities laws.[134]

Let us assume the worst—that there was widespread misappropriation of valuable information by investment professionals and this conduct violates federal securities laws. It still does not follow that making takeovers more difficult is a rational response. Misappropriation of information concerning an imminent takeover bid victimizes the prospective acquirer, not the investors. Such misappropriation may leak information to the market about the future bid. This possible leakage of information may raise the cost to the acquirer of purchasing shares prior to any public announcements. Misappropriation, in other words, decreases the returns to bidders from engaging in takeover activity. The link between takeovers and misappropriation, therefore, is that misappropriation is likely to reduce the number of takeovers.

If the problem is that misappropriation causes too few takeovers to occur, reducing the number of takeovers further by regulation obviously makes no sense as a solution. Yet the *CTS* decision and proposed regulations that would limit the period during which prospective acquirers can purchase shares before public disclosure is likely to have precisely this effect. Nor is lengthening the period an offer must remain open, the effect of the Indiana anti-takeover statute upheld in *CTS* and the new proposed federal legislation, likely to decrease the amount of misappropriation. Prior to the Williams Act and state anti-takeover statutes, there were no waiting periods. Thus bidders could proceed quickly and in secret. Competitive bidding contests were rare, and defeat of offers rarer still. Federal and state regulation of takeover activity, by establishing

---

[133]For an elaboration of the importance of the distinction between consensual and non-consensual use of valuable information, see Carlton & Fischel, The Regulation of Insider Trading, 35 Stan. L. Rev. 857 (1983); Fischel, Investment Analysts and Insider Trading: An Economic Analysis of Dirks v. Securities and Exchange Commission, 13 Hofstra L. Rev. 127 (1985).

[134]Chiarella v. United States, 445 U.S. 219 (1980).

waiting periods, has increased the probability that an outstanding offer will be topped by a higher bid or defeated altogether.[135]

Thus, much more uncertainty currently exists as to whether an offer will be successful than existed prior to federal and state regulation of takeovers. As a result, a new class of professionals has emerged—takeover arbitragers. These individuals attempt to predict the outcomes of takeover contests and make their buy/sell decisions accordingly. Obviously, any information that allows them to make better decisions is very valuable given the huge amounts that are typically at stake. Takeover arbitragers thus have strong incentives to acquire such information, presumably by both legal and illegal means.

This incentive to acquire information, and more generally the importance of takeover arbitragers, would be reduced if less uncertainty existed about the outcomes of takeover contests. This could be accomplished by shortening waiting periods. But *CTS* and proposed federal legislation increase waiting periods and thus the amount of uncertainty. As a result, arbitragers' incentive to acquire and misappropriate information will also increase. Thus the proper solution to the misappropriation problem (assuming it is a problem) is to attack it directly by prosecuting and punishing those who engage in the practice and indirectly by reducing uncertainty.

---

[135]See Jarrell & Bradley, The Economic Effects of Federal & State Regulation of Cash Tender Offers, 23 J. Law & Econ. 371 (1980).

WILLIAM T. PIZZI

BATSON V. KENTUCKY: CURING THE DISEASE BUT KILLING THE PATIENT

A. INTRODUCTION

The Supreme Court's efforts to make all citizens equally eligible for jury service has a long history. In 1880 in *Strauder v. West Virginia*,[1] the Court held unconstitutional as a violation of the defendant's right to equal protection of the laws the murder conviction of a black defendant who had been tried by an all-white jury under a statute that restricted eligibility for jury service to "white male persons." In reaching its result the Court emphasized that the purpose of the Fourteenth Amendment was to prohibit "discrimination because of race or color"[2] and the Court asked rhetorically, "[H]ow can it be maintained that compelling a colored man to submit to trial for his life by a jury drawn from a panel from which the state has expressly excluded every man of his race, because of color alone, however well qualified in other respects, is not a denial to him of equal legal protection?"[3]

William T. Pizzi is Associate Professor of Law, University of Colorado School of Law.

AUTHOR'S NOTE: I am deeply indebted to Professors Albert Alschuler and Richard Collins for helping to improve this article by providing detailed comments on an earlier draft, and I particularly appreciate access to Professor Alschuler's lecture notes on the case, which helped to clarify my arguments—especially when our views differed. I also thank my colleagues Christopher Mueller and Robert Nagel for their many helpful comments; Professor Charles Judd of the Psychology Department of the University of Colorado, for his help in researching the subject of ingroup bias; and John Matthew for his able research assistance.

[1] 100 U.S. 303 (1880).

[2] 100 U.S. at 310.

[3] 100 U.S. at 309.

A year after *Strauder,* in *Neal v. Delaware,*[4] the Court extended the equal protection analysis of *Strauder* to cover a statute that was not discriminatory on its face, but which was administered so as to exclude all blacks from the jury venire. In the years since *Strauder* and *Neal,* the Court has made it clear that the Equal Protection Clause prohibits discrimination on bases other than race, such as national origin.[5] The Court has also eased significantly defendants' difficulties in showing discrimination on the part of the state by ruling that a defendant only need show a prima facie case of discrimination before the burden shifts to the state to prove that there was not deliberate discrimination.[6] The result of these decisions and modern jury selection statutes[7] has been an emphasis on making sure that lists of those eligible for jury service are compiled in neutral ways that help ensure that those citizens called for jury service will come from a cross section of citizens in the community.

Over the past quarter century the battleground over jury selection has shifted from the jury venire to the selection of the petit jury, as defendant after defendant has complained in jurisdiction after jurisdiction[8] that the prosecution used its peremptory challenges on a systematic basis to remove all prospective black jurors with the result that the defendant was tried by an all-white jury. The exact extent of the problem is not known because data on jury demographics at either the state or federal level are sparse,[9] but there is no dispute that it is a serious problem in the criminal justice system,

---

[4]103 U.S. 370 (1881).

[5]See Hernandez v. Texas, 347 U.S. 475 (1954).

[6]See Norris v. Alabama, 294 U.S. 587 (1935). See generally 2 LaFave & Israel, Criminal Procedure §21.2(c) (1984).

[7]The Federal Jury Selection and Service Act of 1968, codified 28 U.S.C. §§1861–69, aims at ensuring that juries are "selected at random from a fair cross section of the community in the district or division wherein the court convenes," 28 U.S.C. §1861. The Act specifically prohibits exclusion from service as a juror "on account of race, color, religion, sex, national origin, or economic status." 28 U.S.C. §1862.

[8]One treatise on jury selection lists lines of cases from Arkansas, Georgia, Louisiana, Maryland, Mississippi, Missouri, North Carolina, Tennessee, Texas, California, Illinois, Massachusetts, Michigan, New Jersey, Pennsylvania, and the federal courts in which all or most blacks were excluded by prosecutorial use of peremptory challenges, Van Dyke, Jury Selection Procedures 156 (1977), but it is doubtful if there are many jurisdictions in which there is not such a line of cases. See also 2 Ginger, Jury Selection in Civil and Criminal Trials §20 (2d ed. 1984).

[9]See Jorgenson, Back to the Laboratory with Peremptory Challenges: A Florida Response, 12 Fla. St. U.L. Rev. 558, 578 n.137 (1984).

especially when one starts with the fact that minorities are often underrepresented on jury panels as an initial matter.[10] The use of peremptory challenges systematically to remove prospective black jurors is most likely to occur when the defendant is black and the prosecution wants to remove jurors who may be sympathetic to the defendant, but it is not limited to such cases. As one treatise explained:[11]

> The prosecution is frequently looking for a juror who is middle-aged, middle-class, and white, on the assumption that this type of juror identifies with the government rather than the defendant and will thus be more likely to convict.

This is consistent with the traditional "folklore" surrounding jury selection which suggests that minorities are more likely to sympathize with plaintiffs in civil cases and with defendants in criminal cases:[12]

> The traditional trial-lawyer lore dictates, for instance, that in complicated cases the young should be preferred over the old and men over women. When a child is either the victim or the plaintiff, women jurors are considered desirable, but when women are parties, female jurors should be avoided because they are hard on their own sex. The Irish, Italians, Jews, French, Blacks, Chicanos and those of Balkan heritage are said to sympathize with plaintiffs in civil suits and defendants in criminal actions. The English, Scandinavian, and Germans allegedly have the opposite perspective.

The major roadblock for the past twenty years to an attack on the use of peremptory challenges to remove prospective black jurors has been *Swain v. Alabama*,[13] a decision issued at the height of the Warren Court era, where the Court refused to extend the equal protection analysis used in the venire cases to cover the use of peremptory challenges in the confines of a single case.[14] But in 1983

---

[10]See Van Dyke, note 8 *supra*, at 28. Among the reasons offered for the underrepresentation of minorities on jury panels is the fact that they are underrepresented on voter registration lists as an initial matter and, in addition, tend to move more frequently than whites so that those voter registrations will often not be accurate. *Id.* at 30.

[11]*Id.* at 152.

[12]*Id.* at 153. See also 1 Lane, Goldstein Trial Technique §§9.45, 9.48 (3d ed. 1984); Simon, The Jury and the Defense of Insanity 111 (1967).

[13]380 U.S. 202 (1965).

[14]See text starting at note 17 *infra*.

the Court hinted that it was preparing to reconsider the issue of the prosecutorial use of peremptory challenges to remove blacks from the trial jury in a trial of a black defendant,[15] and, finally, in 1986 the Court decided *Batson v. Kentucky*[16] and struck down on equal protection grounds the use of peremptory challenges by prosecutors to remove blacks on the basis of race where the defendant is also black. In doing so, the Court avoided the Sixth Amendment ground, which is the issue on which certiorari had been granted.

I. The Discriminatory Use of Peremptory Challenges: The Background to the Problem

A. SWAIN V. ALABAMA

Until *Batson* was decided, the landmark decision on the prosecutorial use of peremptory challenges to remove blacks from the jury was *Swain v. Alabama*,[17] decided in 1965. In *Swain*, a black defendant, convicted of rape and sentenced to death, raised two related challenges. First, he challenged the selection of the grand jurors and the selection of the venire in the county in which he was tried. In support of his argument that his right to equal protection was violated, he showed that blacks were substantially underrepresented on grand juries and on petit jury venires.[18] Secondly, Swain argued that his right to equal protection was violated in the selection of petit jurors. Swain showed that no black had served on a petit jury in his county since 1950[19] and in his particular case, although there were eight blacks on the jury panel, no blacks were on the petit jury that convicted him because two blacks were exempt from service and the prosecutor had used peremptory challenges to strike the other six blacks.[20]

Concerning the underrepresentation of blacks on grand juries and jury panels, the Court concluded that although the selection system was "somewhat haphazard and little effort was made to

---

[15]See text at note 63 *infra*.

[16]106 S.Ct. 1712 (1986).

[17]380 U.S. 202 (1965).

[18]*Id.* at 205.

[19]*Id.* at 222–23.

[20]*Id.* at 210.

ensure that all groups in the community were represented,"[21] the percentage of underrepresentation of blacks was relatively small[22] and the record failed to show purposeful discrimination based on race.

The Court also denied Swain's challenge to the prosecutor's peremptory strikes of prospective black jurors. The Court began by reviewing the long history of peremptory challenges which the Court traced to the Ordinance of Inquests in 1305.[23] The Court then explained that "[t]he essential nature of the peremptory challenge is that it is one exercised without a reason stated, without inquiry and without being subject to the court's control"[24] and it "permits rejection for a real or imagined partiality that is less easily designated or demonstrable."[25] The Court pointed out that peremptories are often exercised on the basis of a prospective juror's looks, gestures, habits, and associations.[26] More importantly, the Court frankly acknowledged that peremptory challenges are often exercised "on grounds normally thought irrelevant to legal proceedings or official action, namely, the race, religion, national origin, occupation or affiliations of people summoned for jury duty."[27]

From these premises concerning the nature of the peremptory challenge and its purpose, the Court concluded that the striking of blacks in a single case could not amount to a denial of equal protection:[28]

> In the quest for an impartial and qualified jury, Negro and White, Protestant and Catholic, are alike subject to being challenged without cause. To subject the prosecutor's challenge in any particular case to the demands and traditional standards of the Equal Protection Clause would entail a radical change in the nature and operation of the challenge.

----

[21]*Id.* at 209.

[22]The methodology whereby Justice White concluded that the underrepresentation of blacks in the county in which Swain was tried was relatively small has been strongly criticized. See Brown, McGuire, and Winters, The Peremptory Challenge as a Manipulative Device in Criminal Trials: Traditional Use or Abuse, 14 New Eng. L. Rev. 192, 201 (1978); Note, 65 Yale L.J. 322, 326 (1965).

[23]380 U.S. at 213.

[24]380 U.S. at 220.

[25]*Ibid.*

[26] *Ibid.*

[27]*Id.* at 220–21.

[28]*Id.* at 221–22.

Any other conclusion, the Court feared, would subject the prosecutor's judgment "to scrutiny for reasonableness and sincerity."[29]

The Court did not close the door entirely on challenges to the alleged misuse of peremptory challenges. It indicated that if it could be shown that in a particular jurisdiction the prosecutors are "consistently and systematically" exercising their challenges to prevent "any and all" blacks on jury panels from serving on petit juries, such a systematic practice would constitute invidious discrimination in violation of the Equal Protection Clause.[30] Since Swain had failed to show under what circumstances the prosecutor in the county at issue had been responsible for striking blacks in cases other than his own, the Court concluded that there had been no violation of Swain's right to equal protection.[31]

Commentators[32] and courts[33] in the years after *Swain* have been highly critical of the opinion. The Second Circuit sarcastically titled a section of an opinion dealing with the showing required by *Swain* "Mission Impossible,"[34] and a state supreme court referred to the burden imposed on defendants to make out an equal protection claim after *Swain* as "Sisyphean."[35] While a number of differing explanations have been offered to account for the failure of black defendants to make the showing required by *Swain*,[36] there is no

---

[29]*Id.* at 222.

[30]*Id.* at 223–24.

[31]*Id.* at 224.

[32]See, *e.g.*, Sullivan, Deterring the Discriminatory Use of Peremptory Challenges, 21 Am. Crim. L. Rev. 477 (1984); Note, 92 Harv. L. Rev. 1770 (1979); Brown, McQuire, and Winters, The Peremptory Challenge as a Manipulative Device in Criminal Trials, 14 New Eng. L. Rev. 192 (1978); Kuhn, Jury Discrimination: The Next Phase, 41 S. Cal. L. Rev. 235 (1968); Note, 39 Miss. L. J. 157 (1967): Comment, 52 Va. L. Rev. 1157 (1966). But see Saltzburg and Powers, Peremptory Challenges and the Clash between Impartiality and Group Representation, 41 Md. L. Rev. 337 (1982).

[33] See, *e.g.*, United States v. Childress, 715 F.2d 1313, 1316–18 (8th Cir. 1983) (en banc), cert. denied, 464 U.S. 1063 (1984); McCray v. Abrams, 750 F.2d 1113, 1120 (2d Cir. 1984), vacated, 106 S.Ct. 3289 (1986); People v. Wheeler, 22 Cal. 3d 258, 148 Cal. Rptr. 890, 583 P.2d 748, 767 (1978).

[34]McCray v. Abrams, 750 F.2d 1120.

[35]Commonwealth v. Soares, 471 Mass. 461, 471 n.10, 399 N.E.2d 499, 509 n.10 (1979).

[36]The lack of success defendants have had under *Swain* is frequently attributed to the fact that an individual defendant is unlikely to have either the time or the resources to compile and analyze the raw data necessary to mount a statistical attack on the prosecution's use of peremptory challenges. See United States v. Childress, 715 F.2d at 1316; United States v. Pearson, 448 F.2d 1207, 1217 (5th Cir. 1971). But with the emergence of strong and organized

dispute that in the years since *Swain*, the number of successful
attacks on the discriminatory use of peremptory challenges to remove blacks on a systematic basis over many cases have been almost
nonexistent. In *United States v. Childress*,[37] decided by the Eighth
Circuit *en banc* in 1983, the court reported that it had found two
such cases,[38] both from the same Louisiana parish, where a defendant had successfully established systematic exclusion of blacks.

B. NEW DEVELOPMENTS UNDER STATE CONSTITUTIONAL LAW: WHEELER AND SOARES

In the late 1970s, after the Supreme Court had extended the
Sixth Amendment right to jury trial to the states[39] and had also
established as part of the right to an impartial jury the right of a
defendant to a jury pool that is drawn from a fair cross section of
the community,[40] two state courts, California and Massachusetts,
using state constitutional analogs to the Sixth Amendment, took a
new approach to the problem raised by the use of peremptory
challenges by the prosecutor to remove blacks from the jury.

In *People v. Wheeler*,[41] the California Supreme Court, using article
I, section 16 of the California Constitution,[42] ruled that it was unconstitutional for a party to employ its peremptory challenges to remove prospective jurors solely on the basis of group bias. The court
reversed the convictions of two black defendants in cases in which
the prosecution had used its peremptory challenges to strike every

---

public defender systems, the empirical difficulties of proof seem somewhat exaggerated. A
more obvious reason why defendants have been unable to show the systematic exclusion by
the prosecution of "any and all blacks" from petit juries in a given jurisdiction is that assuming
a normal mix of cases and a normal cross section of defendants and victims, it would seem
extremely unlikely that there would be many offices in which prosecutors would remove
all blacks from all juries in all cases. There will obviously be cases in which black jurors
would be very desirable from the prosecution's perspective. See Saltzburg and Powers, note
32 *supra*, at 353–65 (arguing that prosecutors try to keep blacks off some but not all juries).

[37] 715 F.2d 1313, 1316 (8th Cir. 1983) (en banc), cert. denied, 464 U.S. 1063 (1984).

[38] State v. Brown, 371 So.2d 751 (La. 1979); State v. Washington, 375 So.2d 1162 (La. 1979).

[39] See Duncan v. Louisiana, 391 U.S. 145 (1968).

[40] See Taylor v. Louisiana, 419 U.S. 522 (1975).

[41] 22 Cal. 3d 258, 148 Cal. Rptr. 890, 583 P.2d 748 (1978).

[42] Article I, section 16 of the California Constitution provides in relevant part: "Trial by
jury is an inviolate right and shall be secured to all. . . ." Cal. Const., art. I, §16.

prospective black juror.[43] While making it clear that a defendant is not entitled to a jury that proportionately mirrors the community nor even to a jury that includes members of his particular ethnic group,[44] the California court explained "that a party is entitled to a petit jury that is as near an approximation of the ideal cross-section of the community as the process of random draw permits."[45] By striking jurors on the basis of what the court referred to as "group bias," which the court defined to include bias against "groups distinguished on racial, religious, ethnic, or similar grounds," the court reasoned that the impartiality that comes from "allowing the interaction of the diverse beliefs and values the jurors bring from their group experiences"[46] would be destroyed. The result of peremptories based on group bias, the court feared, would be a jury "dominated by the conscious or unconscious prejudices of the majority."[47]

Under the procedure set up in *Wheeler,* if a party believes that the other side is using peremptory challenges to strike jurors on the ground of "group bias alone," the party must raise the issue and make a prima facie case of discrimination to the satisfaction of the court.[48] If the court finds a reasonable likelihood that peremptory challenges were used on the ground of group bias alone, the burden shifts to the challenging party to show that the peremptory challenges were not predicated on group bias alone, but were instead based on the "specific bias" of the prospective jurors which the court defined to include "bias concerning the particular case on trial or the parties or witnesses thereto."[49]

The reasoning of *People v. Wheeler* was relied on heavily by the Supreme Judicial Court of Massachusetts in *Commonwealth v. Soares.*[50]

---

[43]The court stated that because members of the venire are not required to indicate their race, religion, or ethnic origin, it was unclear exactly how many blacks had been struck by the prosecution. 583 P.2d at 752.

[44]*Id.* at 762.

[45]*Ibid.*

[46]*Id.* at 761. In another passage in the opinion, the court seemed to suggest that group bias might extend even to groups based on sex, age, education, economic condition, place of residence, and political affiliation. *Id.* at 755.

[47]*Id.* at 761.

[48]*Id.* at 764.

[49]*Id.* at 764–65.

[50]377 Mass. 461, 387 N.E.2d 499, cert. denied, 444 U.S. 881 (1979).

Soares involved a first-degree murder prosecution brought against three black defendants who had scuffled in the early morning hours on the streets of Boston's "Combat Zone" with several members of the Harvard football team—athletes who, after the conclusion of a team banquet, had gone to explore life in and around the topless bars of Boston. During the scuffle, someone had stabbed one of the students, who later died from his wounds. Prior to the trial of the three defendants, the prosecution had used its peremptory challenges to remove twelve of the thirteen blacks on the venire.[51]

The *Soares* court interpreted article 12 of the Massachusetts Constitution, which states in part that no citizen shall be "deprived of his life, liberty, or estate, but by the judgment of his peers, or the law of the land," to provide a right to " 'a petit jury that is as near an approximation of the ideal cross-section of the community as the process of random selection permits.' "[52] This right, the court ruled, is violated when peremptory challenges are used to strike prospective jurors solely on the base of group membership or affiliation, which the court defined to include: sex, race, color, creed, or national origin.[53] Although there is a "presumption of proper use" of peremptory challenges, if there is a "pattern of conduct" whereby members of a cognizable group have been excluded and there is "a likelihood they are being excluded from the jury solely by reason of their group membership," then the burden shifts to the offending party to demonstrate that the strikes were not exercised on the basis of group affiliation.[54] While the court indicated that the party's explanation "need not approximate the grounds required by a challenge for cause," the reason for the challenge "must pertain to the individual qualities of the prospective juror and not to that juror's group association."[55]

Wheeler and *Soares* had at best a mixed reaction in other states, and most states refused to go down the path presented by the

---

[51] The thirteenth black juror remained on the petit jury and was later appointed the jury's foreman by the trial judge. 387 N.E.2d at 508.

[52] *Id.* at 516, quoting from People v. Wheeler, 583 P.2d at 762.

[53] The court used as its source for determining which groups may not be excluded solely on the basis of group affiliation the Equal Rights Amendment of the Massachusetts Constitution. 387 N.E.2d at 516.

[54] *Id.* at 517.

[55] *Ibid.*

decisions.[56] In a dissenting opinion in 1983, Justice Marshall observed that in the five years following *Wheeler* and *Soares*, no other state supreme court had imposed state constitutional limits on peremptory challenges; but in the same period nineteen states had indicated they would continue to follow *Swain*.[57] But in the three-year period between 1983 and the Court's decision in *Batson*, three other states used their state constitutions to reach results similar to those in *Wheeler* and *Soares*.[58]

C. PEREMPTORIES UNDER THE FEDERAL CONSTITUTION

In 1984 Michael McCray, a black who had been convicted of robbery in the New York courts, filed a petition for certiorari in the United States Supreme Court.[59] At McCray's first trial a jury of three blacks and nine whites had hung with either two or all three of the black jury members voting for acquittal.[60] At McCray's retrial, at which he was convicted, the prosecution used eleven or twelve of the state's fifteen peremptory challenges to exclude all blacks and Hispanics from the jury.[61] The state courts had affirmed the conviction on the authority of *Swain*.[62]

---

[56]See, *e.g.*, Flowers v. State, 402 So.2d 1088, 1093 (Ala. Crim. App. 1981); Beed v. State, 271 Ark. 526, 530, 609 S.W.2d 898, 903 (1980); Doepel v. United States, 434 A.2d 449, 457–59 (D.C.), cert. denied, 454 U.S. 1037 (1981); Blackwell v. State, 248 Ga. 138, 281 S.E.2d 599, 599–600 (1981); People v. Davis, 95 Ill.2d 1, 69 Ill. Dec. 136, 447 N.E.2d 353 (1983), cert. denied 464 U.S. 1001; State v. Stewart, 225 Kan. 410, 591 P.2d 166 (1979); Gaines v. State, 404 So.2d 557 (Miss. 1981); Commonwealth v. Henderson, 497 Pa. 23, 438 A.2d 951 (1981); State v. Ucero, 450 A.2d 809, 812–13 (R.I. 1982); State v. Thompson, 276 S.C. 616, 281 S.E.2d 216 (1981); People v. McCray, 57 N.Y.2d 542, 457 N.Y.S.2d 441, 443 N.E.2d 915 (1982), cert. denied, 461 U.S. 961 (1983); Drew v. State, 588 S.W.2d 562 (Tenn. Crim. App. 1979); State v. Grady, 93 Wisc.2d 1, 10–11, 286 N.W.2d 607, 611 (App. 1979); State v. Lynch, 300 N.C. 534, 268 S.E.2d 161 (1980).

[57]See Gilliard v. Mississippi, 464 U.S. 867 (1983) (Marshall, J., dissenting from denial of certiorari).

[58]See Riley v. State, 496 A.2d 997 (Del. 1985); State v. Gilmore, 199 N.J. Super. 389, 489 A.2d 1175 (1985), affirmed 511 A.2d 1150 (N.J. 1986); State v. Neil, 457 So.2d 481, 486 (Fla. 1984). New Mexico had also indicated in 1980 in dicta that it was leaning toward following *Wheeler*. See State v. Crespin, 94 N.M. 486, 612 P.2d 716 (App. 1980). Since the Court's decision in *Batson*, two other states have followed the approach to peremptory challenges pioneered in *Wheeler*. See text at notes 294–97 *infra*.

[59]McCray v. New York, 461 U.S. 961 (1983) (denial of certiorari).

[60]McCray v. Abrams, 750 F.2d 1113, 1115 (2d Cir. 1984), vacated, 106 S.Ct. 3289 (1986).

[61]*Ibid.*

[62]See People v. McCray, 57 N.Y.2d 542, 457 N.Y.S.2d 441, 443 N.E.2d 915 (1982), cert. denied, 461 U.S. 961 (1983).

The Supreme Court denied certiorari,[63] but at the same time the Court hinted that it was interested in reconsidering *Swain*. In an opinion joined by Justices Blackmun and Powell, Justice Stevens explained that the denial of certiorari was intended to enable the state courts to serve as laboratories for further study which would "enable the Court to deal with the issue more wisely at a later date. . . ."[64] Justice Marshall, joined by Justice Brennan, filed an opinion dissenting from the denial of certiorari in which he argued that it was time to reconsider *Swain* in light of intervening developments extending the protections of the Sixth Amendment to the states.[65] The two opinions revealed that at least five justices were concerned about the use of peremptory challenges to strike prospective jurors on the basis of race.

When *McCray* reached the federal district court on habeas corpus, that court took the hint and ruled that the action of the prosecutor in using peremptory challenges to strike black jurors violated both the cross-sectional requirements of the Sixth Amendment and the Equal Protection Clause.[66] On appeal, the Second Circuit reluctantly reversed on the equal protection ground, but affirmed on the Sixth Amendment ruling.[67] The court reasoned that since the Sixth Amendment guaranteed a venire that represents a fair cross section of the community,[68]

> [I]t must logically be because it is important that the defendant have the chance that the petit jury will be similarly constituted. The necessary implication is that the Sixth Amendment guarantees the defendant that possibility. It guarantees not that the possibility will ripen into actuality, but only the fair and undistorted chance that it will.

The result with respect to the use of peremptory challenges is that "the Sixth Amendment's guarantee of trial by an impartial jury allows the prosecution to exercise its peremptory challenges to excuse jurors to whom, on the basis of their personal history or behavior, some bias may be imputed; but it forbids the exercise of

---

[63]See McCray v. New York, 461 U.S. 961 (1983).

[64]*Id.* at 962.

[65]*Id.* at 969.

[66]See McCray v. Abrams, 576 F.Supp. 1244 (E.D.N.Y. 1984).

[67]See McCray v. Abrams, 750 F.2d 1113.

[68]750 F.2d at 1128–29.

such challenges to excuse jurors solely on the basis of their racial affiliation."[69]

Under the procedure set out in *McCray*, a defendant must first establish a prima facie violation of his "right to the possibility of a fair cross section" by showing that in his case (1) the group alleged to be excluded is a cognizable group in the community, and (2) there is a substantial likelihood that the challenges leading to exclusion have been made "on the basis of the individual venirepersons' group affiliation rather than because of any indication of a possible inability to decide the case on the basis of the evidence presented."[70] If the defendant makes such a showing, then the burden shifts to the prosecutor to rebut the presumption of unconstitutional action by showing that "permissible racially neutral selection criteria" supported the peremptory challenge.[71]

The issue was joined when, after certiorari had been granted in *Batson*,[72] the Fifth Circuit issued an *en banc* opinion, *United States v. Leslie*,[73] that challenged the reasoning and the conclusion reached in *McCray*.[74]

Leslie, a prominent fight promoter in the city of New Orleans, was charged with distributing cocaine.[75] During the voir dire the government used its six peremptory challenges to remove six blacks—the only six blacks on the twenty-eight-person panel left after challenges for cause.[76] The defense had challenged ten white jurors with its ten peremptories.[77] The government had also struck the only black on the four-person alternate pool, while the defense had used

---

[69]750 F.2d at 1131.

[70]750 F.2d at 1131–32.

[71]750 F.2d at 1132. The court stated further that the prosecutor's rebuttal need not rise to the level of a challenge for cause because "there are any number of bases on which a party may believe, not unreasonably, that a prospective juror may have some slight bias that would not support a challenge for cause but that would make excusing him or her desirable." *Ibid.*

[72]471 U.S. 1052 (1985).

[73]783 F.2d 541 (5th Cir. 1986), vacated, 107 S.Ct. 1267 (1987).

[74]In Booker v. Jabe, 775 F.2d 762 (6th Cir. 1985), vacated *sub nom.* Michigan v. Booker, 106 S.Ct. 3289 (1986), the Sixth Circuit had adopted the reasoning in *McCray* in ruling that the prosecutor's use of peremptory challenges to exclude prospective black jurors at the trial of a black defendant violated the sixth amendment right to an impartial jury.

[75]783 F.2d at 543.

[76]*Ibid.*

[77]*Ibid.*

its peremptory with respect to alternates to strike one of the three whites in the alternate pool.[78]

The Fifth Circuit began its analysis by arguing that challenges on the basis of race or religion or any other characteristic common to a "cognizable group" were proper as long as the prosecutor acted on the basis of considerations going to the particular case being tried, such as the nature of the crime and the background of the particular defendant. The Fifth Circuit saw this as the teaching of *Swain*. It thus drew a sharp distinction between peremptory challenges exercised for adversary advantage and the complete exclusion of cognizable groups from jury service condemned by the Court in the venire cases:[79]

> To be peremptorily challenged by one side or the other . . . bespeaks a judgment which is neither societal nor even normative, but merely reflects the tactical determination of one contesting litigant's counsel that the challenged person is, under the discrete facts of that particular case, more likely than not to favor the other side.

The court rejected the Sixth Amendment approach pioneered by the Second Circuit and concluded that systematic peremptory challenges of a cognizable group of citizens are not a violation of the right to the "possibility of a cross section of the community" on the jury. It reasoned that although the jury system does embrace "cross-sectional values," such values are embraced in the context of, and are limited by, the overall concept of trial by jury which includes the right to challenge jurors for both individual and group characteristics.[80] The court also refused to bar the use of peremptory challenges by the prosecution on the basis of group affiliation under its supervisory power.[81]

II. BATSON v. KENTUCKY

Three years after the Court hinted that it was preparing to reconsider the issue of the prosecutorial use of peremptory chal-

---

[78] *Ibid.*

[79] 783 F.2d at 554.

[80] *Id.* at 556.

[81] *Id.* at 566.

lenges to strike prospective jurors on the basis of race,[82] the Court decided *Batson v. Kentucky.*[83] Batson was a black defendant charged with second-degree burglary and receipt of stolen goods. In Batson's case, the prosecutor used four of his six peremptory challenges[84] to remove all four prospective black jurors from the jury list. *Batson* was tried and convicted by an all-white jury.[85]

Following his conviction on both counts, *Batson* appealed to the Supreme Court of Kentucky. Conceding that *Swain* foreclosed an equal protection attack on his conviction, *Batson* argued that the prosecutor's act of striking the blacks from his jury violated his right to a jury drawn from a cross section of the community under the Sixth Amendment and its analog in the Kentucky Constitution. The Supreme Court of Kentucky affirmed the conviction in a one-paragraph opinion which relied on *Swain.*[86] The Supreme Court granted certiorari on the Sixth Amendment issue.

But the Court had a major surprise in store. Its opinion in *Batson* turned not on the Sixth Amendment issue, but instead on the Equal Protection Clause of the Fourteenth Amendment. Not surprisingly, this development produced some background skirmishing in the opinions over the propriety of the Court's resolving an important issue of criminal procedure on a theory other than that on which certiorari had been granted.[87]

A. THE OPINIONS IN BATSON

Writing for the seven-person majority, Justice Powell argued that the protection afforded an accused under the Equal Protection Clause does not stop with the exclusion of cognizable racial groups from

---

[82]See text at notes 63–65 *supra.*

[83]106 S.Ct. 1712 (1986).

[84]In noncapital felony cases in Kentucky the prosecution is entitled to five peremptory challenges and the defense is entitled to eight challenges, but where there is an alternate to be chosen, as was the case in Batson's trial, 106 S.Ct. at 1715 n.2, each side receives an additional peremptory challenge. Ky. R. Crim. P., Rule 9.40.

[85]106 S.Ct. at 1715.

[86]*Id.* at 1715–16.

[87]In his dissenting opinion, Chief Justice Burger criticized the majority for departing from normal procedures in order to decide the case on an issue that had not briefed and argued. See 106 S.Ct. 1731, 1731–32. Justice Stevens responded to this criticism in a concurring opinion in which he argued that the issue was properly before the Court because several *amici curiae,* including the Solicitor General in his brief, had raised the issue. See *id.* at 1729.

the jury venire, but rather "the Fourteenth Amendment protects
an accused throughout the proceedings bringing him to justice."[88]
Thus "the State's privilege to strike individual jurors through peremptory challenges, is subject to the commands of the Equal Protection Clause,"[89] and equal protection "forbids a prosecutor from
challenging potential jurors solely on account of their race or on
the assumption that black jurors as a group will be unable impartially to consider the State's case against a black defendant."[90]

Although the majority argued that its decision was a logical extension of *Strauder* and the Court's historical condemnation of discrimination on the basis of race, the majority seemed a bit uncertain
about what to do with *Swain*. The opinion noted that, despite the
denial of relief to the defendant in that case, the *Swain* opinion did
indicate that the Equal Protection Clause placed some limits on
peremptory challenges in certain cases.[91]

The problem with *Swain*, for the majority, was the "interpretation"[92]
of that case so as to place on defendants a "crippling burden of proof"[93]
by making a defendant show systematic exclusion of blacks over a
number of cases in order to establish a prima facie case of discrimination. It was this "evidentiary formulation"[94] which the majority
claimed to reject in *Batson*, because those standards are "inconsistent
with standards that have been developed since *Swain* for assessing a
prima facie case under the Equal Protection Clause."[95]

The standards "developed since *Swain*" to which the Court referred had been developed for assessing equal protection challenges
to jury venires. The Court in *Batson* took the procedures developed
in venire cases for evaluating claims of racial discrimination on the
part of the state and applied them to the petit jury. As in the venire
cases, the defendant must show initially a prima facie case of purposeful discrimination by the prosecutor in the exercise of the state's
peremptory challenges.[96] To establish such a case the defendant

---

[88]*Id.* at 1718.
[89]*Ibid.*
[90]*Id.* at 1719.
[91]*Id.* at 1720.
[92]*Ibid.*
[93]*Ibid.*
[94]*Id.* at 1721.
[95]*Ibid.*
[96]*Id.* at 1722.

must show (1) that he is a member of a cognizable racial group and (2) that the prosecutor has exercised peremptory challenges to remove from the venire members of the defendant's race.[97] In making the requisite showing, the defendant must show facts and circumstances that raise an inference that the prosecutor used peremptory challenges to exclude prospective jurors on account of race. Among the relevant facts which the Court indicated might give rise to an inference of discrimination was a " 'pattern' of strikes against black jurors" or similarly "the prosecutor's questions and statements during voir dire."[98]

Just as with equal protection challenges to the composition of a jury venire, once the defendant has succeeded in raising a prima facie case of discrimination, "the burden shifts to the State to come forward with a neutral explanation for challenging black jurors."[99] Such an explanation, the Court emphasized, "need not rise to the level justifying exercise of a challenge for cause,"[100] but "the prosecutor may not rebut the defendant's prima facie case of discrimination by stating merely that he challenged jurors of the defendant's race on the assumption—or his intuitive judgment—that they would be partial to the defendant because of their shared race."[101]

The Court left to the lower courts the task of working out the procedures to be followed if the prosecutor does not rebut the defendant's prima facie case—whether, for example, to start the jury selection process over with a new panel[102] or to require the reinstatement of improperly challenged jurors.[103] It reasoned that given the variety of jury selection practices followed in state and federal trial courts, it was better not "to attempt to instruct those courts how best to implement our holding today."[104]

Because *Batson* had made a timely objection to the prosecutor's use of peremptory challenges, the case was remanded to permit the

---

[97] *Id.* at 1723.

[98] *Ibid.*

[99] *Ibid.*

[100] *Ibid.*

[101] *Ibid.*

[102] See, *e.g.*, McCray v. Abrams, 750 F.2d at 1132; Booker v. Jabe, 775 F.2d 773; People v. Wheeler, 583 P.2d at 765.

[103] See United States v. Robinson, 421 F. Supp. 467, 474 (Conn. 1976), mandamus granted *sub nom.* United States v. Newman, 549 F.2d 240 (2d Cir. 1977).

[104] 106 S.Ct. at 1724 n.24.

trial court to determine whether the facts had raised a prima facie case of discrimination, and if so, to permit the prosecutor an opportunity to offer a neutral explanation for his actions.[105]

There were four concurring opinions, but two were not directed to the merits of the majority opinion. Justice Stevens's concurring opinion was directed solely to the propriety of the Court's finding a violation of the Equal Protection Clause when the petitioner had not raised that issue in the request for certiorari.[106] Justice O'Connor added a one-paragraph opinion[107] to express agreement with the conclusion of Justice White in his concurrence[108] and of Chief Justice Burger in his dissent[109] that the decision in *Batson* should not be applied retroactively.[110] Justice White was more candid in his concurring opinion than was the majority. He acknowledged at the start of his opinion that the Court was overruling the "principal holding" of *Swain v. Alabama*, which had traditionally shielded a prosecutor's use of peremptory challenges in a particular case from inquiry into the reasons for the exercise of those challenges.[111] But he explained that prosecutors had not heeded the warning implicit in *Swain* "that using peremptories to exclude blacks on the assumption that no black juror could fairly judge a black defendant would violate the Equal Protection Clause."[112] Thus he concluded that because "the practice of peremptorily eliminating blacks from petit juries in cases with black defendants remains widespread, . . . an opportunity to inquire should be afforded when this occurs."[113] If the issue is properly raised by the defendant and the judge "is not persuaded otherwise, the judge may conclude that the challenges rest on the belief that blacks could not fairly try a black defendant."[114]

---

[105] *Id.* at 1725.

[106] *Id.* at 1729. See note 87 *supra*.

[107] 106 S.Ct. at 1731.

[108] *Id.* at 1726.

[109] *Id.* at 1741.

[110] The Court has subsequently ruled that *Batson* is to be applied retroactively to all cases, federal and state, pending on direct review and not yet final, Griffith v. Kentucky, 107 S.Ct. 708 (1987), but *Batson* is not to be applied retroactively on collateral review to cases that had become final before *Batson* was handed down, Allen v. Hardy, 106 S.Ct. 2878 (1986).

[111] 106 S.Ct. at 1725.

[112] *Ibid.*

[113] *Ibid.*

[114] *Ibid.*

Justice Marshall wrote a concurring opinion in which he welcomed the Court's conclusion that use of peremptory challenges to remove blacks from juries violates the Equal Protection Clause, but he questioned the adequacy of the Court's remedy.[115] His analysis of cases in California[116] and Massachusetts[117] following the decisions in *Wheeler* and *Soares* suggested to him that only in a particularly flagrant case will a defendant be able to establish a prima facie case so as to require judicial inquiry into the prosecutor's motives. The result was that "[p]rosecutors are left free to discriminate against blacks in jury selection provided that they hold discrimination to an 'acceptable' level."[118]

Moreover, he argued, even where a prima facie case is found, it will be extremely difficult for a trial judge to second-guess facially neutral reasons for the exclusions—reasons that an unscrupulous prosecutor could always supply.[119] And he worried that, even putting the issue of dishonesty aside, "conscious or unconscious racism" may cause a prosecutor to view a prospective black juror as "sullen" or "distant," and the same source could cause the judge to accept that explanation as well supported.[120]

Since it has often been declared that peremptory challenges are not constitutionally required, Justice Marshall concluded that the best solution would be for the Court to ban the use of peremptory challenges by prosecutors and allow states to eliminate the defendant's peremptory challenges, since "[t]he potential for racial prejudice . . . inheres in the defendant's challenge as well."[121]

---

[115]*Id.* at 1726.

[116]From California, Justice Marshall cited People v. Rousseau, 129 Cal. App.3d 526, 536–37, 179 Cal. Rptr. 892, 897–98 (Cal. Ct. App. 1982), where no prima facie case was found even though the prosecutor had peremptorily struck the only two blacks on the jury panel. 106 S.Ct. at 1727–28.

[117]From Massachusetts, Justice Marshall cited Commonwealth v. Robinson, 382 Mass. 189, 195, 415 N.E.2d 805, 809–10 (1981) where, in a case involving a black defendant, the prosecutor had used one challenge for cause and three peremptory challenges to remove three blacks and a Puerto Rican with the result that the jury that convicted the defendant was all-white. 106 S.Ct. at 1727.

[118]*Id.* at 1728.

[119]*Ibid.*

[120]*Ibid.*

[121]*Id.* at 1729.

Both Chief Justice Burger and Justice Rehnquist filed dissents. On the merits,[122] Chief Justice Burger expressed agreement with *Strauder* and the long line of cases that have found exclusion of cognizable groups from jury venires to be a violation of equal protection, but, relying heavily on *United States v. Leslie*, he maintained that the decisions of the litigants in a particular case to strike prospective jurors stands on a different footing. Peremptory challenges, he explained, are exercised on limited information about the prospective jurors. They are "peremptory" precisely because they are often made on the basis of assumptions and hunches about people and how they might act as jurors in a particular case.[123] Quoting *Swain*, Burger explained that peremptories "are often lodged, of necessity, for reasons 'normally thought irrelevant to legal proceedings or official action, namely, the race, religion, nationality, occupation or affiliations of people summoned for jury duty.' "[124]

Instead of being a logical extension of equal protection principles, Burger argued that the majority in *Batson* was in fact departing from "conventional equal protection principles."[125] In the first place, he maintained, the majority's careful attempt to limit the holding of the case to cognizable racial groups was inconsistent with settled equal protection law which required any such application of equal protection to extend beyond racial groups to embrace exclusions from a petit jury on the basis of sex, religious or political affiliation, mental capacity, number of children, living arrangements, and employment in a particular industry or profession, and so on.[126] In addition, he argued that the Court departed from settled equal protection principles by failing to determine the level of scrutiny to which the state's use of peremptories was subject and then weighing the unrestrained use of peremptories against that test.[127] He expressed his opinion that, given the long history of peremptory

---

[122]The Chief Justice initially argued that it was not proper for the Court to resolve this case on an issue that was not raised by the petitioner. *Id.* at 1731, 1731–34 (Burger, C.J., dissenting). See note 87 *supra*.

[123]106 S.Ct. at 1737.

[124]*Id.* at 1737, quoting from *Swain*, 380 U.S. at 220.

[125]106 S.Ct. at 1737.

[126]*Id.* at 1737.

[127]*Id.* at 1738.

challenges, which he claimed have been in existence almost as long as the concept of trial by jury,[128] and the Court's own statement nearly a hundred years ago that the peremptory challenge is " 'essential to the fairness of trial by jury,' "[129] it may well be that under conventional equal protection analysis, "a state interest of this magnitude and ancient lineage" might well overcome any equal protection objection to the state's unrestrained use of peremptories.[130]

Finally, Burger was highly critical of the majority for giving trial judges a difficult task for which the Court had given them no clear guidelines. He stated, for example, that he was "at a loss to discern the governing principles" that will satisfy the Court's requirement that a prosecutor provide a "neutral explanation" for his challenges, but that such explanation, although it is to be "clear and reasonably specific," "need not rise to the level justifying a challenge for cause."[131] And he concluded that the result of the majority opinion would simply be the interjection of racial matters into the jury selection process as prosecutors and defense attorneys build records to challenge or support the exercise of their peremptories.[132]

Justice Rehnquist argued in his dissent that the majority was doing much more than simply adjusting the "evidentiary burden" on defendants under *Swain*.[133] He objected that the majority was overruling *Swain*, an opinion in which, he pointed out, even the dissenters had viewed the use of race and other group affiliations as a necessary and constitutional means for sorting out potential juror partiality.[134] Justice Rehnquist concluded that as long as the State is treating all defendants the same way—striking Asian jurors when the defendant is Asian, white jurors when the defendant is white, and Hispanic jurors when the defendant is Hispanic—the use of such "crudely stereotypical" strikes "may in many cases be hopelessly mistaken" but does not violate the Equal Protection Clause.[135]

---

[128]*Id.* at 1734–35.

[129]*Id.* at 1738, quoting from Lewis v. United States, 146 U.S. 370, 376 (1892).

[130]*Id.* at 1738.

[131]*Id.* at 1739.

[132]*Id.* at 1740.

[133]*Id.* at 1742, 1744.

[134]*Id.* at 1744. See note 230 *infra*.

[135]*Id.* at 1744–45.

B. EQUAL PROTECTION VERSUS THE SIXTH AMENDMENT

The decision to decide *Batson* on equal protection rather than Sixth Amendment grounds was a surprise because the Sixth Amendment approach to the problem of discriminatory challenges would have offered the Court several advantages. In the first place, under the approach pioneered in *Wheeler* and *Soares*, which views the systematic striking of members of a racial, religious, or ethnic group as violative of the right of a defendant to an impartial jury, any defendant—regardless of the defendant's own racial, ethnic, or religious identity—can challenge the systematic use of peremptory challenges to remove jurors on the basis of race, ethnic origin, or religion. This speaks more completely to the problem the Court was facing, because systematic striking of members of minority groups is not limited to situations where the defendant is also a member of that group.[136] Moreover, the Sixth Amendment approach seems more consistent with the rationale of *Batson*, which turned on the effects of exclusion on those jurors being removed, rather than the effects of exclusion on the defendant's trial. The Court in Batson emphasized that "a defendant has no right to a 'petit jury composed in whole or in part of persons of his own race.' "[137] Instead it is the exclusion of jurors from participation in the process that was the Court's concern.[138]

A second advantage of the Sixth Amendment approach to the problem of discriminatory peremptory challenges is that it more easily allows courts to take a balanced approach to peremptory challenges. A serious distinction between the selection of the venire and the selection of the petit jury is that peremptory challenges are part of the adversary process and, in the battle for a favorable jury, it is sometimes the defendant who is interested in using peremptory challenges to remove jurors on the basis of their race, religion, or ethnic origin. Perhaps recognizing that their opinions were in effect legislating important changes in the rules governing peremptory challenges and thus that a balanced approach to the problems raised by peremptory challenge was important, both *Wheeler* and *Soares* made their rulings applicable to both the prosecution and the de-

---

[136]See text at notes 11–12 *supra*. See also note 190 *infra*.

[137]106 S.Ct. at 1716, quoting from Strauder v. West Virginia, 100 U.S. 303, 305 (1880).

[138]106 S.Ct. at 1724.

fense. While the right to an impartial jury is a right guaranteed to defendants, those courts reasoned that it would be inconsistent if a court were to enforce the right to an impartial jury and the possibility of a fair cross section against the state and at the same time permit the defendant to use peremptory challenges to deprive the state of the same possibility. The California Supreme Court explained:[139]

> [T]o hold to the contrary would frustrate other essential functions served by the requirement of cross-sectionalism. For example, when a white defendant is charged with a crime against a black victim, the black community as a whole has a legitimate interest in participating in the trial proceedings; that interest will be defeated if the prosecutor does not have the power to thwart any defense attempt to strike all blacks from the jury on the ground of group bias alone.

In *Batson*, the Court left for another day the issue of discriminatory peremptory challenges on the part of the defense, stating simply in a footnote, "We express no views on whether the Constitution imposes any limit on the exercise of peremptory challenges by defense counsel."[140] If the Court intends to use the Equal Protection Clause to reach defense challenges, it must confront a state action problem. As one commentator explained, in suggesting that the Court ought not to restrict defense peremptory challenges, "the defendant is not a state actor."[141] This oversimplifies the matter because state action under *Shelley v. Kraemer*[142] seems to have a fairly broad sweep when a private party acts in concert with government officials.[143] It is certainly arguable that the use of peremptory challenges—provided by state rules of procedure and exercised in a state court by "officers of the court" under judicial sanction—would give the Court ample room to conclude that the exercise of such challenges, even by the defense, amounts to state action,[144] but the issue is not beyond doubt.

---

[139]583 P.2d at 765 n.29.

[140]106 S.Ct. at 1718 n.12.

[141]See Note, 92 Harv. L. Rev., note 32 *supra*, at 1786.

[142]334 U.S. 1 (1948).

[143]See Lugar v. Edmundson Oil Co., Inc., 457 U.S. 922 (1982).

[144]In *Lugar, ibid.*, the Court set forth a two-part test for determining if deprivation of a federal right may fairly be attributable to the state, 457 U.S. at 932, and this test would seem to be met when a private defense attorney systematically strikes prospective jurors on the basis of race under state rules of procedure which are enforced by the trial judge.

But even if the state action objection can be met, the Court would need to modify the approach it took in *Batson* if it were to extend its equal protection ruling to defense challenges. Since the state is not a member of a "cognizable racial group," the initial step in the *Batson* analysis would have to be modified or abandoned. Perhaps the state could be permitted to raise equal protection concerns on behalf of prospective jurors who lack standing to vindicate their own rights.

The state action problem raises another major contrast between the Sixth Amendment and the equal protection approaches and a third reason why the Sixth Amendment approach might have seemed a more attractive alternative for controlling discriminatory peremptory challenges. The Sixth Amendment is limited to criminal prosecutions, and thus the Court would be able to limit the impact of its decision to the main area of concern: criminal cases. Having chosen to regulate peremptory challenges under the Equal Protection Clause, *Batson* seems to have obvious implications for any case in which an attorney for the state strikes jurors on the basis of race. Thus, for example, in a civil rights suit against the government in which racial discrimination is alleged, *Batson* and its restrictions on peremptory challenges would seem fully applicable to the exercise of peremptory challenges by the state.[145] And, if the exercise of peremptory challenges by private defense counsel in a criminal case amounts to state action, presumably private attorneys representing private parties in civil cases are subject to constitutional limitations as well.

But although there are a number of reasons that seem to suggest the Sixth Amendment might have provided a better route than the Equal Protection Clause for controlling discriminatory peremptory challenges, there is a major drawback to the Sixth Amendment approach that must have persuaded the Court to use the Equal Protection Clause to control discriminatory peremptory challenges. The fair cross-section approach is based on a myth; the reality is that neither our system of jury selection nor the remedy imposed in *Wheeler* and *Soares* is designed to assure defendants a demographically representative cross section on the jury.

---

[145]In King v. County of Nassau, 581 F.Supp. 493 (E.D.N.Y. 1984), a race discrimination case decided prior to *Batson*, the court held peremptory challenges on the basis of race by the attorney for a public college to be proper under *Swain*. This result would presumably be different after *Batson*.

In the first place, any realistic possibility of obtaining a fair cross section of citizens on the petit jury is incompatible with a system of peremptory challenges where the total number of peremptory challenges the parties are allowed to exercise is, as in Kentucky, in excess of the number of petit jurors to be seated, and where there exist almost no constraints on the exercise of such challenges.[146] As Professor Jon Van Dyke, the author of the leading treatise in the field, explained:[147]

> . . . if we are committed to a completely representative jury, it is anomolous to allow either side to eliminate a juror thought to be unfriendly to its position. The use of peremptory challenges inevitably makes the jury more homogeneous than the population at large—because each side is eliminating the person who are suspected of holding extreme positions on the other side—and to that extent the jury becomes less representative.

This observation led the Fifth Circuit in *United States v. Leslie*[148] to observe that if a fair cross section were really central to the proper function of the jury, "we would take steps" to more nearly ensure that the composition of each jury mirrors that of the community.[149] Instead, the decisions in the area of peremptory challenges have always emphasized that no defendant is entitled to a jury that proportionately reflects his community,[150] nor is any defendant entitled to have even a single juror of his own background or race on the jury.[151]

Wheeler[152] and *Soares*[153] recognize this and instead fall back on the argument that the systematic use of peremptory challenges deprives the defendant, not of his right to a fair cross section of jurors, but rather of his right to " 'as near an approximation of the ideal cross-

---

[146]See Van Dyke, note 8 *supra*, at 162.

[147]*Id.* at 168.

[148]See text starting at note 73 *supra*.

[149]783 F.2d at 555.

[150]See, *e.g.*, Taylor v. Louisiana, 419 U.S. at 538; Apodaca v. Oregon, 406 U.S. 404, 413 (1972). The reason that a cross section has never been required is not the administrative nightmare of a cross-section requirement, but rather the divisive implication that such a concept implies: that without such a system jurors would be unable to be impartial. See Ristaino v. Ross, 424 U.S. 589, 596 n.8 (1976).

[151]See *Strauder*, 100 U.S. at 305.

[152]583 P.2d at 762.

[153]387 N.E.2d at 513.

section of the community as the process of random draw permits.' "[154] This argument has a labored quality to it, but "approximation of the ideal cross-section of the community" is not really
the concern of the courts in *Wheeler* and *Soares*. It is no defense
under those cases to a claimed misuse of peremptories that the actual
jury reflected a cross section of the community.[155] More importantly,
even after those decisions, prosecutors or defense attorneys may
systematically strike important segments of the community—all
college-educated jurors, all union members, all veterans, all Democrats, perhaps even all young people[156]—as long as they do not
systematically strike jurors on the basis of sex, race, color, creed,
or national origin in Massachusetts[157] or on the basis of race, religion, ethnic origin, or "other similar groups" in California.[158] It is
suspect classification that is the real heart of *Wheeler* and *Soares*.[159]
Recognition of this fact led one California judge to suggest that it
might be better "to recognize cross sectional analysis for what it
is—vicarious assertion of an equal protection challenge."[160] And
commentators on *Wheeler* and *Soares* have reached the same conclusion: that it is a concern with values protected by the Equal Protection Clause that drives those cases.[161]

The Court's decision to steer clear of the Sixth Amendment and
the fair cross-section theory was no doubt heavily influenced by
the fact that, at the time that *Batson* was under consideration, it
was also wrestling with *Lockhart v. McCree*,[162] which was handed
down five days after the decision in *Batson*. McCree had been charged

---

[154]387 N.E.2d at 516, quoting from *Wheeler*, 583 P.2d at 762.

[155]See Note, 92 Harv. L. Rev., note 32 *supra*, at 1786.

[156]The exact scope of *Wheeler* is unclear. While the court did not specifically include age
or political affiliation in its list of cognizable groups, 583 P.2d at 761, it left the door open
to a further expansion of the bases which would allow attacks on group-based peremptory
challenges, 583 P.2d at 755.

[157]387 N.E.2d at 516.

[158]583 P.2d at 755.

[159]Although McCray v. Abrams was decided on Sixth Amendment grounds, it was the
court's concern over the use of racial stereotypes in jury selection that was the main factor,
suggesting that equal protection concerns are the heart of the case. 750 F.2d at 1121–22.
See Note, 85 Col. L. Rev. 1357, 1373–74 (1985).

[160]People v. Smith, 186 Cal. Rptr. 650, 664 n.24 (Cal. Ct. App. 1982).

[161]See Note, 85 Col. L. Rev., note 159 *supra*, at 1374–77; Note, 92 Harv. L. Rev., note
32 *supra*, at 1785–89.

[162]106 S.Ct. 1758 (1986).

with capital felony murder in Arkansas and had been convicted, although the jury had rejected the state's request for the death penalty.[163] McCree had argued in his habeas corpus petition that the process of "death qualifying" a jury in capital cases produced juries that were more prone to convict and thus violated the fair cross-section requirements of the Sixth Amendment. In support of his position, McCree's attorneys had introduced into evidence fifteen social science studies which they claimed supported the conclusion that death qualification had the effect of making the jury more inclined to convict.[164]

Although the Court began its opinion by expressing "serious doubts about the value of these studies in predicting the behavior of actual jurors,"[165] the Court concluded that, even assuming their validity, it was "convinced that an extension of the fair cross-section requirement to petit juries would be unworkable and unsound."[166] The Court rejected the notion that an impartial jury must be constructed by assembling a balance of viewpoints and dispositions and stuck to the much more limited view "that an impartial jury consists of nothing more that 'jurors who will conscientiously apply the law and find the facts.' "[167]

The Court's handling of *Batson* and the Court's rejection of the fair cross-section theory in *Lockhart v. McCree* seem to suggest that the Sixth Amendment does not any longer provide an alternative approach for attacking racially based peremptory challenges. The Court will certainly have opportunities to resolve that question in the future as the Second Circuit recently reaffirmed the Sixth Amendment approach it pioneered in *McCray v. Abrams*, concluding that nothing in *Batson* or *McCree* casts doubt on its earlier opinion,[168] and the Sixth Circuit has reached a similar conclusion.[169]

---

[163]*Id.* at 1761.

[164]*Id.* at 1762–63.

[165]*Id.* at 1763.

[166]*Id.* at 1765.

[167]*Id.* at 1767, quoting from Wainwright v. Witt, 469 U.S. 412, 423 (1985).

[168]See Roman v. Abrams, 822 F.2d 214 (2d. Cir. 1987).

[169]See Booker v. Jabe, 801 F.2d 871 (6th Cir. 1986).

III. BATSON AND PEREMPTORY CHALLENGES: PROBLEMS IN THEORY AND PRACTICE

A. THE WAY PEREMPTORY CHALLENGES WORK

The Court's heavy reliance in *Batson* on the long line of venire cases, starting with *Strauder* in 1880, that have attempted to make all citizens eligible for jury service seems at first glance appropriate. The notion that people are being struck from a jury on the basis of race is offensive, and the frequent result of such challenges— trial of a black defendant by an all-white jury—seems to conflict with a system that strives to be race neutral in the way it treats defendants and other citizens. Moreover, if the state cannot constitutionally prevent citizens of a certain race from serving on a jury by discriminating against those citizens on the basis of race in the selection of the venire, it seems only logical that the state should not be permitted to use its peremptory challenges during voir dire to achieve the same result. The constitutional victories over the exclusion of black citizens from the venire seem to be rather hollow, if the prosecutor, armed with several peremptories, can achieve the same result by systematically excluding jurors on the basis of race. Justice Rehnquist, in his dissent, argued that there is "simply nothing 'unequal' " in a system that permits the state to strike black jurors on the basis of race where there is a black defendant, as long as the state strikes Hispanic jurors when the defendant is Hispanic, Asian jurors when the defendant is Asian, and so on.[170] But this seems to miss the point. Except in the most pressing situations, such as cell assignments in prison where safety is a concern[171] or in the interest of maintaining racial balance in public housing,[172] there are very few instances where the state is permitted to differentiate among citizens solely on the basis of race. The naked use of race by the prosecution to remove qualified jurors, taking place as it does in a court of law before a room full of fellow citizens,

---

[170]106 S.Ct. at 1745.

[171]See Lee v. Washington, 390 U.S. 333 (1968). See also Cruz v. Beto, 405 U.S. 319, 321 (1972); Holt v. Hutto, 363 F.Supp. 194, 203 (E.D. Ark. 1973), modified, 505 F.2d 194 (8th Cir. 1974).

[172]See Otero v. New York City Housing Authority, 484 F.2d 1122, 1135–36 (2d Cir. 1973).

simply has no analog. Rehnquist's argument seems to be that many wrongs make a right.[173]

But problems start to emerge when one tries to understand *Batson* in the context of peremptory challenges used to select jurors. It soon becomes clear that the Court has seriously oversimplified the nature of peremptory challenges and their traditional role in the jury selection process. The result is an opinion that sounds nice in theory, but that seems very detached from what happens at trial.

To understand the problems more fully, consider the jury selection process in Kentucky from which *Batson* emerged. Kentucky uses the so-called "struck jury system," in which the first step in jury selection is the questioning of all prospective jurors on the panel.[174] The questioning is conducted by the trial judge, or, in the judge's discretion, by the prosecutor and the defense attorney.[175] If, during the questioning of the jury panel members, there develops "reasonable ground to believe that a prospective juror cannot render a fair and impartial verdict on the evidence," the Kentucky Rules of Criminal Procedure provide that the juror is to be excused for cause.[176]

Only after all challenges for cause have been made and ruled upon and only after completion of the entire voir dire does the exercise of peremptory challenges take place.[177] The task of exercising peremptory challenges is made easier for the lawyers in a struck jury system because the lawyers are given a rather short list of jurors, selected at random from the panel member from which the lawyers are allowed to "strike" prospective jurors. The list is limited to the number of jurors to be seated plus the number of peremptory challenges allowed both sides.[178] In Batson's case, because the court was seeking a jury of twelve and one alternate,[179] the lawyers had twenty-eight names on the list. The prosecutor

---

[173]Justice Rehnquist's starting premise also seems questionable, because there are indications that prosecutors often use peremptory challenges to strike prospective black jurors even when the defendant is not black. See note 190 *infra*.

[174]On the variety of systems in use for the selection of juries, see generally 2 LaFave & Israel, Criminal Procedure §21.3 (1984).

[175]Ky. R. Crim. P. 9.38.

[176]*Id.* at 9.36 (1).

[177]*Ibid.*

[178]*Id.* at 9.36 (2).

[179]106 S.Ct. at 1715 n.2.

was allowed to strike six names from the list and the defense nine.[180] The exercise of peremptories takes place simultaneously with each side striking the jurors not wanted from the list and returning the list to the trial judge.[181] If, after the peremptory challenges are exercised there are more than the number of jurors being sought remaining on the list,[182] the judge eliminates at random the extra jurors to arrive at a jury of twelve (plus alternates).

Contrast the actual process of jury selection in Kentucky with the picture of peremptory challenges offered in the opinions of Justice Powell and Justice White in *Batson*. Justice Powell, for the majority, concluded that it is a violation of the Equal Protection Clause for a prosecutor to strike blacks from a jury on the assumption that "black jurors as a group will be unable impartially to consider the State's case against a black defendant."[183] Justice White in his concurrence similarly condemned prosecutors who use peremptories to exclude blacks "on the assumption that no black juror could fairly judge a black defendant."[184] But the assumption that peremptory challenges are exercised in a system like that in Kentucky on the basis of categorical judgments about the inability of large groups of citizens to be "impartial" or "fair" gives a misleading impression of the nature of peremptory challenges.

The terms "biased" and "unbiased" and "partial" and "impartial" are ambiguous in the context of jury selection. As far as the law is concerned, jurors who are not challengeable for cause are people who are unbiased and impartial with respect to the individual case to be tried. This is clear in Kentucky: those jurors who are not challengeable for cause are those jurors for whom there is no "reasonable ground" to believe that they "cannot render a fair and impartial verdict on the evidence."[185] Obviously, this does not mean that they are all the same in terms of values, religious beliefs, political leanings, experience, sex, race, background, and all those things that make each of us different. But it means that none of

---

[180]See note 84 *supra*.

[181]Ky. R. Crim. P. 9.36 (2).

[182]There would be more than the desired number of jurors if either side chooses not to exercise all of its allotted peremptory challenges or if both sides have jurors in common on their strike list.

[183]106 S.Ct. at 1719.

[184]*Id.* at 1725.

[185]See text at note 176 *supra*.

these people has been shown to be biased in the sense that he or she cannot judge the case before the court on the basis of the evidence and in accordance with the court's instructions.

The characterization of peremptory challenges as involving strikes of jurors because of a belief that they cannot be "impartial" or "cannot fairly judge the defendant" is not an accurate reflection of what happens. This is language appropriate for challenges for cause and not peremptory challenges as traditionally exercised. What really happens at the peremptory challenges stage is comparison shopping, with each side trying to remove prospective jurors who are perceived as being less favorable in the hope of getting jurors who are more favorable on the petit jury. Kentucky, by providing for an initial voir dire of all prospective jurors and then narrowing the list of prospective jurors to twenty-eight jurors from which the final twelve plus an alternate will be seated, makes the process of comparison shopping much easier for the parties. The parties are aware of the full spectrum of jurors from which the petit jury will be selected and can make their decisions as to which jurors they wish to strike accordingly.

What makes a juror favorable or unfavorable in this process depends on the particular case and the people and issues involved in the trial. A lawyer may believe, for example, that a certain prospective juror will be more (or less) sympathetic to the defendant than other jurors, or may be more (or less) sympathetic to the lawyer's arguments, or may be more (or less) sympathetic to a key prosecution witness, or may even be more (or less) sympathetic to the lawyer himself, and so on. But it is important to see that while there may be some jurors struck whom one of the lawyers believes should have been struck by the trial judge from the jury for cause,[186] most of the jurors struck through peremptory challenges will be struck because one of the lawyers believes that he can obtain a juror who will be easier to persuade of the merits of his side of the case.

A prosecutor will obviously try to get people on the jury who will be easiest to convince of the merits of the prosecution's case while the defense will try to get jurors who are likely to be sympathetic to the defendant or the defendant's plight. In trying to decide which jurors are favorable or unfavorable, if a juror shares

---

[186]Judges usually will not excuse jurors for cause unless the showing of bias on the part of the prospective juror is blatant. See Kuhn, note 32 *supra*, at 243–44.

a strong group identity with the defendant, that juror will be viewed with concern or suspicion by the prosecution. If the defendant is a Shiite Muslim, a prosecutor will be worried that a prospective juror who shares the same religion might be more sympathetic to the defendant than someone who has no such common religious ground with the defendant. This is not to say that the prosecutor who strikes a Shiite Muslim prior to the trial is making a judgment that the particular juror struck is "biased" or "partial" to the defendant in the sense that the juror could not decide the case on the basis of the evidence presented and the instructions given. Rather the prosecutor does not want to take the risk that the juror's strong religious identity with the defendant will make it harder for the prosecution to convince the juror of the defendant's guilt than would be the case with a juror who does not share an important emotional bond with the defendant.

The same is true for the defense: if the victim of the crime is a Shiite Muslim, the defense attorney may be worried that a juror who shares the victim's religion may be more sympathetic to the plight of the victim (and the prosecution's case) than a juror without a common group affiliation.

Obviously, it is always open to the prosecution or the defense to inquire into possible bias on the part of a prospective juror due to a shared religious heritage, but a number of factors discourage such questioning. In the first place, such an inquiry is not likely to be fruitful. Few people in our society are likely to admit that they cannot fairly decide the merits of the case before them because of a religious, racial, or ethnic bias.[187] Secondly, such an inquiry requires great tact. The lawyer runs the risk of insulting not just the person asked about bias but other prospective jurors as well.[188]

Thirdly, even if one decides to risk such a delicate inquiry, the answers one receives may not resolve the worry about a juror's inclinations and biases. Besides the problem of juror embarrassment at admitting bias, there is the additional worry that a person may want very much to serve on the jury and may give answers that are not candid or truthful in order to achieve that objective: "Experienced litigators know, and empirical studies have substantiated, that it is part of the psychology of the venire for some people to

---

[187]See Saltzburg and Powers, note 32 *supra*, at 355; Van Dyke, note 8 *supra*, at 163.

[188]Van Dyke, *id.*, at 163.

decide that they want to be on the jury. To that end such people will evade or misconstrue, unconsciously or deliberately, general voir dire questions in order to avoid answering and possibly being struck."[189]

Perhaps a more important reason why voir dire will not satisfy a lawyer's concern over possible bias on the part of prospective jurors is the fact that the bias that a trial lawyer would be concerned about is not just a conscious bias or partiality in favor of one who shares the same religious or ethnic identity but is rather a subconscious predisposition that may influence a juror's reaction to the evidence even where the juror is trying to be scrupulously fair. Because of the subtlety of subconscious influences, most prosecutors (or defense attorneys) would probably be strongly inclined to strike Shiite Muslims from the jury in a situation where the defendant (or the victim) is a Shiite Muslim. It is a traditional function of peremptory challenges to serve as a safety net in order to allow a lawyer to remove jurors whom the lawyer believes may be inclined toward the other side but whom the lawyer cannot show to be biased. Prospective jurors who admit to being prejudiced or biased in favor of one side or the other side will be removed for cause. By contrast, peremptories allow a lawyer to remove a juror who the lawyer believes is either subconsciously biased in favor of the other side and thus will never admit to being biased or a juror who is consciously biased in favor of the other side but who is not being wholly candid in his responses.

When the role of peremptory challenges in the jury selection process is properly understood, one can see that it is not correct for the Court to interpret systematic strikes of prospective jurors because of a shared group identity with the defendant as an assertion that no member of such group "could impartially judge the defendant." Asked on the basis of limited knowledge to rank particular jurors on a panel in terms of their desirability, those who share a strong group identity with the defendant will often be viewed as unfavorable jurors from the prosecution's point of view as compared to jurors who have no strong group identity with the defendant.[190]

---

[189]Babcock, Voir Dire: Preserving "It's Wonderful Power," 27 Stan. L. Rev. 545, 547 (1975).

[190]Although the Court in *Batson* focuses on the striking of black jurors when the defendant is also black, blacks and other minorities are likely to be struck in many cases that involve

B. SOCIAL PSYCHOLOGY AND INGROUP BIAS

There is, of course, a broad literature on jury selection and lit-igators have always tried to categorize citizens so as to give them an edge in selecting a favorable jury. Much of the traditional lawyers' folklore on supposedly desirable jurors for the plaintiff or the de-fense seems incredible. However, the situation on which *Batson* specifically focuses—the striking of prospective jurors because they share a group identity with the defendant—is one as to which there is a considerable amount of empirical evidence that helps explain why a prosecutor (or a defense attorney) might view a juror who has a common bond with the defendant (or the victim) as risky. The reason that litigators might be worried about a shared group identity is the phenomenon of "ingroup-outgroup bias" that is an accepted tenet of social psychology[191] and is discussed in virtually all basic texts in the field.[192] One such text explains the phenomenon as follows:[193]

> We all tend to evaluate ingroup members more positively than outgroup members, partly because assimilation and contrast lead us to misperceive the degree of similarity that exists within and between groups. Instead of looking for similarities we focus on dissimilarities between the groups. This ingroup-outgroup bias doesn't apply just to ethnic groups. . . . It appears to occur whenever people are categorized.

Ingroup-outgroup bias is explained as the inevitable outcome of a desire to maintain a positive self-image; there thus emerges a

---

non-minority defendants, because they are sometimes viewed as being less likely to credit the testimony of the police or as favoring defendants in general. Justice Marshall, in his opinion in *Batson*, noted that an instruction book in a Dallas County prosecutors' office warned that peremptory challenges should be used to eliminate "any member of a minority group." 106 S.Ct. at 1727, quoting from Van Dyke, note 8 *supra*, at 152. See also text at notes 11–12 *supra*. Justice Marshall went on to explain that in 100 felony trials in that county in 1983–84, prosecutors peremptorily struck 405 out of 467 eligible black jurors. 106 S.Ct. at 1727.

[191] A detailed analysis of the experimental literature is contained in Brewer, In-Group Bias in the Minimal Intergroup Situation: A Cognitive-Motivational Analysis, 86 Psychological Bull. 307 (1979).

[192] See, *e.g.*, Baron & Byrne, Social Psychology: Understanding Human Interaction 182–84 (4th ed. 1984); Penrod, Social Psychology 334–35 (2d ed. 1986); Sears, Freedman, & Peplau, Social Psychology 82–83 (5th ed. 1985); Perlman & Cozby, Social Psychology 423–24 (1983); Gergen & Gergen, Social Psychology 139 (2d ed. 1986).

[193] Perlman & Cozby, note 192 *supra*, at 423. See also Gergen & Gergen, note 192 *supra*, at 139.

tendency to emphasize traits of the ingroup that allows members of that group to feel superior to members of the outgroup, with the result that stereotypes of the ingroup tend to be positive and stereotypes of the outgroup negative.[194] So strong is the phenomenon that experimental studies have shown that even where subjects are divided into groups in an arbitrary, trivial, and temporary fashion, having no relationship to any social categories existing outside the experimental setting, the subjects tended to have more positive feelings toward members of their own groups and more negative feeling toward members of the outgroup.[195] These and other studies demonstrate that social categorization per se produces ingroup favoritism.[196]

It is important to emphasize that ingroup bias is a universal phenomenon stemming from the very fact of group identity. But given our history of racial problems and the tension that has existed between races in parts of this country, it may be that ingroup-outgroup bias is more acute between racial groups than is true of some other group affiliations.[197] When one understands the phenomenon of ingroup bias, it is not surprising that an empirical study in mock jury situations concluded that in close cases a white juror is likely to give the benefit of the doubt to a white defendant, but not to a black defendant, and a black juror is more likely to give the benefit of the doubt to a black defendant but not to a white defendant.[198] Perhaps confirming the general experimental conclusion that ingroup favoritism is stronger when a group sees itself as a minority,[199] the same jury study concluded that "black subjects tended to grant the black defendant the benefit of the doubt not only when the evidence is [sic] doubtful but even when there was strong evidence against him."[200]

[194]See Baron & Byrne, note 192 supra, at 183; Perlman & Cozby, note 192 supra, at 424.

[195]See Penrod, note 192 supra, at 334–34; Baron & Byrne, note 192 supra, at 183; Perlman & Cozby, note 192 supra, at 423–24.

[196]See Penrod, note 192 supra, at 334. See Tajfel & Turner, An Interpretive Theory of Intergroup Conflict, in Austin & Worchel, The Social Psychology of Intergroup Relations 38 (1979).

[197]Ingroup favoritism may be especially strong if the ingroup perceives itself to be a minority group. See Gergen & Gergen, note 192 supra, at 139; see also Brewer, note 191 supra, at 318.

[198]See Ugwuegbu, Racial and Evidential Factors in Juror Attribution of Legal Responsibility, 15 J. Experimental Soc. Psychology 133, 139–41 (1979).

[199]See Penrod, note 192 supra, at 334.

[200]See Ugwuegbu, note 198 supra, at 141–42. For a complete review of the social science

C. PEREMPTORY CHALLENGES RELATED TO RACE AFTER BATSON

Empirical studies establishing the phenomenon of ingroup bias do not demonstrate either the wisdom or the necessity of our system of peremptory challenges. But they help explain why, in a system where lawyers are supposed to "deselect" unfavorable jurors, a juror's group affiliations, such as his or her age, race, religion, ethnic origin, and neighborhood background, are central to the exercise of peremptory challenges.[201] *Swain* recognized the important role that suspect classifications have always played in peremptory challenges:[202]

> It [the peremptory challenge] is no less frequently exercised on grounds normally thought irrelevant to legal proceedings or official action, namely, the race, religion, nationality, occupation or affiliations of people summoned for jury duty. For the question a prosecutor or defense counsel must decide is not whether a juror of a particular race or nationality is in fact partial, but whether one from a different group is less likely to be. . . . Hence veniremen are not always judged solely as individuals for the purpose of exercising peremptory challenges. Rather they are challenged in light of the limited knowledge counsel has of them, which may include group affiliations, in the context of the case to be tried.

Swain drew a sharp distinction between the use of race in the selection of the venire and the use of race (and other suspect classifications) as a basis for the exercise of peremptory challenges when exercised for trial-related reasons which the Court upheld as a legitimate basis for the exercise of peremptory challenges.[203]

Although the Court in *Batson* suggested in places that it was simply changing the "evidentiary burden" that *Swain* had placed on defendants if they were to make out a violation of the Equal

---

literature, see generally Johnson, Black Innocence and the White Jury, 83 Mich. L. Rev. 1611, 1625–30 (1985).

[201]See, *e.g.*, 1 Lane, note 12 *supra*, §§9.44, 9.45; Perlman, Jury Selection, in National Institute of Trial Advocacy, Master Advocates' Handbook 59, 77–78 (1985); Kestler, Questioning Techniques and Tactics, §3.20, p. 98 (1982).

[202]380 U.S. at 220–21.

[203]The three dissenters in *Swain* did not challenge the propriety of using race for trial-related reasons as part of the peremptory challenge process. Justice Goldberg's dissent argued that the evidence in the case showed that no black had ever served on a petit jury in the county in which *Swain* had been tried and that this evidence of systematic exclusion of blacks from jury service constituted a prima facie case of racial discrimination requiring the state to disprove such discrimination. 380 U.S. at 238–39.

Protection Clause,[204] in fact *Batson* represented an abrupt break with *Swain*. The Court in *Batson* condemned the exercise of peremptory challenges by a prosecutor on the basis of race even if such challenges were exercised for trial-related reasons. The Court explained this change as follows:[205]

> Although a prosecutor ordinarily is entitled to exercise peremptory challenge "for any reason at all, as long as that reason is related to his view concerning the outcome" of the case to be tried, the Equal Protection Clause forbids the prosecutor to challenge potential jurors solely on account of their race or on the assumption that black jurors as a group will be unable impartially to consider the State's case against a black defendant.

To understand the implications of *Batson*, consider a case with strong racial overtones. In such a case prior to *Batson*, a prosecutor might have used peremptory challenges to remove many or all jurors of the same race as the defendant because he might assume that these jurors would be more sympathetic to the defendant and more inclined to believe his version of the events. But, after *Batson*, should there be a "pattern" of strikes that appear to be based on race, the prosecutor will have to rebut the inference of discrimination. While the prosecutor's reason "need not rise to the level justifying exercise of a challenge for cause," the Court warned that a prosecutor's "assumption" or "his intuitive judgment" that the jurors will be partial to the defendant because of their shared racial background will not rebut such a claim.[206]

How far beyond a prosecutor's "intuitions" and "assumptions" does the Court mean this restriction on peremptory challenge to extend? Obviously, the Court intends to cover the situation where the prosecutor reflexively strikes jurors solely on the basis of race, perhaps even without extensive voir dire. However, the Court presumably intends its ruling to apply to more complicated uses of race. Assume that the prosecutor has managed to engage one of the new breed of jury selection experts. Such experts view the old folklore about desirable and undesirable jurors as too crude and unsophisticated.[207] Instead, they make use of such social science

---

[204]106 S.Ct. at 1714, 1720–21.

[205]*Id.* at 1718–19.

[206]*Id.* at 1723.

[207]"The difficulty with folk wisdom of any kind is that it is too general, too global." 1 Ginger, note 8 *supra*, at §5.2.

tools as community surveys in the jurisdiction where the trial will take place so that the lawyer who is to pick the jury starts with a more sophisticated and accurate picture of the attitudes of different segments of the community. By correlating a subject's answers on the survey with his or her personal characteristics, such as race, religion, marital status, income, occupation, age, and residence, the survey yields a demographic picture of desirable and undesirable jurors in the particular community where the trial will take place.[208]

While this is a more sophisticated (and more expensive[209]) approach to jury selection than simply relying on the trial lawyer's instincts, the difference is one of degree. In the use of social science techniques to aid jury selection, race and other suspect classifications are still important, and in a case with strong racial overtones, race may well be a dominant factor in the demographic picture of desirable and undesirable jurors. For example, in the trial of black militant H. Rap Brown, one of the early cases in which the defense used extensive community surveys to construct a demographic picture of desirable and undesirable jurors, "black people" were listed prominently on the list of the "best jurors for the defense" and "white males over forty-five" were among the "worst jurors for the defense."[210] Presumably, if the prosecution were to use such demographic information to strike, for example, "blacks under thirty" on the basis of a demographic profile suggesting strong resentment toward the prosecution's case among such members of the community, such challenges would be unconstitutional after *Batson*. On the one hand, the prosecutor is not basing his challenges simply on his personal "assumption" that all blacks would "be partial to the defendant because of their shared race," but neither are his challenges neutral as to race and that appears to be what the Court demands, given its heavy reliance on the venire cases.[211]

---

[208]*Id.* at §§5.25–5.38; Van Dyke, note 8 *supra*, at 183–89.

[209]Fees for a community survey run about $35 per person polled with experts preferring to survey at least 250 people and preferably 500 to 1,000. See Couric, Jury Sleuths: In Search of the Perfect Panel, 45 Nat'l L.J., July 21, 1986, at 1 col. 1.

[210]See 1 Ginger, note 8 *supra*, §5.37.

[211]The Court relied heavily on McCray v. Abrams, 750 F.2d at 1132, in explaining the burden that it was placing on a prosecutor after a prima facie case of discrimination had been raised. 106 S.Ct. at 1723–24 n.20. *McCray* was very specific—the prosecution can only rebut a prima facie case of discrimination by showing "permissible racially neutral selection criteria" have produced the result in question. 750 F.2d at 1132.

D. CAN IT BE ENFORCED?

In his dissent, Chief Justice Burger quoted a passage from an essay by Professor Barbara Babcock which bluntly but accurately describes the traditional nature of peremptory challenges:[212]

> The peremptory, made without giving any reason, avoids trafficking in the core of truth in most common stereotypes. . . . Common human experience, common sense, psychological studies, and public opinion polls tell us that it is likely that certain classes of people statistically have predispositions that would make them inappropriate jurors for particular kinds of cases. But to allow this knowledge to be expressed in the evaluative terms necessary for challenges for cause would undercut our desire for a society in which all people are judged as individuals and in which each is held reasonable and open to compromise. . . . Instead we have evolved in the peremptory challenge a system that allows the covert expression of what we dare not say but know is true more often than not.

Whether we should have a system that allows challenges on the basis of "what we dare not say but know is true" is an important question, and one on which Justice Marshall challenged the majority in his concurring opinion when he argued that we should constitutionally abolish peremptory challenges.[213] The problem with *Batson* is that it tries to have things both ways—allow the traditional system of peremptory challenges but insist that the state be race neutral in the selection of the petit jury. The result is an enforcement nightmare. In the venire cases, when a prima facie case of discrimination has been shown by the defense, the burden shifts to the state to show that "permissible racially neutral selection criteria" produced the resulting venire.[214] *Batson* sees the selection of the venire and the selection of the petit jury as quite similar and borrows the language and machinery of those cases and applies it to the issue of peremptory challenges. In three different places the Court stated that a prosecutor who is properly challenged to explain his peremptory strikes must articulate "a neutral explanation" in defense of his challenges.[215]

---

[212]106 S.Ct. at 1735–36, quoting Babcock, note 189 *supra*, at 553–54.

[213]For a discussion of Justice Marshall's proposal to abolish peremptory challenges, see text starting at note 265 *infra*.

[214]See Alexander v. Louisiana, 405 U.S. 625, 632 (1972).

[215]See 106 S.Ct. at 1723; *ibid.; id.* at 1725.

In assembling the venire, we have a good sense of what neutral selection criteria might be. In the world of peremptory challenges, where it is acceptable to challenge jurors based on hunches, body language, pop psychology, political preferences, and economic status, and where lawyers are encouraged to strike jurors on the basis of their subjective feelings and impulses,[216] there is no content to the notion of a "neutral explanation." As Justice Marshall explained in his concurrence,[217]

> [A]ny prosecutor can easily assert facially neutral reasons for striking jurors and trial courts are ill-equipped to second-guess those reasons. How is the court to treat a prosecutor's statement that he struck a juror because the juror had a son about the same age as the defendant, or seemed "uncommunicative," or "never cracked a smile" and "therefore did not possess the sensitivities necessary to realistically look the issues and decide the facts in this case"?

Justice Marshall's concern that the protections erected by *Batson* "may be illusory" was directed not simply at dishonesty on the part of a prosecutor but at "conscious or unconscious racism" which he feared might lead a prosecutor to the conclusion that "a prospective black juror is 'sullen,' or 'distant,' a characterization that would not have come to mind if a white juror had acted identically."[218] He also worried that a "judge's own conscious or unconscious racism may lead him to accept such an explanation as well supported."[219]

The majority's reply to Justice Marshall, that it had "no reason to believe that prosecutors will not fulfill their duty to exercise their challenges only for legitimate reasons,"[220] fails to appreciate the odd and inconsistent world in which *Batson* has placed prosecutors. Prosecutors may strike jurors for any reason they want—their body language, their manner of speech, their sex, their religion, their clothing, their occupation, or their level of education—as long as they don't strike them because of their race. Indeed, they must not

---

[216]See, *e.g.*, James and Starr, Selection of a Jury in a Personal Injury Case, in CLE, Inc. of Colorado, Jury Selection—Picking the Winners 50, 58 (1982); Spence, Some Unscholarly Observations on Jury Selection, contained in Nat'l College for Criminal Defense, Jury Selection Techniques 31, 41 (1980).

[217]106 S.Ct. at 1728 (citations omitted).

[218]*Ibid.*

[219]*Ibid.*

[220]*Id.* at 1724 n.22.

strike jurors because of their race, even in a case that has clear racial overtones, where jury experts would fully support their strikes and where the defense is striking jurors systematically on a racial basis.

One of the first appellate decisions to apply *Batson* demonstrates the difficulty that courts face in resolving an equal protection challenge to the prosecutor's use of peremptory challenges. In *Branch v. State*,[221] the prosecutors at the trial of a black defendant charged with murder used six of their seven peremptory challenges to strike six of the seven blacks on the venire. At a hearing challenging the use of the peremptories, the prosecution offered nonracial explanations for each of the six challenges. One juror was challenged because he was a scientist and it was feared that his background would put too much pressure on the prosecution.[222] A second juror was challenged because he was similar in age and appearance to the defendant and he might have had a relationship to a person arrested in an unrelated criminal case several months earlier.[223] The third juror was struck because she had been unemployed and had a kind of "dumbfounded or bewildered look on her face" as if uncertain about what she was supposed to do.[224] The fourth juror was struck because she was a single female about the same age as the defendant and it was feared that she "might feel as though she were a sister . . . and have some pity on the [defendant]."[225] The fifth juror was challenged because it was the prosecutor's general experience that employees of the company where the juror worked had not been attentive as jurors and some employees at the company were being investigated for a variety of crimes.[226] Finally, the sixth juror was struck because he was unkempt in appearance and gruff in manner, which might place him at odds with other jurors.[227] The trial court found that the prosecution's reasons for its strikes were neutral and legitimate and the appellate court affirmed, concluding that the trial court followed *Batson* "with caution and sensitivity."[228]

---

[221] ___ So.2d ___ (Ala. Crim. App. 1986).

[222] *Ibid.*

[223] *Ibid.*

[224] *Ibid.*

[225] *Ibid.*

[226] *Ibid.*

[227] *Ibid.*

[228] *Ibid.* On certiorari in *Branch*, the Alabama Supreme Court issued procedures and guidelines to try to help trial courts apply *Batson* and remanded the case to the trial court for reconsideration in light of those guidelines. *Ex parte Branch*, ___ So.2d ___ (Ala. 1987).

Branch suggests that Justice Marshall's predictions about the difficulties of enforcement may turn out to be accurate. Evaluating peremptory challenges is an awkward inquiry for an appellate court and *Batson* conceded that because a trial judge's findings with respect to an equal protection claim "largely will turn on evaluation of credibility, a reviewing court should give those finding great deference."[229] Given the traditional control that trial judges have over voir dire and the fact-specific nature of peremptory challenges in general, it seems safe to predict that there will be significant variation in the application of *Batson* from judge to judge. Some judges will be willing to accept facially neutral explanations, like those offered the trial judge in *Branch*, while other judges will find such explanations unacceptable where the result—the striking of six of seven blacks—seems to suggest that race may have been a factor in the decision to strike those jurors.

At the other end of the spectrum from *Branch*, one can expect cases like those that have arisen in California where the California Supreme Court has had to struggle to make its decision in *Wheeler* work.[230] In *People v. Trevino*,[231] for example, the court reversed the defendant's murder conviction. The majority disagreed with the trial court's conclusion that the prosecutor had satisfactorily explained his reasons for peremptorily challenging certain jurors who had Spanish surnames. In *Trevino*, the majority and the dissent went through the peremptory challenges juror by juror, with the majority sometimes indicating that there were "internal inconsistencies" or a "lack of uniformity" in the district attorney's reasoning.[232] More interesting was the appellate court's outright refusal to accept certain reasons offered by the prosecutor as sufficient. An example of the latter was the appellate court's refusal to accept as proper a challenge based on a juror's body language and mode of answering certain questions: in rejecting the challenge, the court stated that although the prosecutor had provided a "specific reason" for his challenge, this did not satisfy the requirement set out in

---

[229]106 S.Ct. at 1724 n.21.

[230]See, *e.g.*, People v. Turner, 42 Cal.3d 711, 230 Cal. Rptr. 656, 726 P.2d 102 (1986); People v. Motton, 39 Cal.3d 596, 217 Cal. Rptr. 416, 704 P.2d 176 (1985); People v. Hall, 35 Cal.3d 161, 197 Cal. Rptr. 71, 672 P.2d 854 (1983).

[231]39 Cal.3d 667, 217 Cal. Rptr. 652, 704 P.2d 719 (Cal. 1985).

[232]704 P.2d at 733.

Wheeler that the prosecutor must base his challenge on "specific bias."[233] *Trevino* makes clear what was implicit in *Wheeler:* that the supreme court was in essence cutting back sharply the traditional rules governing peremptory challenges. Only reasons that come very close to establishing the basis for a challenge for cause will be acceptable when there is an inquiry into a peremptory challenge under *Wheeler.*

IV. BATSON AND OUR SYSTEM OF JUSTICE

The systematic use of peremptory challenges to strike jurors on the basis of race threatens public confidence, especially among minorities, in the criminal justice system. At a time when nearly one out of two persons admitted to prisons in this country is black,[234] when there are deep concerns over racial discrimination in the imposition of the death penalty,[235] and when there is serious concern over renewed racial tension in parts of this country, a system that allows prosecutors to begin a trial by removing all or substantially all the racial minorities on the jury panel sends exactly the wrong message to our citizens.

Against this background, one can certainly understand how Justice Marshall, and others, would welcome the majority's opinion as "an historic step" toward eliminating racial discrimination in the use of peremptory challenges while at the same time acknowledging that the remedy *Batson* offers may be "illusory." I reach a different conclusion on that balance: *Batson* is an unfortunate decision with too many weaknesses, even given the serious problem it was attempting to remedy.

A. THE COSTS OF THE DECISION

To begin with, one has to understand *Batson* in the context of a trial system that has been recognized over and over as one of the most elaborate and expensive in the world.[236] Our trial procedure—

---

[233]*Id.* at 731–32.

[234]See Langan, Racism on Trial: New Evidence to Explain the Racial Composition of Prisons in the United States, 76 J. Crim. L. & Crim. 666 (1985).

[235]See Greenberg, Against the American System of Capital Punishment, 99 Harv. L. Rev. 1670, 1676 (1986). See also McCleskey v. Kemp, 107 S.Ct. 1756 (1987).

[236]See, *e.g.*, Alschuler, Mediation with a Mugger: The Shortage of Adjudicative Services and the Need for a Two-Tier Trial System in Civil Cases, 99 Harv. L. Rev. 1808, 1824

with its pretrial hearings, sophisticated rules of evidence, and heavy reliance on lay juries—is more complicated, more expensive, and more time-consuming than that of any European system. It is so expensive in fact that we do not use it and can not use it in the vast majority of criminal cases. It is plea bargaining, which is estimated to be responsible for about 90 percent of the convictions in this country,[237] that enables the system to keep going. But even with plea bargaining there are often reports of near breakdowns in the system, especially in state trial courts of limited jurisdiction where minor felonies and misdemeanors are tried. It has been reported that in the New York Criminal Court, which handles minor crimes, such as shoplifting, minor assaults, and minor drug offenses, judges have a caseload of 100 cases a day and only one half of 1 percent of their 200,000 cases can be tried.[238] New York is not alone: the inability of the system to keep up with its volume of cases has frustrated efforts in Los Angeles to enforce tougher drunk driving laws[239] and in the District of Columbia to enforce tougher drug laws.[240]

With respect to the intricacies of our trial procedures, one area that is a particular scandal is voir dire. In New York, where lawyers have traditionally controlled voir dire, one study of eleven counties found that the average voir dire took two days and consumed 40 percent of the trial time.[241] In 20 percent of the cases studied, the voir dire took longer than the trial itself.[242] And it is not unusual for jury selection in some felony trials to take weeks and occasionally even months.[243]

(1986); Langbein, Torture and Plea Bargaining, 46 U. Chi. L. Rev. 3, 11 (1978).

[237]See Cramer, Rossman, & McDonald, The Judicial Role in Plea-Bargaining, in Plea Bargaining 139, 139 (McDonald & Cramer eds. 1980).

[238]Editorial, Cattle Car Justice, New York Times, July 2, 1983, at 20, col. 1. Other jurisdictions have similar problems. See, *e.g.*, Bruske and Kamen, Waiting for Justice, Wash. Post, July 24, 1983, at A1, col. 1.

[239]Banks, Courts Struggle with Logjam of Drunk-Driving Cases, Los Angeles Times, August 5, 1983, §II at 1, col. 1.

[240]Bruske, Plea Bargains Erode Drug Law's Intent, Wash. Post, May 12, 1986, at A1, col. 5.

[241]See Who Should Pick Jurors, Attorneys or the Judge, New York Times, June 13, 1984, §II, at 4, col. 3. See also Justice Accelerates, New York Times, June 15, 1984, at A26, col. 1.

[242]See Who Should Pick Jurors, Attorneys or the Judge, note 241 *supra*.

[243]It has been reported that it took nine months to pick a jury in one California murder trial. See Rohrlich, Nine Months Taken to Seat Murder Jury, Los Angeles Times, February 14, 1984, §I, at 3, col. 6.

Against this background, *Batson v. Kentucky* adds a new level of complexity to voir dire and puts pressure on prosecutors to conduct more extensive questioning of prospective jurors in order to be in a position to explain and defend particular peremptory challenges if necessary. The California Supreme Court, in the wake of *Wheeler*, has warned trial courts that it would be unfair to deny counsel a "significant opportunity to probe under the surface to determine the potential juror's individual attitudes" and leave counsel a "Catch-22 alternative of making his decision on the superficial basis we held impermissible in *Wheeler*, or making it on no basis at all."[244]

The exact cost of the decision in *Batson* in terms of trial time consumed by voir dire and challenges to the prosecutor's use of peremptory challenges is uncertain, partly because the contours of the opinion are so vague and partly because it is uncertain how courts will tackle the enforcement problems. A reform that requires trial judges to sift through challenges to "peremptory" challenges continues the present overemphasis on voir dire. It seems a step in the wrong direction as far as the efficiency of the system is concerned.

The closest the majority opinion comes to the subject of cost or strain on the trial system is a single line in which the Court rejected the state's argument that the decision would create "serious administrative difficulties" by explaining that courts that have adopted similar standards for the review of peremptory challenges by the prosecutor—an apparent reference to California and Massachusetts—"have not experienced serious administrative burdens."[245] In support of this assertion, Justice Powell's opinion cited *People v. Hall*,[246] a California Supreme Court decision, in which, according to Justice Powell, "the California Supreme Court found that there was no evidence to show that procedures implementing its version of this standard . . . were burdensome for trial judges."[247] In fact, this summary of *Hall* is not accurate. The California Supreme Court did not find that there was no evidence that the standard announced under *Wheeler* was burdensome, but rather the court stated that "the People have not produced, or called to our attention, any

---

[244]People v. Williams, 29 Cal.3d 392, 174 Cal. Rptr. 317, 628 P.2d 869, 875 (1981).

[245]106 S.Ct. at 1724.

[246]35 Cal.3d 161, 197 Cal. Rptr. 71, 672 P.2d 854 (1983).

[247]106 S.Ct. at 1724 n.23.

empirical evidence in support of their criticism of *Wheeler*."[248] But the reliance on *Hall* is whistling in the dark in any case, because in the two-year period after the Court hinted in *McCray v. Abram* that it might reconsider its stance on peremptory challenges,[249] federal trial judges continued to raise serious doubts about the wisdom and efficacy of requiring judicial scrutiny of peremptory challenges.

In *King v. County of Nassau*,[250] shortly after the federal district court decision in *McCray* was handed down,[251] a federal trial judge in the same district expressed deep concern in a civil case over the impact that overruling *Swain* would have on the trial process. He argued:[252]

> Even assuming the existence of a clear theoretical rule regarding what types of peremptory challenges are legal, enormous difficulties would arise from any attempt to implement such a rule in practice. A great deal of time, effort and expense would be necessary to attempt to determine whether any given peremptory challenge is legal. Any such determination would entail the extremely difficult task of assessing the internal motives of the attorneys. It might also require an inquiry by the Court into the ethnic or religious backgrounds of prospective jurors, thereby promoting the very emphasis on such factors which the rule seeks to avoid. . . . Most important of all, attorneys, confronted with a rule completely or partially restricting their right to act with the internal motive of helping their clients when making peremptory challenges, will be under enormous pressure to lie regarding their motives. Such a rule will foster hypocrisy and disrespect for our system of justice. Indeed, it is even possible that an attorney may lie to himself in an effort to convince himself that his motives are legal. Rather than introduce such a rule, it would be infinitely preferable if the entire system of peremptory challenges were abolished. . . .

Shortly after the Second Circuit issued its opinion in *McCray*,[253] in which it concluded that the exercise of peremptory challenges on the basis of race violated the Sixth Amendment, two federal

---

[248]672 P.2d at 859.

[249]See text at notes 63–65 *supra*.

[250]581 F. Supp. 493, 501–02 (E.D.N.Y. 1984).

[251]See note 66 *supra*.

[252]581 F. Supp. at 501–02.

[253]See text starting at note 67 *supra*.

trial judges in the Southern District of New York, in separate habeas corpus opinions involving codefendants in an arson trial, expressed deep concern over *McCray*. Judge Brieant argued that while prosecutorial abuse of peremptory challenges is unfair, "[t]he transactional costs involved in litigating whether the reasons are 'pretextual' will be vast and the reliability of the results uncertain."[254] Several months later, Judge Goettel expressed his opinion that "although well-intentioned, the *McCray* ruling raises innumerable practical difficulties that outweigh its usefulness."[255] Among the concerns Judge Goettel raised, still unanswered after *Batson*, is the very practical question:[256]

> If . . . the prosecutor uses four of his six peremptory challenges against minority jurors and establishes a non-racial reason for two or three of these challenges, must a mistrial be granted because one or two challenges cannot be supported by a claim amounting to quasi-cause?

While the burden of *Batson* will fall heavily on the trial courts, there are obvious appellate costs as well, because there is not a single aspect of *Batson* that is without fundamental ambiguity—the nature of a prima facie case, the nature of a neutral explanation, the proper remedy, and the applicability of *Batson* to other suspect groupings. When one looks closely at the *Batson* opinion and the number of practical and theoretical questions that the opinion leaves unanswered, it was surely an understatement when Justice White acknowledged in his concurrence that "[m]uch litigation will be required to spell out the contours of the Court's Equal Protection holding."[257]

Balanced against the costs *Batson* imposes on the system, one must keep in mind that the decision in *Batson* delivers quite a bit less than it promises. In defense of its decision, the Court in *Batson* reasoned that "public respect for our criminal justice system and the rule of law will be strengthened if we ensure that no citizen is disqualified from jury service because of his race."[258] But for all the

---

[254]Roman v. Abrams, 608 F. Supp. 629 (S.D.N.Y. 1985), rev'd, 822 F.2d 214 (2d Cir. 1987).

[255]Schreiber v. Salamack, 629 F. Supp. 1433, 1440 (S.D.N.Y. 1985), aff'd, 822 F.2d 214.

[256]619 F. Supp. at 1440.

[257]106 S.Ct. at 1724.

[258]*Id.* at 1724.

effort lower courts will have to put into shaping the uncertain contours of *Batson*, the decision is no more than a modest step in the quest to "ensure that no citizen is disqualified from jury service because of race." In the first place, in those jurisdictions where the venire is unlikely to have more than two or three members of a racial minority, *Batson* may have little or no effect. The equal protection safeguards of *Batson* require as a first step a prima facie case of discrimination. As suggested above, what constitutes a prima facie case is not clear, but as Justice Marshall worried,[259] it seems likely that the use of peremptory challenges by the prosecution to remove one, two, and perhaps even three blacks from the venire will be insulated from scrutiny.

Secondly, *Batson* only applies to situations where the defendant is a member of the cognizable racial group being struck by the prosecution. Thus prosecutors are free to strike blacks or other racial groups of citizens on the basis of race as long as the defendant is not black.[260] This is not an insignificant problem, especially in an urban jurisdiction where there may be tensions between certain minority communities and the police. Justice Marshall in his concurring opinion quoted a Dallas County prosecutors' handbook that urged prosecutors to use peremptories generally "to eliminate any member of a minority group," and the numbers he cites for that county seem to suggest that prosecutors are following this advice.[261] This is consistent with the general trial folklore that views members of minority groups as favorable jurors for plaintiffs in civil cases and unfavorable jurors for the prosecution in criminal cases.[262]

Thirdly, *Batson* deals only with the use of peremptory challenges by prosecutors and says nothing about the use of peremptory challenges by the defense to remove jurors solely on account of race. The majority opinion is careful to "express no views on whether the constitution imposes any limit on the exercise of peremptory

---

[259]See text at notes 116–18 *supra*.

[260]This is one consequence of the Court's decision to apply an equal protection analysis to the situation presented in *Batson*. By contrast, *Wheeler*, which relies on a "fair cross section" analysis, is available to any defendant regardless of whether there is a shared racial identity with the jurors struck. See text starting at note 136 *supra*.

[261]Justice Marshall's statistics from Dallas County would seem to suggest that it is not just in cases where the defendant is black that the prosecution is striking black jurors. See note 190 *supra*. See also text at notes 11–12 *supra*.

[262]See text at note 12 *supra*.

challenges by defense counsel."[263] Thus, at least for the time being, systematic exclusion of jurors on the basis of race by the defense continues to be permitted. Finally, even where the equal protection remedy of *Batson* is fully applicable, there are the general problems of enforceability. If *State v. Branch*[264] turns out to be typical of the way *Batson* enforced, the gains in the number of blacks serving on petit juries may not be substantial.

B.   JUSTICE MARSHALL'S ALTERNATIVE—THE ABOLITION OF PREMEPTORY CHALLENGES

One of the strongest critics of the remedy imposed by *Batson* is Justice Marshall in his concurring opinion. Instead of imposing on trial courts the difficult task of sorting proper from improper peremptory challenges, Justice Marshall suggested that the Court take a more radical approach. He would have the Court deal with discrimination by completely "banning the use of peremptory challenges by prosecutors and by allowing the States to eliminate the defendant's peremptory as well."[265]

In some respects, the abolition of peremptory challenges would be attractive. In the first place, a system of peremptory challenges that forces attorneys to categorize jurors and evaluate them on the basis of group stereotypes, public opinion polls, hunches, demographic predictions, and matters "we dare not say but know to be true"[266] seems offensive to our notions of the way individual citizens—whether they be prospective jurors or defendants—should be judged. The abolition of peremptory challenges would eliminate the use of social science experts and psychologists in jury selection and it would help counter the impression that it is the composition of the jury and not the evidence presented that is fundamental to the determination of guilt or innocence at trial.[267]

Second, there seems a basic fairness in requiring both the prosecutor and the defense attorney to argue the case to a jury selected

---

[263]106 S.Ct. at 1718 n.12.

[264]See text starting at note 221 *supra*.

[265]106 S.Ct. at 1729.

[266]See text at note 212 *supra*.

[267]See Hunt, Putting Juries on the Couch, New York Times, Nov. 28, 1982, §VI, at 70, 82, col. 1 ("Jury selection is one of the most important functions a trial lawyer can perform; some lawyers assert that by the time the jury has been chosen, the case has been decided.")

randomly from the community with only challenges for cause permitted. Our system, which allows peremptory challenges to dominate and distort the jury selection process, ensures that juries rarely
reflect a cross section of the community. The prosecution works
hard to eliminate anyone who might have reason in his or her
background or outlook to sympathize with the defendant or his
plight, while the defense seeks to eliminate anyone who might be
inclined by background or outlook to judge the defendant's behavior
from a more critical perspective or to sympathize with the victim.
Given the large number of peremptory challenges available to each
side in most jurisdictions—eight for the defense and five for the
prosecution in Kentucky,[268] for example—the result is bound to be
the elimination of major segments of society from the jury.

Third, the cost to society in terms of trial time devoted to jury
selection by our system of peremptory challenges is heavy, and
Batson will increase those costs. Eliminating peremptory challenges
would narrow the scope and duration of voir dire and would eliminate some of the expense involved in assembling the extremely
large jury panels that are required to pick a jury in even the most
routine cases. Eliminating peremptory challenges would thus enable
the system to handle more trials more efficiently. In our system,
which has made trial to a jury the exception rather than the rule,
an increase in the number of trials that can be provided defendants
would not be an insignificant achievement.[269]

While there are obvious benefits to abolishing peremptory challenges, the cost of such a proposal in terms of the reliability of trial
process is a difficult question and one which Justice Marshall never
addresses. Despite the rhetoric about the desirability of a "cross
section of citizens" on juries, the present system is designed to
screen out the extremes of the spectrum of jurors at both ends. One
consequence of abolishing peremptory challenges may be more hung
juries as more diverse jurors are permitted to remain on petit juries.
A blend of viewpoints and backgrounds on the jury may sound
poetic, but it may be much more difficult for such diversity to yield
unanimity. The elimination of peremptory challenges might also
increase the risk of false convictions or false acquittals. Peremptory

---

[268]See Ky. R. Crim. P. 9.30 (1) and (2).

[269]See generally Alschuler, Implementing the Criminal Defendant's Right to Trial: Alternatives to the Plea Bargaining System, 50 U. Chi. L. Rev. 931, 1017–20 (1983).

challenges are a hedge against an "unlucky" roll of the jury selection wheel, one which could sometimes result in a jury that is badly distorted so as to favor one side or the other.

Marshall's proposal would leave the prosecutor with only challenges for cause and no other safety net during voir dire. But challenges for cause are usually drafted very narrowly, and it is often extremely difficult to convince a judge to strike a juror for cause unless the showing of bias is blatant.[270] The abolition of peremptory challenges would mean that a prosecutor would be powerless to remove a juror whom the prosecutor correctly believes the trial judge should have removed for cause. And the prosecutor would also be powerless to remove a prospective juror who was strongly biased in favor of the defendant but who gave untruthful answers during voir dire in order to avoid removal for cause. While England has statutorily embraced the concept of nonunanimous verdicts in criminal cases,[271] nonunanimous verdicts are very much the exception in this country[272] and thus the impact that Justice Marshall's extreme proposal might have on jury verdicts should be a serious concern.

Besides being a leap into the unknown, Justice Marshall's resolution of the peremptory challenge problem—a constitutional ban on peremptory challenges exercised by the prosecution—has other problems. In the first place, at least until we have more empirical information about the frequency with which racial discrimination in the exercise of peremptory challenges occurs, a wholesale ban on the exercise of peremptory challenges by prosecutors even in cases where it was clear that race had no bearing on the selection of the jury seems overbroad. Second, at some point it needs to be explained how the Equal Protection Clause demands a ban on the exercise of each and every peremptory challenge exercised by the

---

[270]See Saltzburg and Powers, note 32 *supra*, at 355–57.

[271]By statute, juries in England may return a verdict of conviction by a vote of 10-2 after the jury has deliberated for two hours without reaching a unanimous verdict. Criminal Justice Act 1967, ch. 80, §13, now to be found in the Juries Act 1974, ch. 23, §17.

[272]While the Supreme Court has upheld the constitutionality of nonunanimous jury verdicts in criminal cases, Apodaca v. Oregon, 406 U.S. 184 (1972), among the major jurisdictions still requiring unanimous verdicts are California (Cal. Penal Code §§1149, 1163 (West 1985)), New York (N.Y. Crim. Proc. Law §310,80 (1982)), Texas (Tex. Code Crim. Proc. ann. art 37.04 (1981)), New Jersey (N.J. Rev. Stat. 2A:80–82 (1976)), Pennsylvania (Pa. R. Crim. P. 1120 (b)), Illinois (Ill. Ann. Stat. ch. 38 §115-4 (1977), and Massachusetts (Mass. Crim. R. 27 (a)).

state in criminal cases, but apparently allows the state to exercise peremptory challenges freely in civil cases.

Finally, Justice Marshall's position would lead to a very awkward situation in jury selection until such time as legislatures could address the adversary imbalance that would result from his opinion. The reason for this imbalance is that Justice Marshall, although hostile to peremptory challenges exercised by either the prosecution or the defense, would sweep away peremptory challenges under the Equal Protection Clause only for the prosecution and would "allow" legislatures to abolish peremptory challenge for the defense as well. Presumably, Justice Marshall believes that the Equal Protection Clause is a limit only on the state and does not reach actions by the defense.[273] The immediate result of abolishing peremptory challenges for prosecutors only would be to remove the adversary balance that presently exists in the jury selection process until legislatures could address the imbalance. Thus, for example, in a capital case or a major multi-defendant case that goes to trial in the wake of an opinion abolishing the prosecution's peremptory challenges, defense lawyers might have twenty or more peremptory challenges and the prosecution none.

C. LEGISLATIVE REFORM OF THE PEREMPTORY CHALLENGE PROCESS

The majority opinion of Justice Powell and the concurring opinion of Justice Marshall are reminders that the Constitution can be a blunt instrument for delicate procedural reform. These opinions offer those who are interested in reform of the jury selection process two rather unattractive alternatives—either expand the jury selection process by adding another level of factual hearings and complicated legal issues to the already complicated process of selecting a jury, or abolish peremptory challenges for prosecutors in a single constitutional stroke and hope that the cure does not produce serious adverse side effects.

England has taken a different approach in its efforts to control the peremptory challenge process.[274] At early common law the number of peremptory challenges permitted was thirty-five.[275] England

---

[273]See text starting at note 141 *supra*.

[274]See generally Hughes, English Criminal Justice: Is It Better Than Ours? 26 Ariz. L. Rev. 507, 591–95 (1984).

[275]See Swain v. Alabama, 380 U.S. at 212.

has gradually reduced that number: ten years ago, in response to worries over the ability of defendants to control the ethnic composition of juries,[276] the number of peremptory challenges was dropped from seven to three.[277] One problem with this reduction has been that it has been a one-sided reform, aimed only at defense peremptories because only defendants are permitted to exercise peremptory challenges in England.[278] Instead of having peremptory challenges, the prosecution in England has the ancient common law right to ask individual jurors to "stand aside,"[279] which has no analog in this country. Jurors who are asked to stand aside for the Crown are removed from the jury box as if they have been peremptorily challenged but they remain on the panel from which the jury is selected and could conceivably end up on the jury should all members of the panel be exhausted, which is very unlikely.[280] There is no limit to the number of jurors who may be asked to stand aside, so in effect the English prosecutor has a broader right to challenge jurors than does the defendant.[281] Since there have been no legislative limits placed on the prosecution's traditional power to ask jurors to stand aside, the English reforms of the jury selection process lack balance.

A reduction in the number of peremptory challenges along the lines of the limitation on peremptories enacted in England—except applicable to both the prosecution and the defense—would seem to offer many of the advantages of Justice Marshall's proposal but not nearly as many of the risks. Suppose, for example, that the number of peremptory challenges allowed each side in criminal cases, which presently averages nationally approximately six per side in noncapital offenses,[282] was limited to three or perhaps even two peremptory challenges in such cases. While the Court has always made clear that the peremptory challenge is not protected

---

[276]See Hughes, note 274 *supra*, 591–92.

[277]Criminal Law Act 1977, ch. 45, §43.

[278]Juries Act 1974, ch. 23 (1) (a).

[279]See Walker, The English Legal System ch. 24, 508–09 (1985).

[280]See *ibid*.

[281]See *ibid.*; East, Jury Packing: A Thing of the Past? 48 Mod. L. Rev. 518, 520 (1985).

[282]Note, The Case for Abolishing Peremptory Challenges in Criminal Trials, 21 Harv. C.R.-C.L. L. Rev. 227, 229 (1986) (national average in noncapital felony cases is 6 for the prosecution and 6.8 for the defense).

by the Constitution,[283] continuing to permit two or three peremptory challenges would be consistent with our strong tradition of allowing each side to have some influence over the selection of the jury that will decide the case. It would also provide protection against the occasional juror who is strongly biased but who is clever enough to avoid being challenged for cause. At the same time, a sharp reduction in the number of peremptories would make it much more difficult for one side to remove systematically all jurors of a certain race, religion, or ethnic background.

The advantage of legislation is its flexibility, and it is certainly not necessary that the number of peremptory challenges be reduced to a number that is equal. Allowing the prosecution two challenges and the defense three, for example, would come closer to the ratios of challenges that presently exist in Kentucky[284] and the federal system[285] in noncapital felony cases. And maybe a sharp reduction in the number of peremptory challenges could be made more attractive if it were coupled with expansion of the categories of challenges for cause or with some limited discretion on the part of the trial judge to grant additional peremptories in cases where there is a very unusual problem of possible prejudice.

A sharp reduction in the number of peremptory challenges would certainly not cure all the problems associated with racially based peremptory challenges. In capital cases, even if the large number of peremptory challenges usually available—currently twenty per side in federal court[286]—were drastically reduced, there would still be problems caused by racially based peremptory challenges. But *Batson* is not a cure-all either. And it would seem much the wiser course to place tight legislative limits on the number of available peremptories in noncapital cases and let peremptories be "peremptory," rather than try to attack the problem of racially based peremptory challenges with an expensive and doubtful constitutional remedy.

But while one hopes that *Batson* might spur interest in legislative reform of the jury selection process, there are reasons to be pes-

---

[283]*Batson*, 106 S.Ct. at 1720; *Swain*, 380 U.S. at 212.

[284]See note 84 *supra*.

[285]See Fed. R. Crim. P. 24 (b) (allowing the prosecution six peremptory challenges and the defense ten).

[286]*Ibid.*

simistic about the prospects for bold legislative reforms in the area of peremptory challenges or voir dire in general. In the first place, jury selection is one of those areas in the twilight between substance and procedure where courts and legislatures often share responsibility for legislative reforms, and this can produce tension between these two branches of government. An example is the federal system where the Supreme Court has the authority to make rules of procedure to govern trials in criminal cases, but such rules must then be submitted to Congress, which has the power to modify or even block implementation of such rules.[287] The result over the last fifteen years of this relationship has not been very satisfactory as the Court has seen many of its proposed rule changes delayed or significantly modified by Congress. The uncertain fate that any reform would suffer in Congress hardly encourages bold reforms in a controversial area like jury selection.

An additional and related reason to be pessimistic about the prospects for legislative reform in the area of jury selection is the fact that our trial system has created its own monster in terms of the momentum behind voir dire and peremptory challenges. So strong is the emphasis of the system on jury selection and voir dire that we can expect that any proposal to cut back peremptory challenges or otherwise restrict voir dire would be bitterly fought by trial lawyers. Since England permits no questioning of prospective jurors during the jury selection process,[288] the reduction in the number of peremptory challenges in that country never had to contend with a tradition of aggressive voir dire. But in this country the trial bar can be expected to oppose any restrictions on voir dire. Ten years ago, the Court felt the sting of this lobby when it proposed a change in the federal rules pertaining to peremptory challenges, offered partly to help eliminate the problems that gave rise to *Batson*, that, among other reforms, would have reduced the number of peremptory challenges in felony cases from six to five for prosecutors and from ten to five for defense attorneys.[289] The reform was vigorously opposed and ultimately rejected by Congress.[290]

---

[287]See 18 U.S.C. §3771.

[288]See Hughes, note 274 *supra*, at 592; Walker, note 279 *supra*, at 508.

[289]H.R. Doc. No. 94-464, 94th Cong., 2d Sess. 14 (1976).

[290]See Act of July 30, 1977, Pub. L. No. 95-78 section 2 (c), 91 Stat. 319. See also Note, 92 Harv. L. Rev., note 32 *supra*, at 1774–75.

A more recent legislative battle over voir dire occurred in New York in 1983, when the New York legislature had under consideration a proposal that would have placed some badly needed controls on voir dire.[291] The bill would have modified the New York practice which allows attorneys to control the questioning of jurors and would instead have patterned voir dire on the federal model which empowers the trial judge to conduct the voir dire with discretion to allow questioning by the attorneys.[292] This bill was bitterly fought by the trial bar and was ultimately defeated.[293]

The virtue of *Batson* is that it forces the states to confront a problem that has been smoldering for years, but the cost is the considerable strain that the uncertain contours of the decision place on the system. And when the subject of the reform is a central element of trial procedure, the piecemeal nature of constitutional adjudication whereby the Court decides the issue of race and the constitutionality of the prosecutor's peremptories today, but leaves other issues, such as the applicability of equal protection to other suspect classes or to the defense's use of peremptories, until tomorrow, is very difficult for those who must litigate now.

One way that state courts may avoid some of these uncertainties is for state courts to take control of the issue of peremptory challenges themselves and not wait to see what the Supreme Court does. Forced by *Batson* to confront the issue of discriminatory peremptory challenges, there are early indications that state courts may simply conclude that their Sixth Amendment analogs present, on balance, a more attractive alternative for regulating peremptory challenges than following the Court down the uncertain path of equal protection. In *State v. Gilmore*,[294] a decision by the New Jersey Supreme Court handed down after *Batson*, the court opted for the state Sixth Amendment analog and the rationale of *Wheeler* as the basis for its decision. In its opinion, the court was quite frank in expressing its reluctance to tangle with the uncertainties of *Batson*.

---

[291]See text at notes 241–42 *supra*.

[292]See Editorial, Fast, Fair Ways to Pick Juries, New York Times, September 5, 1984, at A22, col. 1; Chambers, Who Should Pick Jurors, Attorneys or the Judge?, New York Times, June 13, 1984, §II, at 4, col. 3.

[293]*Ibid.*

[294]103 N.J. 508, 511 A.2d 1150 (N.J. 1986).

The court emphasized that "*Batson* is not the final word in this area,"[295] and it quoted Justice White's prediction that " '[m]uch litigation will be required to spell out the contours of the Court's Equal Protection holding.' "[296] More recently, Colorado has also used its state constitutional analog to the Sixth Amendment to regulate peremptory challenges.[297]

V. The Open Question: Racially Based Peremptory Challenges Exercised by the Defense

While *Batson* raised only the issue of the prosecutor's racially based peremptory challenges, it was a mistake for the Court not to have given some indication of where it might go on the issue of defense challenges based on race. Judicial restraint has its virtues, but peremptory challenges are adversary weapons: the aggressiveness with which the Court in *Batson* leapt to confront the issue of racially motivated peremptory challenges on the part of the prosecution and hurried to resolve the issue on a theory not even briefed by the parties stands in contrast to the Court's timidity on the issue of racially motivated defense challenges. Among the majority, it is only Justice Marshall who acknowledged the obvious: "The potential for racial prejudice inheres in the defendant's challenge as well."[298]

No doubt the Court was worried about its ability to reach defense peremptories under the Equal Protection Clause because there is an initial state action problem, and, even with state action, the initial step of the *Batson* analysis—that the party raising the equal protection claim be a member of the cognizable racial group being excluded—would have to be modified or abandoned to allow the state to raise an equal protection claim on behalf of those being systematically excluded. But there are a number of reasons for thinking that it is inevitable that restrictions similar to those laid down in *Batson* will be applied to defense peremptories.

In the first place, the central premise of *Batson*—that "public respect for our criminal justice system and the rule of law will be strengthened if we ensure that no citizen is disqualified from jury

---

[295]511 A.2d at 1157.

[296]*Ibid.*, quoting from *Batson*, 106 S.Ct. at 1725.

[297]See People v. Fields, _____ Colo. _____ , 732 P.2d 1145 (1987).

[298]106 S.Ct. at 1729.

service because of his race"[299]—mandates that the Court finish the job by assuring that public confidence is not undermined by defense peremptories. In this regard, the Court has to be aware of the fact that defense peremptories are a serious threat to public confidence in the system among minority citizens.

Two of the well publicized cases involving defense peremptories have occurred in Florida. In May of 1980, the acquittal of four white police officers[300] who had been on trial for beating to death a thirty-three-year-old black man who had been arrested for a traffic violation sparked the Miami riots.[301] Contributing to the sense of unfairness in the verdict in the so-called "McDuffie case" (the victim of the beating was named McDuffie) was the fact that even though the case was tried in Tampa, which has a sizable black population, by coordinating their peremptories the white police officers were able to remove every black from the venire with the result that the jury that acquitted them was composed solely of whites.[302] Four years later, the problem arose again in *State v. Alvarez*,[303] when a Hispanic police officer, charged with manslaughter in the death of a young black male, was acquitted by an all-white jury.[304] Again there was broad community concern over peremptory challenges[305] which had permitted the defense to remove the only two blacks remaining on the panel after challenges for cause.[306] Against this

---

[299]*Id.* at 1724.

[300]See State v. Diggs (No. 79-21601, Fla. Dade Co. Cir. Ct.).

[301]Crewsdon, 2 Die as Blacks in Miami Protest Police Acquittals, New York Times, May 18, 1980, at 24, col. 1. Eventually 3,600 national guardsmen had to be called out to patrol the city, and the United States Attorney General was sent by the President to Miami to help calm the outrage felt by the black community over the acquittals. Crewsdon, Guard Reinforced to Curb Miami Riot; 15 Dead over 3 Days, New York Times, May 20, 1980, at 1, col. 6.

[302]Miami Times, June 23, 1983, at 1, col. 1. See also Andrews v. State, 438 So.2d 480, 482 (Fla. Dist. Ct. App. 1983), rev'd, 459 So.2d 1018 (1984).

[303]No. 83-3972 (Fla. Dade Co. Cir. Ct.).

[304]See Jorgenson, note 9 *supra*, at 579–80 (1984).

[305]See The Challenge, Miami Herald, March 17, 1984, at 32A, col. 1 (calling for reexamination of the use of peremptory challenges by lawyers); Hampton, Abolish Peremptory Challenges, Miami Herald, March 18, 1984, at 2E, col. 3 (calling for abolition of peremptory challenges). See also Oglesby, Challenged: A Jury Of One's Peers, Miami Herald, January 26, at 29A, col. 1; Fisher, Dade Urges State To Help Keep Blacks on Juries, Miami Herald, March 7, 1984, at 2D, col. 1. See generally, Jorgenson, note 9 *supra*, at 567, 579.

[306]There were originally four blacks on the panel, two of whom were removed for cause and the other two were peremptorily challenged by the defense. See Jorgenson, note 9 *supra*, at 579.

background, it is not surprising that when the Florida Supreme Court, in *Neil v. State*,[307] ruled that the use of peremptory challenges "as a scalpel to excise a distinct racial group" violated the state constitutional right to an impartial jury and ordered a new trial for defendant Neil, the court was careful to explain that both the state and the defense would be entitled in the future to challenge the improper use of peremptory challenges.[308]

Neil suggests another reason why the Court will be under tremendous pressure to extend *Batson* to defense peremptories: to a certain extent the issue has already been resolved by state court decisions like *Wheeler, Soares,* and *Neil* that have emphasized that their restrictions on peremptories apply equally to the prosecution and the defense.[309] While those are state constitutional decisions under analogs to the Sixth Amendment, the conclusion of those courts—that the state as well as the defense is entitled to an "impartial" jury—seems to dictate a similar approach under the Equal Protection Clause. It would be difficult to explain to citizens in a case like *Alvarez*, where the defendant is Hispanic but the victim is black, that "equal" protection prohibits the prosecution from striking Hispanics on a systematic basis, but it permits the defense to remove all blacks on a systematic basis. In an era when our criminal justice system has been heavily criticized for forgetting that there are victims caught in the battle between the defendant and the state, it would be very surprising were the Court not to extend *Batson* to defense challenges aimed at removing jurors who share a racial identity with the victim.[310] The Court may conclude

---

[307]457 S.2d 481, 486 (Fla. 1984).

[308]*Id.* at 487.

[309]In United States v. Leslie, 783 F.2d 541, 565 (5th Cir. 1986), vacated, 107 S.Ct. 1267 (1987), the Fifth Circuit observed that "every jurisdiction which has spoken to the matter, and prohibited prosecution case-specific peremptory challenges on the basis of cognizable group affiliation has held that the defense must likewise be so prohibited." The only exceptions appear to be the federal decisions—*Batson* and McCray v. Abrams, 750 F.2d 1113. The silence of *McCray* on the subject of defense peremptories led one trial judge to protest that such "inequality must lead to abolition or severe reduction of peremptories." See Roman v. Abrams, 608 F.Supp. 629, 630 (S.D.N.Y. 1985), rev'd, 822 F.2d 214 (2d Cir. 1987).

[310]That the prosecution should be restricted in its use of peremptory challenges on the basis of race, but that the defense should have no restrictions on its racially based peremptories, is certainly not without its advocates in the scholarly journals. See, *e.g.*, Massaro, Peremptories or Peers?—Rethinking Sixth Amendment Doctrine, Images, and Procedures, 64 N.C. L. Rev. 500, 560–63 (1986); Note, 92 Harv. L. Rev., note 32 *supra*, at 1786.

that since the interest being protected by *Batson*, whether asserted by the defendant or the state, is the right of non-party citizens to serve on juries on a nondiscriminatory basis, it is appropriate that the state be allowed to raise that issue on behalf of those non-party citizens.

VI. CONCLUSION

Batson is in many ways a paradigm of some of the most serious problems that exist within the system. If one wanted to understand how the American trial system for criminal cases came to be the most expensive and time-consuming in the world, it would be difficult to find a better starting point than *Batson*. *Batson* opens up a new vista of delicate hearings and fascinating legal issues[311] that will occupy courts for years to come. In starting down that path with an opinion that gives almost no consideration to the burden it is placing on the system, the Court in *Batson* seems implicitly to be conceding that trials in this country have come to have largely a symbolic importance that dwarfs interest in trials as an efficient and reliable mechanism for the determination of guilt or innocence.

Besides the burdens the majority opinion places on the system, the lack of balance in the opinion should also be a concern. To put forward a landmark opinion on peremptory challenges that talks glowingly about "public respect for the system" and "ensuring that no citizen is disqualified from jury service because of his race," but that omits any statement about racially based defense peremptories, is startling. Presented with a golden opportunity to show some sympathy for victims in a system frequently criticized for insensitivity in this regard, the decision to avoid any discussion of defense peremptories results in an opinion that is one-sided and naive in its analysis of an important adversary weapon.

To be critical of *Batson* is not, of course, to defend the system of peremptory challenges or to deny that it badly needs reform. The

---

[311]Novel issues are already arising. Recently, the Arizona Court of Appeals ruled that the decision by the prosecution to exercise only four of its six peremptory challenges raised a *Batson* issue because it had the effect of keeping off the jury the only black on the venire, who would have been seated on the jury if the prosecution had used all six of its peremptory challenges. State v. Scholl, Superior Court for Pima County (Bates), __ Ariz. __, 743 P.2d 406 (Ct. App. 1987).

present system of peremptory challenges seems unfair to everyone: unfair to the defendant, unfair to the victim, and unfair to the many citizens who are called for jury duty, often at personal inconvenience and at financial sacrifice, but who wind up being struck by one side or the other. But neither the courts nor the legislatures seem very willing to lead the fight for legislative reforms of the peremptory challenge process that would try to balance fairness, efficiency, and reliability. In the case of peremptory challenges, the legislative vacuum results in an equal protection remedy for racially based peremptory challenges which is laid on top of a system that has as its operating premises arbitrariness and group discrimination. Whether this will prove a consistent and effective remedy is doubtful.

TODD D. RAKOFF

BROCK V. ROADWAY EXPRESS, INC., AND THE NEW LAW OF REGULATORY DUE PROCESS

Over the last seventeen years,[1] the Supreme Court has fashioned a "new" due process applicable to governmental benefits and employment. This past Term, the Court for the first time applied this body of doctrine to the operation of a regulatory program. Without giving the matter overt attention, the Court seems to have transformed the law of regulatory due process, and it may well have set in motion forces that will transform all of the learning concerning due process in administrative proceedings.

I. The General Issue

By what process may government, in the course of regulating the economy, give directions to private persons or firms? The instinctive response of most American lawyers would probably distinguish between making rules and giving orders. They would then say that ordinarily before government may give a particular regulatory order to a particular party, it must hold a hearing on which to base the order. Now, in the modern administrative state, government has considerable latitude to assign this hearing to a court, to an administrative agency, or both. For those matters that are

Todd D. Rakoff is Professor of Law, Harvard Law School.

AUTHOR'S NOTE: I thank Professors Clark Byse and Richard Stewart, and Mitchell Sikora, Jr., Esq. for their thoughtful comments on prior drafts.

[1] Beginning, of course, with Goldberg v. Kelly, 397 U.S. 254 (1970).

assigned to agencies, our lawyers might continue, we should not expect a hearing that contains every jot-and-tittle of a trial. The final decision-maker will not be neutral in the sense a judge is supposed to be; there will be no jury; rules of evidence will be relaxed; and so forth. In unusual circumstances, the agency might be entitled to act first and hear second. But these are details, each to be separately considered. The starting point for analysis—the paradigm of a hearing—is still the courtroom trial.

Nor is this accidental. Warming to their subject, our lawyers might say the common law process is the paradigmatic process because the common law right is the paradigmatic right. We have built our system of regulation to fit into the common law frame even as it departs from it. The compromise struck in both the Progressive and New Deal eras was that statutory substance could deviate in large measure from the law created by the courts, but process and form were more sacrosanct.

Not unexpectedly, like the lawyers, judges have embraced these views in their opinions, and legislators have enacted hundreds of statutes based on such ideas. And administrators, implementing the programs the legislators have established, have acted accordingly. Doubtless a great many of the administrators, legislators, judges, and lawyers involved thought that in adopting this traditional view they were acting under compulsion of the constitutional command of due process.[2]

Since 1970, following the decision in *Goldberg v. Kelly*,[3] the Supreme Court has found a new meaning for administrative due process. At least since 1976, with *Mathews v. Eldridge*,[4] this "new" due process has not regularly required trial-type procedures to satisfy the Due Process Clause.

The cases in which this new law was formulated, however, did not develop out of efforts to regulate the private economy. These cases considered instead a denial of benefits from the welfare sys-

---

[2] The "traditional view," stated with more or less sophistication, forms the core of the basic textual treatments of administrative due process, at least as it stood before 1970. See, *e.g.*, Davis, Administrative Law Treatise §§13.0, 13.13 (2d ed., 1979 & 1982 Supp.); Koch, Administrative Law and Practice §7.3 (1985); Pierce, Shapiro, & Verkuil, Administrative Law and Process §6.3 (1985). Cases upholding summary administrative action are within this tradition as long as they take seriously the need for justification on exceptional grounds.

[3] 397 U.S. 254 (1970).

[4] 424 U.S. 319 (1976).

tem, or a discharge from public employment, or the management of prisons, or discipline in schools. Compared to regulation, the statutory patterns, the institutional contexts, and the social understandings were different. The question was posed, did the new learning apply to government-as-regulator, or for that purpose was the traditional view still sound?[5]

This past Term the Supreme Court finally had to try to answer *that* question. In *Brock v. Roadway Express, Inc.*,[6] it applied the "new" due process to a regulatory proceeding, thus indicating that the traditional view may be not only unsettled but dying.

II. The Case

The issue in *Brock* was the procedural adequacy of the program run by the Department of Labor pursuant to section 405 of the Surface Transportation Assistance Act of 1982.[7] That Act authorized appropriations for various mass transit and highway construction projects and provided for funding various state-run highway safety projects. Of greater present interest, it included in section 405 two substantive legal prohibitions entitled "Protection of Employees." These were, first, that no employee of a commercial motor carrier shall suffer discrimination in his employment for filing a complaint about, or testifying in a proceeding concerning, violation of a commercial motor vehicle safety rule; second, that no such employee shall suffer discrimination in his employment for refusing to operate a vehicle which is in violation of the law, or which he reasonably believes to be unsafe.[8]

---

[5]One index of the uncertainty surrounding this question is the different organization of the subject used in different law-school casebooks. In some, the old due process cases and the new ones are separated and treated as dealing with different matters. *E.g.*, Breyer & Stewart, Administrative Law and Regulatory Policy (2d ed., 1985) (Chapter 6, "Hearing Requirements in Economic Regulation and Taxation" is separated from Chapter 7, "Due Process Hearing Rights and the Positive State"). In others, the old cases and the new are put together and treated as developments within a single doctrinal rubric. *E.g.*, Schwartz, Administrative Law (1977) (single chapter called "Right to Be Heard"); Gellhorn, Byse, Strauss, Rakoff, & Schotland, Administrative Law (1987) (single chapter called "The Constitutional Requirement of an Opportunity to Be Heard").

Hodel v. Virginia Surface Mining, 452 U.S. 264 (1981), also raised the question, but the Court's analysis, *id.* at 298–303, did not clarify the issue.

[6]107 S.Ct. 1740 (1987).

[7]49 U.S.C. App. §2305.

[8]49 U.S.C. App. §§2305(a) & (b).

Implementation of these prohibitions begins with an employee's filing a complaint with the Secretary of Labor. It ends (if the complaint has merit) with an order to abate the violation, to reinstate the employee to his former position and privileges, and to pay backpay, other compensatory damages, and attorney's fees incurred by the employee in bringing the complaint.[9]

In between, the statute provides as follows.[10] First, the company named in the complaint is notified of the filing. Second, the Department of Labor conducts an investigation. Third, "[w]here the Secretary of Labor has concluded that there is reasonable cause to believe that a violation has occurred, he shall accompany his findings with a preliminary order providing the relief prescribed by" the Act. Fourth, either the complainant or the alleged violator may file objections to the preliminary order and request a full adjudicatory hearing.[11] Fifth, the hearing shall be expeditiously conducted, and upon its conclusion a final order shall be issued within 120 days. Sixth, and finally, the filing of objections and the holding of the hearing "shall not operate to stay any reinstatement remedy contained in the preliminary order."

"The issue presented in this appeal," wrote Justice Marshall, "is whether the failure of section 405 to provide for an evidentiary hearing before temporary reinstatement deprives the employer of procedural due process under the Fifth Amendment."[12] In considering that question, he also took into account the administrative rules governing the conduct of the OSHA personnel who initially investigate complaints.[13] These go beyond the statute to provide that the employer have the chance to meet the investigator and give its side of the story, including statements from favorable witnesses. However, neither the statute nor the administrative rules require that the employer be told the names of witnesses favorable to the complainant's charge or the substance of their statements; nor may

---

[9] 49 U.S.C. App. §2305(c).

[10] Ibid.

[11] The statutory term, "request a hearing on the record," implicates the formal adjudicatory process of the Administrative Procedure Act, 5 U.S.C. §554.

[12] 107 S.Ct. at 1744.

[13] Id. at 1746.

the employer cross-examine those witnesses.[14] The district court said that without these protections of an evidentiary hearing, the employer was denied due process.[15]

Held, by Justice Marshall in an opinion announcing the judgment but joined by only three other Justices (Blackmun, Powell, and O'Connor): Roadway Express, Inc., the employer, was entitled by the Due Process Clause to be "informed not only of the nature of the charges but also of the substance of the relevant supporting evidence," and given a chance to respond before the order requiring reinstatement of Hufstetler, the employee, became effective.[16] Thus far, affirmed. However, the district court erred, and would therefore be reversed, when it went further and said the employer also had to be given the right to confront and cross-examine witnesses before "temporary reinstatement" could be ordered.[17]

The other five Justices all concurred in part and dissented in part. Justice White, joined by Chief Justice Rehnquist and Justice Scalia, concluded that the employer need be given only notice of the charges and the chance to present its side of the case. The statute and regulations were fully adequate for due process purposes, and the district court's judgment should be wholly reversed.[18] The remaining two Justices, Brennan and Stevens, wrote separate opinions, each for different reasons supporting the district court's result in its entirety.[19]

Obviously the Court was fragmented. Moreover, the fragments were not entirely unpredictable. Justices, like the Chief Justice, who over the years have tended to defer to legislative judgments concerning proper procedure, did so here. Justices, like Justice

[14]The Solicitor-General's Brief for the Appellants, at 40 n.19, stated that administrative practice went even further: "The Department of Labor informs us that the practice followed by its investigators is to inform the employer of the substance of the evidence supporting the employee's allegations." The Court did not reject this representation, but observed simply that this practice had not been followed in the case before it. 107 S.Ct. at 1749.

[15]Roadway Express, Inc. v. Brock, 624 F.Supp. 197, 203 (N.D.Ga. 1985).

[16]107 S.Ct. at 1749. In Justice White's view, this holding of the plurality opinion necessarily includes giving the employer access to the names of opposing witnesses, *id.* at 1752, but Justice Marshall's opinion does not specifically so state.

[17]*Id.* at 1751.

[18]*Id.* at 1752–53.

[19]*Id.* at 1751–52, 1753–56.

Brennan, who have favored judicial imposition of greater procedural protections, followed form. To emphasize this division, however, is to make the case seem more disjointed than it really is. For all the Justices save Justice Stevens cite the same precedents and use similar conceptual frameworks for analysis.

To see what the other Justices agree about, it is useful to look at Justice Stevens's argument, made in support of requiring a prereinstatement evidentiary hearing.[20] The traditions of due process, he says, require a hearing before deprivation of life, liberty, or property. There are situations where the threat of irreparable injury justifies temporary, emergency action, and other situations in which the efficient management by government of the programs it administers makes it appropriate to postpone adjudication. Here, we are not dealing with beneficiaries of positive programs. As regards the claim that necessity requires quick action (because delay will deter drivers from reporting safety violations), the many weeks the government uses simply to make its own preliminary investigation belies any claim of necessity:[21]

> The Court's willingness to sacrifice due process to the Government's obscure suggestion of necessity reveals the serious flaws in its due process analysis. It is wrong to approach the due process analysis in each case by asking anew what procedures seem worthwhile and not too costly. Unless a case falls within a recognized exception, we should adhere to the strongest presumption that the Government may not take away life, liberty, or property before making a meaningful hearing available.

Justice Stevens, it turns out, thinks much like our hypothetical typical American lawyer. As his further remarks on cross-examination also show, he views trial procedure as the presumptive procedure. The presumption yields only to recognized exceptions. No man's liberty or property are safe when the court simply asks case by case what procedures seem worthwhile and not too costly.

"What procedures seem worthwhile and not too costly" is a fair characterization of the approach taken in all the other opinions. The other Justices disagree with each other, but only within that framework.

---

[20]*Id.* at 1753 *et seq.*

[21]*Id.* at 1755.

The core of Justice Marshall's lead opinion—requiring that the employer be given a chance to respond to the substance of the opposing evidence but not an opportunity to put it to the test in an evidentiary hearing—is that this resolution will allow for those procedures that will most contribute to the reliability of the preliminary determination without so extending the period of investigation as to destroy all practical protection for the employee. In addition to the fact that the propriety of the charges will ultimately be decided in a full hearing where complete cross-examination will be allowed,[22] to provide additional, more formal procedures sooner would threaten the interests furthered by prompt reinstatement. Those interests are the public interest in safety (served by reducing the disincentive for reporting violations) and the individual interest of the employee himself in avoiding the severe deprivation involved in losing his livelihood.[23] For Justice Brennan, this analysis understates the importance of the passage of time. The statute and implementing rules allow six months to pass between the employee's reinstatement and the Secretary's final order, and the Secretary was unwilling to treat even that length of time as a mandatory outer limit.[24] To allow the effects of a streamlined initial procedure (whose result could easily be mistaken) to last that long, is not, for Justice Brennan, due process. Were there a guarantee that the final hearing would be held within a few weeks, the Court's balance might suffice.[25]

On the other side, as the principal reason for not accepting the yet more truncated procedure stipulated in the statute, Justice Marshall's opinion emphasizes the danger of an erroneous determination if the employer is merely given notice of the charges without enough information to permit it to frame a relevant response.[26] For Justice White, this analysis underestimates the need of investigators, in some cases, to keep supporting information, including the names of witnesses, secret until the time of the full administrative hear-

---

[22]*Id.* at 1750.

[23]*Id.* at 1747–48.

[24]*Id.* at 1752.

[25]*Id.* at 1752. Justice Marshall formally declines to decide how much delay is permissible, on the ground that the record on the matter is murky. *Id.* at 1750. At the least this must mean that Justice Marshall considered 180 days, the period clearly allowed by the Secretary's regulations, to be permissible if factually justified.

[26]*Id.* at 1748–49.

ing.[27] The statute concerns employers who may be vindictive: while the investigator might well voluntarily reveal information, he should not be compelled to do so. The employer's interest is adequately protected by requiring the Secretary to make a reasonable cause finding only after hearing the employer's version of what happened. "That is the balance struck by the statute, . . . and Due Process require[s] no more."[28]

In short, what separates the Justices—or at least eight of them—are questions of practical judgment much more than of intellectual structure. In assessing matters of this kind some difference of opinion is to be expected even if, practically speaking, it would doubtless be desirable for the Court's voice to be more unified. But the heart of the law lies in its structure, in the way in which it makes certain matters relevant, in the way in which it gives arguments relative importance. At this level, most of the Justices are in accord.

What lies behind this uniformity of approach is the structure of the "new" due process. *Mathews v. Eldridge*,[29] perhaps the leading modern case on procedural due process, made the question "what procedures seem worthwhile and not too costly?" (somewhat more fully phrased as a three-part test) precisely the relevant one to ask.

Justice Stevens's response appears in a whisper, in the middle of a footnote: "Cases dealing with the pretermination procedures that must be made available to those deprived of employment, benefits, or other forms of 'new property,' are not necessarily controlling on the level of procedures required when the Government exercises its classic police power to interfere with transactions and matters involving private parties."[30]

The voice of the other eight Justices concerning the relationship between the "new" due process treatment of "new property" and the traditional due process of regulation is even quieter than a whisper. Yet in their silence they, too, address the issue. For all the precedents treated by the other Justices as setting the contours of their arguments—*Goldberg v. Kelly*,[31] *Board of Regents v. Roth*,[32] *Arnett*

---

[27]*Id.* at 1753.

[28]*Ibid.*

[29]424 U.S. 319 (1976).

[30]107 S.Ct. at 1754 n.2.

[31]397 U.S. 254 (1970).

[32]408 U.S. 564 (1972).

v. Kennedy,[33] *Mathews v. Eldridge*,[34] and *Cleveland Board of Education v. Loudermill*[35]— concern, in Justice Stevens's words, "forms of 'new property.' " The closest the other Justices come to even citing cases which concern administrative action in the regulatory mode are the references to *Mackey v. Montrym*[36] and *Barry v. Barchi*,[37] both of which concern the revocation of licenses (one for car driving and one for racehorse training). But licensing schemes, which are inherently ambiguous—between being regulation (compared to the alternative of free entry) and being conferral-of-benefit (compared to the alternative of prohibition)—were treated in both cases as the latter, as positive entitlements.[38]

This choice of precedents is not surprising. The due process "revolution" of the last two decades has taken place in government-as-benefit-grantor (taken broadly to include government-as-employer) cases. The closest the Supreme Court has come during that period to giving serious consideration to the process to be used by administrative agencies in regulating otherwise-existing entitlements is in the licensing cases.[39] Indeed, the litigants on both sides of *Brock* had also treated these same cases as their principal precedents.[40]

---

[33]416 U.S. 134 (1974).

[34]424 U.S. 319 (1976).

[35]470 U.S. 532 (1985).

[36]443 U.S. 1 (1979).

[37]443 U.S. 55 (1979).

[38]In *Mackey*, the Court states that "the private interest affected is the granted license to operate a motor vehicle." 443 U.S. at 11. In *Barry* the court explains that a trainer's license may not be suspended at will, but only upon proof of certain matters; hence state law has created an expectancy in the continued enjoyment of the license and the trainer has a legitimate "claim of entitlement." 443 U.S. at 64 & n.11. For the seminal description of licenses as a form of "new property," see Reich, The New Property, 73 Yale L.J. 733 (1964).

[39]The cases since Goldberg v. Kelly that have considered the constitutionality of summary judicial processes for terminating or restricting common law interests have always seemed different precisely because of the different institutional setting. They concern one party suing another for private advantage, and in large part they turn on the question whether in a courtroom setting there must be a judicial judgment before deprivation. See North Georgia Finishing, Inc. v. Di-Chem, Inc., 419 U.S. 601 (1975) and its discussion of Fuentes v. Shevin, 407 U.S. 67 (1972), and of Mitchell v. W.T. Grant Co., 416 U.S. 600 (1974).

[40]The cases cited *"passim"* in the Government's brief were Cleveland Bd. of Education v. Loudermill, Mackey v. Montrym, and Mathews v. Eldridge. Brief for the Appellants at iv. Those cited *"passim"* by the company were Cleveland Bd. of Education v. Loudermill, Goldberg v. Kelly, and Mathews v. Eldridge. Brief for the Appellee at iv.

But what is not surprising is by no means preordained. Precisely because the cases of the last two decades have not concerned government-as-regulator, they might be distinguishable at wholesale, as Justice Stevens suggests. Moreover, in the end the Court did not merely adopt existing doctrine, but reworked it. It may have been the path of least resistance to use the "new" due process, but it was not a path of no resistance.

III. DOCTRINES IN NEED OF EXPLANATION

As a matter of fact, there are quite a few elements of the *Brock* opinion that need to be explained. Most simply, of course, there is the adoption for regulation of the doctrinal framework of the "new" due process. At the center of that structure lies an analytical separation insisted on since *Board of Regents v. Roth*,[41] of the question whether the Due Process Clause applies to a given governmental action, from the question what process is due? if the Clause applies. The first determination, again following *Roth*, depends on whether government threatens to deprive someone of life, liberty, or property. As to the second determination, what process is due, the appropriate approach was described in the much-quoted words of the somewhat later case, *Mathews v. Eldridge;* it[42]

> generally requires consideration of three distinct factors: First, the private interest that will be affected by the official action; second, the risk of an erroneous deprivation of such interest through the procedures used, and the probable value, if any, of additional or substitute procedural safeguards; and finally, the Government's interest, including the function involved and the fiscal and administrative burdens that the additional or substitute procedural requirement would entail.

But it is not just the adoption of this framework in *Brock*, but its detailed application, that calls for understanding.

As to whether the Due Process Clause applies, the existence of a constitutionally protectible interest was not contested by the litigants in *Brock*. Nevertheless, the way in which the point is treated is interesting, indeed somewhat startling. Justice Marshall describes the right of Roadway Express (the employer) which satisfies the

---

[41]408 U.S. 564 (1972).

[42]424 U.S. at 335.

Roth test as a "property right" consisting of "the right to discharge an employee for cause"; this is said to come from the company's collective bargaining agreement with its union.[43] It is fair to say, as the Court points out,[44] that this description was offered by the government in the course of its concession that a protectible interest was at stake,[45] and was accepted by the company.[46] Yet it seems that what has been described as the employer's right is really just the boundary of an agreed limitation on a right. The underlying right, the common law right as it were, is to be free of any obligation to initiate or continue employment except that imposed by agreement.[47] This right comes from participation in the society, not from the positive text of a contract. Indeed, even the description of the right as a "property interest" is noteworthy, because the absence of obligation in the absence of contract is just as typically described as "liberty."

If we turn to the contested question, what process was due upon application of the three factors of the *Mathews v. Eldridge* balancing test, we find other puzzles. The district court had considered the first factor, "the private interest that will be affected by the official action," to be Roadway's interest in not having to reinstate its employee. The protection of employees from retaliatory discharge entered the balance as part of the governmental interest, a combined interest in fairness and public safety.[48] This analysis, wrote Justice Marshall, was in error: The employee's "substantial interest in retaining his job" ought to be considered in the first branch of the *Mathews* test.[49] As a statement of fact, that the employee has a private interest that will be affected may seem far from surprising. But the suggestion that the interests of the employer and the employee are, in this context, comparable and commensurable represents a considerable recasting of the law. The employee is being "deprived" of his job by the employer, a private firm, and that

---

[43]107 S.Ct. at 1746.

[44]*Id.* at 1746–47.

[45]Brief for Appellants at 16.

[46]Brief for Appellees at 16.

[47]Or imposed by generally applicable law; but there is no suggestion in *Brock* that the "for cause" term of the collective bargaining agreement was coterminous with an underlying legal rule.

[48]Roadway Express, Inc. v. Brock, 624 F.Supp. 197, 202–03 (N.D.Ga. 1985).

[49]107 S.Ct. at 1748. Justice White made a similar point, *id.* at 1752–53.

action, considered by itself, would normally be thought—indeed has recently been held—to be beyond the reach of the Due Process Clause.[50] Unless we assume that the employee has an entitlement to regulation, which is certainly not the way the Clause is usually read, the only private entitlement that is at risk of governmental action is the employer's. Thus the Court's treatment of the relevant private interests would appear to be a substantial departure from the traditional view that for these purposes public "deprivation" is different in kind from private "deprivation."

With respect to the second *Mathews* factor, Justice Marshall's opinion asks whether the existing statutory and administrative procedures create an unacceptable risk of error. This is undoubtedly faithful to the "new" due process precedents. For even while the Supreme Court has rejected more extreme theories of deference to the legislature,[51] the milder form of deference to legislative judgment incorporated in the *Mathews* test (of starting where the legislation starts and asking "What's wrong with that?") has persisted. But there are other ways to frame the issue. Indeed, the traditional view, reasserted by Justice Stevens, allocated the burden of persuasion differently: "Is there justification for departing from a trial-type hearing in deciding this matter?" Given Justice Marshall's willingness to reinterpret the *Mathews* test in other respects, even this example of faithfully following the test demands explanation.

Justice Marshall states the third prong of the *Mathews v. Eldridge* test as "consideration of the Government's interest in imposing the temporary deprivation," which then is specified as "the Government's interests in promoting highway safety and protecting employees from retaliatory discharge."[52] The actual *Mathews* phrasing was "the Government's interest, including the function involved and the fiscal and administrative burdens that the additional or substitute procedural requirement would entail." What the *Mathews* court had in mind, as shown by the immediately following citation of *Goldberg v. Kelly*, was a governmental program with substantial operating complexities, such as the administration of welfare benefits, such that the cost of additional procedures and the degree of possible interference with programmatic execution were important

---

[50]Rendell-Baker v. Kohn, 457 U.S. 830 (1982).

[51]See Cleveland Bd. of Education v. Loudermill, 470 U.S. 532 (1985).

[52]107 S.Ct. at 1747.

concerns. The governmental interest, although of course imbued with a public purpose, was tangible, and not merely a restatement of some state of social affairs legislatively determined to be desirable.[53] Thus, Justice Marshall's opinion in *Brock* reconceptualizes not only the private interests involved in the *Mathews* test, but the governmental interest as well.

Finally, Justice Marshall's reliance on government-as-benefit-grantor cases decided under *Mathews*, as indicating the appropriate balance of interest in *Brock*, must be added to the list of matters to be explained. For, as we have just seen, the interests to be balanced in the two situations are really quite different.[54]

To put the matter more broadly, the situation to be considered is this: Eight of the nine Justices in *Brock* share largely or completely a recognizable framework for considering the issues in the case. Clearly this framework represents only one of several possible constructs: it departs very substantially both from the traditional way of framing the issues and from the customary way of using the very line of newer cases it embraces. Yet it is largely non-controversial among Justices who otherwise differ on the outcome of the case. What needs to be done is to explain the forces that created this intellectual structure and then, in light of those forces, to see what its adoption portends for the future.

IV. THE MATRICES OF THE CASE

Why did the Court in *Brock* decide to use the "new" due process, rather than the "traditional" appraoch, as the framework for considering regulatory procedures? Why, if it adopted the new doctrine, did it feel impelled to refashion it? Why, if it had to refashion the new doctrine, did it choose to alter some elements and not others? The legal framework established in *Brock* should

---

[53]The same holds true if one traces the test's lineage to the yet more remote ancestor of Cafeteria & Restaurant Workers Union v. McElroy, 367 U.S. 886, 895 (1961), relied on by *Goldberg* for the statement that "consideration of what procedures due process may require under any given set of circumstances must begin with a determination of the precise nature of the government function involved." The point being made in *Cafeteria Workers* was that government might be entitled to act more summarily in its capacity as the proprietor of military bases.

[54]Indeed, here even Justice White, who otherwise seems to share the conceptual framework of the plurality, expresses his doubts. 107 S.Ct. at 1752.

be understood as the joint product of a doctrinal network and a sociological conception. Some elements of the result can be traced largely to one matrix, some largely to the other, and some to their interaction. To see this, it is useful to begin by understanding the doctrinal commitments the Supreme Court had already made by the time it considered *Brock*.

A. THE DOCTRINAL FRAMEWORK

If we were to assume that the words "life, liberty or property" in the Due Process Clause were limited (in the absence of a more specific constitutional guarantee) to denoting traditional common law interests, then any statute which was not merely declaratory, but rather conferred a benefit, would go beyond those interests. Correspondingly, any method by which that statutory benefit was taken away would not constitute a deprivation of the interests protected by the clause. During the earlier part of this century, something like this view operated, with more or less stringency, to prevent beneficiaries of positive legislative or administrative action from successfully challenging the process by which their benefits could be withdrawn. (This view was often expressed by drawing a distinction between "rights" and privileges," with governmental employment and distribution of largesse constituting only "privileges" in the sense that their denial would not only constitute no deprivation of due process but would also violate no contract and be no taking.) The story of the demise of this view, including the role of Charles Reich's famous article, "The New Property,"[55] has been told often enough, and need not be recounted.[56] All that needs to be remembered is that in its origin the "new" due process, from which *Brock v. Roadway Express, Inc.* grows, was a reaction against a legal vision that gave common law entitlements, viewed as more or less "natural," priority over the benefits granted by the "positive" welfare state.

This older view fell in a series of cases, not just one, but surely the case with the greatest impact on later developments was *Goldberg v. Kelly.*[57]

---

[55]73 Yale L.J. 733 (1964).

[56]See Monaghan, of "Liberty" and "Property," 62 Corn. L. Rev. 405 (1977); Van Alstyne, Cracks in "The New Property": Adjudicative Due Process in the Administrative State, 62 Corn. L. Rev. 445 (1977); Tribe, American Constitutional Law, §§10.8–10.9 (1978).

[57]397 U.S. 254 (1970).

Utilizing a rather fluid balancing approach, *Goldberg* held that a welfare program that allowed for a relatively informal termination of eligibility, to be followed by a full adjudicatory hearing with a full restoration of any funds erroneously withheld, was procedurally deficient. Although a formal trial did not have to be held prior to the termination of benefits, an evidentiary hearing was required. Justice Brennan's opinion emphasized that welfare recipients are on the verge of destitution and that providing assistance to them serves a public purpose, and it minimized (at least in the view of the dissenters) the increased costs entailed by the decision.

But *Goldberg* went beyond both its substance and its form. Its impact was that of a major event. What was eventful about *Goldberg* was that its notions went so far so fast. As a matter of broad social vision, welfare recipients were no longer "others," entitled only to whatever the statute handed out; they were "we" entitled to "our" rights. As a matter of technical procedure, Justice Brennan may have claimed he was not requiring "a judicial or quasi-judicial trial,"[58] but the common judgment was that he had "pull[ed] practically all the procedural stops."[59] Finally, while *Goldberg* mentioned that welfare benefits were "a matter of statutory entitlement," the thrust of the decision was the much more general, nonlegalistic claim that their loss was a "grievous loss" which far outweighed the government's interest in proceeding summarily.[60] From the standpoint of determining the precedential scope of the decision, it seemed to have radical possibilities and no clear stopping point. Any important interest, as determined by the courts, would do.

Goldberg, decided on March 23, 1970, had the misfortune to be caught, rather quickly, by the change which came over the Supreme Court between the late 1960s and the early 1970s. The idea that the Constitution provides positive substantive protection for some minimum property-like entitlements had been suggested in the more radical intimations of some late 1960s' cases such as *Shapiro v. Thompson*.[61] Early in the new decade, however, the possibility that the welfare state had a constitutional authority of this sort was dis-

---

[58]*Id.* at 266.

[59]Friendly, "Some Kind of Hearing," 123 U. Pa. L. Rev. 1267, 1316 (1975).

[60]397 U.S. at 262–63.

[61]394 U.S. 618 (1969).

claimed.[62] This shift affected *Goldberg* (or the spirit of *Goldberg*), because if the Court were to select certain interests as important enough to deserve procedural due process protection, and were to justify that selection by its own assessment of the importance of the interests involved, it might be forced into, or at least drift into, substantive due process protection of these interests as well.[63] Thus, as part of a general movement, the Court determined that even procedural welfare rights had their origins in nonconstitutional law. The case was *Board of Regents v. Roth.*[64]

Roth taught in a state university; he had a one-year contract, which was not renewed. He was given no reason for the decision, and no opportunity to contest it. He sued for a hearing. The district court, after balancing the interests, decided that Roth was entitled to a statement of reasons and at least some form of a hearing.[65] The Supreme Court decided otherwise. It did not reject the district court's balancing, but rather stated that there was a prior question: whether Roth's asserted interest was "within the Fourteenth Amendment's protection of liberty and property."[66]

While this may seem an entirely natural question to pose, the way in which the *Roth* Court stated, and then answered, the question represented an ingenious solution to a complex set of constraints. First, the Court wanted to establish an abstract or doctrinal test for the coverage of the Due Process Clause in order to avoid having to determine the weights to be accorded alternative social interests. Second, the two-year-old result in *Goldberg* had to be maintained even if the case were reinterpreted. Third, the Court

---

[62]*E.g.*, Dandridge v. Williams, 397 U.S. 471 (1970), rejecting "strict scrutiny" of classifications made in welfare laws; James v. Valtierra, 402 U.S. 137 (1971), rejecting "strict scrutiny" of wealth classifications; San Antonio Ind. School Dist. v. Rodriguez, 411 U.S. 1 (1973), rejecting "strict scrutiny" of classifications made in the provision of public education. For a contemporaneous description of the change in mood, see Gunther, Foreword: In Search of Evolving Doctrine on a Changing Court: A Model for a Newer Equal Protection, 86 Harv. L. Rev. 1, 12–15 (1972).

[63]See Stewart & Sunstein, Public Programs and Private Rights, 95 Harv. L. Rev. 1193, 1257–58 (1982).

[64]408 U.S. 564 (1972). The somewhat different account given in Smolla, The Reemergence of the Right-Privilege Distinction in Constitutional Law: The Price of Protesting Too Much, 35 Stan. L. Rev. 69, 69–82 (1982), seems to me to undervalue the more radical possibilities in Goldberg v. Kelly, which were, admittedly, never realized.

[65]Roth v. Bd. of Regents, 310 F.Supp. 972, 976–80 (W.D. Wisc., 1970).

[66]408 U.S. at 570–71.

accepted that it would be out of keeping with modern reality to offer procedural protection only to common law rights. Fourth, any doctrinal basis for cutting off procedural claims would of course be more convincing if it could be grounded in the text of the Constitution.

The core of the Court's solution was to focus on the term "property." As the Court was careful to point out, this was part of the Constitutional text. "[I]t is a written Constitution that we apply. Our role is confined to interpretation of that Constitution."[67] "Property" was then treated as a doctrinal category. "[T]o determine whether due process requirements apply in the first place, we must look not to the 'weight' but to the *nature* of the interest at stake."[68] But it was not a common law category. The Court quite forthrightly said it was not going back to "the wooden distinction between 'rights' and 'privileges' that once seemed to govern the applicability of procedural due process rights."[69] Instead, the term "property" referred to "existing rules or understandings that stem from an independent source such as state law—rules or understandings that secure certain benefits and that support claims of entitlement to those benefits."[70] These understandings were, of course, derived from statutory as well as decisional law—as shown by *Goldberg v. Kelly,* in which welfare recipients "had a claim of entitlement to welfare payments that was grounded in the statute defining eligibility for them."[71] And they could be based on those contractual undertakings which would be considered legitimate claims of entitlement under state law—as was true of the allegations made in the parallel case, *Perry v. Sindermann.*[72] But "property" had no fixed constitutional meaning that the Supreme Court would have to elaborate.

("Liberty," by contrast, was an open-ended concept, to be fleshed out by the Court in the fullness of time. "In a Constitution for a free people, there can be no doubt that the meaning of 'liberty'

---

[67]*Id.* at 579.

[68]*Id.* at 570–71.

[69]*Id.* at 571.

[70]*Id.* at 577.

[71]*Ibid.*

[72]408 U.S. 593 (1972).

must be broad indeed."[73] Merely not being rehired was, however, not a deprivation of liberty, as long as the freedom to take other employment opportunities had not been foreclosed. As for the tension involved in construing two grammatically parallel terms to have such different characteristics, itself indicative of the craft with which the term "property" had been construed, the Court said not a word.)

Perhaps *Roth* was a successful solution to what could be called the Court's constitutional law problem of defending the legitimacy of its judgments. It was not, however, a successful solution to the Court's administrative law problems. Indeed, after *Goldberg* and *Roth* two distinct and identifiable problems remained.

First, while the Court had moved beyond the old order in which statutory entitlements were mere "privileges," the Court had reestablished a system in which the availability to citizens of administrative process was dependent on the presence or absence of a definite entitlement. This gave the companion cases of *Roth* and *Sindermann*, when considered together, a sort of double-or-nothing aspect. If, as Sindermann alleged, there was indeed a demonstrable, even though informal, tenure program in his state college system, the fact that he would have a cause of action in assumpsit in the state courts would also entitle him to an administrative hearing before being discharged.[74] By contrast, Roth, who had no contractual claim to further employment enforceable in court, had no "legitimate claim of entitlement" to serve as the necessary predicate for getting any administrative process. Yet the need for a hearing prior to administrative action would seem to be especially great when an administrator is making a discretionary judgment from which no judicial relief will lie. If the modern administrative state calls for what Professor William Van Alstyne has advocated, a "freedom from arbitrary adjudicative procedures" which is generally applicable[75], *Roth* constituted a square rejection of the need.[76] More broadly, it seemed out of tune with the vast body of admin-

---

[73]*Id.* at 572.

[74]*Id.* at 602–03 & n.7.

[75]62 Corn. L. Rev. at 487.

[76]Indeed, the district judge who was reversed in *Roth* had reached his decision in part because he thought the plaintiff had a general right to be protected against arbitrary nonretention. 310 F.Supp. at 976–80.

istrative law which considered control of discretionary power as its
raison d'être.

Second, *Roth* failed to solve the functional problems in public
administration which *Goldberg* created. Those problems, at least as
they came to be perceived, were famously described by Judge Henry
Friendly in his 1975 lecture, "Some Kind of Hearing."[77] Friendly
began by saying that though there had been few Supreme Court
decisions concerning due process requirements for administrative
action before *Goldberg,* in the five years since "we have witnessed
a due process explosion in which the Court has carried the hearing
requirement from one new area of government action to another."[78]
He ended with the claim that "[i]n the mass justice area the Supreme
Court has yielded too readily to the notions that the adversary
system is the only appropriate model and that there is only one
acceptable solution to any problem . . . . There is need for experimentation, particularly for the use of the investigative model, for
empirical studies, and for avoiding absolutes."[79] If this sort of functional ill-fit was the issue, *Roth* again was no help. The claims it
cut off were chosen in light of the desire to fashion doctrine and
to protect institutional legitimacy. Claimants to hearings in "the
mass justice area" could often pass *Roth's* test, as was indeed inherent
in *Roth's* acceptance of *Goldberg.* If anything *Roth* made things worse:
by insisting as a prerequisite to any process that there be a claim
to "property" of a certain legal dignity, it made it all the more
sensible to assert that any deprivation of that interest should be
treated procedurally as a major event.

In *Mathews v. Eldridge,*[80] the Court chose to resolve the second of
these difficulties at the cost of exacerbating, or at least reinforcing,
the first. The issue in *Mathews* was what procedure could permis-
sibly be employed to terminate Social Security disability benefits.
Under existing procedures, any initial determination of ineligibility
could be disputed and ultimately carried to an administrative law
judge for an evidentiary hearing. If the claimant prevailed, he would
be entitled to full retroactive relief. The only issue was the interim

---

[77]123 U. Pa. L. Rev. 1267 (1975). On the impact of this article, see Davis, 2 Administrative
Law Treatise §13.8 at 498–99 (1979).

[78]123 U. Pa. L. Rev. at 1268.

[79]*Id.* at 1316.

[80]424 U.S. 319 (1976).

loss of payments. That "temporary deprivation" of benefits was imposed after the agency consulted with the recipient's physician, let the recipient know of the impending action and the reasons therefore, and provided an opportunity to submit evidence or arguments in writing. But there was no preliminary trial. The recipient did not, for example, get a pre-termination opportunity to cross-examine the source of any adverse information; or to appear in person and testify as to his medical condition; or to have the initial decision made by an administrative law judge. The Court sustained the procedures.

It was apparent on the face of *Mathews* that the court intended to cauterize *Goldberg*. "In recent years this Court increasingly has had occasion to consider the extent to which due process requires an evidentiary hearing prior to the deprivation of some type of property interest even if such a hearing is provided thereafter. In only one case, *Goldberg v. Kelly*, has the Court held that a hearing closely approximating a judicial trial is necessary."[81] In case you missed the point, "Only in *Goldberg* has the Court held that due process requires an evidentiary hearing prior to a temporary deprivation."[82] And, to make sure, "there is less reason here than in *Goldberg* to depart from the ordinary principle, established by our decisions, that something less than an evidentiary hearing is sufficient prior to adverse administrative action."[83] The Court justified this acceptance of less than an evidentiary hearing by conducting a point-by-point functional consideration of the procedures appropriate to the disability decision to be made, using the existing procedures as the starting point for analysis. It is this process which is restated in the famous three-factored test.

This approach solved the problems identified by Judge Friendly's article, which was more than once cited. As he had suggested, the Court was now "avoiding absolutes." In considering procedures for massive entitlements programs, the lower courts could now consider the practicalities, could now treat *Goldberg* not as paradigmatic but as marginal, could now take as the presumptive starting point not a trial-type hearing but rather the legislatively mandated process.

---

[81]*Id.* at 333.

[82]*Id.* at 340.

[83]*Id.* at 343.

But there was a potential cost to the solution. The practical inquiry mandated by *Mathews* required courts to make an assessment of the significance and substantiality of private interests, and of their weight in comparison to other factors. There was a potential conflict between *Roth's* assertion that only external sources of law determined what property interests were worthy of procedural protection and *Mathews's* assertion that the Court itself could judge what interests had weight.

Mathews resolved this tension by mediating it through the concept of accuracy. The purpose of procedure was to avoid, where reasonable, the "risk of error inherent in the truthfinding process."[84] The balancing test was not at large. It served only to determine what were the sensible procedures to use in determining the presence or absence of the entitlement made relevant by *Roth*.

From the point of view of institutional legitimacy, this mediation is, perhaps, successful. It allows the Court to say, even if it rejects the procedural judgments of other institutions of government, that it is not recognizing substantive entitlements those institutions have not blessed. However, in terms of the first of our administrative law problems—the need for process before important but discretionary decisions are made—it seems wholly off the mark. The concept of error in the determination of an entitlement invokes the image of finding presence or absence, not of exercising discretionary judgment. Or to rephrase the matter, *Mathews v. Eldridge* treats the agency's determination as being essentially similar to the judicial determination of a private right; it is indeed this treatment which justifies the claim of not stepping beyond the bounds of the entitlements elsewhere recognized by the legal system.[85]

By the time *Mathews* said that "the ordinary principle" was that "something less than an evidentiary hearing" would do, *Roth* had already said that the operative category was the grand abstraction, "property," of which common law entitlements and statutory entitlements were equally parts. The particular way in which *Mathews* solved the problem of remaining consistent with the institutional

---

[84]*Id.* at 344.

[85]Occasionally since *Mathews* the Court has nonetheless suggested the value of procedure in informing discretion. At other times it has rejected the idea that any independent claim to administrative process can be so grounded. For its latest statement, saying both things, see Cleveland Bd. of Education v. Loudermill, 470 U.S. 532, 543 & n.8.

legitimacy concerns of *Roth* emphasized that common law and statutory entitlements were alike not because they were both subject to administrative processes, but rather because they were both to be handled on the model of private rights. Accordingly, although *Goldberg, Roth,* and *Mathews* all dealt with substantive entitlements against the government, and were in no way involved with anything that could be conceptualized as governmental regulation of the private sector, they yielded doctrine that said parties "ordinarily" could be deprived of common law rights by something less than trial-type (that is, common law) process. And this conclusion was wrought into the whole carefully constructed doctrinal structure the Court had developed.

Given the degree of doctrinal commitment built into the *Roth-Mathews* framework, and given the great number of cases which the Court has since decided using that framework, and given the fact that within the framework these cases cannot be distinguished simply as being about something other than regulation, the use of the *Roth-Mathews* framework in *Brock* is not hard to understand. Yet even though the doctrinal influences on the result are so clear, there is more to be said.

B. THE SOCIAL CONCEPTION

The *Roth-Mathews* emphasis on understanding the problem of due process as arising when government infringes on private entitlements seems to imply that it is the boundary between the state and civil society which is fraught with danger. Government intervention is what must be policed. Much of what happens in *Brock,* however, derives from a different social vision, in which relationships among parties within civil society are seen as themselves potentially dangerous. Government is now the policeman. As we pursue the impact of this social understanding, we will see that it completes our analysis of the doctrinal choices made in *Brock,* accounts for much of Justice Marshall's rhetoric and use of precedent, explains why the *Mathews* test was rewritten in the way it was, and thus, ultimately, provides much of the persuasive force of the Court's opinion.

The doctrinal history sketched above is not the complete story simply because that very history presents an alternative doctrinal path the *Brock* Court could have followed. This alternative seizes the fact that the Due Process Clause protects not only "property" but also "liberty." If the regulation of the private sector were characterized as implicating a deprivation of "liberty," it might be possible to stay within the confines of *Roth* and still restrict *Mathews v. Eldridge's* test for proper procedure to deprivations of "property." One might then say that the presumptive process for a deprivation of "liberty" is an evidentiary hearing akin to (if not exactly like) a judicial trial. This analysis would make government-as-regulator a distinct category, subject to different restraints. It would reinstate our average lawyer's traditional view of regulatory process and still satisfy the doctrinal needs of the Court.

It is not the force of decided cases that prevents the Court from adopting this view or, yet more telling, keeps Roadway Express's lawyers from even advocating it. There are doctrinal materials that could be used to support this view. We have already noted that *Roth* treats "property" and "liberty" as non-cognate. More important, *Roth* takes as its text for defining "liberty" what was said in *Meyer v. Nebraska*, decided in 1923.[86] There, as quoted in *Roth*, "liberty" was said to include not only freedom from bodily restraint, and freedom to worship according to conscience, but also "the right of the individual to contract."[87] This view, of course, was not new to *Meyer*, where, indeed, the discussion of what "liberty" comprises was followed by a long list of citations, including *Lochner v. New York*. In short, it is formally the position of the Court in *Roth* and thereafter[88] that the same vision of "liberty" that has been repudiated as setting limits on substantive social and economic legislation is the correct view of "liberty" with respect to procedural due process. In that framework, regulation is undoubtedly a deprivation of liberty. The further contention that the appropriate process for a deprivation of liberty should begin with a different presumption than that stated in *Mathews v. Eldridge* would, admittedly, be harder to support. *Mathews* itself could be avoided: when Justice Powell set forth his three-part test, he already had been talking for a couple of paragraphs about the "deprivation of some type of property interest."[89] And the plain assumption that a deprivation of liberty does require an evidentiary hearing appears in the cases, including

---

[86]262 U.S. 390 (1923).

[87]*Id.* at 399, quoted, 408 U.S. at 572.

[88]*E.g.*, Ingraham v. Wright, 430 U.S. 651, 672–73 (1977).

[89]424 U.S. at 333–34.

in *Roth* itself.[90] Some later cases, however, have applied the *Mathews* test to deprivations of liberty; they would have to be—but could be—distinguished.[91] Perhaps it would not be easy, but an opinion supporting this doctrinal route could be written without too much precedential embarrassment.

What would make the task impossible is the way in which established doctrine mixes with our larger understanding of the world. If the Court wanted to make the traditional view of regulatory due process consistent with *Roth* and *Mathews*, doctrine would force the Court to say that when government regulates hiring and firing it infringes the employer's economic freedom, that this is a deprivation different in kind from taking away a government employee's or welfare recipient's property, and that the purpose of drawing the distinction is to show why the employer is entitled to greater procedural protection. What makes this hard to say is not the contention that "liberty" ought to get greater protection than "property." That might be generally accepted. The problem is that what the employer is being prevented from doing does not seem to embody what we understand by "liberty." When the litigants and the Justices in *Brock* simply assume that what is at stake is "property," they are expressing their understanding of the social, even if not narrowly doctrinal, content of the constitutional terms.

---

[90]408 U.S. at 572–75.

[91]To give some indication of what would be involved: There is a line of cases in which prisoners have been said to have "liberty" interests which, however, are protected only by a highly flexible due process. *E.g.*, Superintendent, Mass. Corr. Institution, Walpole v. Hill, 472 U.S. 445 (1985). These could be distinguished as being based on positive statutory or regulatory entitlements, and therefore as being like "property" for these purposes. See Meachum v. Fano, 427 U.S. 215 (1976). There are some other isolated cases in which the *Mathews* test has been applied to what is undeniably a deprivatioin of "liberty," for example, Parham v. J.R., 442 U.S. 584 (1979), which concerned the process to be used in the voluntary commitment of children to mental hospitals. This case could perhaps be viewed as simply being very far afield on its facts, given its stress that truncated process was enough because the question was whether the parental decision to request commitment was wrong, not the incidence of state force *vel non*. See Davis, Administrative Law Treatise, §13.12 at 243–44 (Supp., 1982). That leaves the most famous clearly administrative due process case treated by the Court as involving a deprivation of "liberty," Ingraham v. Wright, 430 U.S. 651 (1977). In that case, the Court held that schools may inflict corporal punishment on students without first holding any sort of hearing. This result was justified by more than one reference to *Mathews*. But the Court treated the plaintiffs as asking for more than the common law remedy of a post-hoc tort trial in court, and the holding was bottomed on the view that the common law was adequate. Whatever may be said as to the practicality of this judgment, which four Justices considered very mistaken, in form the case does not contradict the view that those deprived of liberty deserve a trial-type hearing. *Id.* at 679–80 & n.47.

The content of this social understanding is revealed by the Court's description of the relationship of employer and employee. This relationship, even when the employee is protected from at-will discharge, can be described in many ways, each giving termination of employment a different connotation. "Of course the employer can stop paying an employee when the employee breaches his obligation to perform his tasks faithfully and reasonably." Or, "the employer and the employee are each bound only as far as the terms of their joint contract obligate them." Or, "the employer can terminate the interest of the employee in his job when there is cause to do so." In *Brock*, Justice Marshall describes Roadway's "right" (under the *Roth* test) as "the right to discharge an employee for cause,"[92] and Roadway's "interest" (under the *Mathews* test) as its "interest in controlling the makeup of its workforce."[93] In light of the universe of possible descriptions, the choice of the words "discharge" and "controlling" depicts the employer as the active force in the situation, able to exert power vis-à-vis the employee. This description cannot be dismissed as eccentric, because, as the Court itself rightly indicates,[94] this approach builds on what the district court and the litigants themselves said.

Behind the choice of words lies an appreciation of social reality. It seems appropriate to speak in these terms because, as Justice Marshall informs us early in his opinion, Roadway Express "is a large interstate trucking company."[95] That is why it has a "workforce." Indeed, the sense that we are dealing with large, institutional employers pervades the litigation. For example, when Roadway's brief comes to describe the "immediate tangible consequences" of "forced reinstatement," it does not attempt to portray the personal abrasiveness of having to work shoulder to shoulder with an employee one has tried to discharge. It rather points out that "the reinstatement of Hufstetler to his prior seniority position would carry with it a chain of seniority position displacements, which in turn dictates such matters as bidding for driving assignments with corresponding pay differentials, as well as other seniority related

---

[92] 107 S.Ct. at 1746.

[93] *Id.* at 1748.

[94] *Id.* at 1746–74, 1748.

[95] *Id.* at 1744.

issues such as layoffs, recalls, and vacation selection. Such seniority displacement would result in layoff of the junior-most driver."[96] Similarly, the *amicus* brief filed by the trucking industry simply assumes that employers affected by this statute (and by the upcoming decision) will be in the position of organizing large-scale economic efforts. "As employers of millions of people, the trucking industry is necessarily concerned, as all employers must be, with its rights and responsibilities to discharge dishonest, disruptive employees, who may, by their attitudes and actions, compromise the integrity of the workplace and undermine the productivity and morale of fellow workers."[97]

The idea that the relationship between a large, organized employer and its many employees cannot accurately be described solely in the terms of interpersonal, consensual agreement, but must be viewed as at least in part a coercive relationship, is of course not new.[98] By now, if we ask why it would be hard to frame an appropriate doctrine in terms of "liberty," it is almost enough to say that we can no longer visualize "Roadway Express, Inc." as the "individual" to whom *Meyer v. Nebraska* attributed a valuable "freedom of contract." But the element of power present in the relationship of employer and employee also explains the positive characterization of the employer's "contractual" right as representing "property." Indeed, except on that understanding, the use of the term "property" is hard to comprehend. "The right to discharge an employee for cause" is not something we would, in ordinary speech, "own." One could not, in the ordinary meaning of things, "sell" it. What makes it "property" is the element of "exclusive dominion" it contains, that is, the employer's power to exclude the employee from the job.

The importance of this social vision for the *Brock* opinion goes far beyond the doctrinal characterization of the employer's interest as "property." It colors the Court's use of precedent, and indeed is a logical prerequisite to much of Justice Marshall's heavy reliance on *Cleveland Bd. of Education v. Loudermill.*[99]

---

[96]Brief for the Appellee at 20.

[97]Brief for American Trucking Associations, Inc., *et al.*, *amici curiae*, at 3.

[98]Pound, Liberty of Contract, 18 Yale L.J. 454 (1909); Hale, Coercion and Distribution in a Supposedly Non-Coercive State, 38 Pol. Sci. Q. 479 (1923).

[99]470 U.S. 532 (1985).

The issue in *Loudermill* was "what pretermination process must be accorded a public employee who can be discharged only for cause."[100] This question was a matter of constitutional law, of course, only because government was the employer. The entitlement created by the statutory tenure system was treated as fully comparable to other governmentally established entitlement schemes. Applying *Mathews*, the Court held that the tenured employee, prior to termination, deserved notice, an explanation of the opposing evidence, and a chance to respond. Deprivation of the entitlement was a sovereign act, to which the constraints of the Due Process Clause applied.

Since the issue in *Loudermill* was governmental deprivation of entitlement, it is no surprise that the result in the case is treated by Justice Marshall in *Brock* as an appropriate precedent for helping to set the level of protection to which the employer, Roadway Express, is entitled when deprived of its property right.[101] What is surprising is to find *Loudermill* also used in *Brock* to help measure what the employee deserves.[102]

> We also agree with the District Court that Roadway's interest in controlling the makeup of its workforce is substantial. 624 F.Supp. at 202. In assessing the competing interests, however, the District Court failed to consider another private interest affected by the Secretary's decision: Hufstetler's interest in not being discharged for having complained about the allegedly unsafe condition of Roadway's trucks. This Court has previously acknowledged the "severity of depriving a person of the means of livelihood." *Loudermill*, 470 U.S. at 543; 105 S.Ct. at 1494. "While a fired worker may find employment elsewhere, doing so will take some time and is likely to be burdened by the questionable circumstances under which he left his previous job." *Ibid.* In light of the injurious effect a retaliatory discharge can have on an employee's financial status and prospects for alternative interim employment, the employee's substantial interest in retaining his job must be considered along with the employer's interest in determining the constitutional adequacy of the sec. 405 procedures. The statute reflects a careful balancing of "the strong Congressional policy that persons reporting health and safety violations should not suffer because of this

---

[100]*Id.* at 535.

[101]107 S.Ct. at 1748–49.

[102]*Id.* at 1748.

action" and the need "to assure that employers are provided
protection from unjustified refusal by their employees to perform legitimate assigned tasks." 128 Cong. Rec. S15610 (Dec.
19, 1982) (summary of statute).

It is of course true that in the course of deciding *Loudermill* under
the *Mathews* test, the Court stated: "[T]he significance of the private
interest in retaining employment cannot be gainsaid. We have frequently recognized the severity of depriving a person of the means
of livelihood."[103] But "depriving" meant, in the context of *Loudermill*,
the process of carrying out a constitutional deprivation to which
due process constraints were relevant; that is, it referred to a deprivation carried out by a sovereign. To apply the same statement
to measure the significance of a nongovernmental employer discharging an employee would appear to be a mistake, for it treats
Loudermill as being an "employment" case rather than a "governmental process" case, and it has to be the latter to raise a constitutional issue. It would be a mistake, that is, unless the government's "depriving" through an exercise of sovereignty is not different
in kind from the employer's "depriving" through an exercise of
property. The precise point which this passage exemplifies was
stated more than a half-century ago by Morris Cohen. One cannot
draw a categorical distinction between the use of property and the
exercise of sovereignty, once one views matters in light of the institutional realities of the modern economy.[104]

As the passage also shows, the social understanding which establishes the analogy between governmental deprivation of a private
right and employer deprivation of an employee's job also forms the
basis of the fundamental reinterpretation of the *Mathews* test which
occurs in *Brock:* "the employee's . . . interest . . . must be considered along with the employer's interest in determining the constitutional adequacy of the . . . procedures." For there is no "must"
about this matter if the evil to which the constitutional provision
is addressed implicates only one of these interests; if, that is, public
deprivation of an interest is different from private deprivation. But
Justice Marshall sees them as equal in kind and capable of being
offset against each other. Because employees in the transportation
industry "may be threatened with discharge for cooperating with

---

[103]470 U.S. at 543.

[104]Cohen, Property and Sovereignty, 13 Corn. L. Q. 8 (1927).

enforcement agencies, they need express protection against retaliation for reporting these violations."[105] Government coercion of employers will prevent employer coercion of employees. Thus, while government may have purely administrative interests of its own in the efficient conduct of its business, or may embrace diffuse public interests in, for example, highway safety, it may also be involved in reallocating rights—including procedural rights—in order to achieve a fair balance between conflicting private interests.

The *Mathews* test, as written, conceived of government as a provider of benefits or organizer of institutions, so that the government's interest, quasi-proprietary at least in part, stood on one side, while the private beneficiary stood on the other. (Indeed, in the past the Court had taken pains to avoid framing cases in a way that would make it adjudicate the procedural claims of two groups of statutory beneficiaries with potentially conflicting interests.)[106] By contrast, the *Mathews* test as rephrased and then applied in *Brock* posits government as having a largely regulatory concern, and supposes that more than one private interest is affected by its decision. The details of Justice Marshall's argument are embraced by only four Justices, but this central point also appears in Justice White's opinion[107] for a total of seven. On its face, the Court shows that it understands itself to be dealing with a different social situation. In this latter role, government is an umpire rather than an interested participant. Despite the effort to use similar words, this is a far different model from the government-versus-private-beneficiary dynamics incorporated by implication in the original *Mathews* test.

C. THE JOINT IMPACT

It is notoriously difficult to prove that changes in doctrinal formulation either necessitate, or are necessitated by, changed results. It would be a mistake, nevertheless, to dismiss Justice Marshall's reformulation of doctrine to incorporate a different social dynamic simply as being an accident. To the contrary, the adjustment of

---

[105] 107 S.Ct. at 1745.

[106] See O'Bannon v. Town Court Nursing Center, 447 U.S. 773 (1980). What is done in *Brock* also seems to be in tension with the Court's recent views on judicial control over agency inaction, see Heckler v. Chaney, 470 U.S. 821, 832 (1985).

[107] 107 S.Ct. at 1752–53.

doctrine is intimately connected with giving Justice Marshall's opinion persuasive force. It is, in a sense, part of even the narrow holding.

If the statutory procedure at issue in *Brock* is viewed solely in terms of furthering a governmental interest in public safety, the argument for it is that the promise of prompt reinstatement is a necessary inducement to employees, who can report safety violations but are afraid of retaliation and unable to wait until a full trial-type process takes its course. Employee reports are in turn necessary to the detection of dangerous violations of safety standards. This was the central thrust of the Solicitor General's discussion of how the *Mathews v. Eldridge* balance should be made in *Brock*.[108] Quite apart from whether the supposed string of contingencies was true, the argument was subject to the criticism that government had to investigate the allegation of retaliatory discharge in any case, that no one thought that would happen in a day or a week or even a month,[109] and so, if government spent a little more money, or was a bit more efficient, it could rapidly hold an evidentiary hearing within the same time span. The issue as the company framed it was not safety, but only administrative convenience.[110] On this view, the Court could easily require a prior evidentiary hearing: if the government then sacrificed its own interest in safety through procedural delay, it would be its own fault. The district court, operating within this framework, said that the *Mathews* balance pointed to the need for cross-examination before reinstatement.[111]

---

[108]Brief for the Appellants at 30–38. An occasional sentence in the government's brief, apparently devoid of any doctrinal foundation, also suggested the type of balancing the Court finally adopted. *E.g., id.* at 48.

[109]Newly promulgated regulations required reasonable-cause investigations to be completed within sixty days of the filing of the complaint, which was quicker than the actual practice up to that time. 107 S.Ct. at 1754 n.3.

[110]Brief for the Appellee at 9–11, 34–37. The Appellee's brief was buttressed by a discussion of other statutory programs administered by the Department of Labor for the protection of whistle-blowers. In these programs, reinstatement takes place only after a hearing, but expedited hearings are required. *Ibid.*

[111]In Barry v. Barchi, 443 U.S. 55 (1979), the Court upheld the summary suspension of a racehorse trainer's license after one of his horses was found to be drugged, reasoning that preservation of the integrity of the sport justified immediate action. At the same time, the Court invalidated the statutory scheme before it for failing to provide a prompt postsuspension hearing, the Court stating that "[o]nce suspension has been imposed, the trainer's interest in a speedy resolution of the controversy becomes paramount." *Id.* at 66. Since no real emergency action was being taken in *Brock*, precedents like this supported the company's argument.

By shifting to the two-private-interests framework, Justice Marshall changed the punch line. Now, if reinstatement had to wait and government delayed, the public did not hurt only itself, but also another relevant and particularized private interest. Assuming that delay was predictable, it could not be ignored on an "it is the government's own fault" basis, since "the government" was not suffering the major loss—the employee was. Moreover, this new construct allowed Justice Marshall to identify a demonstrable "error" the district court had made. Naturally its balance was off; it had completely failed to take into account one of the relevant interests.

Of course, all of this might be unpersuasive if it seems that doctrine has been contorted to fit the facts. What keeps Justice Marshall's opinion from appearing to have been forced is that it adopted a way of speaking about regulatory statutes that was already present in the legal culture. While procedural due process claims had long been framed as the state against the citizen, substantive due process claims had long been considered in a framework of conflicting private interests. The contrast appeared, for example, in *NLRB v. Jones & Laughlin Steel Corp.*,[112] one of the foundation cases of the modern regulatory state, which also arose from an order to reinstate employees who were found to have been retaliatorily discharged. There, the company's procedural due process complaint was met by pointing out that quasi-judicial process had to be provided by the Labor Board and "[r]espondent was notified and heard."[113] By contrast, the company's substantive due process claim that the National Labor Relations Act interfered arbitrarily with its right to conduct its business was answered by the statement that "[e]mployees have their correlative right to organize" and "[r]estraint for the purpose of preventing an unjust interference with that right cannot be considered arbitrary or capricious."[114] Thus, Justice Marshall's speaking of plural private interests—with government as umpire—was a way of departing from the specific tradition of procedural due process analysis without doing anything which was, seen from the larger perspective, startling or shocking. Just as the doctrinal basis of *Brock* ultimately drew strength from a social understanding, so, too, did the implicit social vision gain power from its integration into a doctrinal web.

---

[112]301 U.S. 1 (1937).

[113]*Id.* at 47.

[114]*Id.* at 43–44.

Thus the decision and opinion in *Brock* grow from a creative synthesis of doctrinal and sociological frameworks. From the broadest point of view, what makes it possible for the modern doctrinal vision and the modern social vision to interpenetrate each other is that they both represent a reaction to the fall of the older notion of a private realm of civil society radically different from the public realm of government. Yet, lest we be overly sanguine as to the stability of the synthesis, we must also notice that these two views represent different reactions to the past. In the doctrinal vision of the "new" due process, positive enactments of government are as much "property" as the property of the private sphere, but the distinction between creating entitlements and governmental action affecting them remains as the basic opposition. In the social vision, the processes of civil society and government share an inherent likeness, as do the processes of creating entitlements and policing them.

V. Where Do We Go From Here?

The immediate practical issue which *Brock* raises is whether regulatory statutes must provide for trial-type hearings before individual determinations as to the rights of the regulated are made. *Brock* states a framework for considering that issue, and the framework derives from cases that say such an evidentiary hearing is ordinarily not required. This change in framework apparently played an essential part in formulating a persuasive justification for the *Brock* result, which indeed does not require an evidentiary hearing. Assuming that the way *Brock* was solved shows how future cases will be solved, we cannot say that trial-type hearings will never be constitutionally required, but we can say that such a requirement will be much less common.

Or are we overreading the case? Section 405 of the Surface Transportation Assistance Act of 1982, it will be recalled, provided for a full adjudicatory hearing under the Administrative Procedure Act to be held "expeditiously" on request following the Secretary of Labor's finding of reasonable cause. What raised a problem was only the further provision that any reinstatement remedy contained in the preliminary findings would not be stayed. Moreover, what might be considered the formal statement of the holding seems to

be carefully qualified to depend on the statutory requirement of a
later hearing.[115]

> Reviewing this legislative balancing of interests, we conclude
> that the employer is sufficiently protected by procedures that
> do not include an evidentiary hearing before the discharged
> employee is temporarily reinstated. So long as the prereinstate-
> ment procedures establish a reliable "initial check against mis-
> taken decisions," *Loudermill*, [470 U.S. at 545], and complete
> and expeditious review is available, then the preliminary rein-
> statement provision of section 405 fairly balances the competing
> interests of the Government, the employer, and the employee,
> and a prior evidentiary hearing is not otherwise constitutionally
> required.

Future cases legitimately can interpret *Brock* as relating only to the
preliminary steps in what is ultimately a trial-type process. Perhaps
as the Court considers what the consequences of a more expansive
reading will be, it will be led to shun them and settle on this more
narrow construction.

But that will be hard to do. To begin with, the statement made
several times by Justice Marshall, and by Justice White, too, that
all that is being decided is a question of "temporary reinstatement"
or "temporary deprivation" will not logically support a narrow
reading of the opinion. True, the suggestion is that an informal
process is an appropriate basis on which to order an interim sta-
bilization of the situation, which will eventually be straightened
out in a full hearing; the employer's loss, after all, is only temporary.
But this argument confuses two possible meanings of the term
"temporary." The constitutionally relevant deprivation may be
"temporary" in the sense of being more or less short-lived, but it
is not "temporary" in the sense that it will ever be restored. If we
were to say that the employer's liberty were being infringed, self-
evidently the harm would go unrequited. But even if we accept
that the employer has only a property interest—even in the nar-
rowest sense of having to pay wages—the deprivation will never
be recompensed. Unlike the temporary cessation of social security
disability benefits in *Mathews*, which could be fully recouped if the
later hearing proved the deprivation wrongful, here the public treasury will under no circumstances be good for the money. In its

---

[115]107 S.Ct. at 1748. Justice White's opinion also turns on the fact that the employer is
"afforded an adequate post-termination hearing at a meaningful time," *Id*. at 1752.

brief, the government argued that the loss will be insubstantial "because an employer required to pay the wages of a reinstated employee receives the benefits of the employee's labor."[116] Presumably just this argument will block any restitutionary recovery of paid wages in an action against the employee himself. Yet though there is no remedy, quite clearly there will have been in every realistic sense a loss: the employer will have paid permanently for work it did not want to pay for, which it was not contractually bound to accept,[117] and which was furnished by an employee who had a grievance if not a grudge. And this loss is not some ancillary, consequential result of a procedural ruling, nor the inevitable consequence of action justified by the need to meet quickly an imminent danger, but is rather the very deprivation that is ordered by the government in order to benefit someone else.

It does not change matters to suggest that perhaps the Court is using the term "temporary" purely for its rhetorical connotation of "not a large magnitude, under the circumstances." Whether the numbers at stake should be considered large or small is arguable. The typical affected employer may be a large trucking firm, but Hufstetler's own earnings were around $50,000 a year,[118] and the time between the preliminary order and the final determination, even assuming the Department of Labor's compliance with its own timetable, could be six months.[119] Justice Marshall's opinion does indeed state that "at some point" the Court "may" limit the scope of the delay, and therefore of the deprivation, it will allow.[120] But all this only assumes, and therefore confirms, that there is some permanent deprivation of property being authorized on something less than an evidentiary hearing. Since that is so, it is hard to see what would be the sense of a firm doctrinal rule that *Brock* applies only to the preliminary phases of what are ultimately trial-type proceedings.

---

[116]Brief for the Appellants at 13–14.

[117]This point was patent in *Brock*, since by the time a claim was made to the Department of Labor, Hufstetler had already lost his grievance arbitration under the applicable collective bargaining agreement.

[118]App. to Jurisdictional Statement at 37a.

[119]107 S.Ct. at 1752.

[120]*Id.* at 1750.

However, even if we were to accept the Court's analogy of the "temporary deprivation" in *Brock* to the "temporary deprivation" present in government-benefit-granting cases, we would still have good reason to doubt that *Brock* would be carefully cabined. The *Mathews* three-factored test was introduced only after the Court had stated that it "consistently has held that some form of hearing is required before an individual is finally deprived of a property interest," but that the dispute before it "centers upon what process is due prior to the initial termination of benefits, pending review."[121] With time, however, some lower courts did not limit the *Mathews* test to evaluation of the preliminary phases of a process that would end in a trial-type hearing.[122]

Two years ago, in *Walters v. National Ass'n of Radiation Survivors*,[123] the Supreme Court considered statutory provisions that had the effect of keeping lawyers out of the process by which veterans' disability benefits are determined. The process, in the words of the Court, was "designed to function throughout with a high degree of informality."[124] This was true not only of the initial procedure, but also of the internal appeals process, at which there was no formal questioning or cross-examination, and of the judicial review process, which, absent special circumstances, simply did not exist.[125] The absence of lawyers helped contribute to this informality and this, thought the Court, was one of the legitimate purposes of the statute. Beyond the implications of citing *Mathews v. Eldridge* as the governing standard in a case where there would never be a trial-type evidentiary hearing, the Court proceeded to make the point explicit:[126]

> We accordingly conclude that under the *Mathews v. Eldridge* analysis great weight must be accorded to the government interest at stake here. The flexibility of our approach in due process cases is intended in part to allow room for other forms of dispute resolution; with respect to the individual interests at

---

[121]424 U.S. at 333.

[122]*E.g.*, Murray v. Gardner, 741 F.2d 434, 439–40 (D.C. Cir. 1984), cert. denied, 470 U.S. 1050 (1985).

[123]473 U.S. 305 (1985).

[124]*Id.* at 311.

[125]*Ibid.*

[126]*Id.* at 326.

stake here, legislatures are to be allowed considerable leeway
to formulate such processes without being forced to conform to
a rigid constitutional code of procedural necessities.

Thus, despite its origins *Mathews* is not, in the Court's view, a test
applicable only to interim procedural arrangements. There is no
requirement that at some point there has to be a trial-type hearing.
Since *Brock* works from the *Mathews* framework, there is little reason
to think that the cut-off point described in *Brock* will be adhered
to any more strictly.

Indeed, *Brock*'s recasting of the *Mathews* test to make it applicable
to government-as-regulator makes restricting *Brock* even less sensible. For the reasoning in *Brock* highlights the choice between
throwing the burden of unwieldiness of procedure on one private
party or on the other. In that context, if we know how much
procedure will justify imposing a cost of such-and-such a magnitude
on one party in favor of the other, the only relevance of any later,
more formal process would be to justify a yet larger transfer. Thus,
deprivations of the size suffered by the employer in favor of the
employee in *Brock*, based on the degree of procedural informality
allowed in *Brock*, would appear to be equally legitimate whether
they are viewed as an interim matter or, in a particular statutory
pattern, as the whole matter.

If *Brock* is not limited to the determination of the appropriate
interim procedure before a later full hearing, but rather is taken to
state an approach applicable to determining regulatory due process
as a whole, it will have a large impact. For the vision of regulation
incorporated in *Brock* is susceptible of very wide application. Indeed, as we have already noticed, this vision has long been employed
in evaluating due process challenges to the substantive terms of
regulatory statutes. In considering what a series of future cases
decided under *Brock*'s aegis will look like, we ought, then, to inquire
whether the same forces of institutional accommodation which have
turned judicial constitutional control of the substantive terms of
economic regulatory statutes into a dead letter might not be at work
regarding the procedural terms, too.

Justice Stevens warns of the dangers of asking "in each case . . .
anew what procedures seem worthwhile and not too costly," without
some presumption in favor of trial-type procedures.[127] At the other

---

[127] 107 S.Ct. at 1755.

end, Justice White recommends accepting "the balance struck by the statute."[128] The stance taken by Justice Marshall's opinion, however, is that the Court is able to reach a judgment of its own, including a rejection of part of the legislature's design, without having to adopt a presumption of trial-type process for common law rights. It is the stability of this intermediate approach that is in question.

Here is an example of the approach in action:[129]

> Roadway finally argues that requiring an evidentiary hearing as part of the process leading to preliminary reinstatement would not impose a significant additional burden on the Secretary since a subsequent evidentiary hearing must be "expeditiously conducted" in any event. 49 U.S.C. App. § 2305(c)(2)(A). Again, however, Roadway's suggested approach would undoubtedly delay issuance of the Secretary's order of reinstatement. In addition to the extra time required for the hearing itself, this approach would provide an incentive for employers to engage in dilatory tactics. Added delay at this stage of the Secretary's proceedings would further undermine the ability of employees to obtain a means of livelihood, and unfairly tip the statute's balance of interests against them.

What does Justice Marshall mean when he says that Roadway's suggestion would "unfairly tip the statute's balance of interests"? Could he mean that not providing for reinstatement before holding a full hearing would itself be a denial of due process to the employee?[130] The usual practice under the National Labor Relations Act is that reinstatement is ordered only after a full administrative hearing.[131] As was pointed out to the Court, even most "whistle-blower" statutes have provided for formal administrative or district court hearings before reinstatement occurs.[132] It is hard to believe

---

[128]*Id.* at 1753.

[129]*Id.* at 1750.

[130]Who would be being deprived of his "substantial interest in retaining his job" which "must be considered . . . in determining the constitutional adequacy of the section 405 procedures" (*id.* at 1748)?

[131]The Board's authority to seek interim relief on behalf of employees is highly discretionary and rarely used; legislative efforts in the late 1970s to make it the rule failed. See Weiler, Promises to Keep: Securing Workers' Rights to Self-Organization under the NLRA, 96 Harv. L. Rev. 1769, 1798–1803 (1983).

[132]Brief for American Trucking Associations, Inc., *et al, amici curiae* at 8–9 (citing thirteen statutes to this effect, *e.g.*, 42 U.S.C. §7622(b), which provides that any order of the Secretary

that Justice Marshall intended to say that those statutes are unconstitutional. What he must have meant is that, considering the interests involved, it was within the scope of Congress' discretion to determine that requiring an evidentiary hearing before reinstatement would "unfairly tip the statute's balance of interests" against the employee.

Given that, why is it not similarly within Congress' discretion to determine that the only "fair" thing to do is to have the Department of Labor operate with the fewest possible procedural constraints? Or at least to decide against spending the time to explain to the employer the substance of the opposing case, and to listen to the employer's rebuttal witnesses, as the Court requires?

Justice Marshall says that if that is not done, there would be "an unacceptable risk of erroneous decisions."[133] Insofar as he relies on precedent, he relies on governmental employment cases.[134] The interests balanced in those cases, however, are not squarely relevant to his own question, whether one private party's procedural claims must be restrained so that another private party's interests are not "unfairly" infringed.[135] Insofar as he relies on distinguishing the issues, he tries to suggest that holding trial-type hearings, which he does not require, presents primarily a question of delay, while informing the employer and hearing its witnesses, which he does mandate, is really a matter of avoiding error.[136] But retaliatory purpose is the crux of the statutory violation, and the implications of Justice Stevens's riposte—"how is the investigator possibly to decide between conflicting accounts of witnesses without making credibility determinations?"[137]—are hard to deny. Confrontation and

of Labor reinstating an employee who was discriminated against for blowing a Clean-Air-Act whistle "shall be made on the record after notice and opportunity for public hearing," and 29 U.S.C. §660(c), which protects OSHA whistle-blowers by providing that the Secretary of Labor "shall bring an action in any appropriate United States district court," and by giving the district court the power to order reinstatement. As the brief also notes, a fourteenth statute, 30 U.S.C. §815(c), part of the Federal Mine Safety and Health Act of 1977, closely resembles the legislation at stake in *Brock*.)

[133] 107 S.Ct. at 1749.

[134] *Id.* at 1748–49.

[135] As Justice White wrote, "What may have been required in *Loudermill* or *Arnett v. Kennedy* is no guide to resolving the present case." *Id.* at 1752.

[136] *Compare id.* at 1750 *with id.* at 1748–49.

[137] *Id.* at 1755.

cross-examination would be valuable; the full spectrum of procedures raises the problem of balancing risk of error against harm to
the employee through delay.

The only convincing response that Justice Marshall can make is
that the balance of advantage shifts as the procedure in question
becomes more formal.[138]

> Each of these procedures [required by the Court] contributes
> significantly to the reliability of the Secretary's preliminary de-
> cision without extending inordinately the period in which the
> employee must suffer unemployment. To allow the employer
> and employee an opportunity to test the credibility of opposing
> witnesses during the investigation would not increase the reli-
> ability of the preliminary decision sufficiently to justify the
> additional delay.

Can the Court reliably say when it is on one side of the balance,
when on the other? Or to put the matter more precisely, can the
Court reliably say when Congress has gone from one side of the
balance to the other, in the face of a contrary Congressional determination? The issue is, of course, not new. Once the procedural
issues are framed as Justice Marshall frames them, they are struc-
turally analogous to the questions presented by substantive due
process. The legislature is involved in choosing between conflicting
private interests, with no interest having an *a priori* preferred claim
or status.

If this is true, experience would suggest the likelihood that ultimately the Court will be unable to restrain Congress. It is not
conclusive that Justice Marshall second-guesses the legislature to
some extent in this case. Balancing "feels" different when one is
departing from a tradition of established rights from how it will
"feel" when that tradition has faded away. (The initial opinions
which interred economic substantive due process were much more
qualified, or viewed in terms of the Court's role, much more mus-
cular, than those of a short while later.)[139] When there are no longer
"naturally" established rights, and when the issue is the regulation
of private economic intercourse, there is no solid fulcrum on which
the Court can rest its balance save that provided by Congress. Once

---

[138]*Id.* at 1749.

[139]McCloskey, Economic Due Process and the Supreme Court: An Exhumation and Re-
burial, 1962 Supreme Court Review 34, 36–38.

Mathews is applied to regulatory enactments as is done in *Brock*—once, that is, the need for, and cost of, procedures are to be balanced with no presumption given to evidentiary hearings—the "naturally" established procedure of the common law has disappeared.

Indeed, the degree of judicial independence exhibited in *Brock* is already less than it seems. The legislative judgment which three Justices directly uphold, and which four more accept as the starting point for their own calibrations, is not impressive. The general pattern in labor arbitration in the private sector is that an employee must grieve and win before being reinstated. The general pattern in the common law (even in jurisdictions that have moved beyond the "at-will" rule) is that employees must sue and win before they get compensation or their jobs back. Section 405 on its own terms has a very narrow focus, covering only he "who is employed by a commercial motor carrier and who in the course of his employment directly affects commercial motor vehicle safety."[140] It is not part of a broad statutory pattern indicating how unfairly discharged employees should be treated in our society, or even how employees who blow whistles should be protected. The potentially undercompensating features of the "reinstatement-with-back-pay" remedy accepted elsewhere are already addressed separately by the specific additional provision of compensatory damages and attorney's fees. Despite all this, it appears that the statutory provision for interim reinstatement was not based on any articulated finding that whistleblowers in the motor carrier industry face special or peculiar circumstances. The early versions of the statute provided for reinstatement after hearing, with back pay, in the ordinary way.[141] This was true right through the statute described in the Conference Report, which makes no mention of any remedy being ordered prior to conducting a hearing.[142] The very legislative history that the Court recites, while making clear the need to protect employees against retaliation, does not spell out any unusual procedural pattern by which this is to be accomplished.[143] Justice Marshall may write

---

[140]49 U.S.C. App. §2301(2).

[141]S. 1390, 96th Cong., 1st Sess. §109(c)(2)(A) (1979); Amendment No. 1440, §409(c)(2)(A), to S.3044, reprinted in 128 Cong. Rec. S14627 (daily ed. Dec. 14, 1982).

[142]1982 U.S. Code, Cong. and Admin. News 3750.

[143]128 Cong. Rec. S15610 (daily ed. Dec. 19, 1982), thrice cited by the court, contains a summary of the proposed statute which says, anent this matter, simply that "If a violation

that "[t]he statute reflects a careful balancing of the relative interests of the Government, employee, and employer,"[144] but his only citation is to the text of the statute itself, which is of course entirely consistent with the provision's having been inserted at the last minute to please an organized special interest.[145] The care taken in enacting this law is not far different from the hypothetical rationality the Court found present, and sufficient, in the famous substantive due process case *Williamson v. Lee Optical Co.*[146]

It might be thought that Justice Marshall's intermediate approach will survive in the law of the procedural due process of regulation, even though it has not survived in the law of substantive due process, because the Court feels more competent and more comfortable in making judgments about procedural propriety. Whether the Court really is more competent in these matters when the institutional frame is provided by an administrative agency, and not a lower court, is open to question. (Even Professor Davis, in the course of his fervent advocacy for administrative law of what he terms "fair informal procedure," does not suggest how the courts are to make these judgments, but calls instead for the agencies to evaluate their own procedures in light of *Mathews v. Eldridge*.)[147] The larger problem, however, is that as *Brock* frames the matter, the fairness or unfairness which is at issue is not an internal, purely procedural fairness, but a real-world-consequences, substantive balancing of the parties' interests. Once viewed this way, the Court's claim to greater competence here, than in the judging of the substantive terms of statutes, seems dubious.

If the Court's carefully crafted middle ground gives way, what then? For reasons already discussed, conceptual pressures against returning to a world in which the regulation of private rights pre-

---

is discovered, the Secretary of Labor is directed to order" various remedies, with no indication that one of the listed remedies, reinstatement, should take effect at any time different from, or earlier than, the others.

[144]107 S.Ct. at 1746.

[145]The Brief for American Trucking Associations, Inc., *et al, amici curiae*, at 6, asserts that "[t]he Congressional Record is silent as to why, after five years of careful consideration, the legislation was suddenly changed to delete due process procedures when S.3044 was passed by the Senate on December 21, 1982." The Solicitor General's response, that this "provides no grounds for ignoring the plain language of the statute," Reply Brief for the Appellants at 4 n.3, tends rather to confess the assertion.

[146]348 U.S. 483 (1955) (it suffices that "the legislature might conclude").

[147]Davis, 2 Administrative Law Treatise §13.11 at 508 (2d ed. 1979).

sumptively calls for a trial-type hearing will remain quite strong. Thus, it may well be that we will move to a world in which legislatures are little constrained in their specification of the procedural modes by which regulation is accomplished. If so—and assuming that *Goldberg, Roth, Mathews*, and company stay on the books—the legal system will have succeeded in turning itself inside out so that the constitutional procedural protection afforded a "privilege" is indeed greater than that afforded a "right."

Such a world might well be surprising. It would not be inconceivable. Its principal features can be delineated. When government acts to provide a benefit, the legislature has the discretion whether to make the benefit an entitlement. Having created an entitlement, the legislature does not have a free hand in specifying its procedural accoutrements, but is subject to substantial judicial control. When government acts to adjust the relationships of two other-than-governmental economic interests (when it "regulates private rights"), the legislature is able to specify the procedures by which that adjustment takes place free of any substantial judicial control. Finally, we can assume that there will be special protection for certain non-economic rights. So we can specify: when governmental action infringes on matters of special importance to political freedom or to personal individuation, the legislature is once again subject to judicial scrutiny even when it is otherwise adjusting competing social interests.[148]

This set of rules would greatly change the underlying constitutional understanding of statutes far removed from labor relations, whistle-blowing, and discriminatory discharges. Under the Federal Trade Commission Act, for example, the Commission, after issuing a complaint based on the "reason to believe" that a company is engaged in an "unfair or deceptive" commercial practice, must hold a trial-type hearing before issuing a cease-and-desist order that will deprive the company of its otherwise-existing commercial freedom.[149] As was said in one of the early Court of Appeals decisions under the Act: "A hearing is granted before the Commission, and ultimate review by the Circuit Court of Appeals is provided; there-

---

[148]Doctrinally, we might say that before there is a deprivation of "liberty," now defined to exclude purely economic freedoms, there presumptively must be a trial-type hearing.

[149]15 U.S.C. §45.

fore there is no denial of due process."[150] If we now view the matter as balancing the interest of the company in exploiting its commercial advantages against the interest of the consumer in not being deceived into buying something he does not want, and leave the matter to Congress, that body would, on this view, have the latitude to say that the company must cease its practice upon issuance of the complaint (at least for some substantial period of time), with considerable freedom to specify how much investigation must take place before the complaint issues. Congress would, indeed, have the latitude to say that the commercial practice can be stopped, based on an informal procedure of some sort, period.

Of course, the practical consequences may not be nearly so dramatic. Here as elsewhere, the power that Congress constitutionally possesses is not necessarily the power that Congress uses. The coupling of substantial substantive restraints on private interests with substantial procedural restraints on governmental administrative power is a time-honored matter of political compromise and to some extent of political morality. The fear of "administrative absolutism" lies within the Congressional bosom, too.

If, however, one assumes that over time Congress would drift away from considering the evidentiary hearing as its presumptive starting point (perhaps because the Court has told it it can start elsewhere), then the Court might eventually be faced with having to justify the supposed differential between its treatment of government-as-benefit-provider and government-as-regulator. Could it defend judicial imposition of procedural protections in the former situation but not the latter? It might say that when government puts up the money, it is self-interested and less to be trusted in setting the terms on which it adjudicates disputes. While this claim resonates with some Contracts Clause jurisprudence,[151] it seems more attuned to once-and-for-all contractual commitments than it does to the ongoing business of governmental programs which legislatures are free, substantively, to abolish.

Or the Court might say that judges must hesitate to require more procedure in a regulatory setting, because there will be a loser (the interest that would benefit from immediate regulation) as well as a winner, whereas in the benefit-granting situation there is no loser,

---

[150]Chamber of Commerce v. F.T.C., 280 F. 45, 48 (8 Cir. 1922).

[151]Tribe, American Constitutional Law, §9–7 at 473 (1978).

and only a winner. But of course the public fisc can be a loser from delay. While some of the early cases, notably *Goldberg*, seemed to treat these public losses at a discount compared to analogous private costs, the Court has not done so since *Mathews*, and apparently does not want to do so.

Finally, the Court might justify the distinction by saying that private economic interests that are regulated can look after themselves in the legislature, and bargain for proper procedures, whereas the beneficiaries of government largesse need the aid of the Court. It might be hard to accept this argument as a grounding for procedural rights and still reject it as a basis for creating substantive entitlements. Adopting this argument would tend to raise again the problem *Roth* was supposed to bury. In any case, the point is much too narrow for what needs to be shown. For the beneficiaries of governmental action (as Charles Reich pointed out a generation ago) are a much larger group than the poor. It is hard to say realistically that business licensees, or highly unionized government employees, lack political power. In short, the supposed distinction is hard to sustain. If the procedural due process of regulation is confided to the discretion of the legislature, ultimately the procedural due process of positive governmental entitlements may be as well.

In *Brock*, the Court might have, as Justice Stevens suggested, chosen to treat the traditional view of regulatory procedure as the modern constitutional standard. For perfectly understandable reasons, it did not. Instead, it adopted the doctrines of the "new" due process. But since that framework had been developed to govern the procedures for protecting positive claims on the government, it did not fit the context of regulation. To establish a fit, the Court reworked the doctrines, informing them with social images taken from the modern law of the substantive due process of regulation. The consequence, as we have seen, was to create a combination which, even if initially attractive, proves to be unstable. Indeed, it threatens to undermine even the "new" due process from which it grew.

The time may come when the need for procedural protection against the possible designs of the administrative state will be recognized in a new body of doctrine not based on an attempt to carry forward the tradition of common law rights. If so, it may be that April 22, 1987—the day *Brock* was decided—will in retrospect mark as the time that the old constitutional order, long gone with respect to the substance of economic legislation, finally collapsed.

MARY E. BECKER

PRINCE CHARMING: ABSTRACT EQUALITY

Most lawyers, scholars, and judges interested in changing the relative status of women and men assume that there is an appropriate general or abstract standard of equality which should be applied by judges. The debate centers on what standard is most appropriate and how to apply it. Throughout the seventies, most participants agreed that formal equality was the most appropriate general standard,[1] though the more flexible disparate impact standard should perhaps be available in some employment cases. Today, these are the two dominant legal standards. The standard of formal equality is applied in constitutional cases under the Equal Protection Clause of the Fourteenth Amendment. And in Title VII cases, involving discrimination in employment, formal equality is augmented by disparate impact, which is available in some cases.

In the eighties, feminists became increasingly critical of these two legal standards.[2] Within the feminist community, a consensus

Mary E. Becker is Professor of Law, The University of Chicago Law School.

AUTHOR'S NOTE: I thank Al Alschuler, Walter Blum, Richard Epstein, Mary Ann Glendon, Richard Helmholz, Larry Kramer, Christine Littleton, Michael McConnell, Deborah Rhode, Geoffrey Stone, Cass Sunstein, and Anne Weber for helpful comments on an earlier draft and Paul Bryan, Jeannie Polydoris, William Schwesig, and Charles Ten Brink for research assistance. Research support was provided by the Russell Baker Scholars Fund.

[1]See, *e.g.*, Ginsburg, Sexual Equality under the Fourteenth and Equal Rights Amendments, [1979] Wash. U. L. Q. 161; Ginsburg, Gender and the Constitution, 44 U. Cin. L. Rev. 1 (1975); Ginsburg, Sex and Unequal Protection: Men and Women as Victims, 11 J. Fam. L. 347 (1971); Cole, Stategies of Difference: Litigating for Women's Rights in a Man's World, 2 L. & Inequality 33 (1984); Brown, Emerson, Falk, & Freedman, The Equal Rights Amendment: A Constitutional Basis for Equal Rights for Women, 80 Yale L. J. 871 (1971).

[2]In addition to the sources cited in note 3 *infra*, see Rhode, Justice, Gender, and the Justices, in Women, the Court, and Equality 13, 18–19 (Crites & Hepperle, eds., 1987);

seems to be developing that formal equality is inadequate. Some feminists have proposed alternatives.[3]

This debate has, however, assumed a questionable proposition: that a single general standard of equality should be adopted and applied.[4] Rather than attempting to find one abstract standard to solve women's problems, we should identify objectionable aspects of particular situations and argue for particular changes in the appropriate forum, which will often be the legislature. Any general, or abstract, approach is unlikely to effect much real change without seriously risking worsening the situation of many women, especially ordinary mothers and wives. Three cases from the 1986 Term serve to illustrate these points: *California Federal Savings & Loan Ass'n v. Guerra,*[5] *Johnson v. Transportation Agency,*[6] and *Wimberly v. Labor Commission of Missouri.*[7]

I. CONTEMPORARY LEGAL STANDARDS OF EQUALITY

I begin with *Guerra* and *Johnson.* In *Guerra,* the question was the legality of a California statute requiring employers to give workers disabled by childbirth (but not workers otherwise disabled) up to four months unpaid leave. The case arose when Lillian Garland sought to resume working as a receptionist after taking a two-month

---

Finley, Transcending Equality Theory: A Way Out of the Maternity and the Workplace Debate, 86 Col. L. Rev. 1118 (1986). Other feminists have presented more general critiques of liberalism. See Jaggar, Feminist Politics and Human Nature 27–48, 173–203 (1983); Elshtain, Public Man, Private Woman (1981); Wolgast, Equality and the Rights of Women (1980).

[3] See MacKinnon, Sexual Harassment of Working Women (1979); Littleton, Rethinking Sexual Equality, 75 Calif. L. Rev. 201 (1987); Scales, The Emergence of a Feminist Jurisprudence: An Essay, 95 Yale L. J. 1371 (1986); Kay, Models of Equality, [1985] Univ. Ill. L. Rev. 39; Kay, Equality and Difference: The Case of Pregnancy, 1 Berkeley Women's L. J. 1 (1985); Law, Rethinking Sex and the Constitution, 132 U. Penn. L. Rev. 95 (1984). See also Wolgast, Equality and the Rights of Women (1980) (suggesting some ways in which the standard of equality might be improved but not suggesting any one developed equality standard); Note, 95 Harv. L. Rev. 487 (1981) (similar); Freedman, Sex Equality, Sex Differences, and the Supreme Court, 92 Yale L. J. 913 (1983) (similar).

[4] For a somewhat similar analysis see Krieger & Cooney, The Miller-Wohl Controversy: Equal Treatment, Positive Action and the Meaning of Women's Equality, 13 Golden Gate Univ. L. Rev. 513 (1983).

[5] 107 S.Ct. 683 (1987).

[6] 107 S.Ct. 1442 (1987).

[7] 107 S.Ct. 821 (1987).

leave following the birth of her daughter. Her employer told her that her old job had been filled and that there were no similar positions available. Garland was unable to find another job immediately and, because of her unemployment, she lost her apartment and eventually custody of her daughter.[8] When Garland sought to enforce her statutory right before the California Department of Fair Employment and Housing, her former employer, Cal Fed, brought an action in federal district court seeking a declaration that the California statute was inconsistent with and preempted by Title VII.

The feminist community divided sharply on whether employers should be required to give unpaid leave to workers disabled by pregnancy. NOW, the ACLU's Womens' Rights Project, and a number of other feminist organizations (herinafter NOW et al.), argued against permitting states to require disability leaves only for pregnancy.[9] Other feminist groups argued that such statutes should be permissible despite their violation of formal equality.[10] The Supreme Court agreed, and ruled that the California statute guaranteeing jobs only to women disabled by pregnancy was permissible despite Title VII's ban on sex and pregnancy discrimination.[11]

In *Johnson*, the question was the legality of an affirmative action plan for women in promotions to a position previously held only by men. The Santa Clara County Transit District Board of Supervisors adopted an Affirmative Action Plan for the County Transportation Agency in December 1978. The Plan authorized the Agency to consider sex as one factor in deciding which of several qualified applicants to promote to traditionally male job classifications. A year later,

---

[8]See Garland's Bouquet, Time 14 (January 26, 1987).

[9]See Brief Amici Curiae of the National Organization for Women (and six other signatories); Brief of the American Civil Liberties Union (and four other signatories). Both briefs argued that the Supreme Court should extend the statutory benefit to all workers disabled for four months or less.

[10]See, *e.g.*, Brief Amici Curiae of Coalition for Reproductive Equality in the Workplace; Betty Friedan; International Ladies' Garment Worker's Union, AFL-CIO; 9 to 5; National Association of Working Women; Planned Parenthood Federation of America, Inc., California School Employees Association; American Federation of State, County and Municipal Employees, District Council 36; California Federation of Teachers; Coalition of Labor Union Women, Los Angeles Chapter (and thirty other signatories).

[11]Only Justice Scalia declined to reach the merits of the Title VII issue; his concurrence in the judgment rested on preemption grounds. Chief Justice Rehnquist and Justices White and Powell dissented.

in December of 1979, the Agency announced a road-dispatcher opening. Dispatchers assign road crews, equipment, materials, and maintain records of road maintenance jobs. Twelve employees applied for this promotion, including Paul Johnson and Diane Joyce. Joyce was the first woman ever to be a road maintenance worker. She was the only woman in a force of 110 road maintenance workers at the time of the promotion, and the promotion requirements included at least four years of dispatch or road maintenance work. No woman had previously been road dispatcher, a skilled craft position, nor had any woman ever held any of the 238 skilled craft positions at the Agency. Joyce and six men were certified as eligible for promotion after an interview by a two-person board. This board scored applicants on their interview performance. Johnson received a seventy-five; Joyce a seventy-three. (A score over seventy was required to be deemed eligible for the promotion.)

Thereafter, three agency supervisors conducted a second interview. One of these supervisors had been Joyce's supervisor when she began work as a road maintenance worker. He had issued her coveralls (routinely issued to the men) only after she had ruined her clothes on several occasions, complained several times, and finally filed a grievance. Another member of this panel described Joyce as a "rebel-rousing [sic], skirt-wearing person."[12] This member scheduled the interview (apparently deliberately[13]) so as to conflict with Joyce's disaster preparedness class. The three-man panel recommended that Johnson be given the promotion.

James Graebner, the Director of the Agency, was authorized to make the final selection of the new road dispatcher from among those eligible. Graebner, consistent with the recommendation of the Agency's Affirmative Action Coordinator,[14] promoted Joyce. Women's groups unanimously argued that this affirmative action was permissible under Title VII, and the Supreme Court agreed.[15]

---

[12]107 S.Ct. at 1448 n.5.

[13]See id. at 1448.

[14]Joyce contacted the County Affirmative Action Officer prior to the second interview because she was understandably worried about receiving a fair review. Under the terms of the Agency's Affirmative Action Plan, the Affirmative Action Coordinator was responsible for keeping the director informed of opportunities for the Agency to accomplish the Plan objectives, which included achieving "a statistically measurable yearly improvement in hiring, training, and promotion of minorities and women throughout the Agency in all major job classifications where they are underrepresented." 107 S.Ct. at 1447.

[15]Rhenquist, C.J., White & Scalia, JJ., dissenting.

A. FORMAL EQUALITY

Both cases were rightly decided. Yet both are inconsistent with the established standard of formal equality. *Johnson* is obviously inconsistent. There, the Court allowed the employer to treat similarly situated women and men differently, by giving women a "thumb on the scale" in promotion decisions.

The inconsistency of *Guerra* (the pregnancy-leave case) and formal equality is more subtle. At first glance, formal equality might seem consistent with the result in *Guerra* (upholding the statute treating workers disabled by pregnancy differently from other workers). This statute does not violate formal equality for sex-based classifications; it classifies on the basis of pregnancy, not on the basis of sex. Title VII was, however, amended specifically to reject this kind of reasoning.[16] As amended, it provides that discrimination on the basis of sex includes discrimination "on the basis of pregnancy, childbirth, or related medical conditions; and women affected by pregnancy, childbirth, or related medical conditions shall be treated the same for all employment-related purposes . . . as other persons not so affected but similar in their ability or inability to work."[17]

The language of the amended statute indicates that Congress considered pregnant women similar to others who were equal in their ability or inability to work. From this perspective, the outcome in *Guerra* is inconsistent with a standard of formal equality for Title VII: similarly situated pregnant women and other individuals are treated differently under the California statute. Only those tem-

---

[16]In General Electric Co. v. Gilbert, 429 U.S. 125 (1976), the Court had held that Title VII's ban on sex discrimination was not violated by an employer's health plan which covered all medical treatment except treatment related to pregnancy. The Court concluded that a distinction between pregnant and nonpregnant persons was not a distinction on the basis of sex. In response, Congress enacted the Pregnancy Discrimination Act of 1978, which defines sex discrimination to include distinctions based on pregnancy, childbirth, or related medical conditions. According to the reports of both houses on the Pregnancy Discrimination Act, Congress considered the approach in *Gilbert* inconsistent with a proper understanding of Title VII's nondiscrimination mandate. See Amending Title VII, Civil Rights Act of 1964, Sen. Rep. No. 95-331, 95th Cong., 1st Sess. 2–3; Prohibition of Sex Discrimination Based on Pregnancy, H.R. Rep. No. 95-948, 95th Cong., 2d Sess. 2–3 (1978). In Geduldig v. Aiello, 417 U.S. 484 (1974) (challenge to state disability insurance system which specifically excluded pregnancy from list of compensable disabilities), the Supreme Court held that classifications based on pregnancy are not equivalent to classifications based on sex for purposes of equal protection analysis. *Geduldig* remains good law in constitutional cases.

[17]42 U.S.C. 2000e(k).

porarily disabled by pregnancy have any right to a leave of absence; those unable to work for reasons unrelated to pregnancy can be fired.

1. *The inadequacy of formal equality.* These cases illustrate a number of problems with formal equality. First, as the discussion above illustrates, the question of who is similarly situated is hardly susceptible to answer by objective, value-free analysis.[18] There is, for example, a sense in which disabled pregnant workers are similar to other workers disabled for similar periods. From another perspective, it seems strange to consider women and men similarly situated with respect to pregnancy-related disabilities since only women are physically disabled by the onset of parenthood. Which perspective seems appropriate depends on the particular issue and on one's perspective and values.[19] As this example illustrates, formal equality is not capable of discerning discrimination against pregnant people. This, in itself, is a major failing.

As another example of the subjectivity inherent in identifying those similarly situated, consider *Johnson.* Giving Joyce an edge over Johnson at the end of the promotion process is affirmative action only if Johnson and Joyce were similarly situated. If they were not similarly situated, it would not violate formal equality to treat them differently. The notion that they might have been similarly situated is fanciful. Their prior employment experiences were not similar even when they had identical titles. For Joyce, work as the only female road maintenance worker would have involved a constant struggle, including dealing with hazing and harassment. Johnson was one of the boys. It is, however, likely that many male decision makers would neither see what Joyce went through nor appreciate that her unique experiences might be qualifications for promotion. They would be more likely to consider Johnson better qualified because as road dispatcher, Joyce will probably continue to have problems operating in a male world.

---

[18]See Scales, The Emergence of Feminist Jurisprudence: An Essay, 95 Yale L. J. 1371, 1377 (1986); Minow, The Supreme Court 1986 Term—Foreword: Justice Engendered, 101 Harv. L. Rev. 10, 40–45 (1987).

[19]See General Electric Co. v. Gilbert, 429 U.S. 125; Geduldig v. Aiello, 417 U.S. 484. In other contexts, even prior to Congress' overruling *Gilbert* with the Pregnancy Discrimination Act of 1978, see note 16 *supra*, the Court perceived special treatment of pregnancy as a form of sex discrimination. See Nashville Gas Co. v. Satty, 434 U.S. 136 (1977).

To date, standards have not been developed to identify the appropriate perspective from which to decide whether groups or individuals are similarly situated. Typically, judges simply note, in a conclusory fashion, that A and B are (or are not) similarly situated, as though the point was obvious and noncontroversial.[20] In the absence of appropriate standards, women are not likely to be served well by a formal equality standard applied by predominantly male judges on the basis of their subjective values and perspectives.

Second, under formal equality, women who are perceived to be like men are entitled to be treated like men.[21] This "nondiscrimination" rule is not neutral with respect to sex; it is androcentric.[22] Women cannot use formal equality to challenge workplace rules and practices which fit well with men's life-styles, needs, and experiences but less well with women's. Formal equality is not violated by workplace rules under which—as happened in *Guerra*—a new mother loses her job and custody of her daughter because she was the parent who was pregnant. Similarly, when the next Lillian Garland returns to work at Cal Fed following her statutorily-guaranteed pregnancy leave, her employer can ignore that she is primarily responsible for the care of her daughter. Such results are not sex-neutral. As MacKinnon puts it, "day one of taking gender into account" was the day the job was structured with the expectation that its occupant would have no child care responsibilities.[23]

Let me put the same point in another way. Formal equality uses (or misuses[24]) Aristotle's notion of distributive justice to define equality and discrimination. Aristotle defined distributive justice

---

[20]For an extreme example of this problem, see Rostker v. Goldberg, 453 U.S. 57 (1981) (upholding registration only of young men for military service because women were not allowed in combat; men and women were not, therefore, similarly situated).

[21]See MacKinnon, Sexual Harassment of Working Women, at 144–46.

[22]For discussions of the chimera of neutrality, see McConnell, Neutrality under the Religion Clauses, 81 Nw. U. L. Rev. 146 (1986); Minow, The Supreme Court 1986 Term—Foreword: Justice Engendered, 101 Harv. L. Rev. 10; Sunstein, Lochner's Legacy, 87 Colum. L. Rev. 873 (1987).

[23]MacKinnon, Feminism Unmodified 37 (1987).

[24]Aristotle also pointed out that it was unjust to treat similarly people who were not similarly situated. See Nichomachean Ethics V(3) at 112 (Ross trans. 1925). The result, under formal equality, is that women are often treated like men though they are not similarly situated. In addition, Aristotle advocated the use of practical, rather than abstract, reason in attempting to identify the good for humans. Nichomachean Ethics I(3) at 2–5.

as treating similarly situated people similarly.[25] Formal equality defines equality as treating similarly situated individuals similarly. Conversely, discrimination is treating differently individuals who are actually similarly situated. But discrimination is not necessarily the opposite of distributive justice. Discrimination and distributive justice might be quite unrelated things. If discrimination encompasses women's experiences of subordination, then there is more to discrimination than treating differently individuals who are similarly situated: "it is not only lies and blindness that have kept women down. It is as much the social creation of differences, and the transformation of differences into social advantages and disadvantages upon which inequality can rationally be predicated."[26]

Discrimination consists of repeatedly turning real or perceived differences into socially constructed disadvantages for women and socially constructed advantages for men. For example, the fact that only women are disabled by pregnancy does not mean that a policy, like Cal Fed's, under which new mothers (but not new fathers) lose their jobs is not discriminatory. Indeed, it is precisely because only women are disabled by pregnancy that a facially neutral policy like Cal Fed's is part of the system which has kept women subordinate to, because economically dependent on, men.[27]

The fact that only women are disabled by pregnancy does not even explain why women lose their jobs because of the onset of parenthood. The actual difference between the ability of women and men to work at the onset of parenthood need not be transformed into this socially created disadvantage for women. Imagine, for example, the socially constructed advantages women could be given as compensation for (and to facilitate) bearing and rearing children. Statutes could give mothers preferences in employment like those given veterans in many states. Large employers could give mothers extended leaves while their children are young, just as they gave

---

[25]Id., V(3), at 112–14.

[26]MacKinnon, Sexual Harassment of Working Women, at 105.

[27]Although men may sustain as many or more disabilities on the average than women, such disabilities are less likely to lead to parallel male economic dependence on women. Men are likely to sustain more work-related disabilities (because men tend to have more physically hazardous jobs). But work-related disabilities tend to be compensated by workers' compensation systems. Men who sustain them are not, therefore, entirely dependent economically on women. In addition, although social security never affords disability coverage to women temporarily disabled by pregnancy, it often affords disability coverage to workers who sustain other disabilities.

male inductees extended leaves for military service during the draft. Women who care for their children rather than participating full time or at full speed in the wage-labor market could be given social security credits in their own accounts for their contributions to the future rather than having only very contingent claims as their husbands' dependents.[28]

A third major problem is that formal equality is based on a counterfactual assumption; because of this assumption formal equality will, in practice, actually mean inequality. Formal equality assumes that it is possible to ignore an individual's sex. Both common sense and empirical data suggest that we cannot and do not ignore sex in dealing with an individual.[29] Moreover, the empirical data indicate that the routine, unconscious differential treatment of individual women and men tends to dampen ratings of women's competence and potential relative to the ratings of men.[30] To the extent that we cannot treat similarly situated women and men the same, formal equality can mask real, though perhaps unconscious, discrimination.

Johnson illustrates this point. The promotion interviews were conducted entirely by men, who had never promoted a woman to that position before, nor any similar position. One of the interviewers regarded Joyce as a "rebel-rousing [*sic*], skirt-wearing person."[31]

---

[28]Women who care for children (full or part time) could be protected by accounting changes; one need not impose additional taxes on families. During marriage, half of the wages of each spouse could be credited directly to the social security account of the other spouse. See Supplementary Statement by Commissionsers Ball, Keys, Kirkland, Moynihan, and Pepper, from the Report of the National Commission on Social Security Reform, statement (2) at 5–7 (1983).

[29]In addition to the sources cited in note 30 *infra*, see, *e.g.*, Buczek, A Promising Measure of Sex Bias: The Incipendtal Memory Task, 10 Psychology of Women Q. 127 (1986); Schulman & Hoskins, Perceiving the Male Versus the Female Face, 10 Psychology of Women Q. 141 (1986); Deutsch, LeBaron & Fryer, What Is in a Smile, 11 Psychology of Women Q. 341 (1987).

[30]See, *e.g.*, McArthur, Social Judgment Biases in Comparable Worth Analysis, in Comparable Worth: New Directions for Research 53, 55–64 (Hartmann ed. 1985); Gerdes & Garber, Sex Bias in Hiring: Effects of Job Demands and Applicant Competence, 9 Sex Roles 307 (1983); Francesco & Hakel, Gender and Sex as Determinates of Hireability of Applicants for Gender-Typed Jobs, 5 Psychology of Women Q. 747 (1981); Plake, Murphy-Berman, Derscheid, Gerber, Miller, Speth, & Tomes, Access Decisions by Personnel Directors: Subtle Forms of Sex Bias in Hiring, 11 Psych. of Women Q. 255 (1987); Francesco, Gender and Sex as Detriments of Hireability of Applicants for Genders-Typed Jobs, 5 Psychology of Women Q. 747 (1981).

[31]See note 12 *supra*.

Another interviewer had been her first supervisor as a road maintenance worker, the one who issued her work overalls only after she filed a grievance. Those interviews cannot have been precisely equal opportunities for both Joyce and Johnson. In the absence of the affirmative action plan challenged in *Johnson*, it is most unlikely that Joyce would have had a promotion opportunity equal to Johnson's. Yet, after a two-day trial, the District Court found that the Agency had never discriminated on the basis of sex.[32]

A two-day trial could not possibly have afforded a factual basis for concluding that an employer with 238 skilled craft workers and no woman ever in such a position (and one woman out of 110 road maintenance workers) had never discriminated on the basis of sex. Even after the passage of Title VII, women were routinely and overtly excluded from skilled craft positions by both unions and employers. Yet the incredible finding—that the Agency had never discriminated on the basis of sex in hiring skilled craftsmen (as the workers were doubtless originally described)—was not overruled by either reviewing court.

A comparison of *Johnson* and *Steelworkers v. Weber*[33] suggests that systemic discrimination on the basis of sex may be less visible to judges enforcing Title VII than is discrimination on the basis of race. Prior to the affirmative action plan at issue in *Weber*, 1.83 percent (five out of 275) of the skilled craft workers were blacks in Kaiser's plant where *Weber* arose. (Compare zero women out of approximately 238 at the Agency prior to the affirmative action plan at issue in *Johnson*.) In *Weber*, the Court reversed the two lower court decisions holding Kaiser's plan illegal and noted that "[j]udicial findings of exclusion from crafts on racial grounds are so numerous as to make such exclusion a proper subject for judicial notice."[34] Women, too, have been traditionally, explicitly, and routinely excluded from crafts,[35] but—unlike the exclusion of Blacks which was judically noticed in *Weber*—women's exclusion was apparently invisible to all the judges deciding *Johnson*. Justice Scalia relied heavily

---

[32]See Johnson v. Transportation Agency, Santa Clara County, California, No. C-81-1218-WAI (SJ) (N.D. Calif. July 23, 1982).

[33]443 U.S. 193 (1979).

[34]443 U.S. at 198 n.1.

[35]See generally Falk, Women and Unions: A Historical View, 1 Women's Rights L. Reptr. 54 (1973).

on the district court's finding that the Santa Clara Transportation Agency had never discriminated on the basis of sex and apparently believed it. None of the Justices dismissed the finding as incredible and necessarily lacking a factual basis after a two-day trial.[36] Judges can say no woman was ever discriminated against, but saying it cannot make it true.

Justice Scalia would probably respond that even if road maintenance and skilled craft positions had always been open to women, and even if the agency had advertised for women, it is likely that there would never have been a woman actually interested in either position prior to Joyce. This point brings out another problem with formal equality as a solution to sexual inequality. Systemic discrimination against women is often so effective that no woman will apply for a traditionally male job. Perhaps some women do prefer lower-paying women's jobs. But some may think that the job is only nominally open to them.[37] Others may dread the harassment likely to be experienced in breaking into male jobs, especially blue-collar ones;[38] there is no effective remedy for such harassment. Perhaps women have been socialized not to consider rough outdoor jobs but could be interested with a little encouragement. Formal equality ignores all these problems. As long as the job is open to women, so that there is no discrimination by this decision maker today, formal equality is satisfied. Formal equality is often inconsistent with the only means available for overcoming discrimination, whether by co-workers or by our educational system and socialization practices or by the employer's own practices (past or present, conscious or unconscious): taking "affirmative" steps to encourage and facilitate women's entry into traditionally male spheres.

---

[36]The finding may be partly attributable to collusion between the plaintiff Johnson and the defendant employer. Neither would have wanted to give a court a basis for finding that there had been discrimination against women. The courts upholding the affirmative action plan (the Ninth Circuit and the Supreme Court) could have decided the case without any finding on whether there had ever been discrimination against women. That would seem the more prudent course in the absence of an adequate basis for finding such a fact.

[37]Women often presume that blue collar jobs are not open to them but are interested if information is presented in a form indicating that the employer is interested in hiring women. See Roos & Reskin, Institutional Factors Contributing to Sex Segregation in the Workplace, in Sex Segregation in the Workplace: Trends, Explanations, Remedies 237–38, 241, 245 (Reskin, ed. 1984); Walshok, Blue Collar Women 155–70 (1981).

[38]See, e.g., id. at 23, 228–32, 239–40, 259–60.

The "affirmative" action exception to formal equality, both under the Equal Protection Clause of the Fourteenth Amendment and Title VII, alleviates these problems at least a little. In *Johnson*, for example, the Court allowed Joyce's employer to compensate, albeit roughly and indirectly, for the fact that Joyce and Johnson did not have the same opportunities or experiences. "Affirmative" action is troubling because the word "affirmative" implies that, in its absence, women and men would have had equal opportunities. In *Johnson*, "affirmative" conveys the unrealistic notion that had there been no thumb on the scale for Joyce at the very end of the promotion procedure, Johnson and Joyce would have had equal employment opportunities at Santa Clara County's Transportation agency.

Another problem with "affirmative" action is that it is only an exception, a basis for permitting employers to undertake some appropriate but voluntary acts to alleviate the problems faced by women like Joyce. It does not supplement formal equality by offering an alternative model of discrimination for plaintiffs to use in challenging the status quo. Only the disparate impact strand of Title VII offers plaintiff such an alternative.

In sum, formal equality—even with an exception for affirmative action—cannot be expected to transform society by equalizing the status of women and men. In the context of employment, it only opens men's jobs to women on the terms and conditions worked out for men. Further, under formal equality, it is likely that the differences in treatment of women and men will often be invisible to the extent that the differences consist of preferential treatment of men. More specifically, it is likely that a man will appear better qualified when there is no relevant difference between a woman and a man or when the woman is marginally better qualified. And it is likely that a woman's unique qualifications (because of her experiences as a woman) will not be visible, let alone regarded as qualifications.

2. *The case for formal equality, despite its inadequacy.* Despite these flaws, formal equality has an advantage: at least when women are perceived as similar to men, formal equality can be used effectively to challenge rules or requirements expressly restricting entry to privileged male occupations. Throughout the seventies and early eighties, feminists arguing for legal change—either before courts or in pushing for the ERA and other legislative reforms—relied pri-

marily on the concept of formal equality.[39] Because of these efforts, many laws, rules, and practices limiting women's opportunities have been eliminated.[40]

As a result of this experience, a number of feminists continue to insist on strict formal equality.[41] In *Guerra*, NOW et al. filed briefs arguing that California could not require its employers to give unpaid leaves only to women disabled by pregnancy and not to other workers disabled for similar periods. In those briefs, and in the general debate on the issue posed by *Guerra*, these feminists made three major points. First, they argued that "special" treatment of women is dangerous and reinforces traditional sex roles. "Special" treatment has been used to burden as well as to benefit; consider the protectionist legislation of earlier eras. By requiring that pregnant workers be treated like the most similar nonpregnant workers, these feminists would guard against judges' and employers' biases and stereotypes of pregnant women.[42] Maternity leaves (even if nominally for periods of disability) inevitably become child-care leaves. By insisting that parental leaves, if available, are available to both parents, these feminists seek to change the traditional assignment of child care responsibilities primarily to mothers.[43] Second, these feminists have argued that by treating pregnant workers like the most similarly situated nonpregnant workers, we can emphasize what is common about human experience.[44] They argue

[39]See, *e.g.*, Ginsburg, Gender and the Constitution, U. Cincinnati L. Rev. 1 (1975); Brief of the American Civil Liberties Union, Amicus Curiae, filed in Orr v. Orr, 440 U.S. 268 (1979); Brown, Emerson, Falk & Freedman, The Equal Rights Amendment: A Constitutional Basis for Equal Rights for Women, 80 Yale L. J. 871 (1971); Cowan, Women's Rights Through Litigation: An Examination of the American Civil Liberties Union Women's Rights Project, 1971–1976, 8 Colum. Human Rights L. Rev. 373 (1976); Mansbrige, Why We Lost the ERA (1986).

[40]See, *e.g.*, Davis v. Passman, 442 U.S. 228 (1979); Phillps v. Martin Marietta Corp., 400 U.S. 542 (1971); Hishon v. King & Spaulding, 457 U.S. 69 (1984).

[41]See, *e.g.*, Williams, Equality's Riddle: Pregnancy & the Equal Treatment/Special Treatment Debate, 13 N.Y.U. Rev. of L. & Social Change 325 (1985); Williams, The Equality Crises: Some Reflections on Culture, Courts, and Feminism, 7 Women's Rights L. Rep. 175 (1983).

[42]See, *e.g.*, Williams, The Equality Crises, *ibid.*, at 196–97; Brief for American Civil Liberties Union, filed in *Guerra*, at 10–35.

[43]Williams, Equality's Riddle, note 41 *supra*, at 353–56; Williams, The Equality Crises, note 41 *supra*, at 195–96.

[44]Williams, Equality's Riddle, note 41 *supra*, at 326; Williams, The Equality Crises, note 41 *supra*, at 196.

that "special" treatment will unnecessarily alienate women and co-
workers who actually have common concerns, e.g., adequate leave
policies for all disabled workers. Third, these feminists concede
that formal equality in itself cannot always effect needed change,
but maintain that sex-neutral parental-leave legislation is the best
way to achieve such change in law.[45]

3. *The case against formal equality.* There are a number of problems
with these arguments. First, NOW et al.'s arguments in *Guerra* are
undermined by their own position in *Johnson* (the affirmative action
case). Despite their vehement objections to "special" treatment in
Guerra, in *Johnson* these groups favor "affirmative" action. "Affirmative" action—deliberately giving Joyce a "thumb on the scale"
at the end of the decision making process—is as much a form of
"special" treatment as is the pregnancy-disability statute at issue in
Guerra. Affirmative action, perhaps even more than the pregnancy-
disability statute at issue in *Guerra*, divides workers from each other
and makes men resentful.[46] Yet, in the affirmative action cases,
NOW et al. did not consider it so dangerous that it should always
be avoided as a solution to women's problems.[47]

Second, the problem with formal equality is not simply that it
is incapable of radically changing society or of ensuring that similarly situated women and men are treated similarly. Formal equality
has actually hurt many women. Formal equality is likely to help
most, and hurt least, professional women who either have no children or who hire other women to care for their children and are
able to compete with men on men's terms. These women have
tended to control the women's movement. And it is likely to hurt
most mothers and wives who are not well-paid professionals.[48]

Despite the failure of the ERA campaign, formal equality has
been implemented wholly or partially, directly and indirectly,

---

[45]Williams, Equality's Riddle, note 41 *supra*, at 374–80.

[46]See The Supreme Court Puts the Mike in Diane Joyce's Hands, Giving Feminists a
Major Victory, People 49, 53 (April 13, 1987) (quoting Johnson on whether affirmative action
should be used in promotion decision: "You should work for what you get, and if you work,
you should get it.").

[47]See Brief Amici Curiae for NOW Legal Defense and Education Fund *et al.*, filed in
Johnson.

[48]See Woloch, Women and the American Experience 384 (1984) (describing criticisms of
the ERA movement in the twenties); Rothman, Woman's Proper Place: A History of Changing Ideals and Places, 1870 to the Present, at 160 (1978); Hewlett, A Lesser Life (1986),
especially at 202–3.

through legislation and judicial changes in many ways.[49] Because of this trend, women have lost many of the traditional sex-based rules which gave them some measure of financial security and protection. For example, consider the effect on women of the shift from the traditional maternal preference in child custody disputes. During the sixties judges assumed that it was in the best interest of a child of tender years to give custody to its mother.[50] Many jurisdictions have either eliminated this presumption[51] or replaced it with a presumption in favor of joint custody,[52] thus giving a bargaining chip to fathers in negotiations with mothers. Because mothers seem to want custody much more than fathers,[53] the result of giving this bargaining chip to fathers is that mothers who desperately want custody offer economic concessions to settle the custody issue rather than submitting it to a judge.[54]

The gender-neutral custody rules adopted to date have not effected any radical restructuring of parenting roles. Instead, these

---

[49]The ERA would not, necessarily, have to be interpreted as a formal equality standard, see MacKinnon, Excerpts from MacKinnon/Schlafly Debate, 1 L. & Inequality 341, 341 (1983). Nevertheless, the ERA was widely understood as incorporating a formal equality standard. See, *e.g.*, Brown, Emerson, Falk & Freedman, The Equal Rights Amendment, 80 Yale L. J. 871; Ginsburg, Sexual Equality Under the Fourteenth and Equal Rights Amendments, [1979] Wash. U. L. Q. 161.

[50]For a description of the traditional rule, see, e.g., Clark, The Law of Domestic Relations in the United States 17.4 at 584–85 (1968).

[51]See, *e.g.*, Ex Parte Devine, 398 So.2d 686 (1981) (presumption unconstitutional under Supreme Court decisions; court notes presumption has been eliminated in Alaska, Arizona, California, Colorado, Connecticut, Delaware, Georgia, Hawaii, Illinois, Indiana, Iowa, Maine, Massachusetts, Michigan, Nebraska, New York, North Carolina, Ohio, Texas, and Washington and questionable in Kansas, Oregon, Pennsylvania, and Vermont); Legal Rights of Children §6.03 at 236 (Horowitz & Davidson eds. 1984).

[52]See, *e.g.*, West's Ann. Cal. Civ. Code §4600.5 (creating presumption of joint custody on application of either parent); Legal Rights of Children §6.05 at 239–42; Schulman & Pitt, Second Thoughts on Joint Child Custody: Analysis of Legislation and Its Implications for Women and Children, 12 Golden Gate Univ. L. Rev. 539, 545 (1982) (as of March, 1982, 24 states have some form of joint custody statute). Although joint custody can refer to joint physical custody, more often, in practice, it means simply joint legal custody (both parents having the right to make decisions about education, medical care, etc.). See Schulman & Pitt, *id.*, at 542–43. For discussions of problems with joint custody, see, *e.g.*, *ibid.*; Adler & Chambers, The Folly of Joint Custody, 1 Family Advocate 6 (1978).

[53]See, *e.g.*, Weitzman, The Marriage Contract 105–6 & n.* at 105 (1981).

[54]See Schulmann & Pitt, Second Thoughts on Joint Child Custody: Analysis of Legislation and Its Implications for Women and Children, in Joint Custody and Shared Parenting 209 (Folberg, ed. 1984); Scott & Derdeyn, Rethinking Joint Custody, 45 Ohio St. L. J. 455, 478 & n.106 (1981); Pearson & Ring, Judicial Decision-Making in Contested Custody Cases, 21 J. Fam. L. 703, 719 (1982); Neely, The Primary Caretaker Parent Rule: Child Custody and the Dynamics of Greed, 3 Yale L. & Pol. Rev. 168 (1984).

rules may have contributed to the further economic impoverishment of divorced women and their children. The poverty of divorced women and their children (relative to men[55]) is not, of course, entirely attributable to the move away from the maternal presumption. There are no estimates of the effect of movement away from the maternal preference on the post-divorce economic status of women and chidlren. The point is only that notions of formal equality have had a negative economic effect on a group that is not in a good position to bear the cost of social change.

In calculating child or spousal support at the time of divorce, which will typically be paid (if it is paid[56]) by the father to the custodial mother, judges today often assume that the ex-homemaker will find a good-paying job.[57] After all, Title VII and the Equal Pay Act ban wage discrimination; women and men are equal. But full-time female workers continue to earn substantially less than full-time male workers, and a woman who has no recent wage-work experience is likely to have difficulty finding even a decent woman's job. If she is the custodian of small children, as is typically the case when there are small children at the time of the divorce, she cannot enter the workforce unless she either neglects her children or earns a great deal so that she is able to pay for child care. Here, too, treating women and men as though they are equal when, in fact, they are not has worsened the post-divorce economic position of women and children, especially those women (and their children) who are most in need because they are least like men.

Traditionally, during marriage, husbands had a duty to support their wives (and not vice versa). That duty has never been directly

---

[55]See Weitzman, The Divorce Revolution xii (1985); Espenshade, The Economic Consequences of Divorce, J. of Marriage & Fam. 615 (Aug. 1979); Women's Research & Education Institute, Congressional Caucus for Women, The American Woman: A Report in Depth 78–82 (1987) (citing surveys).

[56]Only 4 million women (out of 8.7 million living with children of absent fathers) were to receive child support from fathers in 1983. Of those due payments, half received (about 2 million) the full amount due. About a quarter (1 million) received nothing and an approximately equal number received a partial payment. See U.S. Bureau of the Census, Child Support and Alimony: 1983, Current Population Reports, Special Studies, Series P-23, No. 141 (July 1985). The New York Times recently reported that the average payment for child support droped 12.4 percent from 1983 to 1985. See Average Child Support Payment Drops by 12%, New York Times, §1, p. 26, Aug. 23, 1987. Because of recent federal legislation, women should be receiving more of what is awarded than in the past. See Child Support Enforcement Amendments of 1984, 98 Stat. 1305 (Aug. 16, 1984).

[57]See, e.g., Weitzman, The Divorce Revolution, at 188–89.

enforceable by wives during marriage,[58] but wives' creditors were sometimes able to enforce the duty.[59] In recent cases, in pursuit of formal equality, some judges have imposed a duty on all women to support their husbands, a duty enforceable by creditors.[60] As a result, a widow who has been a homemaker all her life may find, after her husband's expensive final illness, that she is personally liable for his hospital expenses. Ordinary wives are, however, less likely than their husbands to be economically capable of supporting their spouses, especially at age sixty-five or over when the husband dies. Again, treating women and men as though they are similarly situated when they are not hurts many women.

NOW would respond that sex-neutral legislation is the way to solve these problems. And one can imagine sex-neutral rules that would probably be acceptable solutions to most of these issues. But acceptable sex-neutral rules have not been widely adopted in any of these areas. Consider, for example, the appropriate standard for child custody at divorce. The traditional standard, giving an explicit preference to mothers at least during "tender years," created an explicit distinction on the basis of sex and reinforced traditional stereotypes of mothers as the nurturing parent. This standard is not ideal. Under it, for example, mothers were less likely even to consider whether they actually wanted custody, let alone to decide against custody without guilt, than they would have been under a less loaded standard. A gender-neutral rule could lessen these problems. If the new rule awarded custody to the parent likely to want custody most—for example, to the primary caretaker provided only that she were fit—the gender-neutral rule would not significantly affect the bargaining process. Of the many jurisdictions moving from a maternal preference to a gender-neutral rule, however, very few have adopted a rule preferring the parent who has been primary caretaker.[61] In the real world, there is nothing to ensure that the gender-neutral "solution" to an unnecessarily and inappropriately sex-based classification will not further weaken women's economic position.

---

[58]See, *e.g.*, McGuire v. McGuire, 157 Neb. 226, 59 N.W.2d 336 (1953).

[59]See, *e.g.*, Sharpe Furniture, Inc. v. Buckstaff, 99 Wis.2d 114, 299 N.W.2d 219 (1980).

[60]See, *e.g.*, Jersey Shore Medical Center v. Estate of Baum, 84 N.J.2d 137, 417 A.2d 1003 (1980) (rule to be applied in future cases).

[61]See Garska v. McCoy, 278 S.E.2d 357 (1981). In most jurisdictions, the identity of the primary caretaker is only one of many factors considered; see, *e.g.*, Pusey v. Pusey, Utah. Sup. Ct. No. 20365 (August 18, 1987).

In *Guerra* itself, the choice was not between a sex-based rule giving leave only to women disabled because of pregnancy and the ideal parental-leave rule advocated by NOW when lobbying before Congress. Nor was the choice between a sex-based rule giving leave only to women disabled because of pregnancy and a rule giving all workers leaves for disabilities of up to four months, though in its brief NOW argued that the leave policy be extended to all workers.[62] Instead, the choice was between having no statutorily-guaranteed leave for new parents and having leaves at least for women disabled by pregnancy. In other Western industrialized nations, where parenting leaves of one kind or another have been legally mandated for some time, regulation began in the form of maternity leaves. The trend, however, is to expand the policies to parental leaves.[63] Four jurisdictions in this country have adopted parental leave policies, and two of them began with maternity leave policies.[64] Eleven other jurisdictions have maternity leave policies.[65] These states may, in the future, follow the European trend and extend the benefit to include paternity leave.

A number of the decisions hailed as giant steps for women have hurt rather than helped many women by banning sex-based leg-

---

[62]NOW might have preferred the extension of the California statute to all workers, but the Supreme Court was not likely to extend that kind of state statute in the way advocated by NOW, despite its alternative holding to that effect in *Guerra*, see note 145 *infra*. In addition, even if the Court had extended the statute, the California legislature would have been free to repeal it. Further, other legislatures could not, in the future, enact maternal-leave statutes unless willing to give short-term disability leaves to all workers.

[63]Seventy- five countries—including every industrialized country except the United States—have some form of maternal or paternal leave. See Kamerman, Kahn & Kingston, Maternity Policies and Working Women 15 & Table 1.3 at 16–22 (1983); Hewlitt, A Lesser Life 96–100 & 167–74 (1986). Sweden adopted the first (and still most generous) parental leave policy in 1975. Id. at 96; International Labor Office, Maternity Benefits in the Eighties: An ILO Global Survey (1964–1984) at 18–22 (1985). As of 1984, five additional countries (Norway, Denmark, Italy, France, and Portugal) within the European Economic Community had adopted some form of paternity leave in addition to maternity leave. *Ibid.*

[64]The four states are Connecticut, Minnesota, Oregon, and Rhode Island. See Pregnancy and Employment: The Complete Handbook on Discrimination, Maternity Leave, and Health and Safety 98, 102, 104–6 (1987). Of these, two began with maternity leave policies—Connecticut and Oregon. See *id.* at 98 & 104. The Connecticut parental leave statute covers only employees. *Id.* at 98.

[65]Five states have statutes guaranteeing maternity leaves: California, Iowa, Massachusetts, Montana, and Tennessee. *Id.* at 96, 100–01, 105. Six states have regulations guaranteeing maternity leaves: Colorado, Hawaii, Illinois, Kansas, New Hampshire, and Washington. See *id.* at 97, 100–01, 103, 105–06.

islative classifications. And some of the Supreme Court cases striking explicitly sex-based classifications as impermissible forms of discrimination seem shockingly irrelevant to discrimination in the real world. *Orr v. Orr*[66] and *Otis v. Otis*[67] illustrate these points.

In *Orr*, the Supreme Court held that state statutes could not constitutionally provide for alimony to be paid by some husbands to some wives. The Court explained that permissible sex-neutral legislation would either deny alimony to both men and women or extend it to both on the same terms. It postulated two reasons for alimony: (i) because the recipient is needy and (ii) because women were discriminated against during marriage. Both purposes could be served by holding individualized hearings, the Court concluded.

Statutes imposing alimony obligations only on some husbands are hardly the linchpin of systemic discrimination on the basis of sex.[68] Far more important, by any measure, are sex-neutral statutes giving employment preferences to veterans[69] and statutes, rules, and practices which result in the ex-husband's receiving the lion's share of the financial security (including old-age security) accumulated during the ordinary marriage.[70] Yet of these policies, formal equality captures only the relatively trivial case of alimony imposed

---

[66]440 U.S. 268 (1979).

[67]299 N.W.2d 114 (Minn. 1980).

[68]. As of 1978, only 14.3 percent of divorced women had been awarded any alimomy. See U.S. Bureau of the Census, Current Population Reports, Special Studies, Child Support and Alimony, Series P-23, No. 141, at 4, Table E (July 1985).

[69]Such statutes violate neither the Constitution nor Title VII. See Personnel Administrator of Massachusets v. Feeney, 4422 U.S. 256 (1979) (veterans' preference does not violate Equal Protection Clause though women are effectively excluded from top levels of state government); 42 U.S.C. §2000e-11 (exempting veterans' preference statutes from preemption by Title VII).

[70]The financial security accumulated during the marriage includes the present earning power and future earning potential (to the extent accumulated during the marriage) as well as tangible and intangible pension rights and social security credits. Women who are dependent because of their specialization in domestic production and reproduction are not awarded half of these assets. See, *e.g.*, Umber v. Umber, 591 P.2d 299 (1979) (Social Security Act preempts distribution to wife of part of social security account accumulated in husband's name though both worked in family drug store but social security contributions paid only into husband's account); 42 U.S.C. §402(b) (during life of wage earner, divorced spouse receives, at most, 50 cents for every dollar of benefits he is entitled to receive). When a wife is given a share of a pension, she is sometimes "bought out," *i.e.* given cash or other disposable assets to offset the pension rights given the husband. See, *e.g.*, Weitzman, The Divorce Revolution, at 120–21; In Re Marriage of Gillmore, 29 Cal. 3rd 1, 174 Cal. Rptr. 493, 629 P.2d 1 (1981).

only on men. Such statutes are less than ideal; they reinforce notions that women are dependents because they are women. But they are not of much importance in the systemic subordination of women.[71]

More importantly, *Orr v. Orr* has hurt ordinary mothers and wives. During the last twenty-five years, there has been a decrease in alimony awarded even to full-time long-term homemakers.[72] It is likely that *Orr v. Orr* (and the notion of formal equality which both produced it and was reinforced by it) have contributed to this decline. In *Orr v. Orr*, the Court could imagine only two reasons for awarding alimony: a needy recipient and as compensation for discrimination in marriage. The Court never explains what it means by the latter, rather nebulous, concept.[73] The other reason is need. Need is not, in itself, a very compelling reason for post-divorce payments to an ex-spouse. Far more compelling reasons are ignored entirely by the Court.

Consider *Otis v. Otis*, which was decided a year after *Orr* by the Supreme Court of Minnesota. The Otis marriage had lasted over twenty years. The trial judge ordered the husband (who earned over $120,000 a year as a vice-president of Control Data) to pay his ex-wife alimony for four years (at an average rate of $1,500 per month). Ms. Otis quit her job as an executive secretary when her son was born "in order to fulfill the expected, role of wife and hostess for a rising and successful business executive."[74] She played an important role in her husband's career. For example, before his last promotion, she, too, was interviewed. When the board of directors met in Greece for a week in 1977, she was the official hostess. She had wanted to return to work a number of years previously, but her husband said he was " 'not going to have any wife of mine pound a typewriter.' "[75] When she was awarded only short-term

---

[71]. See note 70 *supra* and Weitzman, The Divorce Revolution, at 143–45. Even under a statute imposing equivalent obligations on ex-wives and ex-husbands, very few wives are going to be ordered to pay alimony because, *inter alia*, women usually have custody of the children and earn less than ex-husbands.

[72]See *id.* at 143–83 (California).

[73]The Court does suggest that individualized hearings could be held on whether "the institution of marriage did discriminate against" a particular woman but gives no clue as to what a hearing would actually investigate. 440 U.S. at 281. Because of problems of perspective and bias, women might be better off with sex-based rules than with individualized hearings.

[74]299 N.W.2d at 118 (Otis, J., dissenting).

[75]*Ibid.*

alimony, she was forty-five years old and had been out of the work-place for approximately twenty years. The Supreme Court of Minnesota upheld the award of the trial court because, it explained, post-divorce transfer payments are based on need and Ms. Otis should be able to "rehabilitate" herself within four years.

Ms. Otis's need—in and of itself—is the weakest imaginable reason for awarding her post-divorce transfer payments. Her current need reflects her investment in her husband's career, an investment from which he will continue to profit. Her need reflects the reliance loss she sustained by not working in order to raise their son and further her husband's career (and in order to avoid embarrassing him by typing). Having relied so substantially for so long, she cannot now, at forty-five, recover what she would have had had she put her own career first. Her needs should be met because a reasonable term of their arrangement, with its traditional division of labor, is that in exchange for her reliance in engaging exclusively in non-wage domestic production and reproduction and contributing to his career rather than her own, she would receive a reasonable share of the profit brought in by her husband's career and a reasonable share of the financial security accumulated for their old age.[76]

NOW might argue that ideal sex-neutral post-divorce rules can be imagined. There are, of course, other possible approaches besides tying alimony to sex (thus reinforcing stereotypical notions about women's dependency) and ignoring the life-long economic effects of the division of labor within marriage. *Otis v. Otis* is not, however, unusual. Ideal rules have not been developed to replace sex-linked alimony.[77] Instead, judges have stressed the weakest of reasons for ordering one spouse to make post-divorce income transfers to the other spouse.

---

[76]In *Otis*, the court divided approximately equally the property accumulated during the marriage except that it also awarded Mr. Otis all of his vested pension plan. The court does not attach any specific value to that plan.

[77]Ordinary women may also be hurt by discretionary rules—rules requiring judges to find an appropriate basis for awarding alimony in a particular case—rather than alimony awarded on the basis of sex since bias may affect individual decisions. This problem has been ignored by the Supreme Court which seems unable to perceive any cost, other than administrative, associated with individualized hearings. *Cf.* In re Marriage of Hitchcock, 265 N.W.2d 599 (1978) (wife unsuccessfully tries to repudiate divorce settlement reached after trial judge had made statements indicating that he would award her little as her share of husband's business; among other things, the judge compared her "interest in her husband's business to his own wife's interest in his retirement fund should they be divorced" with the implication that neither wife should receive a share of the specified asset).

Orr v. Orr is not, of course, solely responsible for cases like *Otis v. Otis. Orr v. Orr* reflects and reinforces notions of formal equality which have eliminated the notion that ex-wives should receive alimony because they are women. Judges, like the Justices in *Orr v. Orr*, have been unable to think of any very good alternative reasons for awarding anyone alimony. Many, probably most judges, like the Justices in *Orr v. Orr* have been unable to come up with anything more compelling than simple need. As a result, alimony (even when awarded) tends to be for relatively short periods of time (typically two to four years) and designed only to allow the ex-wife to become self-supporting. In the past, alimony was more often awarded permanently, *i.e.*, until the ex-wife remarried or either spouse died.[78] This change has not been good for most women, especially women who, like Ms. Orr, were homemakers for twenty years or more. Many women would have been better off if feminists had argued for needed economic rights and greater economic security for women (in recognition of their domestic production and reproduction) rather than for strict formal equality in family law matters.

NOW, or someone else, might argue that women have been hurt just about as much as possible under strict formal equality. They should, therefore, try at least to get its benefits, having paid the price. There are, however, still some sex-specific rules, statutes, and practices. These are still, at least arguably, permissible because we have not yet adopted strict formal equality as the appropriate standard. Further movement towards a formal equality standard would jeopardize such classifications. For example, a few jurisdictions retain a weakened form of the maternal preference;[79] even in those jurisdictions in which it has been formally changed, individual judges continue to use it in actually deciding cases.[80] Public schools still have separate sports programs for girls and women.[81] In many

---

[78]If alimony is basically a form of expectation-reliance (contract) damages for the needy traditional wife when a marriage breaks up, it should not necessarily terminate entirely with her remarriage. Thus, I do not mean to suggest that traditional rules could not be improved upon.

[79]See, *e.g.*, Pellegrin v. Pellegrin, 478 S.2d 306 (Miss. 1985) (error to award custody to mothers solely on the basis of children's tender years); In Re Marriage of Kershner, 400 So.2d 126 (Fla. 1981) (where all other factors are equal, custody of children of tender years should go to mother (dicta)).

[80]See Weitzman, The Divorce Revolution, at 235–36; Report of the New York Task Force on Women in the Courts 162–65 (1986).

jurisdictions, unwed fathers who have never lived with or supported a child cannot take a newborn away from its mother or interfere with her decision to let the child be adopted.[82] In a few jurisdictions, the obligation of husbands to support their spouses has not been extended to wives.[83] In many jurisdictions, clubs for women only are permissible.[84] All these rules, and others, would be threatened by further movement towards formal equality.[85]

In addition, formal equality has yet to permeate effectively our entire culture. Women can, therefore, be harmed by increased acceptance of formal equality in the surrounding culture. For example, even in the jurisdictions that have formally abolished the maternal custody preference, individual judges deciding individual cases often—consciously or unconsciously—consider mothers the more appropriate custodian for a child of tender years. Similarly, some judges deciding post-divorce economic issues recognize that most women cannot earn as much as men. Despite the fact that courts regard protectionist legislation as preempted by Title VII,[86] some women working in factories continue to enjoy some of the advantages (such as limits on what they can be required to lift) initially implemented through protectionist legislation.[87] Such re-

---

[81]*Cf.* Vorchheimer v. School District of Philadelphia. 532 F.2d 880 (3rd Cir. 1976) (Equal Protection Clause challenge to "separate-but-equal" public high schools for boys and girls), aff'd by an equally divided court, 430 U.S. 703 (1977)).

[82]See Krause, Child Support in America 139–52 (1981). The trend is, however, *contra.* "Modern" judges tend to equalize the status of new fathers and new mothers despite the obvious disparity between their contributions to, and involvement with, the newborn. See, *e.g.*, Collinsworth v. O'Connell, No. BQ-305 (Fla. 1st Dist. 1987); In re Baby Girl Eason, No. 44709 (Ga. 1987).

[83]See, *e.g.*, Schilling v. Bedford Co. Mem. Hospital, 303 S.E.2d 905 (Va. 1983) (abolishing duty); Marshfield Clinic v. Discher, 314 N.W.2d 326 (Wis. 1982) (retaining traditional doctrine with qualification that wives are ordinarily responsible for their own necessities).

[84]See Rhode, Association and Assimilation, 81 Nw. U. L. Rev. 107, 115 (1986).

[85]Perhaps such distinctions are already unconstitutional. The Supreme Court has not, however, decided cases squarely on these points. It can at least be argued that the Court might allow these distinctions to survivew their middle tier scrutiny applied in sex-discrimination cases.

[86]See, *e.g.*, Rosenfeld v. Southern Pacific Co., 44 F.2d 1219 (1971).

[87]See Hewlett, A Lesser Life, at 202–3; *cf.* Bielby & Baron, Undoing Job Discrimination: Job Integration and Comparable Worth, in Ingredients for Women's Employment Policy 211, 221–22 (Bose & Spitze, eds., 1987) (discussing continuing job segregation by sex; authors stress "the tendency for organizational arrangements to be inert in the absence of profound environmental shocks").

sults might become more tenuous in a world with greater stress on formal equality. As this suggests, the real-world negative effects of formal equality are difficult to see, let alone predict.

In the end, there are two distinct kinds of problems associated with formal equality. One is that formal equality cannot be the basis for implementing the kinds of changes that must be made if the status of women and men is to be equalized. The other is that the limited changes effected by formal equality will often hurt many women, especially ordinary mothers and wives.

Formal equality is dangerous for women in a way in which it is not dangerous for other minority groups. Few, if any, traditional racially explicit classifications ever had either the purpose or overall effect of benefiting a racial minority. There is, for example, no racial analogy to the maternal preference standard in custody disputes, no traditional racial classification which, despite its reinforcement of a stereotype, also gave a racial minority a better bargaining position in negotiations with nonminorities than would race-neutral rules. Because the legal system has protected women better than it has protected other minorities (though not, of course, as well as it has protected men), formal equality is dangerous for women in a unique way.

The trend, throughout law, is strongly towards strict formal equality. There is, at the same time, another legally accepted model of discrimination, a model available for Title VII cases: disparate impact.

B. DISPARATE IMPACT

Under Title VII, a plaintiff can use disparate impact to challenge a practice or requirement that disproportionately disqualifies women from employment opportunities.[88] For example, under Title VII, women can challenge height and weight requirements on the ground that such requirements are likely to disqualify more women than men.

Some feminist students and litigators have argued that disparate impact should be generally available as a basis for challenging dis-

---

[88]See Griggs v. Duke Power Co., 401 U.S. 424 (1971) (race case).

criminatory policies and practices.[89] There are, however, a number of limitations which prevent disparate impact from being a solution to the problems of formal equality. In order to use disparate impact, one has to have a perspective and some basis for comparison. For example, when disparate impact is used to challenge a height and weight requirement, one looks to see whether more female than male applicants fail to qualify because of the height and weight requirements. One assumes that in the absence of the challenged requirement, women and men would qualify in proportion to their numbers in the applicant pool.[90] One can, therefore, compare the actual pass (or qualifying) rate and the assumed pass rate (*i.e.*, the proportion of women in the pool) to see whether the test or requirement has a disparate impact.

In other settings, there is no single reference for comparison. Even assuming a basis for comparison, often one can imagine many solutions which could be implemented by various defendants. Consider, for example, *Wimberly v. Labor and Industrial Relations Commission*, a third case from the 1986 Term and one factually much like *Guerra* except that it arose in Missouri, which had no statute analogous to California's. Like Garland, Linda Wimberly was not rehired after her pregnancy leave because there were no suitable openings. She filed a claim for unemployment benefits with the Missouri Division of Employment Security. The agency denied her claim because, under Missouri law, unemployment benefits were never available to a claimant who "left his work voluntarily without good cause attributable to his work or his employer." Wimberly challenged the decision, arguing that the Missouri rule violated a federal requirement that states not deny unemployment compensation claims "solely on the basis of pregnancy or termination of pregnancy."[91] The Supreme Court unanimously held that Missouri

---

[89]See Williams, Equality's Riddle, note 41 *supra*, at 364–65, 372–74; Stone, Comparable Worth in the Wake of AFSCME v. State of Washington, 1 Berkeley Women's L. J. 78 (1986) (arguing for comparable worth as a form of disparate impact); Siegel, Employment Equality Under the Pregnancy Discrimination Act of 1978, 94 Yale L. J. 929 (1985) (arguing for general availability of disparate impact under Pregnancy Discrimination Act); Brief of State of California at 14–21 filed in *Guerra*.

[90]See Dothard v. Rawlinson, 433 U.S. 206 (1977) (height and weight requirements are impermissible because of disparate impact on women; employer must test directly for strength).

[91]This provision applies to states participating in the federal-state unemployment compensation program and is codified at 26 U.S.C. §3304(a)(12) (1982).

law was consistent with the federal requirement since Missouri did not deny claims solely on the ground the employee quit because of pregnancy. Instead, Missouri denied claims like Wimberly's on the more general ground that unemployment compensation was available only to workers who quit their jobs for work-related reasons. But the Missouri law can be viewed as having a disparate impact on pregnant workers relative to other possible policies. Under the Missouri plan workers who lost their jobs because of pregnancy and childbirth are never eligible for unemployment compensation. A policy extending unemployment benefits to all workers—once able to work again—who lost their jobs because of physical disability (lasting up to four months) would not have so negative an impact on new mothers.[92]

No court is likely to recognize a disparate impact claim in this situation;[93] the claim, the remedy, the proper defendant, are all too indeterminate. One solution has just been suggested: to order the Labor and Industrial Relations Commission of Missouri to extend benefits to all workers who lost their jobs because of short-term disabilities lasting four months or less. Alternatively, the Commission could be ordered to extend coverage only to women disabled because of pregnancy or only to individuals who lost their jobs because of a disability lasting two months or less. Or Wimberly's employer could be ordered to reinstate her after her period of disability; that too would eliminate some of the disparate impact of the current Missouri policy. Alternatively, Wimberly's employer could be ordered to give leaves to all workers disabled up to two months (or up to four months or up to six weeks) or to give leaves to all new parents. Indeed, although one can imagine more desirable policies, any disparate impact on pregnant workers would be elim-

---

[92]One can, of course, imagine other policies which would also be preferable from the perspective of pregnant workers, e.g., a plan which considered all reasonable quits (including pregnancy) as covered by the plan.

[93]Wimberly did not frame her claim in terms of disparate impact. Instead, she argued that the federal provision mandated "preferential teatment for women who leave work because of pregnancy." 107 S.Ct. at 825. Something like disparate impact has, however, been recognized in the context of the Free Exercise Clause. States must extend umemployment benefits to workers who are fired for refusing to work on their Sabbath. See Sherbert v. Verner, 374 U.S. 398 (1963); Hobbie v. Unemployment Appeals Commission of Florida, 107 S.Ct. 1046 (1987).

inated by ordering all Missouri employers to require that every man in Missouri take an (unpaid) paternal leave when his child is born equal to the length of time the mother of his child is disabled by childbirth.

As another example, consider the argument, made by the state of California in its brief in *Guerra*, that the state statute was permissible because an employer's failure to give at least four months disability leave for pregnancy would necessarily have a disparate impact on pregnant workers.[94] The ACLU Women's Project in their amicus brief in *Guerra* responds that "[i]n fact, the average number of days lost from work due to disability, including childbirth and illness during pregnancy, is remarkably similar for men and women workers."[95] The ACLU women's project cites evidence that "men workers experience an average of 4.9 days of work loss due to illness or injury per year while women experience 5.1 days per year."[96] Men lose more days of work from all injuries than women do because, among other things, men tend to work at more dangerous jobs and suffer more job-related disability. In their amicus brief, the California Women Lawyers, et al., respond that this is the wrong comparison. One needs to ask whether disability leaves inadequate for most pregnancies (the average length of pregnancy disability may be six weeks) have a disparate impact on women. The fact that women have an average of only 4.9 days of disability a year and men and average of 5.1 days a year is irrelevant to the question of whether the lack of leaves adequate for most pregnancies has a disparate impact on women.[97]

If the question is whether a no-leave policy has a disparate impact on women, there is a sense in which each of these litigants is right. There is no one perspective from which to judge disparate impact

---

[94]See Brief of California at 14–21 filed in *Guerra*.

[95]See ACLU *et al.* brief, note 9 *supra*, at 25.

[96]*Id.* at 26.

[97]See Brief of California Women Lawyers, *et al.*, note 10 *supra*, at 12–13. On the other hand, workers who sustain work-related disabilities are less likely (than workers disabled by pregnancy) to lose their jobs. Employers are usually anxious to avoid charges that employees were fired in retaliation for filing a work-related disability claim and are anxious to do everything possible to limit the size of the claim. Both these purposes are served by allowing the worker to return to work at the earliest possible date. Indeed, California prohibits employers from terminating employees because of work-related disabilitites. Cal. Labor Code §132a, cited in Brief of California, filed in *Guerra*, at 18–19 n.16.

on women in this situation.[98] In addition, changes could be made by a number of different entities; disparate impact does not give a court any guidance about who is a proper defendant. At least to date, even supposedly activist judges have not been willing to develop standards for choosing among various policies to be implemented by various defendants.

There is another problem with disparate impact. Like formal equality, disparate impact refers to male performance levels. Women are, at most, entitled to succeed at men's rates.[99] This antidiscrimination rule (like formal equality) has a male reference point; it is not neutral with respect to sex. Disparate impact cannot, for example, afford a basis for challenging promotion requirements designed by and for men as long as women, by dint of whatever efforts are necessary given their typically greater domestic responsibilities[100] and other disadvantages, are nevertheless as successful as men.

Only a few feminists (other than litigators) have argued for a disparate impact standard in contexts outside hiring or promotion requirements.[101] Instead, most feminists disenchanted with contemporary standards of equality have tried to develop alternatives.

II. Feminist Alternatives

For purposes of this discussion, feminist alternatives may be put under three headings: first, Catharine MacKinnon's inequality approach;[102] second, Christine Littleton's acceptance ap-

---

[98]Because Title VII specifically defines sex discrimination as including discrimination on the basis of pregnancy, perhaps the disparate impact question in this Title VII case should focus on whether a no-leave policy has a disparate impact on pregnant workers rather than women workers. The State of California argued that the appropriate focus was pregnant workers, see Brief of California, at 14–22, especially n.16 at 18–19. The ACLU considered the appropriate focus women workers, not pregnant workers. See ACLU Brief, at 23–35.

[99]Cf. MacKinnon, Sexual Harassment, at 145–46 (noting that inequality is buried in standards, such as the height and weight standard at issue in *Dothard*, which was actually average male height and weight).

[100]Even in families in which both spouses work, women are primarily responsible for domestic tasks. See, *e.g.*, Blumstein & Schwartz, American Couples 144–46 (1983); Gilbert, Men in Dual Career Couples: Current Realities and Future Prospects 60–90 (1985); Pleck, Men's Family Work: Three Perspectives and Some New Data, 28 The Family Coordinator 481 (1979).

[101]See sources cited in note 89 *supra*.

[102]See, *e.g.*, MacKinnon, Sexual Harassment, especially at 101–41; MacKinnon, Feminism Unmodified, especially at 32–45.

proach;[103] and third, formal equality with limited special treatment.[104] Some feminists have suggested other approaches to equality in recent years but have not elaborated judicially enforceable standards. Instead, they have primarily attempted to expand the kinds of arguments that might be made to employers and legislators.[105] This discussion is limited to judicially enforceable feminist approaches.[106]

A. THE INEQUALITY APPROACH

The inequality approach, developed by MacKinnon in the seventies, is a powerful and influential model, as well as being, itself, a devastating critique of formal equality. The inequality model begins with the seemingly obvious observation that when we use the word "discrimination," we are referring to "systematic disadvantagement of social groups."[107] As already noted, formal equality assumes that distinctions based on relevant differences are not discriminatory. But systemic discrimination consists primarily of turning differences, real or perceived, into socially constructed disadvantages for women and socially constructed advantages for men.

MacKinnon refuses, therefore, to focus on the rationalizations for distinctions which, however "reasonable," are part of the systemic subordination of women to men. Instead, she focuses on whether a particular practice or rule "participates in the systemic social deprivation of one sex because of sex. The only question for litigation is whether the policy or practice in question integrally

---

[103]Littleton, Reconstructing Sexual Equality, 75 Cal. L. Rev. 201 (1987).

[104]See Kay, Models of Equality, [1985] Univ. Ill. L. Rev. 39; Law, Rethinking Sex and the Constitution, 132 Univ. Pa. L. Rev. 955 (1984); Kay, Equality and Difference: The Case of Pregnancy, 1 Berkeley Women's L. J. 1 (1985); Law, Rethinking Sex and the Constitution, 132 U. Pa. L. Rev. 95 (1984). Ann Scales also advocated this approach in an early article, see Scales, Towards a Feminist Jurisprudence, 56 Ind. L. J. 375 (1981), but in more recent work has advocated MacKinnon's inequality approach. See Scales, The Emergence of Feminist Jurisprudence: An Essay, 95 Yale L. J. 1373 (1986).

[105]Finley, Transcending Equality Theory: A Way out of the Maternity and the Workplace Debate, 86 Col. L. Rev. 1118 (1986); Wolgast, Equality and the Rights of Women (1980).

[106]I do not discuss the "choice" standard advocated by Kirp, Yudof, and Franks in Gender Justice (1986). As Lucinda Finley points out in her review, the choice approach is a reformulation of conventional liberalism. See Finley, Choice and Freedom: Elusive Issues in the Search for Gender Justice, 96 Yale. L. J. 914 (1987).

[107]MacKinnon, Sexual Harassment, at 116.

contributes to the maintenance of an underclass or a deprived position because of gender status."[108]

At least one feminist, Ann Scales, has argued for MacKinnon's inequality standard as a general, judicially enforceable approach to discrimination.[109] Although MacKinnon describes the "question to be litigated" as whether a practice or policy contributes to women's subordinate status, it is unlikely that MacKinnon understands inequality as a general judicially enforceable standard for challenging any practice or policy that contributes to the subordination of women.[110]

Despite Scales's optimism, the inequality approach is not a general solution to the problems raised by formal equality and disparate impact. Typically, a policy or practice contributes to women's subordinate status because of its interaction with other policies, practices, and social mores. Typically, one can imagine many changes to the status quo, implemented by many different entities, which would result in less systematic subordination of women. Inequality's "question to be litigated" does not identify either the appropriate defendant or the appropriate change. Each of the points made in the earlier discussion of disparate impact and pregnancy policies could be made again here.

As an example, consider whether the inequality standard would be violated when a worker disabled by pregnancy is fired. Her employer fires all workers disabled for more than two weeks for reasons that are not work related. Such a policy contributes to the subordination of women, by tending to make them dependent on men after childbirth. But even giving the worker an unpaid leave of absence during pregnancy-related disability tends to contribute to the subordination of women, by tending to make them dependent on men while temporarily disabled by pregnancy. There are a number of ways in which these policies could be changed so as to make

---

[108]*Id.* at 117.

[109]See Scales, The Emergence of Feminist Jurisprudence: An Essay, note 107 *supra.*

[110]Certainly, MacKinnon has not taken such an approach. In Sexual Harassment of Working Women, she used her inequality approach in arguing that policies of sexual harassment that explicitly treat women and men differently are forms of sex discrimination because they contribute to the inequality of women. But in her attempts to have pornography recognized as a form of sex discrimination, she has used inequality analysis as a basis for arguing for legislative change, rather than as a judicially-enforceable abstract standard of equality capable, in itself, of affording a remedy for such discrimination.

women more independent. Employers could be required to give women leaves for pregnancy-related disabilities with full pay. Alternatively, employers could be required to give women unpaid leaves and state unemployment compensation systems could be changed to give women unemployment compensation during the period of pregnancy-related disability. Or employers could be required to give all new parents a period of paid leave for six months. Alternatively, employers could be required to give new parents six months of unpaid leave and some new state-mandated insurance system could provide financial benefits to parents taking such leaves.

Identifying current policies as contributing to the subordinate status of women simply does not identify a single defendant or one appropriate change. Like disparate impact, inequality as a general standard is simply too indeterminate to expect judges to use it in the foreseeable future.[111]

B. THE ACCEPTANCE STANDARD

Christine Littleton suggests that judges apply equality in terms of an acceptance standard. She identifies men's power to determine what is of value as an essential element of the inequality of the sexes. She proposes to "rescue equality" by "making sex difference not make a difference in equality, by making difference 'costless' (or at least cost less)."[112] In applying an acceptance standard, judges would make difference cost less by equalizing the resources (money, status, and access to decision making) allocated on the basis of "gendered complements."[113]

For example, under Littleton's acceptance standard, comparable worth would be appropriate in disputes about pay because male and female job categories should be paid equally. In other contexts, acceptance would be implemented by "inventing complementary structures containing female norms."[114] For example, an employer with a job-related height requirement (tending disproportionately to disqualify women relative to men) would be required to restruc-

---

[111]For a similar analysis, see Law, Rethinking Sex and the Constitution, 132 Univ. Pa. L. Rev. at 1005–06.

[112]Littleton, Reconstructing Sexual Equality, 75 Cal. L. Rev. at 238–43.

[113]*Id.* at 244, 253

[114]*Id.* at 248.

ture the job (or offer equal job opportunities) to accommodate the disqualified women.[115] In the context of pregnancy, Littleton would require that, in the workplace, "money, status, and opportunity for advancement flow equally to the womb-donating woman and the sperm-donating man."[116] Littleton argues that motherhood and military service could be established as gendered complements; this would mean "requiring the government to pay mothers the same low wages and generous benefits as most soldiers."[117] Littleton suggests that this could "mean encouraging the use of motherhood [like the use of military service today] as an unofficial prerequisite for governmental office."[118]

Littleton's standard adds another level of indeterminancy to disparate impact analysis. In addition to eliminating those policies and practices which have a disparate impact on women in terms of money, status, or access to decision making, judges must initially identify appropriate gendered complements.

Consider a worker who stops working when her first child is born, works on a part-time basis at low-paying jobs intermittently for the next ten years, and then resumes full-time work when her youngest child enters first grade. It is unrealistic to think that judges can or will order changes equalizing her and her husband's (or the average man's?) access to money, status, and decision making. What is the gendered complement for the various stages of her life? Should she receive soldier's pay (what rank?) and benefits until her youngest child is eighteen? Even after the youngest is eighteen, she will probably continue to receive lower wages because she took time off from wage work to care for her children. After twenty years of motherhood, should she be entitled to military retirement benefits? Although Littleton's acceptance standard suggests arguments that might be made to legislatures, it is unrealistic to think that judges will be willing to implement so nebulous a standard.

---

[115]*Id.* at 248 (no remedy would be available under Title VII, as currently interpreted, for the policy described in text because the height requirement is job related).

[116]*Ibid.*

[117]*Id.* at 251.

[118]*Id.* at 251–52 n.260 (by changing media treatment of female political candidates and by establishing preferences for employment similar to those granted veterans).

C. FORMAL EQUALITY WITH LIMITED "SPECIAL" TREATMENT

Through the early eighties, the current feminist movement relied primarily on formal equality in pressing for change both in courts and in other arenas. In recent years, a number of feminists have argued that formal equality should be qualified by allowing for policies treating women differently from men in very limited circumstances centering on the biological fact that only women bear children.[119] These feminists would uphold the California statute challenged in *Guerra,* since women are given "special" treatment only when—on the level of physical reality—they are situated differently from men: they are disabled by pregnancy.

This approach can be criticized both by those who would never permit "special" treatment (other than "affirmative" action) and by those who think "special" treatment in such limited circumstances too narrow a standard. (I have already summarized and responded to the objections of the first group, feminists like Wendy Williams and the leadership of the National Organization of Women, who argue for strict formal equality with no exceptions other than "affirmative" action.) "Special" treatment in such limited circumstances does not go very far towards rectifying the many, and I think devastating, reasons for rejecting formal equality, reasons already discussed in detail. If "special" treatment is permissible only when warranted by physical, biological differences, the standard remains one of formal equality in almost all instances augmented by "special" treatment only in the most narrow of circumstances.

Formal equality augmented by such limited special treatment will not effect nearly enough beneficial change and will often result in change detrimental to most women. Few of the criticisms of formal equality, elaborated above, were limited to the use of formal equality when there is actually a biological difference. Even with

---

[119]See Scales, Toward a Feminist Jurisprudence, 56 Ind. L. J. 375 (women should be regarded as having rights different from men only with respect to sex-specific conditions that are completely unique to women, *i.e.* pregnancy and breast feeding); Law, Rethinking Sex and the Constitution, 132 U. Pa. L. Rev. 955; Kay, Equality and Difference, 1 Berkely Women's L. J. 1 (1985); Kay, Models of Equality, [1985] Ill. L. Rev. 39. In a 1986 article, Scales moved from the limited-special-treatment view to share MacKinnon's dominance approach. See Scales, The Emergence of a Feminist Jurisprudence, 95 Yale L. J. 1371, especially at 1381 n.46.

an exception for biological differences, formal equality affords no basis for challenging rules which structure the work place to fit men's life experiences and needs, but not women's. This limited exception does nothing to correct the male bias inevitable in a standard of formal equality applied mostly by men. It still accepts actual or perceived differences as justifications for further differential treatment. The exception does not help make visible discrimination which is often invisible under a standard of formal equality.

Most importantly, the limited exception for differential treatment based on biological differences will not preclude the use of formal equality though the result may be to further disadvantage many ordinary mothers and wives. True, under this standard, a court would not overrule a statute giving women pregnancy leaves. But courts would continue to strike down the maternal preference in custody and judges would tend increasingly (in a world with greater acceptance of formal equality) to regard fathers as equally appropriate custodians of young children and to regard mothers as equally capable of supporting children financially.

III. An Impossible Dream?

We use equality to refer to a number of things, including both (i) the situation in an ideal (nonsexist) world and (ii) a legal standard to be applied by judges (based either in the Constitution or in a statute such as Title VII). Hopefully, (ii) should be a means to get from this world to the ideal world imagined in (i).

We cannot, today, know what an "ideal" world with equality between the sexes would look like, let alone how best to get there. This is another difference between race and sex. With race, we can at least imagine a world in which Blacks and whites are equal. We can imagine a world in which race is no more important than eye color. We cannot so easily imagine a world in which women and men are equal or in which sex would matter no more than eye color. Most of us would not want to live in a world in which sex was no more important or relevant than eye color. Perhaps equality could occur in a world in which sex still matters, but in different ways from the ways in which it matters in this world. Few of us can imagine what that world might look like.

For those, including myself, who think that whatever it might look like, a reasonably ideal world would look rather different from this one, formal equality must be rejected. Formal equality is not capable of producing enough change in the status quo, and is likely to impose significant costs on those women most in need of change because most unlike men.

Perhaps formal equality's proponents regard harm to some women (especially ordinary mothers and wives) as a justifiable cost of effecting social change. If the economic position of ordinary women (especially after divorce, an ever present danger today) becomes tenuous enough, fewer women will be willing to fulfill traditional roles or (as is often the case) attempt to combine traditional roles and some (often limited) wage work. As a result of greater insecurity, more women will work, even while their children are small, will regard their own jobs as important as their husbands', and will refuse to be primarily responsible for either child care or other domestic duties. Also, if their chances of having post-divorce custody are no greater than their husbands', they will invest less in their children during marriage, thus equalizing fathers' and mothers' investments in raising children.

There are, however, a number of problems with such justifications for formal equality. First, formal equality tends to help most exceptional professional women, with the costs borne by another group. The elite who lead the feminist movement should be reluctant to press for change they consider desirable by imposing its costs on other women.

Second, it is likely that a majority of women would consider this "solution" unacceptable. It is, for example, unlikely that most women would want to be only as involved with children as their husbands. Perhaps this is the result of their socialization, and a form of false consciousness about their own best interests. We should, however, be reluctant to use false consciousness as the basis for ignoring women's desires. One important aspect of women's subordination has been that others have defined who women are and what they want. Feminists have generally stressed the importance of listening to what women say rather than dictating what women should say and feel.

Most women might prefer other means to other ends. True, one way of effecting change is to make traditional roles (even when combined with limited employment) too risky. But one could, instead, improve the position of ordinary women by making women's traditional roles less risky, empowering women by making them less dependent on men. Is "our" goal a world in which there is more respect for and reward of those traits, skills, and contributions traditionally associated with women? Or should we try to discourage these traits, skills, and contributions so that women will be more like men? Feminists today are deeply divided on these issues[120] and, were it possible to ask all women for their views, they too would have vastly different responses. Formal equality should be rejected because it takes one particular approach to a number of complicated questions about which women disagree vehemently.

Third, our young people continue to have different expectations about their futures—and different futures—depending on their sex.[121] As long as we continue producing girls and boys with different expectations, it is fundamentally unfair to treat women, once they are grown, as though they were like men in order to foster change. Change could be more effectively and fairly fostered by changing socialization than by making motherhood, child care, and domestic work riskier through implementation of strict formal equality.

Fourth, if—as feminists have suggested—women tend (more than men) to define themselves in terms of others,[122] it may be very unrealistic to think that women will respond to increased insecurity by taking steps in their own individual self-interest despite harms to the interests of those closest to them. Yet increased risks associated with traditional roles will effect an appropriate level of change only if women act in their individual self interest.

Fifth, making traditional roles more costly as a means of effecting change assumes that women will assess correctly the risk associated

---

[120]There is a great deal of controversy even among those who would identify with the word "feminist" about how and why women are different from men, the causes of any differences, and what changes to the current order are desirable. As Jane Flax has pointed out, "Feminist discourse is full of contradictory and irreconcilable conceptions of the nature of our social relations, of men and women and the worth and character of sterotypcially masculine and feminine activities." Flax, Postmodernism and Gender Relations in Feminist Theory, 12 Signs 621, 638 (1987). See also Gerson, Emerging Social Divisions Among Women: Implications for Welfare State Politics, 15 Politics & Society 213 (1986–87); Rosenfelt & Stacey, Second Thoughts on the Second Wave, 13 Feminist Studies 341 (1987).

[121]See, e.g., Marini, Sex Differences in the Determination of Adolescent Aspirations: A Review of Research, 4 Sex Roles 723 (1978); Marini & Greenberger, Sex Differences in Occupational Aspirations and Expectations, 5 Sociology of Work and Occupations 147 (1978); Lyson, Race and Sex Differences in Sex Role Attitudes of Southern College Students, 10 Psychology of Women Q. 421 (1986); Waite, Haggstrom, & Kanouse, Changes in the Employment Activities of New Parents, 50 Am. Soc. Rev. 263 (1985).

[122]See, e.g., Chodorow, The Reproduction of Mothering (1978).

with traditional roles given the probability of divorce. Although some women, especially remarried women, seem to take the risk of another divorce into account in making decisions about wage-work versus full- or part-time homemaking, many women (especially women who have never been divorced) seem irrationally confident that divorce will not happen to them.

For all these reasons, as well as the reasons stated earlier, formal equality should not be regarded as the solution to women's problems and should not be too rigidly applied in challenges to sex-based classifications. To date, we have not developed any workable and satisfactory general alternative to formal equality, any alternative which judges would be willing to use and which would effect significant change. The remaining question is whether we should continue to seek another general standard for equality, or substitute therefore, as a solution to women's problems.

It is not feasible to prove an abstract negative: that we cannot possibly imagine a workable satisfactory general standard of equality (or substitute therefore) to replace formal equality and to be applied by judges. That may, however, be the case. I suspect it is, at least for the foreseeable future. Any standard capable of effecting real change would have to be based on a notion of both the desired end and of the appropriate means. If we do not know what equality means, we cannot know where we are going nor how to get there. How, then, can we give judges a standard of equality that will ensure our arrival? Women are not a homogenous group with widely-shared beliefs on these issues. Instead, women are a large group of very different people with vastly different interests and concerns. I suspect that for the foreseeable future, any abstract standard capable of effecting real change would implement one subgroups's notion of equality with the risk that other subgroups would bear most of the cost.

IV. CURRENT STANDARDS, INSTITUTIONAL CONCERNS, AND CHANGE

A. THE CONSTITUTIONAL STANDARD

Even if we could imagine a satisfactory general standard capable of effecting real change, we should be hesitant about adopting it as a constitutional standard to be enforced by judges, at least for the foreseeable future. Judges are, and are likely to remain for the foreseeable future, mostly older, relatively conservative males. They are powerful members of the established order. One cannot realistically expect them to use a general abstract standard to implement much real change in the relative status of women and men. More importantly, as the experience with formal equality suggests, one must worry that an abstract standard will be implemented in ways that will hurt women. Harmful decisions are then enshrined as part of constitutional law and difficult to change.

A flexible constitutional standard, allowing a fair amount of leeway to legislatures—rather than a rigid one like formal equality— is, of course, dangerous. Under a flexible standard, a legislature may enact legislation which expressly discriminates between women and men in a way detrimental to women, and the Constitution would afford no reliable basis for striking the statute. But formal equality illustrates that using an abstract standard to overrule legislation creating distinctions between women and men is also dangerous. Under such a standard, courts can replace standards distinguishing between women and men with sex-neutral standards which worsen the position of many women (especially ordinary mothers and wives), because women and men are not similarly situated.

The current constitutional standard, although it has gone a ways towards formal equality, is still fairly flexible. I would suggest that it has gone too far already; we should not push for futher movement towards either strict formal equality for sex-based classifications (analogous to the standard for racial classifications) or for any alternative general standard as a constitutional matter.

I do not mean to suggest that feminists should be content with the current constitutional standard. That standard is seriously flawed, and it may be possible to fashion concrete refinements which make it more effective while retaining some flexibility. We should not, however, expect even a refined constitutional standard to solve all, or even many, of women's problems.

For example, MacKinnon suggests one possible refinement to the current constitutional standard. Women might be better off were the current constitutional standard modified so that, instead of permitting express distinctions between women and men based on reasonable differences, express distinctions would be permitted only when they would pass muster under MacKinnon's inequality standard. Judges would decide whether a distinction between women and men was part of the system subordinating women.[123] One could not expect to see any radical restructuring of society with a standard which would only examine express classifications to see if they contribute to the subordination of women. This refinement might, nevertheless, be better than the current standard; it might be less dangerous to entrust the question of whether an express classification contributes to the subordination of women to judges than for judges to continue to uphold express distinctions based on sex whenever supported by a difference perceived as relevant. Thus, for example, were *Johnson* (the affirmative action case) a constitutional challenge to an affirmative action plan designed to increase the number of women in traditionally male jobs, a court could use a refined equal protection standard to uphold it, because such a plan is much more likely to empower women than it is to contribute to their subordination; the alternative to affirmative action is not sex-neutral treatment but invisible discrimination in favor of men.

Other refinements might be possible. For example, it might be possible to expand equal protection coverage of sex discrimination to include other distinctions which are typically part of the systematic subordination of women though not distinctions expressly between the sexes. Thus, for example, a court could recognize pregnant-nonpregnant as a classification as suspect as male-female, since distinctions based on pregnancy have traditionally been used to subordinate women. A statute like that in *Guerra* (requiring disability leaves for only pregnant persons) could then be challenged under the Equal Protection Clause of the Fourteenth Amendment.

Such a statute should, under the refinement suggested above, pass constitutional muster. The statute would be permissible because not part of the systematic subordination of women. Granted, the statute reinforces stereotypical notions connecting mothers, more than fathers, with small infants. And equality may be difficult,

---

[123]Granted, it is not always easy to distinguish benefits (empowerment) from burdens (disempowerment), and women may be hurt if burdens are judged benefits. In addition, as has been noted repeatedly here, often a policy helps some women and hurts others. On the other hand, as the affirmative action cases illustrate well, it is not always impossible to judge that it is likely that a certain policy benefits more women than it hurts. This standard might work out to be much like that proposed by Suzanna Sherry in Selective Judicial Activism in the Equal Protection Context: Democracy, Distrust, and Deconstruction, 73 Georgetown L. J. 89 (1984) (only disfavored classes should be able to bring equal protection challenges).

perhaps impossible, to achieve as long as only women are the primary caretakers of young infants.[124] The stereotype that mothers care for infants remains, nevertheless, overwhelmingly accurate. Ideally, a statute would provide for temporary leave for any new mother or father. But we do not live in an ideal world. We must choose, for the time being in California at least, between letting employers deny all employees short-term disability leaves and requiring that employers give workers disabled by pregnancy up to four months disability leave. Women—who are, after all, the only parents temporarily out of commission because of the onset of parenthood and who are primarily responsible for the care and feeding of newborns in the vast majority of relationships[125]—are less dependent on men under the California statute than they would be under employer policies such as those of Cal Fed. A major part of the systematic subordination of women has consisted of giving them few options other than relying on men for financial security after having children. This statute empowers women by facilitating the combination of motherhood and wage work.

I would not, however, expect even an improved Fourteenth Amendment standard to offer a remedy whenever women are, in fact, subordinated by a rule, policy, or practice.

B. THE TITLE VII STANDARD: *JOHNSON* AND *GUERRA*

Title VII should also be interpreted as a fairly flexible standard, allowing for some distinctions on the basis of sex in at least some instances, as in both *Johnson* and *Guerra*.

In *Johnson*, the question was whether an employer's voluntary affirmative action plan—which took sex into account in promoting Joyce to a position previously held only by men—was a form of sex discrimination barred by Title VII.[126] Had the Court never

---

[124]Several feminists have suggested that as long as women are the primary caretakers of young children, we will have difficulty relating to women as individuals. See, *e.g.*, Chodorow, The Reproduction of Mothering (1978); Dinnerstein, The Mermaid and the Minotaur (1976).

[125]See, *e.g.*, Gilbert, Men in Dual Career Couples: The Current Realities and Future Prospects 60–90 (1985); Pleck, Men's Family Work: Three Perspectives and Some New Data, 28 Family Coordinator 481 (1979), reprinted in Work and Family (Voydandor ed. 1984).

[126]Although the defendant was a public employer, Johnson did not use the Fourteenth Amendment to challenge the affirmative action plan. Perhaps he did not use equal protection because, in the context of sex, an equal protection challenge might have been even weaker

decided an affirmative action case, this would have been a difficult question of statutory construction.[127] Justice Brennan was, however, able to rely on *Steelworkers v. Weber*[128] in writing the opinion of the Court upholding Joyce's promotion as a permissible form of affirmative action.

Justice Brennan began by specifying the three *Weber* criteria for a permissible voluntary affirmative action plan. The plan must (i) remedy a " 'manifest imbalance' that reflect[s] underrepresentation of women in 'traditionally segregated job categories' ";[129] (ii) not trammel "the rights of male employees or create[] an absolute bar to their advancement";[130] and (iii) be "intended to *attain* a balanced work force, not to maintain one."[131] Justice Brennan found the first requirement satisfied because women were underrepresented at the Agency in those areas in which " 'women have not been traditionally employed in significant numbers.' "[132] Specifically, he noted that none of the 238 skilled craft positions was held by a woman and that " '[a] plethora of proof is hardly necessary to show that women are generally underrepresented in such positions and that strong social pressures weigh against their participation."[133] (In *Weber*, in contrast, five out of 273 skilled craft positions had been held by Blacks at Kaiser's Gramercy plant prior to the affirmative action plan.[134]) Both Blacks and women have traditionally been excluded from skilled crafts. At the end of the World War II, for example,

---

than the Title VII challenge. *Cf.* Kahn v. Shevin, 416 U.S. 351 (1974) (upholding Florida statute giving property tax preference to widows but not to widowers). Because he did not challenge the Agency's affirmative action plan on equal protection grounds, the Court did not reach the equal protection standard for permissible affirmative action. See 107 S.Ct. at 1449–50 n.6. That standard might, of course, be different for sex and race.

[127]See Meltzer, The *Weber* Case: The Judicial Abrogation of the Antidiscrimination Standard in Employment, 47 U. Chi. L. Rev. 423 (1980).

[128]443 U.S. 193 (1979).

[129]107 S.Ct. at 1452, quoting *Weber*, 443 U.S. at 4383.

[130]*Id.* at 1455.

[131]*Id.* at 1456.

[132]*Id.* at 1453.

[133]*Id.* at 1453 & n.12. Justice Scalia would have interpreted *Weber* as allowing affirmative action only as a remedy for an employer's own past discrimination. See *id.* at 1467. He relied heavily on the district court's finding that the Agency had not discriminated on the basis of sex.

[134]443 U.S. at 198.

many women were fired from traditionally male—and often skilled—jobs to make room for returning soldiers.

Secondly, Justice Brennan found that the plan did not trammel on the rights of male employees because it did not close any employment opportunities categorically to men and because it set only rather modest goals once fully implemented. True, the initial plan created, as a long-term goal, a workforce in which major job classifications mirrored the available work force. But the plan required the formulation of annual short-term goals in light of a number of factors, such as the number of openings during the coming year and the percentage of women and minorities in the local workforce qualified for the position. At the time Joyce was promoted over Johnson in 1980, no annual goal had been established for skilled craft positions. But, as Justice Brennan noted, the Agency's Plan emphasized "that the long-term goals were not to be taken as guides for actual hiring decisions."[135] Instead, "supervisors were to consider a host of practical factors in seeking to meet affirmative action objectives, including the fact that in some job categories women were not qualified in numbers comparable to their representation in the labor force."[136] Graebner, the person who made the decision to promote Joyce over Johnson, testified: "I tried to look at the whole picture, the combination of her qualifications and Mr. Johnson's qualifications, their test scores, their expertise, their background, affirmative action matters, things like that . . . . I believe it was a combination of all those."[137]

Justice Brennan also noted, though in the margin, that the plan had not, in fact, trammelled the rights of male employees. Of the 111 new skilled craft positions filled at the Agency between 1978 and 1982, "105, or almost 95%, went to men."[138] Indeed, when the Agency first set a numerical goal for hiring women into skilled crafts (for the year 1982) that goal was a modest 5.4% of new hires (three out of 55).[139] Certainly the effort to bring women into skilled

---

[135] 107 S.Ct. at 1454.

[136] *Ibid.*

[137] Quoted at 107 S.Ct. at 1448. In his dissent, Justice Scalia stresses that Johnson would have received the promotion rather than Joyce but for the affirmative action plan. Sex was therefore the determinative factor in this case. *Id.* at 1468. It is true, of course, that under any affirmative action plan having any effect, some decisions will come out differently because of sex or race.

[138] 107 S.Ct. at 1456.

[139] *Ibid.*

crafts in *Johnson* was much more restrained than the effort at issue in *Weber,* where the employer established a skilled-craft training program and filled half the trainee positions with Blacks.

Finally, Justice Brennan discussed whether the Agency's plan was intended to attain a balanced workforce or to maintain one. The plan did not have any explicit termination date; it could have been better drafted. Justice Brennan refused to invalidate the plan for this reason, however, concluding that the absence of an explicit end date was understandable given the Agency's flexible approach which, as the evidence just cited suggests (given its modest goals), was not expected to yield immediate success. Given the glacial "speed" of the plan—under which only three women were, for example, to be among the fifty-five skilled workers hired in 1982— the failure to specify an end date was irrelevant to anything that might happen during this century and entirely understandable.

Although *Johnson* was a fairly straightforward application of *Weber,* it was the first time that the Supreme Court actually upheld an affirmative action plan in the context of sex. As discussed earlier, however, there is little reason to distinguish between *Johnson* and *Weber* in terms of the need for "affirmative" action if women (like Blacks) are ever to enjoy equal employment opportunity. Women, like Blacks, have traditionally been excluded from the skilled crafts and are likely to be significantly underrepresented in the foreseeable future even with affirmative action.[140]

Guerra does not represent quite as straightforward an application of *Weber.* The California statute gave pregnant workers a permanent preference. The Court nevertheless upheld the California statute on a *Weber*-like rationale. Justice Marshall, speaking for the Court, reasoned that Congress, in requiring that employers treat pregnant workers like other workers similar in their ability to do the job, intended to create a floor below which treatment of pregnant workers could not drop, but that Congress did not intend to create a ceiling above which beneficial treatment could not rise.[141] The Cal-

---

[140]It is often suggested that women do not want traditionally male skilled-craft jobs. The evidence suggests, however, that women are interested in such jobs if they think that such jobs are actually open to them. See, *e.g.*, Walshok, Blue Collar Women (1981).

[141]The ACLU Women's Project had argued that the California statute, like protectionist legislation in an earlier era, would "reinforce[ ] stereotypical attitudes [towards pregnancy and women's biological nature] which threaten women's employment status in subtle but significant ways." Brief of ACLU Women's Project, *et al.*, at 18 and generally at 11–23. Justice Marshall, speaking for the Court, rejected this argument, noting that "unlike pro-

ifornia statute was therefore permissible because it "promotes equal employment opportunity" which was, after all, Congress' purpose in enacting Title VII.[142]

Although the preference permitted for pregnant workers in *Guerra* is permanent, this extension of *Weber*'s rationale[143] is easily justified in the context of sex. *Weber* allows, in order to achieve equality, some preference as long as a minority group is substantially underrepresented in a position from which it has traditionally been excluded. In general, once a minority group successfully integrates a traditionally closed position, it should (we hope) be possible for members of the minority group to continue to enjoy access for a number of reasons.[144] Women face an additional problem, however. It is not just that some jobs have been formally or informally closed to women. Another access problem (inter alia) is that rules and practices have been structured with the expectation that workers would not be new mothers. This problem is not solved simply by hiring women in appropriate numbers. It can only be solved by changing workplace policies and practices so that it is easier for women to combine wage work and reproduction. *Weber* should, therefore, be extended to allow statutes which guarantee pregnant workers their jobs during pregnancy-related disability.

Guerra and *Johnson* suggest two ways in which Title VII's apparently absolute ban on sex discrimination should be construed so as to permit some distinctions based on sex. Perhaps, in the

---

tective labor legislation prevalent earlier in this century, [the California statute] does not reflect archaic or stereotypical notions about pregnancy and the abilities of pregnant workers" because it covers only the "period of *actual physical disability.*" 107 S.Ct. at 694.

[142]*Ibid.* As an alternative ground for decision, Justice Marshall noted that even if Title VII banned leave policies giving preferential treatment to pregnant workers, California employers could obey both Title VII and the California statute by offering leaves to all workers disabled for up to four months.

[143]This is not to suggest that *Guerra* should be labelled an "affirmative action" case. As discussed earlier, "affirmative" action is misleading. In his opinion, Justice Marshall did not to refer to the California statute as a form of affirmative action. Instead, he stressed that the effect of the California policy was to equalize the situation of working women and men since, "by 'taking pregnancy into account,' California's pregnancy disability leave statute allows women, as well as men, to have families without losing their jobs." 107 S.Ct. at 694. *Cf. id.* at 696 ("preferential treatment") (per Stevens, J.).

[144]For example, those hiring will no longer have unconscious expectations that members of the excluded minority group are uninterested in the position or not competent to hold it. In addition, the "old boy" hiring network should be operating to bring in members of the minority group once they are represented in the job in sufficient numbers.

future, additional refinements will also be suggested for Title VII, refinements which will make it a more effective means to achieving equality between the sexes. *Johnson* and *Guerra* might not be sufficient to promote real equality.

Certainly, as of today, the statute—despite the flexibility afforded by *Guerra* and *Johnson*—is inadequate as the solution to women's problems in achieving equality in the wage-labor market. It does not afford any way to challenge much of what needs to be challenged. For example, the statute (like the Constitution) does not provide a means for women to challenge the use of employment requirements and standards which are well adapted to male life-styles and poorly adapted to female life-styles. Nor does it provide a means of challenging the undervaluation of jobs traditionally performed by women.[145]

C. CHANGE THROUGH THE POLITICAL PROCESS

Since it is unlikely that we will be able to imagine one abstract standard capable of providing an effective means for resolving all such problems, much change in the legal system must occur (if it is to occur at all) as a result of legislative change, often piecemeal legislative change. This "solution" will not, however, be easy.

A responsive political process would seem an ideal forum for resolving women's conflicting visions of equality and how to get there. There are other advantages to legislative forums. One can make all kinds of arguments. Effective arguments need not be traditional arguments. Disparate impact arguments can be effective in this setting and need a label no more esoteric than the simple word "fairness." A legislature can choose which of many policies to modify to effect a desired change. Unlike a court, a legislature can choose the appropriate "defendant." Specific legislative reform—such as changing the social security system so that homemakers receive credits in their own accounts for their contributions (based, perhaps, on their husbands' wages)—is often the only way to effect needed changes. Only a legislature will do the kind of detailed tinkering necessary to implement many of the changes needed if the legal system is to be as responsive to women's needs as it is to

---

[145]See, *e.g.*, Becker, Barriers Facing Women in the Wage-Labor Market and the Need for Additional Remedies: A Reply to Fischel & Lazear, 53 U. Chi. L. Rev. 934, 942–43 (1986).

men's. Many needed changes simply cannot and will not be ordered by a court pursuant to an abstract standard of equality. A final advantage of the legislative forum is that legislatures can experiment with various approaches more easily than courts. It may not always be apparent whether a certain change would be desirable or not. Or a change, desirable at one time, may become obsolete or undesirable at another. It is easier for legislatures than for courts to take different approaches at different times.

Unfortunately, it is not going to be easy to change the status of women through the legislative process, for two major reasons. The first is that the political process itself is not responsive to women, in part because women are not a homogenous group. A number of factors make it difficult for women to operate as a cohesive political force: women are geographically dispersed; women are members of different classes; women identify with male interests because of relationships that are often only temporary; women are still raised to consider the home (rather than the public arena) their special sphere of interest; women still do not enter politics in proportion to their numbers in the population; women tend (more than men) to define themselves in terms of the interests of others (their husbands and children), and may therefore be less likely than other groups to push for their own interests in the legislative arena; women tend to have less time and money (than men) to spend lobbying; legislatures are still predominantly male enclaves and not, one imagines, much easier for individual women to break into, or to effect change within, than the all-male road maintenance gang on which Joyce worked. In addition, many issues of special concern to women are state-law issues, and many state legislatures are very conservative, even hostile, to "women's lib," a label likely to taint any change designed to equalize the status of women and men.

The second major problem is that even when women succeed in effecting legislative change, the new laws will be more or less general and will typically require judicial implementation. Judges may fail fully to implement the desired change. To some extent, this problem can be avoided by careful drafting and detailed legislative history. But, to be effective, the groups interested in change must continue to monitor the situation after the desired legislation is enacted and, when necessary, begin another round of lobbying for additional legislative reform.

Legislative change, especially piecemeal legislative change, is not a miraculous solution. If, however, for the foreseeable future, it is the only solution to many of women's problems with the current legal structure, surely it is better to face squarely that fact and attempt to implement piecemeal legislative change than to continue to strive to implement some vague and abstract standard of equality which will effect too little good and too much harm.

V. CONCLUSION

To date, we have not discovered any abstract standard of equality (or substitute therefore) with the potential for real change. Formal equality (with and without limited exceptions when there are biological differences)—the leading contender as the general standard—can effect only limited change. It cannot, for example, ensure that jobs are structured so that female workers and male workers are equally able to combine wage work and parenthood. Nor can it ensure that social security, unemployment compensation, and other safety nets are structured so as to provide for women's financial security as well as they provide for men's. Moreover, women, especially ordinary mothers and wives, have been harmed by the changes effected to date by the movement towards formal equality. Further movement in that direction could bring additional harm. Any other satisfactory and workable general standard to be applied by judges is as yet unimagined and likely to be so for the foreseeable future.

Women do not share a single vision of equality or one view of how to get there from here. Women are not a homogenous group with homogenous values, concerns, and interests. Were the legislative process more responsive to women, it would be a good forum for women to resolve their conflicting interests and visions of equality. Unfortunately, it is unresponsive, and certainly far from ideal. Nevertheless, piecemeal legislative change, especially in the area of economic rights, is likely to be more effective in improving the lives of many women than is the development of any abstract standard of equality.

LARRY KRAMER
ALAN O. SYKES

MUNICIPAL LIABILITY
UNDER §1983: A LEGAL AND
ECONOMIC ANALYSIS

Corporations are a legal fiction representing a network of legal, usually contractual, arrangements. "Corporations" thus do not act, do not make contracts, sell property, or commit torts; their agents do. For convenience, we sometimes describe the acts of such agents as acts of the corporation. But if an agent commits a tort and the tort is said to have been committed by the corporation (meaning that damages will be paid out of the corporate treasury), the corporation's liability is necessarily vicarious.

Vicarious liability may be imposed on any number of theories. At common law, corporate vicarious liability typically rests on the doctrine of *respondeat superior*, which holds principals liable for torts committed by their agents within the scope of employment.[1] In *Monell v. Department of Social Services*,[2] the Supreme Court held that the doctrine of *respondeat superior* is inapplicable to municipal corporations in suits brought under 42 U.S.C. §1983. "Instead," the

Larry Kramer and Alan O. Sykes are Assistant Professors of Law, The University of Chicago.

AUTHORS NOTE: We are grateful to Albert Alschuler, Walter Blum, Richard Craswell, David Currie, Daniel Fischel, Fred McChesney, Geoffrey Miller, Richard Posner, Geoffrey Stone, David Strauss, and Cass Sunstein for their helpful comments. Special thanks are due to Stephanie Dest for her indefagitable research assistance. Financial assistance for this paper was provided by the Lynde and Harry Bradley Foundation and by the Olin Foundation.

[1] See Keeton, Dobbs, Keeton & Owen, Prosser and Keeton on the Law of Torts 501-08 (5th ed. 1984).

[2] 436 U.S. 658 (1978).

Court explained in a much quoted passage, "it is when execution of a government's policy . . . , whether made by its lawmakers or by those whose edicts or acts may fairly be said to represent official policy, inflicts the injury that the government as an entity is responsible under §1983."[3]

Like the "scope of employment rule" or the "independent contractor rule" at common-law, the "policy rule" of *Monell* limits the circumstances in which a municipal employer may be held liable for tortious acts committed by agents or employees. Unfortunately, the Court in *Monell* did not define the concept of policy: elaboration of the policy rule was left to future litigation.[4] The result has been confusion about the limits of municipal liability under §1983. The factual patterns in which issues of §1983 municipal liability arise are extremely diverse, involving everything from employment decisions to licensing decisions to police misconduct. Even a small sampling of the numerous lower court decisions applying *Monell* reveals the absence of any clear understanding of what policy is or means.[5] Recent Supreme Court decisions have only added to the confusion. In each of the last three Terms, the Court agreed to hear cases for the purpose of elaborating the policy requirement, but was unable to put together a majority in any.[6]

That such uncertainty remains and indeed is growing suggests that a reexamination of the policy rule is in order. The policy rule has been extremely difficult to apply coherently, and there is no reason to continue the exercise. The *Monell* Court read the language and legislative history of §1983 erroneously. Rather than define the precise limits of liability, Congress intended to create a federal common-law tort remedy for deprivations under color of state law of federally protected rights. That conclusion raises the question how the federal courts should exercise their common-law power in determining the scope of municipal liability. We contend that this

---

[3] *Id.* at 694.

[4] *Id.* at 695.

[5] See, *e.g.*, Spell v. McDaniel, 824 F.2d 1380 (4th Cir. 1987); Nahmod, Civil Rights and Civil Liberties Litigation: The Law of Section 1983 ch. 6 (2d ed. 1986).

[6] The cases are City of Oklahoma City v. Tuttle, 471 U.S. 808 (1985); Pembaur v. City of Cincinnati, 475 U.S. 469 (1986); and City of Springfield v. Kibbe, 107 S.Ct. 1114 (1987). The Court recently heard argument in City of St. Louis v. Praprotnik, No. 86-772, which raises a question suggested by *Pembaur:* whether a municipality is liable under §1983 for unconstitutional actions taken by non-policymaking municipal employees acting within the scope of delegated authority when these actions are not subject to further *de novo* review.

question cannot be answered without due regard for the economic consequences of municipal liability, and that economic analysis may be dispositive. We conclude that *Monell's* policy rule—which has the effect of immunizing the municipality where there is no policy and making it strictly liable where there is policy—is economically inefficient.[7] We suggest the adoption of a negligence rule for the imposition of municipal liability, requiring the plaintiff to show that the municipality (*i.e.*, municipal officials who supervise the tortfeasor) failed to take reasonable (*i.e.*, cost-effective) measures to avert the tort, or, alternatively, the adoption of conventional *respondeat superior*. With respect to cases in which the individual tortfeasor enjoys immunity, we tentatively conclude that immunity ought also to extend to the municipality.

I. A Reexamination of Municipal Liability Under Monell

A. THE POLICY RULE

The Court's post-*Monell* efforts have produced two competing views of what constitutes "policy" for purposes of municipal liability under §1983, neither of which has been accepted by a majority of the justices.

One view, developed in Part IIB of Justice Brennan's opinion in *Pembaur v. City of Cincinnati*[8] (a part joined only by a plurality[9]), focuses on the status of the decisionmaker. This view conceptualizes "policy" as encompassing decisions that are made by persons designated to speak the last word for the municipality. A second view, implicit in Justice Rehnquist's plurality opinion in *City of Oklahoma City v. Tuttle*[10] and elaborated in Justice Powell's dissent in *Pembaur,*

---

[7]This paper uses the term "efficiency" in the Hicks-Kaldor sense: liability rule A is more efficient that liability rule B if the members of society who prefer A to B can compensate the members of society who prefer B to A and remain better off themselves, whether or not such compensation is actually paid. This notion of efficiency underlies applied "cost/benefit" analysis as it is generally practiced and is the concept of efficiency typically employed in economic analyses of tort law. See generally Landes & Posner, The Economic Structure of Tort Law (1987).

[8]475 U.S. 469 (1986).

[9]In *Pembaur,* Justice Brennan delivered an opinion for six justices in Parts I and IIA, for four justices in Part IIB, and for five justices in Part IIC. Justices White, Stevens, and O'Connor each wrote separate opinions disagreeing with particular aspects of Justice Brennan's analysis. Justice Powell dissented, joined by Chief Justice Burger and Justice Rehnquist.

[10]471 U.S. 808 (1985).

emphasizes the nature of the decision and the process by which it is made. This view limits "policy" to formal rules, usually of general applicability, established through careful deliberation.

Pembaur highlights the difference between these views. In that case, county police officers sought entry to plaintiff's medical clinic to execute a capias (a form of arrest warrant) for two witnesses thought to be at the clinic. When plaintiff refused to allow them to enter, the officers contacted their supervisor, who advised them to call the prosecutor for instructions. The prosecutor commanded them to " 'go in and get [the witnesses],' " a command subsequently held to violate the Fourth Amendment. The liability of the county turned on whether this order constituted "policy" under *Monell*. The evidence showed that county police had never before used force to gain access to a third-person's property while serving a capias, that the police handled such matters on a case-by-case basis, and that the practice of the county police department was to refer such matters to the county prosecutor and follow his instructions.[11]

Justice Brennan concluded that the prosecutor's order constituted policy under *Monell*. He understood the policy rule as intended "to distinguish acts of the *municipality* from acts of *employees* of the municipality, and thereby [to] make clear that municipal liability is limited to action for which the municipality is actually responsible."[12] Decisions by some municipal employees are acts "of the municipality" while other decisions are merely acts "of employees of the municipality." Liability depends entirely on who makes a decision: "where the decisionmaker possesses final authority to establish policy with respect to the action ordered," the decision can fairly be said to represent a decision of the municipality itself and the imposition of liability is not vicarious.[13]

Justice Powell argued in dissent that the plurality's view constituted nothing less than a partial overruling of *Monell*. By focusing exclusively on the status of the decisionmaker, "local government

---

[11]475 U.S. at ____, 106 S.Ct. at 1294–96.

[12]*Id.* at ____, 106 S.Ct. at 1298.

[13]*Id.* at ____, 106 S.Ct. at 1298–1300. Justice Brennan did not explain how it is possible to determine who is a policymaker without first determining what makes something "policy," although he did distinguish between policymaking power and discretion (apparently including discretion to make unreviewed decisions). *Id.* at ____, 106 S.Ct. at 1299–1300. The Court may clarify the distinction in City of St. Louis v. Praprotnick, No. 86-772.

units are now subject to *respondeat superior*, at least with respect to a certain class of employees, *i.e.*, those with final authority to make policy."[14] Justice Powell argued that the Court should focus on the characteristics of the decision at issue. Thus, for Justice Powell, "policy" is established "when a rule is formed that applies to all similar situations—a 'governing principle [or] plan.' . . . When a rule of general applicability has been approved, the government has taken a position for which it can be held responsible."[15] In rare instances, a rule not of general applicability may constitute municipal policy according to Justice Powell, but only if that rule was formulated through a properly deliberative process.[16] Because the prosecutor's order was directed to the specific case only and was "an off-the-cuff answer to a single question," it did not constitute policy for purposes of §1983.[17]

Both the plurality and the dissent in *Pembaur* read *Monell* as holding that municipalities cannot be vicariously liable under §1983, and both reason that municipal liability is direct rather than vicarious only when a tort is committed pursuant to policy. The argument in *Pembaur* thus turns on whether a particular definition of policy successfully limits municipal liability to situations where the municipality is directly responsible for the tort or whether it has the effect of imposing liability vicariously.

Justice Powell is surely correct when he characterizes Justice Brennan's approach as imposing a form of vicarious liability: the municipality must pay for the wrongful acts of certain of its employees. But exactly the same thing can be said of Justice Powell's approach. The only difference between the two formulations is that Justice Powell would impose vicarious liability only if the employee whose acts are to be attributed to the municipality expressed himself in general terms or chose his course of action carefully.

The problem is that municipal action is always—can only be—carried out by persons employed by the municipality. Municipal liability is necessarily vicarious, and there is no such thing as "policy" that can make a municipality directly rather than vicariously responsible for a constitutional tort. "Policy" is merely a conclusion

---

[14]475 U.S. at ____, 106 S.Ct. at 1308.

[15]*Id*. at ____, 106 S.Ct. at 1309.

[16]*Id*. at ____, 106 S.Ct. at 1309.

[17]*Id*. at ____, 106 S.Ct. at 1310.

about which activities by which municipal employees should be vicariously attributed to the municipality for purposes of §1983. It is therefore senseless to try and define policy as the Court has done, as something that distinguishes acts "of the municipality" from acts of "employees of the municipality."

But *Monell* did not hold that all forms of vicarious municipal liability are improper. *Monell* held only that "a municipality cannot be held liable *solely* because it employs a tortfeasor—or, in other words, a municipality cannot be held liable under §1983 on a *respondeat superior* theory."[18] Thus, the proper question is not whether we can define policy in such a way as to prevent imposing vicarious liability, but whether we can define policy in such a way as to prevent imposing a particular form of vicarious liability—*respondeat superior.*

This refinement does little to solve the problem of defining "policy." There are several semantically plausible definitions of policy.[19] The problem is to choose which of these definitions best serves the purpose underlying the "policy" concept as it is used in the context of §1983 municipal liability. But *Monell* tells us only that municipal liability must rest on more than *respondeat superior,* and all of the competing definitions of policy satisfy this requirement. For example, Justice Brennan's approach in *Pembaur* is more than *respondeat superior,* because the municipality is not liable for acts by every municipal employee; it is *respondeat superior* "plus," with the plus factor being the limitation to those employees who make policy. Similarly, Justice Powell's approach limits the scope of *respondeat superior* to a particular kind of act by policymaking employees. Indeed, every definition of policy that in any way limits the ordinary scope of *respondeat superior* will satisfy *Monell* by not imposing liability "*solely* because [the municipality] employs a tortfeasor."[20] It is, therefore, not surprising that courts have had difficulty implementing *Monell's* policy rule. By limiting municipal liability to acts pursuant to "policy" without saying anything more than policy is something different from *respondeat superior,* the Supreme Court

---

[18]436 U.S. at 691; see also *id.* at 692 & n.57.

[19]Consider, for example, the different dictionary definitions cited and relied upon by the Justices. *Compare Pembaur,* 475 U.S. at ___, 106 S.Ct. at 1299, n.9 (opinion of Brennan, J.) *with id.* at ___, 106 S.Ct. at 1309 (Powell, J., dissenting) and City of Oklahoma City v. Tuttle, 471 U.S. 808, 823 n.6.

[20]436 U.S. at 691.

established a vague category susceptible to many plausible definitions.

Should the policy rule therefore be abandoned? The Court in *Monell* deliberately chose not to elaborate the meaning of policy, and it may be that the reasoning which led the Court to reject *respondeat superior* suggests ways of refining the policy rule. Reexamining *Monell*, however, demonstrates only that the Court's reasons for rejecting the use of *respondeat superior* under §1983 were mistaken.

B. MONELL

Monell offered two propositions to support its conclusion that Congress did not intend municipalities to be liable under §1983 unless a tort resulted from action pursuant to municipal policy. First, the Court suggested that this limitation was implicit in the language of §1983. Second, it contended that the application of *respondeat superior* to municipalities would be inconsistent with §1983's legislative history.

1. *Monell's Analysis of the language of §1983*. Section 1983 holds liable "[e]very person who, under color of [state law] subjects, or causes to be subjected" any person to the deprivation of a federally protected right.[21] *Monell* overruled the holding of *Monroe v. Pape* that municipal corporations are not "persons" within the meaning of this language.[22] At the same time, the Court found significance in the phrase "subjects or causes to be subjected." According to the Court, "that language cannot be easily read to impose liability vicariously on governing bodies solely on the basis of the existence of an employer-employee relationship with a tortfeasor. Indeed, the fact that Congress did specifically provide that A's tort became B's liability if B 'caused' A to subject another to a tort suggests that Congress did not intend §1983 liability to attach where such causation was absent."[23]

---

[21]In its entirety, §1983 provides: "Every person who, under color of any statute, ordinance, regulation, custom, or usage, of any State or Territory, subjects, or causes to be subjected, any citizen of the United States or other person within the jurisdiction thereof to the deprivation of any rights, privileges, or immunities secured by the Constitution and laws, shall be liable to the party injured in an action at law, suit in equity, or other proper proceeding for redress." 42 U.S.C. §1983 (1982).

[22]See *Monell*, 436 U.S. at 664–89; Monroe v. Pape, 365 U.S. 167, 187–92 (1961).

[23]436 U.S. at 692.

The Court does not explain why the municipality "causes" the constitutional tort only if the tort is committed pursuant to official policy. The practical effect of the policy rule is to limit vicarious liability to cases in which high-level municipal employees participate in the tort. But even if there is reason to treat the acts of high-level employees differently from the acts of lower-level employees, that reason has nothing to do with causation and thus nothing to do with the language upon which the Court focused. The municipality has not "caused" the tort more in one situation than in the other.

More importantly, the Court was wrong to suppose that the language of §1983 conveys such subtle limitations on liability. That language, which was proposed and debated as §1 of the Civil Rights Act of 1871, was borrowed from §2 of the Civil Rights Act of 1866.[24] The wording was given little thought or attention by its drafters, who were primarily concerned with the more controversial provisions of sections two through four.[25] For similar reasons, §1 was largely ignored during the bitter and extensive floor debate concerning the 1871 Civil Rights Act.[26] Supporters said only that §1 was to be "liberally and beneficently construed" by the courts.[27] The only opponent of the Act to address §1 in any detail was Senator Thurman, and his chief complaint was that its language was vague and raised more questions than it answered.[28]

The reason so little attention was paid to the wording of §1 is suggested by a colloquy between Senators Thurman and Edmunds about another provision of the Act at a later point in the debate: Edmunds (who sponsored the 1871 Act) responded to Thurman's charge that the Act omitted certain essential safeguards by stating that these need not be included by Congress since they were already

---

[24]Adickes v. S.H. Kress & Co., 398 U.S. 144, 162–63 (1970); Cong. Globe, 42d Cong., 1st Sess. app. at 68 (1871) [hereinafter Globe] (statement of Rep. Shellabarger); Nahmod, note 7 *supra*, at §1.03.

[25]For the history of the Civil Rights Act of 1871, see Fairman, VII History of the Supreme Court of the United States ch. 3 (1987); Comment, 46 U. Chi. L. Rev. 402, 407–17 (1979); see generally Globe, note 24 *supra*.

[26]See Globe, note 24 *supra*, *passim*; *Monell*, 436 U.S. at 665.

[27]Globe, note 24 *supra*, app. at 68 (statement of Rep. Shellabarger); see also *id.* at 800 (statement of Rep. Perry). Similar statements are collected and cited in *Monell*, 436 U.S. at 684–85 & n.45.

[28]Globe, note 24 *supra*, app. at 216–17.

provided by the common law.[29] In other words, the language of §1983 was not intended to define fully the extent of liability, which would be determined by the courts through common-law adjudication.[30]

2. *Monell's analysis of §1983's legislative history.* The holding in *Monell* does not rest solely on the Court's textual argument. Indeed, the Court relied "[p]rimarily"[31] on a second proposition: that the limitation of municipal liability to action pursuant to official policy is mandated by the legislative history of the Civil Rights Act of 1871, in particular, the debate over the so-called "Sherman amendment."

The history of the Sherman amendment, which was twice modified by conference committees before being passed, is recounted in great detail in *Monell*.[32] The relevant portion of that history is the House debate in which the first conference report was rejected.[33]

---

[29]See Globe, note 24 *supra*, at 771. Senator Thurman responded that common-law doctrines should not be read into a statute. *Ibid.* See also the colloquy between Senators Sherman, Edmunds, Thurman, and Frelinghuysen in which Senator Sherman explains that an amendment to his proposed amendment is unnecessary because the common-law already contains such a provision. *Id.* at 707.

[30]In addressing other questions under §1983, the Court has recognized that the statute should be "read against the background of tort liability." Monroe v. Pape, 365 U.S. 167, 187 (1961). *Accord* Carey v. Piphus, 435 U.S. 247, 258 n.13 (1978); Imbler v. Pachtman, 424 U.S. 409, 418 (1976). See also Nahmod, Section 1983 and the "Background" of Tort Liability, 50 Ind. L. J. 5 (1974); Comment, 46 U. Chi. L. Rev. 935, 939 (1979); Comment, 37 U. Chi. L. Rev. 494, 507–08 (1970).

[31]See *Pembaur*, 106 S.Ct. 1292, 1298 (1986).

[32]See *Monell*, 436 U.S. at 665–83.

[33]Globe, note 24 *supra*, at 755; see also *Monell*, 436 U.S. at 703–04. The bill which became the Civil Rights Act of 1871 was proposed as H.R. 320 by Representative Shellabarger on March 28, 1871. Globe, note 24 *supra*, at 317. Senator Sherman introduced his amendment immediately prior to the vote in the Senate. *Id.* at 663, 686. As proposed, the Sherman amendment would have added a provision to the Act making any inhabitant of a municipality liable for damage inflicted within municipal boundaries by any persons "riotously and tumultuously assembled" for the purpose of depriving the victim of federally protected rights. *Id.* at 663. Under the Senate's rules, no discussion of the amendment was allowed and it passed without debate. *Id.* at 704–09.

The House refused—also without debate—to acquiesce in the Sherman amendment by a vote of 45–132 and requested a conference on this and several other amendments made by the Senate to H.R. 320. *Id.* at 725. Despite the overwhelming rejection of the Sherman amendment by the House, the Senate voted not to recede and agreed to confer. *Id.* at 727–28. The conferees submitted an alternative version of the Sherman amendment to the Senate the very next day. The debate over this proposal, which modified the original proposal to give the victim an action against the municipality itself, was thus the first open debate in Congress on the merits of the Sherman amendment.

This report proposed adding to the 1871 Act a section that would provide victims of injuries inflicted by "any persons riotously and tumultuously assembled together" an action for damages against the municipality in which the injuries were inflicted. The municipality, in turn, was given an action for indemnity against the wrongdoers.

As explained in *Monell*, the Representatives who voted against this proposal—in particular, the moderate Republicans who held the balance of power in the House[34]—did so because they thought that it was unconstitutional.[35] Congress sought in the 1871 Act to stop groups such as the Ku Klux Klan from using violence to prevent individuals from exercising their constitutional rights. The Sherman amendment went beyond the Act's provisions for federal intervention and sought by imposing liability to compel municipalities to assist the federal government in this effort. Opponents of the Sherman amendment contended that, while Congress could create federal mechanisms for enforcing constitutional rights, it could not obligate state and local governments to allocate their resources to the task.[36]

This understanding of the limits of federal power was consistent with then-existing Supreme Court precedents such as *Collector v. Day*[37] and *Prigg v. Pennsylvania*.[38] In fact, the moderate Republicans

---

The Senate agreed to the conference report by a vote of 32–16, essentially identical to the 38–24 vote that had approved Senator Sherman's initial proposal. *Id.* at 707, 779. The House again voted the amendment down, this time by the somewhat closer margin of 74–106. *Id.* at 800. A second conference was held and the amendment was drastically altered: the second conference version did not mention municipalities; it imposed liability on individuals who knew that a wrong was to be committed and had power to prevent it but failed to act. *Id.* at 801, 802, 819–20. This version easily passed both Houses of Congress. *Id.* at 804, 808, 831. It is currently codified as 42 U.S.C. §1986.

[34]See Comment, note 24 *supra*, 46 U. Chi. L. Rev., at 414–20.

[35]*Monell*, 436 U.S. at 669–83.

[36]Globe, note 24 *supra*, at 795 (statement of Rep. Blair). This position was espoused by all of the Republicans who spoke against the Sherman amendment. See *id.* at 791 (statement of Rep. Willard); *id.* at 793 (statement of Rep. Poland); *id.* at 795 (statement of Rep. Burchard); *id.* at 799 (statement of Rep. Farnsworth).

[37]*Collector* held that the federal government could not tax a state court judge because this would enable the federal government to cripple or destroy the "means and instrumentalities employed [by the states] for carrying on the operations of their governments." 11 Wall. 113, 125–126 (1871).

[38]*Prigg* held that, while the Fugitive Slave Clause empowered Congress to enact legislation for the return of escaped slaves, Congress could not require state officers to execute such legislation but must provide federal means of doing so. 16 Pet. 539, 615–16 (1842).

whose votes defeated the first conference report cited and discussed these cases as the source of their opposition.[39]

Although the Sherman amendment had nothing to do with §1 of the 1871 Act, Justice Brennan found the reasons for its rejection pertinent to the imposition of municipal liability under §1983. He argued that *respondeat superior* imposes an obligation on employers to prevent their employees from committing torts that is much like the obligation to prevent Klan violence imposed on municipalities by the Sherman amendment.[40] It follows, therefore, that "creation of a federal law of *respondeat superior* would have raised all the constitutional problems associated with the obligation to keep the peace, an obligation Congress chose not to impose because it thought imposition of such an obligation unconstitutional."[41]

This reasoning proves too much. Justice Brennan asserts that *respondeat superior* under §1983 would have raised the same constitutional objections as the Sherman amendment because it too imposes an obligation on municipalities. But if all such obligations suffer the same constitutional infirmity, why was it not also unconstitutional for Congress to impose an obligation to obey the Constitution on individual state officers? The only difference between requiring an individual officer not to violate the Constitution and requiring a municipality to insure that its employees do not violate the Constitution is that the individual officer is made responsible only for his own behavior, while the municipality is made responsible for the behavior of agents. But that distinction has

---

[39]See, *e.g.*, Globe, note 24 *supra*, at 795 (discussing *Prigg* and Collecter v. Day) (statement of Rep. Blair); *id.* at 793 (discussing Collecter v. Day) (statement of Rep. Poland); *id.* at 799 (discussing Collecter v. Day) (statement of Rep. Farnsworth).

[40]436 U.S. at 693–94.

[41]*Id.* In a footnote, Justice Brennan added that the Sherman amendment was the only form of vicarious liability presented to Congress and concluded that "combined with the absence of any language in §1983 which can easily be construed to create *respondeat superior* liability, the inference that Congress did not intend to impose such liability is quite strong." 436 U.S. at 693 n.57. On the contrary, any such inference depends on erroneous assumptions. The nature of the liability to be imposed by the Sherman amendment was significantly different from *respondeat superior*, and its rejection cannot reasonably be interpreted to say anything at all about the question. The Sherman amendment would have made the municipality liable for unlawful acts committed by anyone—citizens, employees, or strangers— within municipal boundaries. Although a few states and England may have had similar "riot acts," see Globe, note 24 *supra*, at 760–61 (statement of Sen. Sherman); *id.* at 792 (statement of Rep. Butler), this was an unusually severe form of vicarious liability. *Respondeat superior*, on the other hand, was an already long-established and unexceptionable common-law rule. See City of Oklahoma City v. Tuttle, 471 U.S. 808, 835–39 (1985) (Stevens, J., dissenting).

nothing to do with the constitutional principles that made the Sherman amendment objectionable. Indeed, the cases relied upon by the opponents of the Sherman amendment—*Collector v. Day* and *Prigg v. Pennsylvania*—involved federal efforts to impose duties on individual state officials. The Sherman amendment's opponents were able to make their argument only by claiming that municipalities were identical to individual officers as regards the principle of dual sovereignty recognized in these cases.[42]

Thus, if Justice Brennan is right—if Congress would have found the imposition of a duty on municipalities to prevent their employees from violating the Constitution subject to the same objections as the Sherman amendment—then Congress would have also opposed the imposition of an obligation to obey the Constitution on individual state officials. Yet everyone agreed that §1983 was intended to do just that.[43] The moderate Republicans whose votes defeated the Sherman amendment voted in favor of §1983.[44]

These votes can, however, be reconciled. The opponents of the Sherman amendment distinguished between imposing an entirely new obligation on a state officer, and requiring a state officer to discharge obligations already imposed by state law in accordance with the Constitution. The federal government could not add to the duties imposed on state agents by state law an additional duty to prevent Klan violence, but the federal government could require state agents to discharge duties the state had already placed on them in accordance with the Constitution.[45] In other words, the argument that the federal government had no power to impose obligations on state agents did not include the obligation to obey the Constitution in the pursuit of ends established by state law.

---

[42]See, *e.g.*, Globe, note 24 *supra*, at 795 (statement of Rep. Blair): "It was held also in the case of Prigg v. Pennsylvania (I speak from recollection only) that it was not within the power of the Congress of the United States to lay duties upon a State officer; that we cannot command a state officer to do any duty whatever, as such; and I ask gentlemen to show me the difference between that and commanding a municipality, which is equally the creature of the State, to perform a duty."

[43]*Monell*, 436 U.S. at 682–83; see, *e.g.*, Globe, note 24 *supra*, at 334 (statement of Rep. Hoar); *id.* at 365 (statement of Rep. Arthur); *id.* at 367–68 (statement of Rep. Sheldon); *id.* at 385 (statement of Rep. Lewis).

[44]*Compare* Globe, note 24 *supra*, at 522 *with id.* at 800.

[45]This distinction was drawn by a number of opponents to the Sherman amendment. See, *e.g.*, Globe, note 24 *supra*, at 794 (statement of Rep. Poland); *id.* at 795 (statement of Rep. Blair); *id.* (statement of Rep. Burchard); *id.* at 799 (statement of Rep. Farnsworth). *Cf.* Levin, The Section 1983 Municipal Immunity Doctrine, 65 Georgetown L. J. 1483, 1520–31 (1977).

This distinction may sound hollow to the modern ear. After all, requiring a state officer not to violate the Constitution while performing duties imposed by state law is still imposing an obligation—the obligation to obey the United States Constitution. In both cases, a state officer is being required by the federal government to act in a particular way. The distinction may be justified, however, by the difference in degree of intrusion by the federal government into the operation of state government. In any event, and however weak or strong the distinction may appear today, it was recognized and accepted by the members of the Forty-Second Congress.

What this means, moreover, is that the constitutional objections to the Sherman amendment have no bearing on whether a municipality may be liable under §1983 on a *respondeat superior* theory. Under *Collecter v. Day* and *Prigg v. Pennsylvania*, it was thought that Congress could not impose obligations on individual state officers. But there was no constitutional impediment to holding such officers liable if they violated the Constitution while performing tasks delegated to them by the state. For purposes of *Collector v. Day* and *Prigg*, there was no distinction between individual and corporate agents of the state.[46] Thus, by analogy to these same cases, Congress could not impose affirmative obligations on municipalities. However, still reasoning by analogy, there would have been no constitutional impediment to holding municipalities liable for constitutional violations committed by municipal employees performing tasks delegated to the municipality by the state.

II. METHODOLOGICAL ISSUES IN INTERPRETING §1983: TOWARD A COMMON-LAW FOUNDATION FOR MUNICIPAL LIABILITY

What follows from the conclusion that *Monell*'s analysis is unsound? Does the inadequacy of its reasoning imply that *respondeat*

---

[46]This was Representative Blair's argument cited *supra* at note 42. This conclusion is also consistent with the prevailing legal theory, which held that a municipal corporation is merely an agent of the state to which some of the duties of governing have been assigned. See, *e.g.*, Shearman & Redfield, The Law of Negligence §§116–22 (2d ed. 1870); Dillon, The Law of Municipal Corporations §§29–39 (1872); Cooley, Constitutional Limitations, 211 (1868); Cooley, General Principles of Constitutional Law 344–45 (1880).

Interestingly, Justice Brennan relied on the identity between individual and corporate agents in Part I of *Monell* to explain why the objections to the Sherman amendment did not support the conclusion that municipalities could never be liable under §1983. See 436 U.S. at 682; Mead, 42 U.S.C. §1983 Municipal Liability: The Monell Sketch Becomes a Distorted Picture, 65 N.C. L. Rev. 517, 535–36 (1987).

superior should be fully applicable to municipalities? Other commentators and one Justice have reached this conclusion, arguing that if the language and legislative history of §1983 do not preclude municipal liability on a *respondeat superior* theory, then the fair assumption is that it was intended to apply to suits under §1983.[47] These commentators note that the doctrine of *respondeat superior* was used against municipalities in 1871 and argue that the members of the Forty-Second Congress were familiar with common-law principles and presumably intended them to apply.

This is a conventional method of statutory construction. Courts often assume that if the language and legislative history of a statute are silent on a question, the legislature intended to incorporate then-prevailing rules of law. Hence, it is certainly plausible to interpret §1983 to incorporate nineteenth-century principles of *respondeat superior*.

The argument is plausible, but incomplete. To be sure, municipal corporations sometimes incurred liability under *respondeat superior* at the time §1983 was enacted.[48] But more commonly, municipal corporations were insulated from liability by various immunity doctrines not applicable to private corporations. For example, municipal corporations were not liable for wrongs committed by municipal employees performing "governmental" rather than "corporate" (we would now say "proprietary") activities.[49] This limitation on municipal liability is significant here because, while the classification of municipal activities as "corporate" or "governmental" was often controversial,[50] the vast majority of §1983 claims probably

---

[47]See, *e.g.*, *Pembaur*, 475 U.S. at ____, 106 S.Ct. at 1303 (Stevens, J., concurring in part and concurring in the judgment); Mead, note 46 *supra*, at 538–42; Blum, From Monroe to Monell: Defining the Scope of Municipal Liability in Federal Courts, 51 Temp. L. Q. 409, 413 n.15 (1978); Comment, 47 Brook. L. Rev. 517, 552–57 (1981); Comment, note 30 *supra*, 46 U. Chi. L. Rev. at 952–55; Comment, 64 Iowa L. Rev. 1032, 1045–52 (1979); Note, 7 Hofstra L. Rev. 893, 917–21 (1979).

[48]See Cooley, The Law or Torts 619–27 (1879) (citing cases); Dillon, note 46 *supra*, at §§752–802 (citing cases); Shearman & Redfield, note 46 *supra*, ch. 8 (citing cases). See also *Pembaur*, 475 U.S. at ____, 106 S.Ct. 1292, 1303 (1986) (Stevens, J., dissenting); City of Oklahoma City v. Tuttle, 471 U.S. at 834–36 (Stevens, J., dissenting); Mead, note 46 *supra*, at 527; Blum, note 47 *supra*; Comment, note 30 *supra*, 46 U. Chi. L. Rev. at 956–61.

[49]See Dillon, note 46 *supra*, at §§753–55, 764, 778–80; Cooley, note 48 *supra*, at 619–20; Shapo, Municipal Liability for Police Torts: An Analysis of a Strand of American Legal History, 17 U. Miami L. Rev. 475, 478–79 (1963); Note, 30 Am. St. Rep. 376 (1892) (citing cases); see also Owen v. City of Independence, 445 U.S. 622, 644–47 (1980).

[50]See Dillon, note 46 *supra*, §766 at 724.

involve municipal functions that were traditionally classified as governmental.[51]

The "governmental functions" immunity apparently was not available if the wrongful act "was expressly authorized by the governing body of the corporation, or where, without such special authorization, it . . . has been ratified by the corporation."[52] This is rather similar to the policy rule of *Monell*. Consequently, and somewhat ironically, proponents of the view that §1983 should be interpreted consistently with common-law principles in use when it was enacted may find themselves reaffirming the policy rule after all. In any event, advocates of this interpretation of §1983 must explain why municipalities can no longer rely on the common-law immunities.[53]

Simply posing this question suggests another: why should liability under §1983 depend upon—or have anything to do with—the common law of 1871? Why, in other words, should congressional silence on the issue of municipal liability be interpreted to incorporate and freeze then-existing common-law rules?[54]

---

[51]Levin, note 45 *supra*, at 1521 n.156.

[52]Dillon, note 46 *supra*, §770 at 728 & n.2 (citing cases). See also Cooley, note 48 *supra*, at 621; Shearman & Redfield, note 46 *supra*, §120 at 148. Shearman and Redfield went farther than this and asserted in 1869 that the distinction between governmental and corporate activities had been "entirely repudiated." *Ibid*. However, they did not support this assertion with any authority, and, in light of the cases cited by Dillon, Cooley, and others, it appears that Shearman and Redfield were trying to shape rather than describe law. Although inaccurate at the time, Shearman's and Redfield's assertion subsequently became the law in most states. See note 54 *infra*.

[53]In Owen v. City of Independence, 445 U.S. 622 (1980), the Supreme Court held that the common-law "governmental functions" immunity is not available to municipalities sued under §1983. Tracing the source of this doctrine to the principle of sovereign immunity, the Court explained: "the municipality's 'governmental' immunity is obviously abrogated by the sovereign's enactment of a statute making it amenable to suit. Section 1983 was just such a statute. By including municipalities within the class of 'persons' subject to liability for violations of the Federal Constitution and laws, Congress—the supreme sovereign on matters of federal law—abolished whatever vestiges of the State's sovereign immunity the municipality possessed." *Id*. at 647–48 (footnote omitted). This is *ipse dixit*. The fact that Congress could have abrogated this municipal immunity does not mean that it did so. In precisely the same way, Congress could have abrogated the traditional common-law immunities of individual officials. Yet the Supreme Court has held that Congress did not abolish these immunities in enacting 1983. See notes 64–68, 76–86 *infra* and accompanying text.

[54]The rules of municipal liability in the states have undergone profound changes in the last 117 years as a product of both judicial and legislative efforts. See Prosser & Keeton, note 1 *supra*, at 1051–52; Shapo, note 49 *supra*. See also Owen v. City of Independence, 445 U.S. at 680–82 (Powell, J., dissenting).

The language and legislative history of §1983 say nothing about a great many issues in addition to municipal liability that arise under the statute. To name only a few, the statute and its legislative history do not indicate what defenses are available,[55] who bears the burdens of pleading and persuasion,[56] what kinds of damages are recoverable,[57] or whether exhaustion of state remedies is required.[58] Surely Congress must have been aware that cases under §1983 would raise many issues not answered by the text. The legislative history suggests an explanation for Congress' silence on these issues. Supporters of the 1871 Act wanted a federal remedy for injuries associated with the denial under color of state law of federally protected rights. Once the existence of a remedy was established, however, the Act's supporters were content to allow the courts to develop its boundaries as part of the federal common law of torts. Thus, on the few occasions when opponents pointed to the omission of particular details from the Act, supporters answered that such provisions were "not necessary because the common law gives a remedy."[59]

One can, of course, read these references to the common law as evidence that Congress thought it was incorporating then-existing common law into the statute. Far more likely, however, is the conclusion that Congress intended the federal courts to shape and develop this tort as part of the general common law. It was the heyday of *Swift v. Tyson;*[60] the existence of an evolving common law and of federal judicial power to share in its development was a given. Indeed, some members of Congress apparently understood §1983 as nothing more than a grant of federal jurisdiction over common-law tort actions that had previously been heard exclusively

[55]See, *e.g.*, Tenny v. Brandhove, 341 U.S. 367, 376 (1951); Pierson v. Ray, 386 U.S. 547, 554–55 (1967).

[56]See, *e.g.*, Gomez v. Toledo, 446 U.S. 635 (1980).

[57]See, *e.g.*, Memphis Community School District v. Stachura, 106 S.Ct. 2537 (1986); Smith v. Wade, 461 U.S. 30 (1983); City of Newport v. Fact Concerts, Inc., 453 U.S. 247 (1981); Carey v. Piphus, 435 U.S. 247 (1978).

[58]See, *e.g.*, Patsy v. Bd. of Regents, 457 U.S. 496 (1982).

[59]See Globe, note 24 *supra*, at 707 (statement of Sen. Sherman); see also *id.* at 771 (statement of Sen. Edmunds); notes 24–30 *supra* and accompanying text.

[60]16 Pet. 1 (1842).

by state courts.[61] Thus, while the issue is not free from doubt, the sounder view is that—as with the Sherman Act and the federal habeas corpus statute—Congress intended not only to allow the common law to inform §1983, but also to permit the common-law interpretation of the statute to evolve with the rest of the common law.

The Supreme Court has sometimes said that it does not have common-lawmaking powers under §1983.[62] Where the language and legislative history do not make congressional intent clear, the Court has said, §1983 should be interpreted by assuming that the "members of the 42d Congress were familiar with common-law principles . . . and that they likely intended these common-law principles to obtain, absent specific provisions to the contrary."[63] Notwithstanding such statements, the Court has seldom hesitated to abandon historical inquiry into congressional intent in favor of its own analysis of sound public policy.

Consider the cases on official immunity.[64] The language and legislative history of §1983 do not indicate whether state officials may assert immunities, and the Court has engaged in an official-by-official analysis of whether immunity is available. In its early encounters with this question, the Court simply asked whether there was an analogous tort immunity at common-law and assumed that if Congress had wished to abrogate that immunity it would have said so.[65] But the Court did not adhere to this approach in subse-

---

[61]Senator Thurman began his remarks in opposition with the statement that §1 of the 1871 Civil Rights Act "creates no new cause of action. Its whole effect is to give to the Federal Judiciary that which now does not belong to it—a jurisdiction that may be constitutionally conferred upon it, I grant, but that has never yet been conferred upon it." Globe, note 24 *supra*, app. at 216. See also Butz v. Economou, 438 U.S. 478, 502, n.30 (1978), quoting District of Columbia v. Carter, 409 U.S. 418, 427–28 (1973).

[62]See, *e.g.*, Malley v. Briggs, 475 U.S. 335, ____, 106 S.Ct. 1092, 1097 (1986); see also Wood v. Strickland, 420 U.S. 308, 316 (1975).

[63]City of Newport v. Fact Concerts, Inc., 453 U.S. 247, 258 (1981). See also, *e.g.*, Malley v. Briggs, 475 U.S. 335, ____, 106 S.Ct. 1092, 1097 (1986); Briscoe v. LaHue, 460 U.S. 325, 330, 334 (1983); Pierson v. Ray, 386 U.S. 547, 553–55 (1967) ("Congress would have specifically so provided had it wished to abolish" common-law doctrines).

[64]The pattern described here is not limited to the issue of official immunity but can be found in the Court's solution to other questions not resolved by the language or legislative history of §1983. See Kreimer, The Source of Law in Civil Rights Actions: Some Old Light on Section 1988, 133 U. Pa. L. Rev. 601, 611 (1985). See, *e.g.*, cases cited at notes 55–58 supra.

[65]See, *e.g.*, Tenny v. Brandhove, 341 U.S. 367, 376 (1951); Pierson v. Ray, 386 U.S. 547, 554–55 (1967).

quent cases. In some cases, the Court ignored or disregarded the common law and resolved the question of immunity solely on the basis of policy considerations such as whether liability would have an undue chilling effect on decisionmaking.[66] In other cases, the Court examined the common law to see whether it provided immunity, and asked whether the considerations supporting the common-law rule likewise warrant immunity under §1983.[67] In still other cases, the Court discussed both common-law and public policy considerations, without explaining how these considerations are related.[68] In none of these subsequent cases did the Court limit its examination of the common law to the period before 1871.

The inconsistency between these cases and statements that §1983 should be presumed to incorporate common-law doctrines well-established in 1871 is striking. Whatever it may say, the Court does not adhere to the common-law as it stood in 1871. Nonetheless, the Court continues to deny that it can make—and has been making—federal common-law pursuant to §1983. This reticence is unnecessary. Congress left all but the most basic questions of liability unresolved when it enacted §1983. It anticipated that the common law would fill the gaps and in no way suggested that the Courts should not depart from the common-law as it existed in 1871.[69]

---

[66]See, e.g., Procunier v. Navarette, 434 U.S. 555, 561–62 (1978); Harlow v. Fitzgerald, 457 U.S. 800 (1982).

[67]See, e.g., Imbler v. Pachtman, 424 U.S. 409, 424–25 (1976).

[68]See, e.g., Malley v. Briggs, 475 U.S. 335 (1986); Tower v. Glover, 467 U.S. 914 (1984); Wood v. Strickland, 420 U.S. 308, 318–22 (1975); Scheuer v. Rhodes, 416 U.S. 232, 242–49 (1974). In Malley and Tower, the Court did explain that the " 'initial inquiry is whether an official claiming immunity under §1983 can point to a common-law counterpart to the privilege he asserts,' " and that if such a privilege is found to exist, " 'the Court next considers whether §1983's history or purposes nonetheless counsel against recognizing the same immunity in §1983 actions.' " Malley, 106 S.Ct. at 1095 (quoting Tower, 467 U.S. at 920). Although this tells us the order in which to ask questions about history and policy, it does not explain what in "§1983's history or purposes" will trump the common-law or why. Nor does this description explain the cases in which history but not policy or policy but not history was relied upon.

[69]Cf. Kreimer, note 64 supra, at 630. In Smith v. Wade, 461 U.S. 30 (1983), the Court held that a plaintiff could recover punitive damages against state officials who acted with reckless indifference to plaintiff's federal rights. Both Justice Brennan's opinion for the Court and Justice Rehnquist's dissent included extensive discussion of nineteenth-century common-law authorities. In a separate dissent, Justice O'Connor came close to advocating this approach to interpreting §1983. She agreed that it made sense to look to the common-law as it existed in 1871 "when there was a generally prevailing rule of common law, for then it is reasonable to assume that Congressmen were familiar with that rule and imagined that it would cover

III. An Introduction to the Economic Analysis

The conclusion that *Monell* is unsound and that the rules of municipal liability should be developed as part of the federal common law obviously does not establish who should incur liability when a municipal employee commits a tort. Should liability be imposed on the employee, the municipality, or both? We now turn to familiar tools of economic analysis to explore this problem.[70]

Put simply, economic analysis asks how to design a liability rule that will maximize the net economic value of municipal activity—the excess of its economic benefits over its economic costs. This inquiry, in turn, requires attention to three components of economic value. The first component is the efficiency of the precautions or deterrent measures that result under alternative liability rules. This is really a rather simple notion: liability rules create incentives to take precautions against accidental injuries and stand as a deterrent to intentional harms. These precautions and deterrent measures produce benefits in the form of a reduction in the number and magnitude of injuries, but they also impose costs on the individuals and institutions subject to liability. Economic analysis undertakes to identify the net gain from precautions or deterrent measures under alternative liability rules and, other things being equal, prefers the rule for which the excess of benefits over costs is at a maximum.

---

the cause of action they were creating." But, she continued, "when a significant split in authority existed, it strains credulity to argue that Congress simply assumed that one view rather than the other would govern. . . . Once it is established that the common law of 1871 provides us with no real guidance on this question, we should turn to the policies underlying §1983 to determine which rule best accords with those policies." *Id.* at 93.

[70]A number of recent papers analyze rules of vicarious liability from the economic perspective, but do not directly address the liability of municipalities. See Kraakman, Corporate Liability Strategies and the Costs of Legal Controls, 93 Yale L. J. 857 (1984); Kraakman, Gatekeepers: The Anatomy of a Third-Party Enforcement Strategy, 2 J. L. Econ. & Org. 53 (1986); Landes & Posner, Joint and Multiple Tortfeasors: An Economic Analysis, 9 J. Legal Stud. 517 (1980); Sykes, The Economics of Vicarious Liability, 93 Yale L. J. 1231 (1984) [hereinafter The Economics of Vicarious Liability]; Sykes, The Boundaries of Vicarious Liability: An Economic Analysis of the Scope of Employment Rule and Related Doctrines, 101 Harv. L. Rev. 563 (1988) [hereinafter The Boundaries of Vicarious Liability]. Some of the principles developed in this literature apply directly to the public sector, but others do not—as discussed below, the imposition of vicarious liability on governmental entities raises several difficult issues that do not arise in the private sector. Economic issues relating to municipal liability are addressed briefly in Kornhauser, An Economic Analysis of the Choice Between Enterprise and Personal Liability for Accidents, 70 Calif. L. Rev. 1345 (1982).

A second component of economic value is the effect of alternative liability rules on scale of activity. Actors in the marketplace—individual or corporate, public or private—are limited in their ability to carry on activities by the resources available to them. Damages payments consume resources and thus tend to affect the scale of activity of those who are liable for damages (as well as those to whom they are paid). Other things being equal, economic analysis will prefer the liability rule that adjusts everyone's scale of activity so that the marginal benefit of an increase in scale is equal to its marginal cost—if such a rule exists.

The third component of value is the effect of different liability rules on the efficiency of risk bearing. Some individuals or organizations are better able to bear risk than others because, for example, they can better diversify the risk or can more easily lay it off on a superior risk bearer (such as an insurance company). Other things being equal, economic analysis will prefer the liability rule that allocates risk to institutions that are close to risk neutral and that shifts risk away from risk-averse individuals.

The importance of these considerations to the choice of liability rules seems self-evident.[71] The real question is whether the economic analysis is dispositive, or whether other, non-economic considerations also require attention. For example, economic analysis makes no allowance for purely distributional objectives like the provision of compensation to injured persons without regard to the effect of compensation on prevention, scale of activity, and risk bearing. Arguably, the pursuit of compensation for its own sake should not play an important role in the common-law jurisprudence of §1983. The legislative history of §1983 makes abundantly clear that Congress enacted §1983 to deter state officials from depriving state residents, particularly the newly freed slaves and Southern Republicans, of federally protected rights; there was no talk of enacting this statute to provide needed compensation to victims of constitutional torts.[72]

---

[71]The congruence between the economic theory of liability and the common law of torts has been well documented, see, *e.g.*, Landes & Posner, note 7 *supra*; Posner, Economic Analysis of Law (3d ed. 1986), including the considerable congruence between economic efficiency and the common law of vicarious liability, Sykes, The Economics of Vicarious Liability, note 70 *supra*.

[72]See Globe, note 24 *supra*, *passim*; see also Developments in the Law, Section 1983 and Federalism, 90 Harv. L. Rev. 1133, 1142–52 (1977).

Nonetheless, some readers may find our analysis incomplete as a normative basis for policymaking due to the omission of express attention to "compensation" or some other conceivable policy objective. In any event, the issues that we address are by all accounts central to—if perhaps not exhaustive of—the policy debate.[73]

IV. RULES OF OFFICIAL IMMUNITY

The vicarious liability of employers in the private sector is almost always joint and several with their employees. With very few exceptions, plaintiffs cannot reach the employer of the tortfeasor unless they can also establish the tortfeasor's individual liability. Of course, the individual liability of the injurer is not sufficient to allow the plaintiff to reach the injurer's employer—rules like the scope-of-employment rule and the independent contractor rule act as limitations on the scope of the employer's vicarious liability. Thus, depending upon the circumstances in which an employee commits a tort, the employee may be liable alone or the employer may be jointly and severally liable with the employee, but liability on the employer alone is extremely uncommon.

The existing rules of liability that apply to municipalities and to their employees under §1983 are often parallel. A plaintiff may seek damages from an employee who committed the tort. But, as in the private sector, the liability of the employee may not be sufficient for municipal liability since the plaintiff cannot recover from the municipality without also satisfying the policy rule of *Monell*. In these cases, the policy rule functions like the familiar limits on vicarious liability mentioned above.

Another class of §1983 cases finds little parallel in the private sector. Rules of official immunity sometimes allow public officers to escape individual liability under §1983. But *Owen v. City of Independence*[74] provides that municipalities cannot raise official immunity as a defense to their own liability. As a result, municipalities

---

[73]There is, of course, much more that could be said about the role of economics in developing legal rules. See, *e.g.*, Dworkin, Is Wealth a Value, 9 J. Legal Stud. 191 (1980); Kronman, Wealth Maximization as a Normative Principle, 9 J. Legal Stud. 227 (1980); Posner, The Value of Wealth: A Comment on Dworkin and Kronman, 9 J. Legal Stud. 243 (1980); Posner, Utilitarianism, Economics, and Legal Theory, 8 J. Legal Stud. 103 (1979).

[74]445 U.S. 622 (1980).

may incur liability under §1983 even if the individual tortfeasor is immune. Here, too, of course, the municipality's liability is contingent on the plaintiff's ability to satisfy *Monell*'s policy rule.

Our analysis will not question the efficiency of these rules of immunity where they apply. The doctrine of official immunity raises a number of difficult legal and economic issues,[75] but we shall assume that rules of official immunity are immutable and direct our inquiry to how the rule of vicarious liability should be designed given the existing rules of immunity. We must digress briefly, therefore, to sketch the limits of official immunity.

Certain classes of individual defendants are "absolutely" immune from damages actions under §1983. Specifically, absolute immunity has been conferred upon state legislators when acting in a legislative capacity,[76] upon judges when not acting in the clear absence of jurisdiction,[77] and upon prosecutors when acting as advocates in the criminal process.[78]

Otherwise, all public officials can assert a defense of qualified immunity under §1983.[79] At first, this qualified immunity had both a subjective and an objective element; an official could be held liable for committing a constitutional tort if the official "knew or reasonably should have known that the action he took . . . would violate the constitutional rights of the [plaintiff], or if he took the action with malicious intention to cause a deprivation of constitutional rights or other injury. . . ."[80] Because this formulation,

---

[75]See, *e.g.*, Epstein, Private Law Models for Official Immunity, 42 L. & Contemp. Probs. 53 (1978).

[76]Tenny v. Brandhove, 341 U.S. 367 (1951); see also Lake Country Estates, Inc. v. Tahoe Regional Planning Agency, 440 U.S. 391 (1979) (absolute immunity for regional legislators acting under authority of interstate compact).

[77]Stump v. Sparkman, 435 U.S. 349 (1978); Pierson v. Ray, 386 U.S. 547 (1967).

[78]Imbler v. Pachtman, 424 U.S. 409 (1976). In both *Imbler*, 424 U.S. at 430–31, and *Pembaur*, 475 U.S. at _____, 106 S.Ct. at 1295 n.2, the Supreme Court expressly reserved judgment on whether a prosecutor is entitled to absolute immunity when he acts as an administrator or investigator rather than as an advocate.

[79]Although the Supreme Court has not issued a blanket holding that all state and local officials are entitled to at least qualified immunity, it has extended such immunity to every public official who has sought it. See, *e.g.*, Pierson v. Ray, 386 U.S. 547 (1967) (police officers); Scheuer v. Rhodes, 416 U.S. 232 (1974) (executive officials); Procunier v. Navarette, 434 U.S. 555 (1978) (prison officials); O'Connor v. Donaldson, 422 U.S. 563 (1975) (mental hospital administrators); Wood v. Strickland, 420 U.S. 308 (1975) (school board members).

[80]*Id.* at 322. Although the Court in *Wood* limited its holding to school board members, subsequent cases relied upon *Wood* as a general statement of the qualified immunity test. *E.g.*, Procunier v. Navarette, 434 U.S. at 562–63; see also Harlow v. Fitzgerald, 457 U.S. 800, 815, n.25 (1982).

particularly its subjective element, made it difficult for public officials to obtain summary judgment, the Court revised the qualified immunity standard in *Harlow v. Fitzgerald*.[81] *Harlow* eliminated the subjective element and made the objective element more favorable to defendants. Government officials now enjoy immunity from liability for civil damages "insofar as their conduct does not violate clearly established statutory or constitutional rights of which a reasonable person would have known."[82] Public officials have a duty to follow clearly settled law, but are immune from suit if their actions were of uncertain legality under an objective standard when they were taken.[83] Qualified immunity is also referred to as "good faith" immunity: acts that satisfy the *Harlow* test are said to be acts in "good faith"; acts that do not meet the test are said to be in "bad faith."

As noted, municipalities cannot claim the same immunity as their officials under §1983.[84] This is true whether that immunity is absolute or qualified.[85] The vast majority of municipal liability cases, however, involve acts by officers who are entitled only to good faith immunity.[86]

---

[81]457 U.S. 800 (1982).

[82]*Id.* at 818. See also Davis v. Scherer, 468 U.S. 183 (1984).

[83]*Cf.* Mitchell v. Forsyth, 472 U.S. 511, 530–35 (1985); Bennis v. Gable, 823 F.2d 723, 732–33 (3d Cir. 1987); Llaguno v. Mingey, 763 F.2d 1560, 1569 (7th Cir. 1985). See generally Nahmod, note 5 *supra*, at §8.06.

[84]Owen v. City of Independence, 445 U.S. 622 (1980).

[85]Reed v. Village of Shorewood, 704 F.2d 943, 953–54 (7th Cir. 1983); Hernandez v. City of Lafayette, 643 F.2d 1188, 1194–1200 (5th Cir. 1981).

[86]Prior to the Supreme Court's decision in *Lake Country Estates*, 440 U.S. 391 (1979), local—as opposed to state—legislators were given only qualified immunity. See, *e.g.*, Thomas v. Younglove, 545 F.2d 1171 (9th Cir. 1976); Lane v. Inman, 509 F.2d 184 (5th Cir. 1975); Curry v. Gillette, 461 F.2d 1003 (6th Cir.), cert. denied, 409 U.S. 1042 (1972); Nelson v. Knox, 256 F.2d 312 (6th Cir. 1958). In *Lake Country Estates*, which dealt with the immunity of regional legislators acting under an interstate compact, the Court left the issue of local legislators' immunity open; Justice Marshall noted in dissent that, as a practical matter, the Court's reasoning resolved the question in favor of absolute immunity. 440 U.S. at 408–09 (Marshall, J., dissenting). Since that decision, a number of courts of appeals have held that local legislators are entitled to absolute immunity. See, *e.g.*, Aitchison v. Raffiani, 708 F.2d 96 (3d Cir. 1983); Reed v. Village of Shorewood, 704 F.2d 943 (7th Cir. 1983); Hernandez v. City of Fafayette, 643 F.2d 1188 (5th Cir. 19981); Bruce v. Riddle, 631 F.2d 272 (4th Cir. 1980). See generally Nahmod, note 5 *supra*, at §7.05. Nonetheless, these cases are relatively rare. Also rare are cases in which a plaintiff sues a municipality for the act of a municipal judge or a local prosecutor. The combined number of cases in all three of these categories does not compare to the number of cases filed against police officers and other municipal officials who have only good faith immunity.

V. The Scope of Municipal Liability for "Bad Faith" Acts by Municipal Employees

Setting aside for the moment any consideration of "good faith" acts, and assuming that a cause of action against the individual official for bad faith acts is efficient,[87] we now examine whether the policy rule of *Monell* is an economically sensible criterion for the imposition of vicarious liability on municipalities. We conclude it is not. The application of common-law agency principles, including the doctrine of *respondeat superior*, would likely produce improvement. Moreover, we contend that a negligence-based approach to municipal liability for bad faith acts might do better still.

A. THE SIGNIFICANCE OF THE CHOICE BETWEEN PERSONAL LIABILITY AND VICARIOUS LIABILITY

It is perhaps tempting to assume that the choice between vicarious liability (a regime in which employers and employees are jointly and severally liable) and personal liability (a regime in which only employees are liable) is always important on the premise that a judgment against the employee under personal liability will have little or no impact on the employer. Recent work on the economics of vicarious liability, however, suggests that the choice between vicarious liability and personal liability has no economic consequences if two conditions prevail: (1) the employee has sufficient assets to pay any conceivable judgment against him in full (perhaps with the aid of insurance or contractual indemnification from the employer), and (2) the transaction costs of employment contracts that include terms to allocate liability between the employer and the employee are small.[88] The intuition that underlies this proposition is quite simple.[89]

Suppose that a rule of personal liability prevails, so that only the employee incurs liability for the employee's torts. In negotiating

---

[87]The assumption that the cause of action against the individual employee is efficient implies that economic welfare is greater when the cause of action is allowed that when it is barred. Without this assumption, potentially difficult second-best issues complicate the analysis.

[88]See Sykes, The Economics of Vicarious Liability, note 70 *supra*, at 1239–43.

[89]The analysis assumes that there are no systematic errors in the assignment of liability or the computation of damages under either personal liability or vicarious liability: in either regime, expected liability is equal to the actual costs suffered by injured parties.

an employment agreement, the employer and the employee can nonetheless include provisions that allocate the risk of liability judgments against the employee between the employer and the employee. Perhaps the employer will agree to assume some or all of the risk of liability, or perhaps the employee will agree to bear this risk in exchange for higher wages or other benefits. The precise terms of this agreement will depend upon each party's attitude toward risk-bearing, upon the need to create proper incentives for the employee, upon each party's bargaining power, and so on.

Now suppose that the liability rule is changed to vicarious liability. The employer and the employee must renegotiate their employment agreement to take account of the fact that judgments may now be rendered against the employer. The total amount paid to the plaintiff by the employer and the employee remains the same, however, for if employees can pay adverse judgments in full under personal liability, all judgments will be satisfied under either liability rule. That being true, the renegotiated employment agreement under vicarious liability *can* exactly replicate the division of liability agreed to by the employer and the employee under personal liability.

Moreover, if the second condition above is met, if the transaction costs of replicating the division of liability and all other terms and incentives contained in the employment agreement negotiated under personal liability are small, then the employment agreement under vicarious liability *will* tend to replicate the preferred agreement under personal liability.[90] At least the change to vicarious liability is unlikely to have any systematic or predictable effect on the employment agreement.

Whichever rule prevails, then, injured parties are fully compensated, the incentives facing employees are likely to be the same,

[90]Of course, the analysis works in reverse if the liability rule changes from vicarious liability to personal liability, thus establishing the equivalence of the two regimes. Formal models of bargaining developed by game theorists typically embody an assumption—known as the "independence of irrelevant alternatives"—that leads directly to this result. See, *e.g.*, Nash, The Bargaining Problem, 18 Econometrica 155 (1950); Sykes, The Economics of Vicarious Liability, in Two Essays in the Economics of Law (unpublished Ph.D. dissertation 1987). One can also show that if employees can pay all judgments in full under personal liability and the transaction costs of contracting are negligible, then any employment agreement that is Pareto optimal from the perspective of the employer and the employee under personal liability is also Pareto optimal from their perspective under vicarious liability. *Ibid.*; Kornhauser, note 70 *supra*.

and the ultimate allocation of risk (in contrast to the initial allocation created by the legal rule) is likely to be the same. It follows that the efficiency of resource allocation is invariant to the liability rule.

This analysis seems at first to be equally applicable to employment relationships in the public and private sectors. One need only assume that the employer and the employee each have preferences among the alternative employment agreements that jointly determine, along with each party's bargaining power, the terms of their agreement. Then, if the mutually preferred employment agreement under one liability rule can be reconstructed at little cost under the other rule, the choice between the two rules is unlikely to have any systematic effect on the terms of the employment relationship or the resulting allocation of resources.

This conclusion is at odds with recent literature on governmental liability and immunities. This literature implies that, even if employees are able to pay judgments against them in full, and even if the transaction costs of employment agreements are low, a rule of personal liability will have a perverse effect on the incentives and productivity of government workers.[91] Employees in the public sector, the argument runs, perform tasks that benefit the public as a whole, not just themselves or the organization that employs them. Personal liability, by contrast, is a cost that is borne entirely by the employee. Personal liability thus encourages overcautious behavior or inaction by the employee: while the employee enjoys all the benefits associated with his reduced exposure to civil liability, the costs of excessive caution or inaction fall on the public as a whole. Proponents of this argument conclude, therefore, that personal liability is undesirable, and implicitly assume that the adverse effects of personal liability will not be eliminated by contract (for example, by the use of indemnity agreements). They recommend greater immunity for government employees, coupled with expanded governmental liability.

This analysis is flawed. All employers, public or private, face incentive problems. It is usually too costly for employers to observe the behavior of each employee at all times, and thus impossible to

---

[91]See, e.g., Mashaw, Civil Liability of Government Officers: Property Rights and Official Accountability, 42 L. & Contemp. Probs. 8, 26–28 (1978); Schuck, Suing the Government (1983); Schuck, Suing Our Servants: The Court, Congress, and the Liability of Public Officials for Damages, 1980 Supreme Court Review 281.

design an incentive structure that perfectly harmonizes the behavior of employees with the interests of the employer. The result is the familiar problem of "agency costs," the costs of shirking, of imprudence, of overcaution, of inaction, and so on. To a large extent, these costs fall on the employer whether the employer is public or private.

Because employees' incentives are seldom perfectly aligned with employers' interests, the imposition of personal liability on an employee may lead to an exercise of caution that is excessive from the employer's perspective:[92] the employee will perceive benefits from excessive caution in the form of reduced exposure to liability, while the costs of excessive caution—decreased productivity—fall, in the first instance, on the employer. The employer can respond to this problem by altering the employee's incentive structure to encourage him or her to perform more desirably. For example, if a truck driver for Sears is personally liable for his or her motor vehicle torts, Sears can discourage overcautious driving by rewarding the driver for timely deliveries or penalizing late deliveries. Similarly, if a policeman for the City of Chicago is personally liable for the unintended use of excessive force, the City can try to discourage timidity or inaction in the pursuit of suspects by rewarding policemen with distinguished arrest records or penalizing policemen whose arrest records suggest ineffectiveness.

Of course, some incentive problems are more difficult than others. It may be easy to determine when a delivery is late, but quite difficult to ascertain when police conduct is timid. Thus, in our hypotheticals, Sears may find it easier to remedy the incentive problem than the City of Chicago (though Chicago can always ameliorate the problem by indemnifying its policemen). But that observation is irrelevant: the fact remains that it is in the interest of any employer, public or private, to utilize whatever cost-effective incentives are available to eliminate the undesirable consequences of personal liability.

Moreover, as explained above, the ultimate allocation of risk—and the attendant set of incentives facing employees—will not be

---

[92]This problem may not arise if personal liability attaches only to harms that the employee intends to cause. Because the employee need only refrain from deliberate misconduct to avoid liability, he or she has no incentive to become overcautious. Consequently, there may be no adverse effect on employee productivity. The possibility of frivolous lawsuits predicated on intentional misconduct, however, might induce overcaution even under these circumstances.

affected by the choice between personal liability and vicarious liability so long as judgments would be paid in full under either liability rule and the transaction costs of contracting are low enough to permit the employment agreement that would prevail under personal liability to be reconstructed under vicarious liability (or vice-versa). Under these conditions, the initial locus of liability simply does not affect the mutually preferred set of contractual incentives,[93] including the ultimate division of liability between the employer and the employee.

To be sure, the incentives contained in the employment contract may not be socially optimal. In the public sector, for example, poor performance by governmental employees may impose considerable costs on members of the general public while imperfections in the political process insulate public agencies from any substantial pressure to eliminate these costs. Consequently, employment agreements in the public sector may work poorly at motivating employees to serve the public interest. But such problems with the performance of public sector employees are not affected by the choice between personal liability and vicarious liability when employees are able to pay adverse judgments in full and the transaction costs of contracting are low—the terms of employments agreement, including the existence or non-existence of indemnification agreements and the like, will be the same under either regime. Of course, these two conditions may not be satisfied, in which case the choice between personal and vicarious liability can have significant effects on resource allocation, problems to which we now turn.

B. THE EFFICIENCY OF VICARIOUS LIABILITY WHEN THE EMPLOYEE IS
   JUDGMENT-PROOF

Municipal employees are often unable to pay adverse judgments in full. Judgments in §1983 cases are frequently quite large; amounts

---

[93]The concept of "incentives" here is quite broad. For example, suppose that a vicariously liable employer decides to establish a training program to instruct employees on precautions against accidents. The employer finds the program desirable because its cost is less than the reduction in his expected liability. Would the training program also be desirable under personal liability? If employees can pay judgments against them in full, the answer is yes. Employees can finance the program through a reduction in wages, and it is advantageous for them to do so because the cost is again less than the reduction in their expected liability. Unless transaction costs prevent the employees from bargaining for the program, then, it will be established whatever the liability rule.

in excess of several hundred thousand dollars are not uncommon.[94] Plainly, such judgments will usually exceed the personal assets of municipal employees.[95]

The fact that municipal employees are often judgment-proof may have profound effects on resource allocation. It can affect the scale of municipal activity; the degree of supervision, training, and other incentives that discourage constitutional torts; the productivity of municipal employees; and the efficiency of risk allocation. To understand these effects, and their implications for the choice between personal and vicarious liability, it is instructive to begin by examining the inefficiencies that arise when employees are judgment-proof under a regime of personal liability.

1. *The inefficiencies of personal liability. a) The private sector.* In the private sector, the inefficiencies of personal liability for torts when employees are judgment-proof may be readily identified. Under such circumstances, a rule of personal liability allows the business enterprise to "externalize" costs of doing business by passing off all or part of the losses occasioned by the commission of a tort onto the victim.[96] One result of cost externalization is that the incentive to exercise care to avoid the occurrence of torts may be inadequate, either for the employer or the employee. Alternatively, even though

---

[94]*Cf.* Nahmod, note 5 *supra*, at §4.03.

[95]Of course, municipal employees exposed to the risk of large judgments under a rule of personal liability may seek employment agreements that provide indemnification. Indeed, some municipal employees are indemnified by their state governments. See, e.g., N.Y. Pub. Off. Law §18 (McKinney 1984). Municipalities will be reluctant to provide indemnification for "bad faith" behavior that consists of knowing, intentional torts by the employee; the attendant moral hazard would likely be unacceptable. E.g., *id.* at §18(4) (b) (excluding indemnification for "intentional wrongdoing or recklessness"). But many bad faith acts that give rise to liability are merely negligent—the failure of a policeman in the heat of the moment to abide by the strictures of the Fourth Amendment, for example, or the unwitting failure of supervisors to provide constitutionally required process before discharging a subordinate. Employees may succeed in obtaining indemnification for liability that arises from such behavior. By agreeing to indemnify employees, the municipality (or its state government) in effect imposes vicarious liability on itself by contract. Any judgment will generally be satisfied in full, and, as suggested above, the choice between personal liability and vicarious liability likely becomes a matter of indifference. The "policy rule" of *Monell* has no practical effect.

[96]This discussion assumes that the tort is "caused" by the employment relationship in the following sense: If the employment relationship dissolves and the employee remains unemployed, the probability of the tort is reduced to zero. Under this assumption, the tort is properly viewed as a cost of production for the business enterprise. See Sykes, The Boundaries of Vicarious Liability, note 70 *supra*.

a judgment-proof employee does not bear the full cost of the injuries that he causes, the prospect that a judgment could render him bankrupt may motivate the employee to exercise an inefficiently high level of care if he is risk averse. If the employer cannot eliminate this incentive for excessive care except through indemnification—potentially very costly to the employer—the employer may decide simply to tolerate the excessive level of care.

In addition, if either employees or prospective injured parties are risk averse, the allocation of risk under personal liability may be inefficient. Risk allocation could be improved if the risk of injury were shifted to a more efficient risk bearer such as an insurance company or, in many cases, the employer.

Finally, in a competitive market, the added profitability that results from cost externalization attracts new entry and encourages the expansion of existing firms until the prevailing price falls to the level of private marginal costs. Because the externalization of liability implies that private marginal costs are below social marginal costs, the resulting scale of business activity is excessive.[97]

Despite these inefficiencies, the externalization of liability can prove worthwhile from the perspective of the employer and the employee. The resulting increment in expected profits to the business enterprise can be divided between the employer and the employee (in the form of higher wages) to make them both better off at the expense of the injured party whose judgment goes wholly or partially unsatisfied. For this reason, rational profit-maximizing or utility-maximizing employers and employees will often enter employment agreements that do not provide the employee with indemnification and that expose the employee to a risk of bankruptcy.

b) The public sector. To a considerable extent, the inefficiencies and incentives for liability externalization that arise in the private sector under a rule of personal liability also arise when the employer is a municipality. But there are important differences as well.

Consider first the incentive to externalize liability. As explained above, cost externalization is often profit-maximizing for a private firm. With the possible exception of certain independent, proprietary government entities, however, municipal agencies are not usually motivated by the desire to maximize profits.

---

[97]But see note 113 *infra.*

Yet municipalities (or, more accurately, municipal officials) are to some extent motivated by a desire to provide public services at minimum cost. Most elected officials confront demands for both increased levels of public services and lower taxes. Although the response to these pressures may be somewhat unpredictable and imperfect, opportunities for cost reduction are likely to be explored. The externalization of liability is one such opportunity.

Of course, any costs that are "externalized" will fall to a large extent on citizens of the municipality—the voters. For a variety of reasons, however, voters may not act as an effective check on liability externalization and the inefficiencies that may accompany it even if they bear the brunt of the externalized costs. Injuries caused by municipal employees may be relatively low-probability events about which most voters are poorly informed, and which consequently do not have much influence on voting. Moreover, even well-informed voters probably view the problem of injuries caused by municipal employees as unimportant by comparison to other issues, and thus of little moment in deciding how to vote. By contrast, the tax assessment is all too familiar to most voters, many of whom will reward officials who minimize it.

Finally, and perhaps most importantly, the costs of uncompensated injuries may fall disproportionately on segments of the population with limited political power. The costs of police misconduct, for example, may fall primarily on the poor, on minorities, and on individuals with prior convictions, while the costs of compensating such injuries through tax revenues will be more broadly dispersed. The result may well be that a majority of the electorate, even if well-informed, will prefer liability externalization despite the attendant inefficiencies.

Consequently, even though municipalities will rarely be motivated to externalize liability by the pursuit of "profit," powerful incentives to take advantage of the opportunity to externalize liability may nonetheless arise. The fact that liability externalization occurs in the public sector rather than the private sector warrants no presumption that it is efficient or otherwise in the overall public interest.

Given the incentive to externalize liability that may arise on the part of municipalities, then, will externalization lead to the same inefficiencies as in the private sector? The answer is yes, and no.

First, as in the private sector, cost externalization by municipalities and their employees may result in inadequate incentives to take precautions against wrongdoing. Employees may exercise inefficiently little care in performing their duties or, with respect to intentional harms, the level of deterrence may be inadequate.[98] Similarly, as in the private sector, the externalization of liability diminishes the incentives of municipalities to institute training, supervision and monitoring, or otherwise to dissuade wrongdoing through injury-contingent contractual penalties. On the other hand, it is conceivable that municipal employees may exercise inefficiently high levels of care due to the conjunction of risk aversion with personal liability, or to the fact that the burden of overcautious behavior falls on the general public and not on the employees. As noted, municipalities have an incentive to correct this problem, and the most obvious way to do so would be by indemnifying employees. But the costs of indemnification may be too high from the municipality's perspective (it requires forgoing the benefits of cost externalization), and effective alternatives to indemnification may not exist.

Although the problem of excessive care surely exists in the abstract, we doubt its significance with respect to "bad faith" constitutional torts. Many of these torts involve intentional harms, and others involve reckless behavior or other conduct that reflects complete inattention or indifference to constitutional requirements. It therefore seems unlikely that personal liability for such torts will often induce overcautious behavior or inaction, as the employee can avoid liability with minimal effort.[99] Rather, the problems of un-

---

[98]Bad faith constitutional torts may be either intentional or negligent. If a supervisor discharges a subordinate on the basis of race, for example, or a policeman deliberately brutalizes a suspect, the tort is plainly intentional. By contrast, if a policeman carelessly exceeds his authority under a search warrant, or a supervisor unthinkingly discharges an employee without an adequate hearing, the injury is not intentional but negligent or reckless.

[99]This is true of the factual issue on which §1983 claims are typically based as well as the question of immunity under *Harlow*. The factual component in §1983 cases invariably concerns intentional action by a state official, such as whether an official searched a plaintiff's home. The uncertain element in such cases is the legal effect of this intentional action and the official's knowledge of the law: should the official have known that he lacked probable cause to search? Until recently, claimed deprivations of due process were an exception to this rule and could be based on allegations that a government official acted negligently. Parratt v. Taylor, 451 U.S. 527 (1981). In Daniels v. Williams, 106 S.Ct 662 (1986), however, the Supreme Court overruled *Parratt* and held that injuries inflicted by governmental negligence do not violate the Due Process Clause. The Court reserved the question "whether

derinvestment in care and underdeterrence are probably far more serious inefficiencies of personal liability for these torts.

A second consequence of cost externalization that may arise in the public sector as well as in the private sector is inefficiency in risk allocation. The costs of injuries fall on the victim and the individual wrongdoer who, as in the private sector, are often risk averse. Here too, then, the efficiency of risk bearing can be improved by shifting the risk to a risk neutral (or less risk averse) entity. Of course, even a risk averse wrongdoer is an efficient "risk" bearer in cases involving intentional injuries[100] and, as noted,[101] many bad faith constitutional torts involve intentional misconduct. But if the wrongdoer is unable to pay judgments against him in full, the risk still falls on the risk averse victim in many cases, and risk allocation remains inefficient.

With respect to the third possible inefficiency of personal liability in the private sector, distortion in the scale of activity, the situation in the public sector is significantly different. As noted above, economic theory predicts that cost externalization in a competitive market will lead (other things being equal) to an inefficiently large scale of activity as prices fall below social marginal costs of production. No such prediction can be made about the effects of cost externalization on the scale of governmental activity for the simple reason that economists have no generally accepted theory of how the scale of public sector activity is determined in the first place.

If the scale of activity is determined by majority vote, for example, the preferences of the "median voter" might be decisive.[102] Whether the scale of government activity established by the "median voter" is efficient depends upon a variety of factors that determine how the costs and benefits of government activity are dis-

---

something less than intentional conduct, such as recklessness or 'gross negligence,' is enough to trigger the protections of the Due Process Clause." *Id.* at 667 n.3. As to "good faith" torts, see notes 122–32 *infra* and accompanying text.

[100]If the employee knows that particular behavior will produce an actionable injury with certainty, and knows that he can avoid the injury with certainty by refraining from the behavior in question, then the employee does not bear any "risk" if he incurs personal liability for such behavior. Such a deterministic relationship between the behavior and the existence of an actionable wrong is characteristic of most "intentional" misconduct. It follows that aside from any risk of exposure to baseless litigation, there is no inefficiency in risk allocation if the wrongdoer bears the full cost of any injury that he "intentionally" causes.

[101]See notes 98–99 *supra* and accompanying text.

[102]See, *e.g.*, Atkinson & Stiglitz, Lectures on Public Economics 299–326 (1980).

tributed among members of the voting public. If the benefits of government activity accrue to a minority of citizens but the costs are widely dispersed, for example, then the scale of activity determined by majority vote may be inefficiently small. The reverse possibility also exists.

To complicate matters further, direct majority voting only rarely determines the scale of government activity. More commonly, the scale of activity is determined by elected representatives and appointed bureaucrats who respond to complex and widely divergent incentives. A variety of theories have been advanced that directly or indirectly purport to explain the resulting scale of government activity—theories of budget-maximizing bureaucrats, theories of voters who "vote with their feet" by relocating to find a preferred mix of public services, and many others.[103] Some of these theories predict that the scale of government activity will tend to be inefficiently high while some predict the opposite; some yield no determinate prediction about the efficiency of scale.[104]

Assuming, therefore, that cost externalization by the public sector tends to increase the scale of government activity,[105] it is unclear whether the resulting increment in scale will enhance or worsen the efficiency of resource allocation. In some cases, cost externalization may cause government activity to expand from an already excessive base; in other cases, the expansion may offset conditions that would otherwise produce an inefficiently small scale of activity.

Thus, at least two of the inefficiences associated with a rule of personal liability when employees are judgment proof are found in the public as well as the private sector: the reduction of incentives to avoid committing torts and an inefficient allocation of risk. With respect to the third inefficiency in the private sector—an inefficient

---

[103]For a partial survey, see Mueller, Public Choice (1979).

[104]The Niskanen model of the budget-maximizing bureaucrat, for example, predicts overprovision of public services. Mueller, note 103 *supra*, at 156–63. The theory of public goods by contrast, implies some tendency for under-provision of public goods due to free-rider problems. See, *e.g.*, Malinvaud, Lectures on Microeconomic Theory 211–19 (1972).

[105]Whatever the details of the public choice process, it seems likely that an increase in the cost of government services to the public treasury will usually (though perhaps not always) lead voters or their representatives to economize on those costs through some reduction in the scale of government activity. Conversely, a reduction in the cost of government services to the public treasury will tend to produce an expansion in the scale of government activity.

increase in the scale of activity—no prediction can be made with respect to the public sector.

2. *The consequences of vicarious liability.* Under the common law of torts, the imposition of vicarious liability on employers usually occurs pursuant to the doctrine of *respondeat superior.*[106] *Respondeat superior* is a form of "strict" liability: the plaintiff need not show that the employer was negligent or otherwise culpable, and, once the employee's liability is established, the derivative liability of the employer follows without more.

In some cases, however, the employer cannot be held liable unless the plaintiff proves that the employer breached a duty to the plaintiff, for example, the limited duty of an employer to control the conduct of an employee acting outside the scope of employment.[107] Derivative liability on the basis of negligent failure to supervise a wrongdoer or otherwise to prevent a wrong is also quite common outside the employment relationship.[108] Strictly speaking, of course, such liability is not "vicarious" at all, as the derivatively liable party breached its own duty of care. For convenience of exposition, however, we refer below to two types of "vicarious" liability: strict vicarious liability and vicarious liability based on negligence.

More precisely, we understand "strict" vicarious liability to be the application to municipalities of the same common-law agency principles that govern the liability of private sector employers. The doctrine of *respondeat superior* is the most important of these principles.

A "negligence" approach to the liability of the municipality would, by contrast, require the plaintiff to prove that municipal employees with supervisory authority over the wrongdoer failed to adopt some cost-effective measure to avert the constitutional tort and that the absence of such a measure proximately caused the injury. For example, if the constitutional tort arose in connection with an illegal police search, the plaintiff might show that the police officers were inadequately trained or supervised or that the police department

---

[106]See generally Prosser & Keeton on the Law of Torts, note 1 *supra*, at 501–08.

[107]See Restatement (Second) of Torts §317 (1965).

[108]See Sykes, The Boundaries of Vicarious Liability, note 70 *supra*. For example, the version of the Sherman Amendment that was finally passed imposes liability on individuals who know that someone else will commit a constitutional tort and have power to prevent it but fail to act. See 42 U.S.C. §1986. There are many other examples.

neglected to establish reasonable internal policies to deter illegal searches.[109]

To some, the negligence approach might seem peculiar—the municipality escapes liability for the wrong of one employee, while it incurs liability for the wrong of a second employee. But upon reflection, the result is not peculiar at all.

Personal liability on the active wrongdoer operates directly upon his incentives, but not upon the incentives of supervisors. And, because of transaction costs (discussed below) or because the active wrongdoer is judgment proof, personal liability may produce little or no indirect pressure for cost-effective supervision. To generate such incentives under these circumstances, the scope of liability must be expanded.

One option would be to impose personal liability on the negligent supervisors. We reject that option, principally because it would involve potentially intolerable litigation costs. Specifically, although plaintiffs might reasonably be expected to explain how better training, monitoring, or supervision of the tortfeasor could have prevented their injury, it might be extraordinarily difficult for them to identify which supervisory officials were responsible—indeed, a colorable claim of negligence might be advanced against numerous officials at various stages of the hierarchy. A rule imposing personal liability on negligent supervisors would thus tempt plaintiffs to implead any number of municipal officials. Each might well want his own attorney, and the ensuing litigation over which official was the "negligent" one would consume considerable resources. Compounding the problem is the fact that supervisors themselves may be judgment proof, so that the imposition of personal liability upon negligent supervisors may still fail to create adequate incentives for supervision.

We therefore conclude that incentives for cost-effective supervision within the municipal hierarchy can be created more efficiently by a rule that imposes liability on the municipality rather than upon negligent supervisors individually. The more difficult question is whether those incentives should be created through a rule of strict vicarious liability for bad faith torts, or whether the victims of bad faith torts should be required to show that the tort

---

[109]Justice O'Connor adopted a variation of this approach in her dissent from the dismissal of the petition for certiorari in City of Springfield v. Kibbe, 107 S.Ct. 114 (1987).

also resulted from an act of negligence somewhere within the administrative hierarchy.

Either type of vicarious liability can ameliorate certain inefficiencies that arise under personal liability when municipal employees are judgment-proof. Take the problem of underinvestment in care by the employee or the employer or the problem of underdeterrence of intentional harms. If, as is almost certainly the case, fiscal pressures produce incentives for municipalities to minimize the cost of delivering municipal services, strict vicarious liability will motivate the municipality to adopt cost-effective measures to reduce the incidence of misconduct.[110] But much the same incentives for taking cost-effective measures to prevent misconduct will arise if vicarious liability is imposed on the basis of negligence, assuming that "negligence" is defined in accordance with the Learned Hand test as the failure to take cost-effective precautions.

Indeed, by singling out negligent supervisory officials and identifying the measures that they should have taken, a negligence-based approach to vicarious liability might be more effective than strict vicarious liability at motivating cost-effective monitoring, training, and similar measures: negligence cases would generate a body of information about required precautionary measures for the guidance of other municipalities.

The negligence approach also has disadvantages. First, it requires an expenditure of resources to litigate the issue of negligence, although the total number of lawsuits under a negligence regime will likely be smaller.[111] Second, and in contrast to strict vicarious liability, the negligence approach places the court in the position of second-guessing municipal officials about what measures should be taken to guard against constitutional torts, a process that may introduce significant error costs. Finally, although both strict vicarious liability and vicarious liability based on negligence will ameliorate the inefficient allocation of risk that results under personal liability, strict vicarious liability appears to do this better. Strict

---

[110]These measures may include greater supervision of employees, better training programs, improved penalty/reward incentives conditioned on the occurrence/avoidance of misconduct, and so on. If the transaction costs of such measures are high, however, shifting liability from the employee to the employer may actually increase the incidence of negligent or intentional harms. See Section I-C *infra*.

[111]See Landes & Posner, note 7 *supra*, at 65–66.

vicarious liability automatically redistributes the risk of loss from typically inefficient risk-bearers (victims[112] and municipal employees) to a typically superior risk bearer that can distribute the risk broadly among the taxpaying public. Under the negligence approach, by contrast, losses are redistributed only when the municipality is shown to have been negligent.

Yet another difference exists between the two approaches: they are likely to have differing effects on the scale of municipal activity. In the private sector, a potential advantage of either strict or negligent vicarious liability is that it increases the degree of cost-internalization by business enterprises whose judgment-proof employees cause injuries. Other things being equal, this improves resource allocation by encouraging businesses to operate at a more efficient scale. And, because there is less cost-internalization under a negligence-based approach to vicarious liability than under strict vicarious liability, the scale of private sector activity that results from vicarious liability based on negligence would be less efficient (other things being equal[113]) than the scale of activity that results from strict vicarious liability.

In the public sector, however, it is unclear whether greater cost internalization by municipal agencies would, other things being equal, improve or worsen resource allocation. The problem lies in the issue discussed above: the scale of municipal activity resulting from political and bureacratic decisions may be too large or too small. We simply have no way of knowing. Therefore, even if greater cost internalization would reduce the scale of activity, it is impossible to know whether such a reduction would be beneficial.[114]

---

[112] First-party insurance is not an entirely satisfactory method of risk redistribution, as the injuries caused by constitutional torts are often uninsurable in the first-party insurance market. Loss of public employment and loss of liberty and income due to unlawful confinement are illustrative of these uninsurable injuries.

[113] Of course, other things may not be equal. Greater cost-internalization by injurers under strict vicarious liability accompanies reduced cost-internalization by victims. But in some cases, it may be more efficient for victims to reduce the scale of their activities than for injurers to reduce the scale of their activities. See, e.g., Shavell, Strict Liability vs. Negligence, 9 J. Legal Stud. 1 (1980). Yet the observation in the text with respect to the difference between the public and private sectors remains valid. Whatever the desirability of cost internalization by victims, the greater cost internalization by injurers under strict vicarious liability has some benefit in the private sector (perhaps offset by other costs), but may have no benefits whatsoever in the public sector.

[114] In other words, a "second-best" issue arises with respect to cost-internalization in the public sector that does not arise in the private sector. Technically, this "second-best" issue

To summarize: either strict vicarious liability or vicarious liability based on negligence is an improvement over personal liability with respect to the efficiency of deterrent and precautionary measures to reduce the incidence of constitutional torts. Both would also likely improve the efficiency of risk allocation, but strict vicarious liability is probably better than a negligence-based approach in this regard. Finally, the greater degree of cost-internalization produced by strict vicarious liability has highly ambiguous effects on resource allocation. It would almost certainly lead to a greater reduction in the level of municipal services than the negligence-based approach, but the efficiency of this reduction is questionable. We therefore reserve judgment on the choice between the two approaches for the moment, pending an exploration of transaction cost issues.

It seems clear, however, that either approach is superior to personal liability when employees are judgment-proof and the transaction costs of contractual incentives are low (as assumed throughout this section). The only possible disadvantage of vicarious liability arises from the possibility that, in some instances, the greater degree of cost-internalization under vicarious liability could inefficiently reduce the scale of municipal activity. Yet, it is also possible that the increased cost-internalization under vicarious liability would efficiently reduce the scale of municipal activity. Hence, it seems that the economic case for pockets of personal liability must rest on transaction costs, if the case can be made at all.

C. THE PROBLEM OF TRANSACTION COSTS

Although vicarious liability may ameliorate some inefficiencies of personal liability by eliminating cost externalization, it may result in other inefficiences if certain transaction costs of employment agreements are significant. One possible inefficiency associated with vicarious liability, whether strict or negligent, is that the employee's incentive to avoid the occurrence of the wrong may be diluted, or at least the costs of motivating the employee to avoid the wrong will increase.

---

also complicates the analysis of precautionary behavior and deterrent measures under the alternative liability regimes. In particular, although either strict vicarious liability or vicarious liability based on negligence will motivate cost-effective precautions and deterrent measures, what is "cost-effective" may depend upon the scale of activity, and thus may differ between the two regimes. We assume throughout the analysis to follow, however, that such differences do not weigh systematically in favor of one regime or the other.

Under vicarious liability, successful plaintiffs tend to collect their judgments from the deep pocket (the municipal defendant) even if the individual wrongdoer remains jointly and severally liable. But if employees do not bear the costs of their wrongdoing, their incentive to avoid misconduct will decline. The municipality can avoid this decline only by introducing contractual incentives that will motivate precautions against accidental harms and deter intentional harms.

Absent transaction costs to negotiating and enforcing such contractual incentives, a municipality could establish adequate alternatives to personal liability. For example, the municipality can preserve the incentive to avoid wrongdoing that is created by personal liability with a clause in the employment agreement requiring the wrongdoer to indemnify the municipality for the consequences of the wrongdoer's acts.

But the limited empirical evidence suggests that employers very rarely pursue indemnity actions against their employees even when they have a legal or contractual right to indemnity.[115] To some extent, the unwillingness of employers to pursue indemnity actions may reflect implicit risk sharing agreements motivated by the risk aversion of employees or the existence of alternative incentive devices that are superior to indemnity. In that case, the unwillingness of employers to seek indemnity would not evidence any inefficiency of vicarious liability. It is also possible, however, that indemnity actions are simply not worth the effort, because the costs of bringing them and pursuing recovery thereafter may exceed the anticipated recovery from an employee with limited assets.[116] Under these conditions, the reduction in the incentives of employees to avoid wrong-

---

[115]See The Economics of Vicarious Liability, *supra* note 70, at 1243, and sources cited.

[116]. If an employee's assets are too meager to justify the pursuit of indemnity by the employer under vicarious liability, then a prospective plaintiff under personal liability may also find it unprofitable to bring suit. If so, then the imposition of vicarious liability will not dilute the employee's incentives to avoid wrongdoing. For a variety of reasons, however, plaintiffs may find it worthwhile to file suit even if the employer does not. The plaintiff may have an emotional or dignitary interest in filing an action that the employer lacks. Alternatively, the employer may decline to pursue indemnity for fear that it will disrupt otherwise amicable relations with the workforce—an indemnity action that sends an employee into personal bankruptcy could send a signal to the workforce that the employer has little interest in the personal welfare of his employees, affecting morale and productivity adversely.

doing may not be outweighed by other benefits, and vicarious liability may be inefficient.

Moreover, even if the employer can maintain the same incentive to avoid wrongdoing that exists under personal liability through indemnity actions or some other device, vicarious liability requires the employer to incur the transaction costs[117] of doing so. Vicarious liability also adds an additional party to litigation, and may thus increase litigation costs significantly. Unless these costs are offset by some other benefit of vicarious liability, such as a reduction in the number of wrongs committed due to greater monitoring and supervision by the employer, vicarious liability will ultimately reduce economic welfare. More generally, the economic benefits of vicarious liability (if any) are greater, the smaller the transaction costs to the employer of creating effective incentives for employees to avoid wrongdoing.

1. *The nature and magnitude of transaction costs.* A variety of factors affect the transaction costs of establishing contractual incentives to prevent misconduct. One important factor is the observability of employee performance. It is usually quite inexpensive to deter misconduct that the employer can cheaply observe before a wrong occurs: the employer simply intervenes to correct misbehavior before it causes injury. If behavior is unobservable or costly to observe, by contrast, ex-post rewards or penalties contingent upon the occurrence or non-occurrence of a wrong may be the only options available to establish proper incentives. Such ex-post incentives, however, may be quite costly. Consider, for example, the possibility of requiring the employee to indemnify the municipality: because litigation and other costs of pursuing an employee's assets are often quite high relative to the value of the assets, indemnity will often be uneconomical.

The expected duration of the employment relationship is another factor that affects the transaction costs of establishing incentives to

---

[117]The absolute magnitude of transaction costs is often less important than their relative magnitude. For example, the absolute costs of negotiating and enforcing a collective bargaining agreement between a municipality and its police force may be considerable, yet the existence of the agreement and of the attendant opportunity to bargain carefully on a wide range of issues may enable the municipality and its police officers to agree upon training, monitoring, and other incentive mechanisms that cheaply and effectively dissuade constitutional violations by the entire police force.

avoid misconduct. If the employee anticipates a long association with the employer and cannot easily secure equally attractive alternative employment, the employer can incorporate effective incentives against wrongdoing into routine decisions about career advancement—decisions about promotions, firings, salary increases, and so on. Such decisions must be made anyway, and it costs very little to condition them in part upon an employee's history of wrongdoing. If, however, the anticipated duration of employment is brief, or if equally attractive alternative employment is easily available, incentives pertaining to career advancement will likely be ineffective.

A third factor affecting transaction costs is the extent to which various employees confront the employer with similar or distinct incentive problems. If a large number of employees perform similar functions and pose similar risks of malfeasance, a single system of incentives that applies to all of these employees may dissuade misconduct satisfactorily, and the employer may achieve considerable "economies of scale" with such a system. If each employee performs distinct tasks, by contrast, a costly process of customizing the incentives for each employee may be necessary.

Finally, the employer's knowledge of the risk of misconduct and the opportunities to avoid it will affect the magnitude of transaction costs. If the employee performs a highly skilled function that the employer understands poorly, it may be quite expensive for the employer to design and enforce effective incentives against misconduct. If the risk of misconduct involves behavior that is quite familiar to the employer, the cost of instituting incentives is lessened.

2. *Implications for the rule of municipal liability.* As noted at the outset, the factual patterns that give rise to constitutional tort claims are tremendously diverse. Consequently, it is difficult to generalize about the transaction costs of incentives to avoid these torts. Two examples may be instructive.

Example (i): Police activity is perhaps the most frequent target of constitutional tort actions. Most of this police conduct occurs on the streets and is difficult for police supervisors to observe before the tort occurs, a factor that increases the transaction costs of preventing it. On the other hand, most police officers are career employees who are deeply concerned about prospects for promotion, and who cannot move easily to equally remunerative alternative employment. Cheaply administered rewards and penalties built into career advancement decisions, therefore, may be quite effective at inducing appropriate behavior. In addition, because the risk of misconduct is similar for every police officer, customized incentives are probably unnecessary. Finally, the nature of police misconduct is quite well understood by supervisory employees, making it easy to design training programs and police manuals that establish detailed guidelines for line officers to follow.

On the whole, therefore, the costs to the municipality of negotiating and enforcing reasonably effective incentives to dissuade constitutional violations by the police are probably modest. The use of costly incentive mechanisms such as indemnity suits against individual police officers is unnecessary, because training programs, careful supervision, and injury-contingent penalties relating to career advancement can probably suffice to prevent most misconduct.

It follows that the imposition of vicarious liability on the municipality is unlikely to dilute the incentives of police officers to avoid constitutional violations. On the contrary, vicarious liability will likely motivate municipalities to adopt a variety of cost-effective devices to reduce the incidence of police malfeasance. These devices may not be adopted in the absence of vicarious liability because police officers are often judgment-proof which, as explained above, allows municipalities to externalize the costs of constitutional violations and thereby dilutes their incentives to economize on the costs of injuries.

Example (ii): Hiring and firing decisions are also common targets of constitutional tort litigation. For concreteness, imagine a small municipality with a city attorney's office; the office has a small staff, and the city attorney is ordinarily responsible for hiring and firing members of the staff. The city attorney discharges a female staff attorney, purportedly because she is incompetent. The discharged employee claims, however, that she was fired because of her sex.

If—as seems quite likely—senior municipal officials (the mayor, the city manager, and so on) lack the expertise necessary to evaluate the legal skills of staff attorneys in the city attorney's office, it is difficult to imagine what type of monitoring or other supervisory measures they might cost-effectively employ to avoid invidious discrimination in the hiring and firing decisions of the city attorney. Any attempt to interfere in such decisions might simply undermine the ability of the city attorney to assemble the best possible staff.

Of course, vicarious liability will likely motivate the municipality to do what it can to avoid hiring a sexist city attorney, but such proclivities on the part of candidates for the position may be undetectable during the hiring process. And, while the municipality can always establish a policy of firing any city attorney who is successfully sued under §1983, even that sanction may be relatively ineffective if the city attorney can earn a comparable income in private practice.

Under these circumstances, the imposition of vicarious liability upon the municipality may not do much to ameliorate any problem of unlawful hirings and firings. Indeed, it may exacerbate the problem if its only effect is to insulate potential wrongdoers, like the city attorney in our hypothetical example, from personal liability. Vicarious liability may then be counterproductive.

These examples illustrate how transaction costs vary from job category to job category. And, depending upon the transaction costs of available contractual incentives, the imposition of vicarious liability may lead to an amelioration of serious inefficiencies that arise under personal liability or may actually worsen those inefficiencies.

We now return to an issue raised in the last section, whether a negligence-based approach to the imposition of vicarious liability upon municipalities is more or less efficient than strict vicarious liability. What follows suggests that the possible existence of significant transaction costs tends to support adoption of the negligence approach.

The transaction costs of contractual incentives are directly relevant to a negligence analysis. Under a negligence standard, the question is whether supervisory employees could have employed cost-effective measures to prevent the constitutional tort. Where the transaction costs of contractual incentives are high, cost-effective measures to prevent the tort may not exist, and thus negligence is less likely to be found. Where transaction costs are low, cost-effective measures to prevent the tort may well exist, and a finding of negligence is more likely. In short, the negligence approach tends to result in the imposition of vicarious liability in precisely those situations where transaction costs are lowest and the economic benefits of vicarious liability are greatest.

Strict vicarious liability, on the other hand, imposes vicarious liability whenever it is determined that the employee who committed the wrong was a servant of the municipality acting within the scope of his employment, a condition that is almost always satisfied in constitutional torts cases. Thus, a danger exists that strict vicarious liability may at times reduce the incentives of municipal employees to avoid misconduct, or at least increase the costs of dissuading misconduct, with little or no offsetting benefits.[118]

For this reason, the negligence-based approach is perhaps the better alternative, although the choice is a close one. The negligence approach creates incentives for municipalities to adopt cost-effective measures to prevent constitutional torts, while preserving the incentives created by personal liability for individual employees to avoid misconduct when municipalities cannot substitute alternative incentives at reasonable cost or when municipalities have exhausted all reasonable measures to prevent misconduct.

One last issue requires attention. If vicarious liability is limited as under the negligence-based approach, there will be more cases in which the employee is held personally liable and must pay damages out of his own pocket. This observation brings the analysis full circle to an issue addressed earlier: whether personal liability inefficiently reduces the productivity of municipal employees by causing overcautious, self-protective behavior. If the transaction costs of contractual incentives to avoid misconduct are high—contrary to the assumption embodied in our prior discussion of this issue—the same may be true of the transaction costs of contractual incentives to discourage undue timidity or inaction by municipal employees. One must therefore inquire whether a rule of personal liability might create inefficiencies that cannot be averted by contract.

---

[118]Of course, strict vicarious liability is not necessarily inconsistent with an approach to vicarious liability that is sensitive to the transaction costs problem. The common-law of agency and torts creates categories of employment relationships, and imposes vicarious liability or not depending upon the category into which the employment relationship falls—*respondeat superior* applies to the master-servant category. One of the authors has argued elsewhere that this approach often (though by no means always) leads to vicarious liability when transaction costs of contracting are low and vicarious liability is relatively more efficient. See Sykes, The Economics of Vicarious Liability, note 70 *supra*, at 1259–79. In effect, then, an implicit (though more sweeping and categorical) negligence analysis appears to underlie the common-law categories.

As noted in the text, however, almost all constitutional torts are committed by servants under the common-law definition. The city attorney in our illustration, for example, almost certainly fits the definition of a servant, yet we are uneasy about vicarious liability under the hypothesized circumstances. We are therefore hesitant to embrace the common-law categories as an adequate solution to the problem of transaction costs.

As noted above, bad faith constitutional torts usually involve intentional harms or reckless behavior that reflect indifference to well-settled constitutional requirements. Most of these torts are easily avoidable, and few municipal employees need fear that they will accidentally commit them.[119] The likelihood of overcautious behavior under personal liability seems small, therefore, even when the transaction costs of contractual incentives against it are high.

In addition, the costs of any overcautious behavior under personal liability must be weighed against the costs of shifting liability to the municipality in circumstances where the municipality cannot cost-effectively create equivalent contractual incentives against misconduct. Especially where the danger of inducing overcautious behavior under personal liability is quite low, as is seemingly the case for bad faith constitutional torts, the balance would seem to favor personal liability.

In short, although a negligence-based approach to vicarious liability would assuredly insulate the municipality from liability in some cases, it does so in precisely those cases where vicarious liability is least likely to be beneficial, and where personal liability produces valuable incentives that may be lost or that will be costly to replicate under vicarious liability. Strict vicarious liability, as well as some of the alternatives proposed by other writers,[120] lacks this important quality.

D. THE POLICY RULE

Is the policy rule of *Monell* an economically sound basis for the imposition of vicarious liability upon the municipality? The above analysis suggests that the answer is no.

In Part I, we noted that the policy rule is somewhat unsettled and that recent Supreme Court decisions vacillate between two interpretations of "policy." One interpretation focuses upon the position of the wrongdoer in the municipal hierarchy; the tort was committed pursuant to "policy" only if the decision that led to the

---

[119]To the extent that overcautious behavior might be induced by a fear of baseless litigation, municipalities can avoid the problem by agreeing to assume the litigation costs of employees sued for constitutional violations, or at least the costs of employees who successfully defend themselves.

[120]See note 91 *supra*.

tort was made by a high-ranking municipal official in a policymaking position. The second interpretation focuses on the nature of the decision that led to the tort; the tort was committed pursuant to "policy" only if that decision amounted to or resulted from a rule of general applicability, formulated through a deliberative process. Neither of these understandings of the policy rule is economically satisfactory.

The view that requires the decisionmaker to be a policymaker with final authority in the municipal hierarchy obviously excludes the possibility of municipal liability for most torts caused by low-level employees. It does so even when training, monitoring, or injury-contingent contractual penalties provide a cost-effective means to avoid the tort or to reduce the incidence of such torts, and despite the fact that the municipality may lack the incentive to utilize these measures under personal liability. There is no apparent economic justification for this limitation.

Concomitantly, municipal liability for constitutional torts caused by high-level municipal officials may sometimes do little to reduce the incidence of these torts (or may even increase their incidence) because of the potentially high transaction costs associated with establishing contractual incentives to dissuade misconduct. The higher the official in the municipal hierarchy, the more likely that the official occupies a specialized and relatively autonomous position. As a consequence, other municipal officials will often lack the expertise to monitor or supervise the official effectively. In addition, because the duties of officials high in the municipal hierarchy are often unique, a costly process of negotiating customized contractual incentives applicable to only the one official will often be necessary.

Consequently, the transaction costs of contractual incentives against misconduct are probably, on average, relatively great for high-level municipal officials in policymaking positions. A rule of municipal liability that limits liability to torts caused by these officials may at times produce outcomes opposite to those that would result under the negligence-based approach that we advocate above.

The alternative interpretation of the policy rule, which emphasizes the nature of the decision that causes the constitutional tort, is no better. It is true that municipal liability for the consequences of rules of general applicability will perhaps motivate more careful deliberation over the formulation of these rules, and thus reduce the number of constitutional torts that result from them. But no economic basis exists for limiting municipal liability so narrowly. To the extent that the incidence of constitutional torts can be reduced cost-effectively through training, monitoring, and injury-contingent contractual incentives, it should not matter whether the torts result from some generally applied rule.

In sum, the policy rule of *Monell*, in both of its present variations, is economically unsound as a rule of vicarious liability for bad faith constitutional torts. As noted, a number of commentators have suggested abandoning the policy rule in favor of *respondeat superior*.[121] Our analysis shows that such an approach would certainly be preferable to existing law. But a rule of "vicarious" liability based on the negligent failure of the municipality to take measures to prevent the tort is also economically superior to existing law, and is at least arguably superior to *respondeat superior* as well.

VI. The Scope of Municipal Liability for "Good Faith" Acts by Municipal Employees

Good faith torts arise from actions of municipal employees that are determined to be unconstitutional ex post but were not clearly unconstitutional ex ante. In many of these cases, municipal employees or their supervisors undoubtedly recognize that the behavior in question falls within a gray area of the law.[122] In other cases, however, the courts make new law or reverse old law and apply the change retroactively, with the result that behavior may ultimately be found unconstitutional even if it appeared certainly constitutional beforehand.[123]

As noted earlier, municipal employees enjoy individual immunity for good faith constitutional torts. But under *Monell* and *Owen*, municipalities incur liability for good faith torts committed pursuant to official policy.[124] Thus, in this class of cases, the policy rule of *Monell* does not simply determine whether a municipality is vicariously liable for a constitutional tort, it determines whether the tort is actionable at all.

---

[121]See authorities cited in note 47 *supra*.

[122]See *e.g.*, Mitchell v. Forsyth, 472 U.S. 511 (1985); Evers v. Custer County, 745 F. 2d 1196 (9th Cir. 1984); Walters v. City of Ocean Springs, 626 F.2d 1317 (5th Cir. 1980).

[123]See, *e.g.*, *Pembaur*, 475 U.S. 469; Owen v. City of Independence, 445 U.S. 622.

[124]See notes 74, 84–86 *supra* and accompanying text.

A. THE JUSTIFICATION FOR INDIVIDUAL IMMUNITY

The policy rationale for individual immunity is the familiar concern about self-protective behavior. Without immunity, the courts suggest, a fear of personal liability would cause municipal employees to become overcautious in the performance of their duties.[125]

This concern is legitimate where, for whatever reason, the municipal employer cannot be sued: If the law is unsettled, municipal employees cannot determine with confidence ex ante which of their actions may later be judged unconstitutional. To subject them to personal liability under these conditions may well encourage them to avoid taking actions that they believe create an appreciable risk of liability, with adverse effects on job performance and on overall social welfare.

Of course, as explained above, the municipality might eliminate this problem through indemnification agreements or other contractual incentives that motivate better job performance.[126] But the municipality may view indemnification as undesirable because it eliminates the cost externalization that accompanies the use of judgment-proof employees. And other incentives for improved job performance may operate quite imperfectly, especially if the quality of job performance is difficult or costly to observe. As a result, it is possible that municipalities will simply tolerate the adverse effects of personal liability on job performance. If so, personal liability could lead to serious inefficiencies.

By discouraging behavior of uncertain legality, of course, personal liability can also reduce the incidence of good faith constitutional torts. The benefits of this reduction in the number of torts, however, may well be outweighed by the inefficiencies of uncorrected self-protective behavior. It may then be economically desirable to provide individual immunity—at least so long as the employer is not amenable to suit.

---

[125]See *e.g.*, Imbler v. Pachtman, 424 U.S. at 424–29; Wood v. Strickland, 420 U.S. at 319–21; Scheuer v. Rhodes, 416 U.S. at 242–49. In addition to this policy rationale, the Supreme Court has sometimes justified the official immunity doctrine on the ground that the Forty-Second Congress would have explicitly abolished common-law tort immunities had it intended to do so. See *e.g.*, Tenny v. Brandhove, 341 U.S. at 376; Pierson v. Ray, 386 U.S. at 554–55. (1967). As we suggested in Part II, however, this is an incorrect way to interpret §1983.

[126]See notes 96–99 *supra* and accompanying text.

If the municipal employer can be sued, however, the case for individual immunity is considerably weakened, whether or not the transaction costs of contractual incentives are significant. Consider first the case of low transaction costs. As the analysis in Section V indicates, the choice between vicarious liability and personal liability has no economic importance if employees can pay judgments against them in full and the transaction costs of contractual incentives are low. Precisely the same analysis establishes that the choice between municipal liability with individual immunity and municipal liability without individual immunity has no significance if municipalities can pay judgments against them in full and the transaction costs of contractual incentives are low. Because most municipalities generally can pay adverse judgments, therefore, our prior analysis establishes that the rule of individual immunity will have no effect on resource allocation when transaction costs are low.

When transaction costs are high, individual immunity is still largely superfluous. For whether the employee enjoys individual immunity or not, successful plaintiffs will usually collect from the deep-pocket defendant (the municipality) rather than the employee. Hence, even if the problem of self-protective behavior makes it inefficient to place personal liability on the employee, a costly reallocation of liability to the municipality by contract is usually unnecessary. Alternatively, if it is efficient for the employee to bear some amount of liability, a costly employment agreement to accomplish that result will be necessary regardless of whether the employee enjoys personal immunity.

It follows that a rule of individual immunity has no impact if the municipality is amenable to suit. It does no harm, but neither is it essential to prevent self-protective behavior. If individual immunity serves some valuable purpose, therefore, that purpose must relate to cases in which the municipal employer is also immune. This conclusion contrasts starkly with the conclusions of other writers,[127] who argue that individual immunity is an important component of the liability regime, even when the municipality is subject to suit.

B. THE CASE FOR MUNICIPAL IMMUNITY

The remainder of our analysis will assume, as do the courts, that a serious problem of self-protective behavior would arise if personal

---

[127]See authorities cited in note 91 *supra*.

liability were imposed in cases involving good faith torts and that a rule of individual immunity is therefore efficient for such cases if the municipality is also immune from suit. We have established as well that if the municipality can be sued, the existence or non-existence of individual immunity is largely a matter of indifference. The analysis is thereby considerably simplified, and only one question remains: should there be a cause of action against municipalities for good faith constitutional torts?

A review of cases involving good faith torts suggests that many of them involve actions which, ex ante, appear almost certainly to be legal. Cases in which changes in the law are applied retroactively are illustrative.[128] Obviously, the imposition of municipal liability for these actions will have little impact on the ex ante behavior of municipal employees and their supervisors. It will simply impose costs ex post that tend to reduce the scale of municipal activity, with highly ambiguous implications for economic welfare, while at the same time creating significant litigation costs.

To be sure, liability also redistributes the risk of associated injuries, and may therefore provide some risk-sharing benefits if municipalities are better risk bearers than injured parties. But risk sharing benefits alone rarely suffice to justify the imposition of civil liability, since civil litigation is ordinarily far more costly than alternative mechanisms for the redistribution of risk, such as social insurance schemes.

Other good faith constitutional tort cases involve actions that are known ex ante to fall within gray areas of the law.[129] If liability attaches in such cases, municipal employees and their supervisors may well perceive a substantial possibility of an adverse judgment in the event of litigation. This prospect, in turn, will induce some efforts to avoid actions of questionable legality altogether and to accomplish tasks by alternative means. The question is whether these efforts are efficient.

That question is quite difficult to answer. The prospect of liability will discourage actions that would ultimately prove constitutional as well as actions that would ultimately prove unconstitutional. In other words, a problem of self-protective behavior arises yet again as municipalities strive to avoid liability, with potentially adverse effects on the quality of municipal services. It is impossible to know

---

[128]See note 123 *supra*.

[129]See note 122 *supra*.

whether the inefficiencies of self-protective behavior by municipalities will exceed the efficiencies associated with a reduced number of constitutional torts. But the danger of self-protective behavior
certainly weakens the case for the imposition of liability, and the
distinct possibility arises that municipal liability for these good faith
torts is also inefficient.[130]

This conclusion again contrasts markedly with the analysis of
other writers,[131] who suggest that self-protective behavior is a problem that arises mainly under personal liability, and that it can be
eliminated by expanded governmental liability coupled with immunity for individual officials. On the contrary, inefficient self-
protective behavior is by no means unique to a regime of personal
liability, and its emergence under vicarious liability may justify
governmental immunity just as its emergence under personal liability may justify individual immunity.

In the end, because the efficiency of municipal liability for good
faith constitutional torts is very much in doubt, a rule of municipal
immunity for such torts is perhaps as attractive as any alternative.
At a minimum, immunity would avoid some costly litigation, eliminate some inefficient self-protective measures, and protect municipalities in some cases against liability that cannot be anticipated at
all ex ante and that consequently would impose considerable burdens on the municipal treasury ex post with no attendant reduction
in the number of constitutional violations.[132]

VII. CONCLUSION

The rules presently governing the imposition of municipal
liability in constitutional tort cases are hopelessly flawed. Contrary

---

[130]This analysis provides no support, however, for the policy rule of *Monell*, inasmuch as
the risk of self-protective behavior is no smaller for "policy" decisions by high-level officials
than for other decisions by municipal employees.

[131]See note 91 *supra*.

[132]A possible objection to immunity for good faith constitutional torts is that it would
destroy the incentive for litigation over actions that fall within gray areas of the law, and
thus perpetuate legal uncertainty. Municipal liability would create an incentive to litigate
such actions and thereby promote the resolution of uncertainties. But the resolution of
uncertainty is not in itself advantageous, as the costs of associated litigation may be great.
Besides, the incentive to litigate is considerable even in the absence of municipal liability
for good faith torts. Little would be lost, arguably, if "good faith" constitutional torts were
no longer actionable.

to the analysis in *Monell*, there is no evidence in the Civil Rights Act of 1871 or its legislative history that the Forty-Second Congress intended to limit vicarious liability for the torts of municipal employees to actions that are taken pursuant to "policy." Instead, the historical evidence suggests that Congress intended to leave the standards for the imposition of vicarious liability to the federal common law.

More importantly, the "policy rule" of *Monell* serves no intelligible purpose. It is largely incompatible with the policy objectives that the Supreme Court itself invokes on occasion as the basis for the enactment of §1983, such as the effective deterrence of wrongdoing.

Thus, the Court, through its common-lawmaking authority, should adopt an alternative approach to municipal liability. We have developed an economic analysis that provides some support for the proposal by other writers that the policy rule be abandoned in favor of common-law agency principles, including the doctrine of *respondeat superior*, but our analysis suggests still other alternatives. With respect to the most egregious constitutional torts, those committed in "bad faith," a negligence approach to municipal liability is arguably as good or better from an economic standpoint than *respondeat superior*. And with respect to more innocent "good faith" torts, for which municipal officials enjoy individual immunity, the extension of immunity to the municipality is perhaps the best option.

WILLIAM E. LEE

THE SUPREME COURT
AND THE RIGHT TO
RECEIVE EXPRESSION

In several cases in the 1960s, the Warren Court articulated a First Amendment right to receive expression.[1] Most notably, the Court held that restriction on the freedom of broadcasters was justified because the rights of broadcast listeners were paramount.[2] The Burger Court relied upon the right to receive expression, for example, to invalidate restrictions on commercial speech[3] and on cor-

William E. Lee is Associate Professor, Henry W. Grady School of Journalism and Mass Communication, University of Georgia.

AUTHOR'S NOTE: Research for this paper was supported by grants from the American Cable Publishers Institute and the University of Georgia. The views expressed are solely those of the author.

[1] Red Lion Broadcasting Co. v. FCC, 395 U.S. 367 (1969); Stanley v. Georgia, 394 U.S. 557 (1969); Lamont v. Postmaster Gen., 381 U.S. 301 (1965). The right to receive was briefly mentioned in several decisions prior to the 1960s, but it did not play a significant role in those decisions. See Thomas v. Collins, 323 U.S. 516, 534 (1945) (stating that the law in question imposed a restriction upon the speaker's rights and the rights of the audience to hear); Martin v. City of Struthers, 318 U.S. 141, 143 (1943) (stating that freedom of speech and press has broad scope; it embraces the right to distribute literature and necessarily protects the right to receive it). Cf. Marsh v. Alabama, 326 U.S. 501, 507 (1946) (regardless of the ownership of a town, the public has an interest in the functioning of the community in such manner that the channels of communication remain free). For a discussion of the intellectual ferment in the 1940s that led to many government actions designed to promote the right to receive expression, see Baldasty & Simpson, How Pessimism Rewrote the First Amendment, 56 Wash. L. Rev. 365 (1981).

[2] Red Lion Broadcasting Co. v. FCC, 395 U.S. 367, 390 (1969). See text and notes accompanying notes 158–73 infra.

[3] Virginia State Bd. of Pharmacy v. Virginia Citizens Consumer Council, 425 U.S. 748 (1976). See text and notes accompanying notes 58–76 infra.

porate expression.[4] But the Burger Court's commitment to a right
to receive expression wavered. In *Board of Education v. Pico*,[5] a plurality found that students had such a right in a school library.[6] But
four members of the Court joined dissenting opinions rejecting the
right.[7] More recently in *Pacific Gas & Electric Co. v. Public Utilities
Commission*,[8] the Court found the requirement that a utility include
the messages of a consumer group in its billing envelopes a violation
of the utility's First Amendment rights. And in *Posadas De Puerto
Rico Associates v. Tourism Co.*,[9] the Court gave extraordinarily deferential review to a restriction of casino gambling advertisements.

Posadas and *PG & E* have the potential to affect a variety of First
Amendment cases. For example, *PG & E* was based on principles
that conflict with the fairness doctrine.[10] *PG & E* also conflicts with

---

[4]First Nat'l Bank v. Bellotti, 435 U.S. 765 (1978). See text and notes accompanying notes
129–57 *infra*.

[5]457 U.S. 853 (1982).

[6]Justice Brennan, joined by Justices Marshall and Stevens, concluded that the First Amendment imposes limitations on a school board's discretion to remove books from libraries. *Id.*
at 863–72. Justice Blackmun joined in all parts of the plurality opinion except that dealing
with the right to receive expression. In a concurring opinion, Justice Blackmun stated that
the issue was narrower than the right to receive expression identified by the plurality. *Id.*
at 878 (Blackmun, J., concurring in part and concurring in the judgment). Justice White
concurred in the judgment but believed that the plurality's discussion of the First Amendment
limits on the school board was premature. *Id.* at 883–84 (White, J., concurring in the
judgment). See text and notes accompanying notes 110–28 *infra*.

[7]Chief Justice Burger, joined by Justices Powell, Rehnquist, and O'Connor, issued a
dissenting opinion criticizing the right to receive. Justice Rehnquist's dissent, joined by Chief
Justice Burger and Justice Powell, also criticized the right to receive information. See text
and notes accompanying notes 110–28 *infra*.

[8]106 S.Ct. 903 (1986). See text and notes accompanying notes 202–28 *infra*.

[9]106 S.Ct. 2968 (1986). See text and notes accompanying notes 84–109 *infra*.

[10]In FCC v. League of Women Voters, 468 U.S. 364 (1984), the Court noted that technological advancements may have rendered the spectrum-scarcity rationale for broadcast
regulation obsolete, but that a signal from Congress or the FCC would be required before
the Court altered its approach to broadcast regulation. *Id.* at 376 n.11. The Court also stated
that if the fairness doctrine reduces rather than enhances speech, it would be forced to
reconsider the constitutionality of that doctrine. *Id.* at 378 n.12.

In 1985, the FCC concluded that the information marketplace was sufficiently diversified
to attenuate the need for the fairness doctrine, and that the doctrine indeed created a chilling
effect. 102 F.C.C.2d 143, 158–221 (1985). The Commission, however, deferred to the judgment of Congress as to whether the fairness doctrine should be repealed. *Id.* at 246. In 1986,
the D.C. Circuit held that the fairness doctrine was not a binding statutory obligation.
Telecommunications Research and Action Center v. FCC, 801 F.2d 501, 517–18 (D.C. Cir.
1986), cert. denied, 107 S.Ct. 3196 (1987). In response to the D.C. Circuit, legislation to
codify the fairness doctrine was passed by both the Senate, 133 Cong. Rec. S5232 (daily
ed. Apr. 21, 1987), and the House of Representatives, 133 Cong. Rec. H4160 (daily ed.
June 3, 1987). President Reagan vetoed the legislation, claiming the fairness doctrine is

cable must-carry and access channel requirements, both of which
will be tested in the next wave of cable litigation.[11] The key principle
from *Posadas*—that the government can manipulate private behavior
through restrictions on truthful advertisements for legal products
or services—could diminish protection for all commercial speech.
Posadas is part of the impetus behind the current legislative proposal
to ban all advertisements for tobacco products.[12] In light of these
broad implications, it is critical to understand the doctrine of the
right to receive expression.

Slightly more than a decade ago, Professor Thomas Emerson
described the contours of the right to receive as "obscure."[13] The
question addressed here is whether it is better defined today.[14] At

---

"antagonistic to the freedom of expression guaranteed by the First Amendment." 133 Cong.
Rec. S8438 (daily ed. June 23, 1987). Following the veto, the FCC eliminated the fairness
doctrine. 63 Rad. Reg.2d (P & F) 541 (1987). Congressional advocates of the fairness doctrine
then announced that they would try to attach a fairness doctrine provision to a bill that the
President would be reluctant to veto. Wall St. J., Aug. 5, 1987, at 8, col. 3.

[11]The FCC's must-carry requirements, which forced cable systems to carry certain television signals, were found unconstitutional in Quincy Cable TV, Inc. v. FCC, 768 F.2d
1434 (D.C. Cir. 1985), cert. denied, 106 S.Ct. 2889 (1986). The FCC adopted a new version
of must-carry in 1986. 61 Rad. Reg.2d (P & F) 792 (1986), modified, 62 Rad. Reg.2d (P &
F) 1251 (1987). The new rules are being challenged in Turner Broadcasting System, Inc. v.
FCC, No. 86-1682 (D.C. Cir. filed Dec. 12, 1986).

Municipal cable franchises frequently require that cable publishers provide access channels
for certain purposes. The Cable Communications Policy Act of 1984, 47 U.S.C. §521 (1985)
also contains access provisions. *Id.* at §§531–32. In Preferred Communications, Inc. v. City
of Los Angeles, 754 F.2d 1396 (9th Cir. 1985), aff'd and remanded, 106 S. Ct. 2034 (1986),
the Ninth Circuit commented that while it was not addressing the constitutionality of access
requirements, the provisions posed "particularly troubling constitutional questions." 754
F.2d at 1401 n.4. The constitutionality of access requirements will be challenged at trial in
Preferred. Two federal courts recently concluded that access channel requirements violate
the First Amendment. Group W Cable, Inc. v. City of Santa Cruz, No. C-84-7456-WWS,
slip op. at 30–33 (N.D. Cal. Sept. 10, 1987); Century Federal, Inc. v. City of Palo Alto,
No. C-85-2168 EFL, slip op. at 3–8 (N.D. Cal. Sept. 1, 1987). But see Erie Telecommunications, Inc. v. City of Erie, 659 F. Supp. 580, 598–601 (W.D. Pa. 1987) (access channels do
not violate First Amendment).

[12]H.R. 1272, 100th Cong., 1st Sess., 133 Cong. Rec. H836 (daily ed. Feb. 25, 1987). The
bill, sponsored by Representative Synar, was described by his legislative assistant as a
response to the *Posadas* decision. Telephone interview with John Hollar (Mar. 2, 1987).

[13]Emerson, Legal Foundations of the Right to Know, 1976 Wash. U.L.Q. 1, 3. See also
Note, 82 Colum. L. Rev. 720, 733 (1982) (describing the right to receive as well established,
but stating that it has received little attention in the case law); Note, 34 Wash. & Lee L.
Rev. 1115, 1123 (1977) (claiming that the right to receive is an ill-defined concept).

[14]It is important to distinguish the right to receive expression from the right to gather
information, although both combine in the right to know. Emerson, note 13 *supra*, at 2.
Some commentators have described information gathering as an active right, while the receipt

the outset, it is important to note that the concept has been applied in two markedly different types of cases. First, it has been applied where the government restricts communication between private parties. An example is *Virginia State Board of Pharmacy v. Virginia Citizens Consumer Council*,[15] where the Court held that a ban on pharmacist advertising of prescription drug prices was unconstitutional. Second, the right to receive is a rationale for those government regulations that seek to enhance the flow of expression by limiting the exercise of "private censorship." An example of this type of case is *CBS, Inc. v. FCC*,[16] where the Court sustained a federal requirement that broadcasters provide time to federal can-

---

of expression is a passive right. See, *e.g.*, Note, 4 Hastings Con. L.Q. 109, 137–38 (1977); Note, 82 Yale L.J. 1337, 1347 n.66 (1973). This distinction assumes that intent to disseminate information motivates information gathering. But the Supreme Court's protection of a right to gather information does not rest solely upon the value of dissemination of information. See, *e.g.*, Press-Enterprise Co. v. Superior Court, 464 U.S. 501, 508 (1984) (stating that the value of open court proceedings lies in the fact that people not actually attending trials can have confidence that standards of fairness are being observed; the knowledge that anyone is free to attend gives assurance of the fairness of the proceeding). Moreover, while audience members may be passive in that they do not initiate communication, they may actively seek to receive expression.

The right to receive expression exists only when a willing speaker wishes to communicate; it cannot be used by a listener to force a potential speaker to communicate. Professor Nimmer's comment on the distinction between the right to gather information and the right to receive expression is helpful. He stated: "The right to gather information is sometimes also referred to as a right to 'receive information and ideas.' This too leads to confusion, because the latter formulation may be understood as simply a recognition of the audience interest in the freedom of a given communication. In that broad sense, any denial of speech involves a denial of the potential audience's right to 'receive information and ideas.' The right to gather information is both broader and narrower in its scope. It is broader than the audience interest in speech in that it may arise even if the 'information' to be gathered is not contained in speech, either written or oral, but consists instead of an event or of observable facts, which will become 'speech' only when the information gatherer communicates that which he has observed. When the information to be gathered is contained in speech, the information gathering right is narrower in scope than the general audience interest in speech in that it assumes that the speech has either already occurred (and is recorded in some form), or that it will occur in that a willing speaker will engage in speech without interference. . . . The only issue posed is as to the right of the press or public to be in such physical propinquity with a setting or event, or with a document or speaker, so as to make possible the gathering of the 'information' contained therein." Nimmer, Nimmer on Freedom of Speech §4.09[B] at 4-42-43 (1984). As Professor Nimmer indicates, any restriction on speakers could also be regarded as an infringement of the audience's right to receive expression. Only those First Amendment cases where the Court considered audience rights as part of its analysis are considered here.

[15]425 U.S. 748 (1976). See text and notes accompanying notes 58–76 *infra*.

[16]453 U.S. 367 (1981). See text and notes accompanying notes 178–89 *infra*.

didates. In both settings, the right to receive seeks to promote a well-informed public.

Although the Court claims that the right to receive is well established,[17] the Court has done little more than point to the right.[18] It has never explained the theoretical basis of the right. The right to receive is a catchall phrase. The right consists of different doctrinal strands not always reconcilable, due in part to the Court's failure to ground the right in a cohesive theory of freedom of expression. Another explanation is that the right was developed in disparate and unique contexts. It will be shown that the primary utility of the right to receive is in those peculiar settings where speakers[19] are free from government restraint but where the government burdens the receipt of expression. When used to confer standing upon an audience to challenge restraints on speakers, the right to receive merely increases the number of parties who may challenge such restrictions. It does not alter the First Amendment analysis of those cases. It will be shown, too, that the concept of audience rights ought to be abandoned as a rationale for restricting the expression of speakers.

I. GOVERNMENT RESTRICTIONS ON THE FREE FLOW OF EXPRESSION

A. SANCTIONS AGAINST THE RECIPIENT OF INFORMATION

1. *The curious beginning:* Lamont. The first case in which the Court found that a law violated the right to receive was *Lamont v. Postmaster General.*[20] At issue was a federal statute requiring the postal service to detain "communist political propaganda" until the addressee was notified of the mail and requested delivery. The government claimed that the senders of the mail, foreign governments, were not persons with First Amendment rights,[21] and that the statute was justified because many members of the public were offended by mail of this

---

[17]Stanley v. Georgia, 394 U.S. 557, 564 (1969). See note 45 *infra*.

[18]Similarly, lower courts also only point to the right to receive expression. See, *e.g.*, Minarcini v. Strongsville City School District, 541 F.2d 577, 583 (6th Cir. 1976).

[19]In this paper, I use "speaker" and "speech" generically, instead of changing terms to reflect the particular communicative activity involved in a given case.

[20]381 U.S. 301 (1965).

[21]Brief for Appellee at 12.

content.[22] Lamont asserted that the First Amendment protects the right to receive a communication.[23] He also challenged the statute as a licensing system designed to discourage communication of "politically offensive" expression.[24] Justice Douglas's opinion for the Court briefly mentioned the danger of administrative officials "sitting astride" the flow of mail,[25] but rested on the narrow ground that the burden of requesting delivery of mail was an abridgment of the addressee's First Amendment rights.[26] The unique context of *Lamont*, along with the terseness of the majority opinion, suggest that the right protected is not readily transferable to other settings.

A fundamental problem in *Lamont* was the statute's targeting expression of political ideology for disfavored treatment. This, Justice Douglas stated, was at war with the uninhibited debate contemplated by the First Amendment.[27] Douglas's use of the phrase "uninhibited debate" derives from *New York Times Co. v. Sullivan*,[28] decided a year earlier. In *New York Times*, the Court elaborated on the relationship between government and citizenry[29] and sought to

---

[22]*Id.* at 13.

[23]Brief for Appellant at 15. Commentators had previously articulated a right of addressees to receive mail. See Schwartz, The Mail Must Not Go Through—Propaganda and Pornography, 11 UCLA L. Rev. 804, 824 (1964); Note, 68 Harv. L. Rev. 1393, 1406 (1955).

[24]Brief for Appellant at 17.

[25]381 U.S. at 306. In a subsequent case involving censorship of mail sent and received by prisoners, the Court held the interests of prisoners and their correspondents in uncensored communication by mail was grounded in the First Amendment. Procunier v. Martinez, 416 U.S. 396, 418 (1974). Although the right to receive expression was an aspect of the process of communication at issue in *Martinez*, the Court also noted the way in which the censorship affected the speech of nonprisoners. The Court stated: "The wife of a prison inmate who is not permitted to read all that her husband wanted to say to her has suffered an abridgment of her interest in communicating with him as plain as that which results from censorship of her letter to him. In either event, censorship of prisoner mail works a consequential restriction on the First and Fourteenth Amendment rights of those who are not prisoners." *Id.* at 409. By approaching the case from this perspective, the Court avoided questions concerning prisoner's rights. *Id.* at 408. *Martinez* is more important for its criticism of standardless censorship, *id.* at 415–16, than for its brief comments about the right to receive expression.

The Court recently sustained a state prison regulation limiting correspondence between prisoners. Turner v. Safley, 107 S. Ct. 2254 (1987). The Court distinguished *Martinez* from *Turner* because the latter involved a content neutral regulation affecting only prisoners. *Id.* at 2259–60. Applying a deferential standard of review, the Court concluded that the regulation in *Turner* was reasonably related to legitimate governmental interests. *Id.* at 2264.

[26]381 U.S. at 307.

[27]*Ibid.*

[28]376 U.S. 254 (1964).

[29]See, *e.g.*, *id.* at 269–76.

temper the inhibiting effect of postpublication penalties.[30] The concern about inhibiting effects also animated the *Lamont* decision. Justice Douglas stated that addressees "might think they would invite disaster if they read what the Federal Government says contains the seeds of treason."[31] Read with *New York Times*, the *Lamont* decision shows that an uninhibited debate requires innovative doctrines, certainly more than protection from prior restraints.

Lamont is not instructive as to the precise contours of the right to receive or the strength of the right in other settings.[32] A likely limitation on the right's contours comes from the fact that the case involved the postal system, a communications facility occupying a special position in our society.[33] But the Court's opinion is bereft

---

[30]See *e.g.*, *id.* at 279–83.

[31]381 U.S. at 307. See also Meese v. Keene, 107 S. Ct. 1862, 1877 (1987) (Blackmun, J., dissenting) (film labeled by the government as "political propaganda").

[32]One commentator claimed that the Court's reliance on Thomas v. Collins, 323 U.S. 516 (1945) (holding unconstitutional a requirement that labor organizers register with the government prior to making speeches) may indicate that no limitation on the right to receive is permissible. The Supreme Court, 1964 Term, 79 Harv. L. Rev. 56, 156 (1965). This misreads the majority opinion. The Court's reliance on *Thomas*, like its reliance on Murdock v. Pennsylvania, 319 U.S. 105 (1943) reveals that there are certain requirements that may never be imposed on the exercise of First Amendment rights. But this is not the same as saying that the right to receive expression is absolute.

The *Lamont* Court did not address the question whether an addressee may assert the rights of others who are not party to the action. The district court had held that the plaintiff could not invoke the rights of third parties. 229 F. Supp. 913, 920–21 (S.D.N.Y. 1964).

[33]The Court noted the special nature of the postal system by quoting Justice Holmes's famous statement that " 'The United States may give up the Post Office when it sees fit, but while it carries it on the use of mails is almost as much a part of free speech as the right to use our tongues . . . .' " *Lamont*, 381 U.S. at 305, quoting Milwaukee Social Democratic Publishing Co. v. Burleson, 225 U.S. 407, 437 (1921). Since *Lamont*, the Court has continued to treat the postal service as a special form of communications. See Bolger v. Youngs Drug Products Corp., 463 U.S. 60 (1983) (invalidating a statute prohibiting the mailing of unsolicited contraceptive advertisements); Blount v. Rizzi, 400 U.S. 410 (1971) (holding unconstitutional an obscenity law empowering the Postmaster General to prohibit mailing matter he deemed obscene).

The limited reach of the right to receive set forth in *Lamont* is illustrated by Kleindienst v. Mandel, 408 U.S. 753 (1972), where appellees argued that their right to receive was violated by denial of a visa to a foreign scholar. The Court upheld the government action: "[P]lenary congressional power to make policies and rules for exclusion of aliens has long been firmly established. In the case of an alien excludable under §212(a)(28), Congress has delegated conditional exercise of this power to the Executive. We hold that when the Executive exercises this power negatively on the basis of a facially legitimate and bona fide reason, courts will neither look behind the exercise of that discretion, nor test it by balancing its justification against the First Amendment interests of those who seek personal communication with the applicant." *Id.* at 769–70. The Court's deference shows the right to receive has minimal value in the visa context. Justices Marshall and Brennan dissented because the Court's deference "departs from its own best role as the guardian of individual liberty in the face of governmental overreaching." 408 U.S. at 785.

of the type of analysis, such as a comparison of the government's interests with the burden on expression,[34] that would have been useful for future cases. The lack of comparison, plus reliance on *Thomas v. Collins*[35] and *Murdock v. Pennsylvania*,[36] suggest that the statute imposed a condition that is always impermissible in this setting. In a later case Justice Blackmun referred to the statute at issue in *Lamont* as imposing an "unjustifiable" burden,[37] an indication that the government could never justify the restriction.

Curiously, Justice Douglas did not explain the new First Amendment right to receive expression, nor did he cite or quote earlier opinions that referred to a right to receive expression.[38] But Justice Brennan stated the following in a concurring opinion:[39]

> It is true that the First Amendment contains no specific guarantee of access to publications. However, the protection of the Bill of Rights goes beyond the specific guarantees to protect from congressional abridgment those equally fundamental personal rights necessary to make the express guarantees fully meaningful. . . . I think the right to receive publications is such a fundamental right. The dissemination of ideas can accomplish nothing if otherwise willing addressees are not free to receive and consider them. It would be a barren marketplace of ideas that had only sellers and no buyers.

Brennan's language foreshadowed Douglas's opinion for the Court in *Griswold v. Connecticut*,[40] decided two weeks after *Lamont*, in which Douglas stated that the "specific guarantees in the Bill of Rights have penumbras, formed by emanations from those guarantees that help give them life and substance."[41]

Because Justice Douglas's *Lamont* opinion is so terse, it is only Justice Brennan's concurring opinion that illuminates the basis for the

---

[34] In his concurring opinion in *Lamont*, Justice Brennan addressed the government's asserted interests and the availability of less restrictive means. 381 U.S. at 310.

[35] 323 U.S. 516 (1945). See note 32 *supra*.

[36] 319 U.S. 105 (1943). See note 32 *supra*.

[37] Kleindienst v. Mandel, 408 U.S. 753, 763 (1972).

[38] Of the previous opinions referring to a right to receive, see note 1 *supra*, Justice Douglas did cite Thomas v. Collins, 323 U.S. 516 (1945), but only as an illustration of an impermissible requirement imposed upon a speaker. 381 U.S. at 306. The language from *Thomas* referring to listener rights was not cited or quoted in *Lamont*.

[39] 381 U.S. at 308.

[40] 381 U.S. at 479 (1965).

[41] *Id.* at 484.

right to receive expression. Justice Brennan stated that the "dissemination of ideas can accomplish nothing" if the audience is not free to receive them. This, along with the reference to the specific guarantee of the First Amendment, indicates that the right to receive is the corollary of the right to speak, that the rights of the audience are derived from the rights of the speaker. Justice Brennan had articulated this view in a speech made two years before *Lamont*.[42] After *Lamont* he quoted his concurring opinion in a discussion of the right to receive as the corollary of the right to speak.[43] But there is a fundamental problem with this treatment of the right to receive—it ignores the facts of *Lamont*. How can a right to receive exist as the corollary of the right to speak when the speakers, foreign governments, did not have a right to speak? Justice Brennan acknowledged that it would be a troublesome case if the addressees sought to establish First Amendment protection for the expression originated by foreign governments,[44] but left the link between the audience and the speaker unexplained. Conceivably Justice Brennan was writing beyond the facts of the case so his concurring opinion would serve to signal that speakers are only as free to speak as their audiences are to listen. Or Justice Brennan, and the Court for that matter, may have sidelined an explanation of the relationship between the rights of the speaker and the rights of the audience in order to make a statement about the impermissibility of viewpoint-based regulations.

2. Stanley *and the right to possess information.* In *Stanley v. Georgia*,[45] the Court reversed on First Amendment grounds a conviction for

---

[42]In a 1963 speech, Justice Brennan described the right to receive expression as follows: "One of the liberties we Americans prize most highly is our freedom to read what we wish when we wish. It is hard to realize that nothing in the body of the Constitution or the Bill of Rights says anything in terms about a freedom to read, or to listen, or even to think. Yet we know that such liberties are there just as surely as if they were expressly written into the First Amendment. For the freedom to speak would be meaningless without the corollary freedom to listen. And in the same way, freedom of the press which we have cherished throughout history would be a hollow right without a corresponding freedom to read without fear of prosecution, censorship, or suspicion. The author and publisher are only as free to write and to print as their readers are to read." Brennan, Law, Liberty and Libraries, in Book Selection and Censorship in the Sixties 268 (Moon ed. 1969).

[43]Board of Educ. v. Pico, 457 U.S. 853, 867 (1982). See text and notes accompanying notes 113–14 *infra*.

[44]381 U.S. at 307–08.

[45]394 U.S. 557 (1969). Curiously, the opinion refers to the right to receive as being well established. *Id.* at 564. Of the three cases cited by Justice Marshall as direct support for this proposition, only *Lamont* expressly relied upon the right to receive as the basis for the decision.

possession of obscene material. Writing for the Court, Justice Marshall stated that the right to receive ideas, regardless of their social worth, is fundamental to our free society.[46] This is a stunning statement which led several lower courts to conclude that if an individual has the right to receive expression regardless of its social worth, then someone must have the right to distribute it.[47] To reverse Justice Brennan's phrase from *Lamont*, it would be a barren marketplace that had only buyers and no sellers. In several obscenity cases decided after *Stanley*, the Court stated that *Stanley* did not create a right to receive obscenity, or a right to distribute it.[48] In non-obscenity cases, though, *Stanley* is commonly cited as protecting a right to receive ideas.[49]

Just what did the Court protect in *Stanley?* At oral argument, the appellant's attorney claimed that insofar as mere "possession"

---

[46]394 U.S. at 564.

[47]In United States v. Reidel, 402 U.S. 351 (1971), the Court reversed a district court's sweeping interpretation of *Stanley*. Respondent was charged with distributing obscene materials through the mails and a district court concluded that a federal statute prohibiting such dissemination could not be applied where the material was sent to a willing adult recipient. *Id.* at 355. The Court stated that the right to receive in *Stanley* "is not so broad as to immunize the dealings in obscenity in which Reidel engaged here . . . ." *Ibid.* Similarly, in United States v. Thirty-Seven Photographs, 402 U.S. 363 (1971), the Court addressed a federal statute prohibiting the importation of obscene materials. A district court read *Stanley* as protecting the right to receive obscene expression and declared the statute unconstitutional. The Court reversed, stating, "That the private user under Stanley may not be prosecuted for possession of obscenity in his home does not mean that he is entitled to import it from abroad . . . ." *Id.* at 376. The Court again addressed the importation issue in United States v. 12 200-foot Reels of Super 8MM Film, 413 U.S. 123 (1973). The district court had relied upon the district court's opinion in *Thirty-Seven Photographs*. The Court reversed, stating that it would not extend the limited holding of *Stanley* to permit importation of obscene material intended for private use. *Id.* at 128. Finally, in United States v. Orito, 413 U.S. 139 (1973), a district court relied upon *Stanley* for the proposition that nonpublic transportation of obscene materials was permissible. The Court held that *Stanley* applied only to the home. *Id.* at 141–42.

[48]See note 47 *supra*. The Court's position on the scope of *Stanley* was summarized in Smith v. United States, 431 U.S. 291, 307 (1977). Justice Stevens, in dissent, recently criticized the Court's decisions that have "adopted a restrictive reading of *Stanley* . . . ." Pope v. Illinois, 107 S.Ct. 1918, 1930 (1987). "[The] crabbed approach offends the overarching First Amendment principles discussed in *Stanley*, almost as much as it insults the citizenry by declaring its right to read and possess material which it may not legally obtain." *Ibid.*

[49]See, *e.g.*, Board of Educ. v. Pico, 457 U.S. 853, 867 (1982); Virginia State Bd. of Pharmacy v. Virginia Citizens Consumer Council, 425 U.S. 748, 757 (1976). Lower courts also commonly cite *Stanley* as protecting a right to receive expression. See, *e.g.*, Cruz v. Ferre, 571 F. Supp. 125, 130 (S.D. Fla. 1983), aff'd, 755 F.2d 1415 (11th Cir. 1985).

is concerned, "there is no such thing as 'obscenity.' "[50] The Court's rejection of the state's justifications for the statute,[51] as well as its belief that the power to regulate obscenity does not extend to possession in the home,[52] indicate agreement with that argument. Thus, Justice Marshall's loose statement about the social worth of ideas really refers to a right to possess sexually explicit materials, rather than a right to receive those materials.

Stanley is best understood if one ignores the language about a right to receive expression and focuses instead on the concept animating the decision, a First Amendment right of privacy.[53] As Justice Marshall stated, "If the First Amendment means anything, it means that a State has no business telling a man, sitting alone in his house, what books he may read or what films he may watch. Our whole constitutional heritage rebels at the thought of giving government the power to control men's minds."[54] This concern for privacy, though, did not create a zone of protection that extended beyond the home. *Stanley* is replete with references to private possession and the home,[55] and subsequent efforts to extend *Stanley* outside the home have been rejected by the Court.[56] The subsequent

---

[50]67 Landmark Briefs and Arguments of the United States Supreme Court 827 (Kurland & Casper eds. 1975).

[51]Georgia sought to defend the statute by asserting a right to protect the individual's mind from the effects of obscenity. This, the Court stated, was wholly inconsistent with the philosophy of the first amendment. 394 U.S. at 565–66. Georgia further claimed that exposure to obscene materials may lead to deviant sexual behavior, a claim the Court rejected for want of empirical basis. *Id.* at 566–67. But see Paris Adult Theatre I v. Slaton, 413 U.S. 49, 60–61 (1973). Finally, Georgia argued that prohibiting possession was necessary to efforts to prohibit distribution. The Court was not convinced that it would be difficult to prove intent to distribute or that distribution occurred. 394 U.S. at 567–68. The Court's rejection of the state's interests led some to question whether obscenity legislation could ever be justified. The Supreme Court, 1968 Term, 83 Harv. L. Rev. 7, 149 (1969). Between 1969 and 1972 more than 50 cases in the lower federal courts considered the effect of Stanley on obscenity law. Note, 81 Yale L.J. 309, 313 n.32 (1971).

[52]394 U.S. at 568. See also United States v. Reidel, 402 U.S. 351, 356 (1971) (stating that the personal constitutional right to possess and read obscenity in the home does not depend upon whether the materials are obscene).

[53]This is not to say that autonomy and similar aspects of a right of privacy are not relevant to a right to receive expression. See text accompanying notes 75–76 *infra*.

[54]394 U.S. at 565.

[55]See, *e.g.*, *id.* at 561, 564, 565, 567, 568. See also Paris Adult Theatre I v. Slaton, 413 U.S. 49, 66 n.13 (1973).

[56]See, *e.g.*, United States v. Thirty-Seven Photographs, 402 U.S. 363, 376 (1971).

limitations placed on the reach of *Stanley* prompted Justice Black's dissent that *Stanley* would be "good law only when a man writes salacious books in his attic, prints them in his basement, and reads them in his living room."[57] A careful reading of *Stanley* and its progeny shows that the First Amendment does not protect a right to distribute obscene expression or a right to receive it.

B. RESTRICTIONS ON COMMERCIAL EXPRESSION

1. *The audience interest in* Virginia Pharmacy. The right to receive expression was central in *Virginia State Board of Pharmacy v. Virginia Citizens Consumer Council*,[58] where the Court held a ban on prescription drug advertising by pharmacists was unconstitutional.[59] In their briefs, appellees claimed their First Amendment right to receive price information was not derived from the rights of speakers to disseminate that information.[60] But at oral argument, counsel for appellees stated that the right to receive was the correlative of the right to speak.[61] This prompted a response from the Court that the Constitution protects the right to know by guaranteeing the right to speak.[62] In contrast, the appellants argued that if courts were to rely upon the concept of audience interests in expression, they would once again be deciding whether legislation is wise.[63]

The threshold question for the Court was one of standing. If there was First Amendment protection for prescription drug advertising, did this apply to the consumer as well as the pharmacist? Justice Blackmun stated that where a willing speaker exists, the

---

[57]*Id.* at 382.

[58]425 U.S. 748 (1976).

[59]In his dissenting opinion, Justice Rehnquist emphasized that the ban applied only to pharmacists; thus, consumer groups could acquire and publish prescription drug price information. *Id.* at 782. Appellees were not asserting their right to receive information, Justice Rehnquist stated, they were asserting the right of some third party to publish. *Ibid.* In response, the Court stated that it was not aware of a "general principle that freedom of speech may be abridged when the speaker's listeners could come by his message by some other means . . . ." 425 U.S. at 757 n.15.

[60]Brief of Appellees at 10.

[61]86 Landmark Briefs and Arguments of the United States Supreme Court 196 (Kurland & Casper eds. 1977).

[62]*Ibid.*

[63]Brief of Appellants at 18.

First Amendment protects both the source and the recipient.[64] This meant that audience members could assert their right to receive, rather than asserting the right of a speaker who was not before the Court. But the right to receive was the consequence of a speaker's freedom. With the question of standing resolved, the Court analyzed the ban just as though the challenge was brought by a speaker. The right to receive did not increase the government's burden of justification for the ban, nor did it alter the Court's balancing methodology.[65] By finding that audience members had standing, the Court merely increased the number of parties that could challenge the ban.

The nature of the right to receive recognized in *Virginia Pharmacy* can be explained by three contrasting definitions of the right. First, the right could be defined so that audience members are not harmed as long as they are able to receive drug price information from another speaker, such as a consumer group.[66] As Alexander Meiklejohn once stated, "What is essential is not that everyone shall speak, but that everything worth saying shall be said."[67] This definition, though, illustrates a primary drawback of treating expression solely in terms of the listener's interests: a restraint on a speaker or class of speaker may be justified when the audience can acquire the same content from another speaker. Second, the right to receive could be defined in affirmative terms so that audience members could demand that a particular pharmacist communicate to them. Obviously, this would denigrate a speaker's interest in being free from coercion. The *Virginia Pharmacy* Court adopted a definition that falls somewhere between the first two. The Court defined the right to receive as the reciprocal of a willing pharmacist's freedom to speak.[68] Thus, for purposes of standing, the appellees were as-

---

[64]425 U.S. at 756. The Court was not invoking that aspect of overbreadth analysis where a "litigant whose own activities are unprotected may nevertheless challenge a statue by showing that it substantially abridges the First Amendment rights of other parties not before the court." Village of Schaumburg v. Citizens for a Better Environment, 444 U.S. 620, 634 (1980). Rather, the Court held that the ban violated the rights of the appellees.

[65]Once the Court resolved the standing question and concluded that commercial speech was entitled to First Amendment protection, it engaged in the type of balancing frequently employed in the First Amendment context; the ban was examined to determine if it narrowly and directly advanced interests sufficient to justify the effects of the ban. 425 U.S. at 766–70.

[66]See note 59 *supra*.

[67]Meiklejohn, Political Freedom 26 (1960).

[68]425 U.S. at 757.

serting their own right, but it was inextricably tied to the pharmacist's freedom to speak.

Apart from the standing issue, the right to receive appears to have been a device for the Court to expand the constitutional value of commercial expression.[69] That is, given the difficulty of fitting protection for commercial speakers into a theoretical framework of free speech,[70] the interests of the audience, instead of the speaker, provided justification for First Amendment protection.[71] By focusing on the right to receive and the accompanying marketplace images, the Court avoided the difficult theoretical questions posed by affording First Amendment protection to commercial speakers.[72]

---

[69]For example, the Court stated that the consumer's interest in the free flow of commercial information may be "as keen, if not keener by far, than his interest in the day's most urgent political debate." *Id.* at 763. See also *id.* at 765 (it is a matter of public interest that private economic decisions be well informed). Professor Farber believes that the Court overstated the consumer's interest in commercial expression. Farber, Commercial Speech and First Amendment Theory, 74 Nw. U.L. Rev. 372, 379–80 (1979). Dean Yudof believes that the right to receive is "little more than artistic camouflage to protect the interests of a willing speaker." Yudof, When Government Speaks 46 (1983).

[70]See, *e.g.*, Baker, Commercial Speech: A Problem in the Theory of Freedom, 62 Iowa L. Rev. 1, 3 (1976) (complete denial of First Amendment protection for commercial speech is required by First Amendment theory); Jackson & Jeffries, Commercial Speech: Economic Due Process and the First Amendment, 65 Va. L. Rev. 1, 14 (1979) (commercial speech falls outside the accepted reasons for protecting freedom of speech). But see Neuborne, A Rationale for Protecting and Regulating Commercial Speech, 46 Brooklyn L. Rev. 437, 454 (1980) (while a commercial speaker has no cognizable First Amendment interest of his own, the First Amendment's protection flows from the constitutional interest of listeners); Redish, The First Amendment in the Marketplace: Commercial Speech and the Values of Free Expression, 39 Geo. Wash. L. Rev. 429, 431 (1971) (arguing that no adequate justification exists for excluding certain types of commercial speech from the scope of the First Amendment).

[71]The Court continues to emphasize that protection for commercial expression is not justified because of the benefit such speech provides to speakers. Rather, such protection "is justified principally by the value to consumers of the information such speech provides . . . ." Zauderer v. Office of Disciplinary Counsel, 471 U.S. 626, 651 (1985). See note 72 *infra*.

[72]Apart from briefly noting that advertising is the sine qua non of commercial profit, 425 U.S. at 772 n.24, *Virginia Pharmacy* is bereft of analysis of why such expression is important to speakers. That the Court was willing to modify key First Amendment doctrines, such as the prohibition against prior restraint, *id.*, indicates that the Court is not entirely comfortable with First Amendment protection for commercial expression. See also Central Hudson Gas & Elec. Corp. v. Public Serv. Comm'n, 447 U.S. 557, 571 n.13 (1980) (suggesting that utility advertisements be subject to government review prior to dissemination). Professor Baker, note 70 *supra*, at 54, states that the Court's willingness to allow such unusual regulations indicates "that the problem and doctrine of commercial speech have not yet been thought through . . . ."

One key aspect of *Virginia Pharmacy* that is closely related to the right to receive is the Court's rejection of the argument that the public can be "kept in ignorance" to prevent lawful conduct that the government deems harmful.[73] The alternative to the paternalism advanced by the government, the Court stated, is to assume that "people will perceive their own best interests if only they are well enough informed, and that the best means to that end is to open the channels of communication rather than to close them."[74] Or, stated differently, the right to speak and the corollary right to listen cannot be restrained on the ground that the listeners will be persuaded by the speech to engage in legal actions the state disfavors.

Implicit in this anti-ignorance principle is a perception of individual autonomy and the limited powers of the state. Although undeveloped by the *Virginia Pharmacy* Court, the concept of individual autonomy provides a powerful theoretical framework for the right to receive expression. As one scholar described it, autonomy means that individuals have sovereignty in matters of choice. Therefore, individuals also have a right to receive expression that is relevant to their decision making; the state distorts decision making by restricting expression. "Persons who see themselves as autonomous see themselves as having a right to make up their own minds, hence a right to whatever is necessary for them to do this. . . ."[75] While one finds a measure of autonomy in *Virginia Pharmacy*, the Court's commitment to the concept, and its rejection of paternalism, was narrow. For example, the Court acknowledged the state's legitimate power to protect citizens from false or misleading commercial speech.[76]

The anti-ignorance principle was also used by the Court in the commercial speech cases of *Linmark Associates v. Township of Wil-*

---

[73]425 U.S. at 769–70.

[74]*Id.* at 770. Professor Nimmer calls this the "anti-ignorance principle." Nimmer, note 14 *supra*, at §2.05 [B](2) at 2–32. Professor Schneider claims that paternalism is not all bad. Schneider, Free Speech and Corporate Freedom: A Comment on First National Bank of Boston v. Bellotti, 59 S. Cal. L. Rev. 1227, 1241–42 (1986).

[75]Scanlon, A Theory of Freedom of Expression, 1 Phil. & Pub. Aff. 204, 221–22 (1972). Professor Schauer noted that Scanlon's theory "is best characterized not as a right to speech, but rather as a right to receive information and, more importantly a right to be free from governmental intrusion into the ultimate process of individual choice." Schauer, Free Speech: A Philosophical Inquiry 69 (1982).

[76]425 U.S. at 771 & n.24.

lingboro,[77] *Carey v. Population Services International,*[78] *Bates v. State Bar of Arizona,*[79] and *Bolger v. Youngs Drug Products Corp.*[80] A significant implication of *Central Hudson Gas & Electric Co. v. Public Service Commission,*[81] however, is that truthful expression concerning lawful activities may be suppressed if the government's methods narrowly advance a significant interest.[82] Justices Blackmun and Stevens concurred in the Court's judgment in *Central Hudson* but did not join the opinion because they disagreed with the idea that the government may attack problems indirectly by depriving the public of information.[83] As shown next, the *Posadas* Court held that the government may manipulate private behavior by suppressing information about lawful conduct.

---

[77]431 U.S. 85, 96–97 (1977) (ban on "For Sale" signs in residential community).

[78]431 U.S. 678, 701 (1977) (ban on contraceptive advertising).

[79]433 U.S. 350, 374–75 (1977) (a ban on attorney advertising).

[80]463 U.S. 60, 74 (1983) (ban on mail distribution of unsolicited contraceptive advertisements).

[81]447 U.S. 557 (1980).

[82]In *Central Hudson*, the Court articulated a four-part analysis for restrictions on commercial speech: "At the outset, we must determine whether the expression is protected by the First Amendment. For commercial speech to come within that provision, it must at least concern lawful activity and not be misleading. Next, we ask whether the asserted governmental interest is substantial. If both inquiries yield positive answers, we must determine whether the regulation directly advances the governmental interest asserted, and whether it is not more extensive than is necessary to serve than interest." *Id.* at 566. Because the *Central Hudson* Court found that a ban on utility advertisements did not directly affect the fairness and efficiency of the utility's rates, *id.* at 569, and that the ban was more extensive than necessary to protect the state's interest in energy conservation, *id.* at 569–71, it did not directly address the issue of using restrictions to manipulate consumer behavior. See note 83 *infra.*

[83]"If a governmental unit believes that use or overuse of air conditioning is a serious problem, it must attack that problem directly, by prohibiting air conditioning or regulating thermostat levels. Just as the Commonwealth of Virginia may promote professionalism of pharmacists directly, so too New York may *not* promote energy conservation 'by keeping the public in ignorance.' " 447 U.S. at 579 (Blackmun, J., concurring), quoting *Virginia Pharmacy,* 425 U.S. at 770. Justice Stevens stated: "The justification for the regulation is nothing more than the expressed fear that the audience may find the utility's message persuasive. Without the aid of any coercion, deception, or misinformation, truthful communication may persuade some citizens to consume more electricity than they otherwise would. I as ume that such a consequence would be undesirable and that government may therefore prohibit and punish the unnecessary or excessive use of electricity. But if the perceived harm associated with greater electrical usage is not sufficiently serious to justify direct regulation, surely it does not constitute the kind of clear and present danger that can justify the suppression of speech." *Id.* at 581. Justice Brennan joined the opinions of Justices Blackmun and Stevens.

2. *Diminished status for speaker and audience rights in* Posadas. Although the Court has applied divergent levels of scrutiny to commercial speech cases,[84] *Posadas De Puerto Rico Associates v. Tourism Co.*[85] is the nadir of the Court's deference to a legislature. Justice Rehnquist, author of the *Posadas* opinion, had previously expressed his opposition to any First Amendment protection for commercial speech[86] and *Posadas* may be read as effectively gutting the protection established in *Virginia Pharmacy*. Alternatively, the case may be precedent for only those bans on advertising for certain products the government allows but disfavors, such as alcoholic beverages. Under either reading of *Posadas*, the importance of the anti-ignorance principle is diminished. Additionally, *Posadas* shows that the consumer's interest in being well informed, which provides the ostensible justification for first amendment protection of commercial expression,[87] can be overcome easily in the Court's balancing methodology.

Posadas entailed a facial challenge to a Puerto Rico statute prohibiting casino gambling advertisements directed at Puerto Rican residents.[88] Since the proscribed advertising concerned lawful activity, and the government's interest—reducing demand for casino gambling by Puerto Ricans—was assumed to be related to a reduction of problems such as prostitution, the Court devoted little attention to the first and second steps in the customary commercial

---

[84]*Compare* Friedman v. Rogers, 440 U.S. 1, 13–15 (1979) (deferential treatment of legislature's conclusion that a trade name would mislead the public), *with* Bolger v. Youngs Drug Products Corp., 463 U.S. 60, 73–74 (1983) (concluding that a ban on mailing unsolicited contraceptive advertisements would provide only the most limited support for the asserted governmental interest).

[85]106 S.Ct. 2968 (1986).

[86]See, *e.g.*, Rehnquist, J., dissenting in Central Hudson Gas & Elec. Corp. v. Public Serv. Comm'n, 447 U.S. 557, 598 (1980); Bates v. State Bar, 433 U.S. 350, 404 (1977); Virginia State Bd. of Pharmacy v. Virginia Citizens Consumer Council, 425 U.S. 748, 790 (1976).

[87]See note 71 *supra*. In *Posadas*, the appellant argued that the advertising restriction affected not only the casino's rights, but also the public of Puerto Rico had a right to receive truthful information concerning legalized gambling. Brief for the Appellant at 43–44.

[88]Casinos were permitted to advertise to tourists, but not to Puerto Rican residents. 106 S.Ct. 2968, 2974 (1986). Justice Stevens dissented on this point, claiming that the regulation discriminated on the basis of the location of the publisher and intended audience. *Id.* at 2986–87. Advertising for other legalized gambling activities, such as dog racing and cockfighting, could be directed at residents. The Court found this permissible, 106 S.Ct. at 2977, but Justice Brennan claimed that the appellee failed to show that casino gambling presents risks different from those associated with other gambling activities. *Id.* at 2983.

speech analysis.[89] On the issue of the fit between the ends and the means chosen by the legislature, Justice Rehnquist wrote:[90]

> The Puerto Rico Legislature obviously believed, when it enacted the advertising restrictions at issue here, that advertisements of casino gambling aimed at residents of Puerto Rico would serve to increase demand for the product advertised. We think the legislature's belief is a reasonable one . . . .

Notice that the Court did not assess whether the restriction actually advanced the governmental interest. Rather, the Court concluded that the legislature's belief as to the effectiveness of the law was reasonable. This approach duplicates that taken by some lower courts in cases involving cigarette[91] and alcohol[92] advertising restrictions. Under such analysis, the effectiveness of the restriction is not subject to empirical measurement; instead, the critical inquiry is whether the measure conforms to "common sense."[93] Given the Court's assumption that advertising influenced consumer behavior in *Posadas*, virtually any advertising restriction will be believed to reduce demand for products.

---

[89]106 S.Ct. at 2976–77. Justice Brennan sharply disagreed with the majority on the issue of the government's interest. He stated, "Neither the statute on its face nor the legislative history indicated that the Puerto Rico legislature thought serious harm would result if residents were allowed to engage in casino gambling; indeed, the available evidence suggests exactly the opposite. Puerto Rico has legalized gambling casinos, and permits its residents to patronize them." *Id.* at 2983. Where First Amendment rights were at stake, he argued that the Court could not speculate about the valid reasons a government might have for enacting restrictions. *Id.* at 2984. For additional criticisms of this aspect of the Court's opinion, see Kurland, Posadas de Puerto Rico v. Tourism Company: " 'Twas Strange, 'Twas Passing Strange; 'Twas Pitiful, 'Twas Wondrous Pitiful," 1986 Supreme Court Review 1, 7–8.

[90]106 S.Ct. at 2977.

[91]Capital Broadcasting Co. v. Mitchell, 333 F. Supp. 582, 585 (D.C. 1971) (stating that it is enough that there is an evil at hand for correction and that it might be thought that the particular measure was a rational way to correct it) (quoting Williamson v. Lee Optical, 348 U.S. 483 487–88 (1955), aff'd, 405 U.S. 1000 (1972).

[92]Dunagin v. City of Oxford, 718 F.2d 738, 750 (5th Cir. 1983) (stating that sufficient reason exists to believe that advertising and consumption are linked to justify a restriction on alcohol advertising, whether or not "concrete scientific evidence" exists to that effect), cert. denied, 467 U.S. 1259 (1984). For a discussion of *Dunagin* and other alcohol advertising ban cases, see, Note, 85 Colum. L. Rev. 632 (1985).

[93]The Court reached a similar conclusion in Metromedia, Inc. v. City of San Diego, 453 U.S. 490, 509 (1981) (stating that the Court is hesitant to disagree with the accumulated, common-sense judgments of local lawmakers that billboards are a substantial hazard to traffic safety).

In his dissenting opinion, Justice Brennan said the ban was seriously flawed because even if it reduced residents' patronage of casinos, the harmful effects associated with gambling, such as prostitution, likely would continue because gambling was promoted to tourists.[94] He felt that without a showing that the ban would advance the government's interest in controlling the harmful activities accompanying gambling, Puerto Rico could not restrict the casino advertisements.[95]

On the issue of less restrictive alternatives, the Court rejected the argument that demand for casino gambling among residents could have been reduced "not by suppressing commercial speech that might encourage such gambling, but by promulgating additional speech designed to discourage it."[96] Again applying a deferential posture, the Court stated that it is up to the legislature to decide whether or not a "counterspeech" policy would be as effective as a restriction on advertising.[97] This provoked a sharp response from Justice Brennan:[98]

> Where the government seeks to restrict speech in order to advance an important interest, it is not, contrary to what the Court has stated, "up to the legislature" to decide whether or not the government's interest might be protected adequately by less intrusive measures. Rather, it is incumbent upon the government to *prove* that more limited means are not sufficient to protect its interests, and for a *court* to decide whether or not the government has sustained this burden.

In this case, the record did not show that the legislature considered the efficacy of alternative measures, nor was it shown that alternative measures would be inadequate.[99]

One of the stunning aspects of the majority opinion is its lack of analysis of the value of the advertisements to residents of Puerto Rico. In cases such as *Virginia Pharmacy*, the Court concluded that

---

[94]106 S.Ct. at 2985.

[95]*Ibid.*

[96]106 S.Ct. at 2978.

[97]*Ibid.* Justice Rehnquist added, "The legislature could conclude as it apparently did here, that residents of Puerto Rico are already aware of the risks of casino gambling, yet would nevertheless be induced by widespread advertising to engage in such potentially harmful conduct." *Ibid.* See text accompanying note 99 *infra.*

[98]*Id.* at 2985 (Brennan, J., dissenting).

[99]*Ibid.*

advertisements helped citizens make well-informed choices. Implicit throughout *Posadas* is the Court's approval of the legislature's belief that casino advertisements will cause residents to make the "wrong" choices. Rather than directly attacking the problems accompanying gambling, Justice Rehnquist found it appropriate for the government to manipulate consumer choice by depriving consumers of information. This paternalism was criticized by Justice Brennan, who noted that commercial speech assists consumers and furthers the societal interest in the fullest possible dissemination of information.[100] Drawing upon Justice Blackmun's concurring opinion in *Central Hudson*[101] and *Virginia Pharmacy*,[102] Justice Brennan observed that a ban designed to manipulate behavior strikes at the heart of the First Amendment and should be subject to strict scrutiny.[103] In essence, advertisements for casino gambling promote a viewpoint. For the Court to approve of a blatant viewpoint restriction with only cursory analysis is troubling.

Posadas may be read narrowly.[104] The Court emphasized that the government's power to restrict the advertising was based upon its

---

[100]*Id.* at 2981. A dispute over paternalism was an aspect of the Court's recent decision in Meese v. Keene, 107 S.Ct. 1862 (1987). Under the provisions of a federal statute, three films produced by a foreign government were labeled as "political propaganda." By a 5-3 vote, the Court reversed a district court's prohibition of the labeling. Writing for the Court, Justice Stevens stated that the injunction withheld information that would better enable the public to evaluate the films. In Justice Stevens's view, the injunction was similar to the paternalistic strategy followed by the legislature in *Virginia Pharmacy*. *Id.* at 1871–72. In dissent, Justice Blackmun said there was a significant difference between a ban on information, such as in *Virginia Pharmacy*, and a prohibition of the government labeling at issue in *Keene*. The injunction lifted a disclosure requirement so that the films would not be constrained by government condemnation. *Id.* at 1877–78. Justice Blackmun added, "It is the Government's classification of those films as 'political propaganda' that is paternalistic. For that government action does more than simply provide additional information. It places the power of the Federal Government, with its authority, presumed neutrality, and assumed access to all the facts, behind an appellation *designed* to reduce the effectiveness of the speech in the eyes of the public." *Id.* at 1878.

[101]See note 83 *supra*.

[102]See text accompanying notes 73–74 *supra*.

[103]106 S.Ct. at 2981–82. Justice Brennan felt that there was no reason why commercial speech should be afforded less protection than other categories of expression where the government seeks to deprive citizens of accurate information concerning lawful activity. *Id.* at 2982.

[104]Chief Justice Burger and Justices White and Powell joined the majority in *Virginia Pharmacy* and *Posadas*. None issued separate opinions in *Posadas* attempting to reconcile their votes in the two cases.

greater power to restrict completely casino gambling.[105] This was followed by references to regulation of other products or activities deemed harmful, such as prostitution and alcoholic beverages.[106] Moreover, the Court may have been especially willing to defer to the judgment of the legislature due to the "unique cultural and legal history of Puerto Rico."[107] But it is hard to reconcile any First Amendment protection for commercial speech with the central principle of *Posadas*—that the government may attack problems indirectly by depriving citizens of information. Whether *Posadas* leads to a complete denial of protection for all types of commercial speech, it will be exceedingly difficult to limit its scope to only a small number of products such as cigarettes and alcoholic beverages. The potential scope of *Posadas* is troubling when one recalls that if the restriction in *Central Hudson* had been narrowly tailored, the Court presumably would have permitted the government to attack the problem of energy conservation by limiting advertising.[108] After *Posadas*, protection for commercial expression may exist only where the underlying conduct, such as the sale of contraceptives, is constitutionally protected.[109]

C. BOOK REMOVAL AND THE SCHOOL LIBRARY

Can the right to receive expression be violated in settings where there is no right to speak? This question is addressed in *Board of Education v. Pico*,[110] where a school board removed certain "filthy" books from junior and senior high school libraries. A plurality composed of Justices Brennan, Marshall, and Stevens held that if the removal were motivated by a desire to suppress ideas, the stu-

---

[105] 106 S.Ct. at 2979. Professor Kurland, note 89 *supra*, observes that this is a perversion of First Amendment law because almost all areas of economic activity are subject to government regulation. "Presumably, then, under *Posadas*, there is no advertising that is not subject to government censorship." *Id.* at 13.

[106] 106 S.Ct. at 2979–80.

[107] *Id.* at 2976 n.6.

[108] In his concurring opinion in *Central Hudson*, Justice Blackmun observed that the test adopted by the majority would allow suppression of truthful expression concerning lawful activity. 447 U.S. at 573, 574, 579. See note 83 *supra*.

[109] See *Posadas*, 106 S.Ct. at 2979 (distinguishing a ban on gambling advertisements from bans on contraceptive and abortion clinic advertisements).

[110] 457 U.S. 853 (1982). For a scorecard of the votes in *Pico*, see notes 6–7 *supra*.

dents' right to receive expression would be violated.[111] The plurality described the right to receive expression as "an inherent corollary of the rights of free speech and press that are explicitly guaranteed by the Constitution . . . ."[112]

Elaborating on the concept of the right to receive as a corollary to the right to speak, Justice Brennan first stated that the right to receive follows "ineluctably from the sender's First Amendment right" to speak.[113] This statement is out of place in this case. As Chief Justice Burger and Justice Rehnquist observed in their dissenting opinions, there can be no reciprocal right to receive expression in a place where no speaker has the right to speak.[114] More appropriate to the facts of *Pico* is Justice Brennan's second basis for a right to receive expression. He described it as a "necessary predicate to the recipient's meaningful exercise of his own rights of speech, press, and political freedom."[115] Stated differently, if citizens are to offer informed expression to society, they must have the opportunity to receive the expression of others. This is a new perception of the right to receive expression, one which was not present in *Lamont, Stanley,* or *Virginia Pharmacy.*

For Justice Brennan to include this second basis for the right to receive in a discussion of corollary rights is a misapplication of the word corollary. Of greater importance, though, is the morass created when the right to receive is viewed as the predicate to informed expression. Consider the following: to offer informed expression, A must receive B's expression. If the protection for B's expression stems from A's rights as a potential speaker, then the nature of B's expression is irrelevant. Therefore, if A wants to offer well-informed

---

[111]457 U.S. at 872. The Court addressed only the First Amendment rights of students; it did not address the issue of academic freedom for librarians and teachers also raised by the respondents. See Respondents' Brief at 6.

[112]457 U.S. at 867.

[113]*Ibid.*

[114]See, *e.g., id.* at 888 (Burger, C.J., dissenting); *id.* at 912 (Rehnquist, J., dissenting). The school board also argued that the right to receive expression exists only as a reciprocal right to the right of another to communicate. "Publishers and authors do not have such a right with respect to the public schools and students do not possess its reciprocal." Petitioners' Brief at 28.

[115]457 U.S. at 867. The plurality added that "just as access to ideas makes it possible for citizens generally to exercise their rights of free speech and press in a meaningful manner, such access prepares students for active and effective participation in the pluralistic, often contentious society in which they will soon be adult members." *Id.* at 868.

views on the topic of obscenity, A would have a right to receive
B's obscenity. Or, if the receipt of B's expression is the predicate
to A's expression, A's right to receive can be harmed in settings,
such as public libraries, where B has no right to speak. Once A's
right to receive is no longer dependent upon B's right to speak, a
host of problems arise, ranging from First Amendment protection
for previously unprotected categories of expression to judicial management of libraries. To avoid such results, so many constraints
must be placed on the right to receive that it becomes, as Justice
Powell stated in his *Pico* dissent, a "meaningless generalization."[116]

A central problem with the plurality opinion is that it accepted
the principle that public schools may inculcate certain values,[117]
while also accepting the student's right to receive expression. By
defining the case in these terms, it was necessary for the plurality
to draw arbitrary lines around the right to receive, otherwise the
latter right would sharply limit, if not eliminate, a school board's
discretion in a host of areas, such as curriculum. The plurality
confined the right to receive to the school library, described as a
unique place,[118] and further stated that only book removal motivated
by a desire to suppress ideas was inappropriate.[119]

These limitations, though, are highly suspect. Justice Blackmun,
in a concurring opinion, questioned the validity of the distinction
between book removal and book acquisition, and felt that the harm
of suppression of ideas was not peculiarly associated with libraries.[120] And the description of the right to receive expression as a
predicate to informed discussion has potentially sweeping applications; government restrictions in a host of other settings would
implicate audience rights,[121] as would restrictions not motivated by

---

[116]*Id.* at 895.

[117]457 U.S. at 864.

[118]*Id.* at 868–69. For criticism of the plurality's distinction between a library and classrooms, see Note, 35 Stan. L. Rev. 497, 508 (1983).

[119]457 U.S. at 872.

[120]*Id.* at 878 & n.1 (Blackmun, J., concurring in part and concurring in the judgment).
See also *id.* at 892 (Burger, C.J., dissenting); *id.* at 915 (Rehnquist, J., dissenting).

[121]For application of the listeners' rights concept where a public television station cancelled
a program, see Barnstone v. University of Houston, 514 F. Supp. 670 (S.D. Tex. 1980),
rev'd, 660 F.2d 137 (5th Cir. 1981), aff'd on rehearing en banc *sub nom.* Muir v. Alabama
Educ. Television Comm'n, 688 F.2d 1033 (5th Cir. 1982), cert. denied, 460 U.S. 1023 (1983).
See generally Case Comment, 36 Miami L. Rev. 779 (1982) (claiming that the Fifth Circuit's
opinion does not sufficiently protect viewers' interests).

a desire to suppress ideas. Also troubling about the plurality's perception of the right to receive expression are the affirmative obligations that may be imposed on the government. As Chief Justice Burger stated in dissent, the need to be informed "would support a constitutional 'right' of the people to have public libraries as part of a new constitutional 'right' to continuing adult education."[122]

The plurality identified two permissible reasons, vulgarity and educational suitability, for book removal.[123] These reasons, however, pose certain dangers. Vulgarity falsely assumes that ideas can be separated from form and that objection to form is not also an objection to the idea being expressed.[124] For Justice Brennan to identify vulgarity as a permissible reason for book removal is strange because he previously recognized in his dissent in *FCC v. Pacifica Foundation* that the "idea that the content of a message . . . can be divorced from the words that are the vehicle for its expression is transparently fallacious."[125] And educational suitability is a content-based criterion that is sufficiently subjective to mask efforts to suppress ideas.

Despite its awkward attempt to balance the inculcative function of schools against the right to receive, the plurality eventually got to the heart of the case by stating its objection to government efforts to create an orthodoxy of ideas.[126] More to the point, Justice Blackmun separately argued that the central problem in the case was not interference with a right to receive expression; he stated that the government may not suppress ideas for the sole purpose of suppressing ideas.[127] Justice Blackmun's emphasis on the suppression of ideas offers better guidance for future school cases than the plurality's ill-conceived notions of a right to receive as the predicate

---

[122]457 U.S. at 888. He further stated that "if the need to have an informed citizenry creates a 'right' [to receive expression], why is the government not also required to provide ready access to a variety of information?" *Ibid*. Justice Blackmun wrote, "I do not suggest that the State has any affirmative obligation to provide students with information or ideas, something that may well be associated with a 'right to receive.' " *Id*. at 878 (concurring in part and concurring in the judgment).

[123]457 U.S. at 871.

[124]See Lee, Lonely Pamphleteers, Little People, and the Supreme Court: The Doctrine of Time, Place and Manner Regulations of Expression, 54 Geo. Wash. L. Rev. 757, 776–81, 802–05 (1986).

[125]438 U.S. 726, 773 (1978).

[126]457 U.S. at 872.

[127]*Id*. at 877 (concurring in part and concurring in the judgment).

to informed discussion. This aspect of the right to receive can create unmanageable[128] and perhaps unforeseeable problems unless it is arbitrarily confined.

D. CORPORATE EXPRESSION

As in *Virginia Pharmacy*, the Court in *First National Bank v. Bellotti*[129] based its decision on the value of expression to the audience, rather than to the speaker. At issue in *Bellotti* was a Massachusetts statute prohibiting corporate expenditures intended to influence voting on referendum proposals, unless the proposal materially affected the corporation's business, property, or assets. The right to receive expression was central to the appellants' argument. The key point about the First Amendment, they stated, is that it protects the right of the listener to receive expression.[130] From the listener's perspective, "it is of little or no significance whether the source of the information is a media or non-media source. It is the right to receive the message which counts."[131]

In a opinion joined by four other members of the Court, Justice Powell stated that by asking whether corporations have First Amendment rights, the Massachusetts Supreme Judical Court posed the wrong question.[132] Shifting the inquiry away from corporate rights, Justice Powell asked if the statute abridged expression protected by the First Amendment. Since the appellants wanted to "speak" on governmental issues, he described their expression as at the heart of the First Amendment's protection.[133] By restricting this type of expression, the statute interfered with the "informational purpose"[134] of the First Amendment, a purpose Justice Powell distinguished from the individual's interest in self-expression.[135] Since the *Bellotti* Court did not pursue questions concerning the value of expression to a corporation, the opinion rests on the self-

---

[128]*Id.* at 889 (Burger, J., dissenting) (stating that schools ought not be made a slavish courier of the material of third parties).

[129]435 U.S. 765 (1978).

[130]Brief for Appellants at 40.

[131]*Id.* at 41–42.

[132]435 U.S. at 776.

[133]*Ibid.*

[134]*Id.* at 782 n.18.

[135]*Id.* at 777 n.12.

governing function of free speech. Justice Powell stated that because the people are entrusted with the responsibility for judging arguments, the government is forbidden from restricting access to expression "lest the people lose their ability to govern themselves."[136] Thus, the implicit value protected in *Bellotti* is the autonomy of audience members. It is not the speaker that is protected. Rather, speech that is of value to the audience is protected. By stating the case in these terms, Justice Powell avoided any analysis of whether corporations can actually speak, or similar questions about the nature of corporations posed by the case.[137]

Justice White in dissent criticized the majority's analysis because it proved too much. He stated, "Any communication of ideas, and consequently any expenditure of funds which makes the communication of ideas possible, it can be argued, furthers the purposes of the First Amendment."[138] Justice White claimed that ideas which are not the product of individual choice, and therefore do not contribute to an individual's self-realization, should receive diminished protection.[139] Thus, the public's right to receive corporate communication was not "of the same dimension" as its right to receive other forms of expression and a restriction on corporate speech would not significantly harm the public because other speakers remained free to "communicate any ideas which could be conveyed by means of the corporate form."[140] Presumably Justice White would find a restriction on a corporation unacceptable if it had the effect of depriving the public of an idea.[141] But how is the Court to measure whether an idea is sufficiently available to the public? The majority rejected Justice White's line of analysis by defining the right to receive in terms of the audience's particularized interest in receiving

---

[136]*Id.* at 783.

[137]As Professor O'Kelley noted, "[I]t would be fair to describe the majority opinion as dismal. The result is correct, but the analysis is defective and incomplete. The opinion essentially ignores precedent and the realities of what a corporation is." O'Kelley, The Constitutional Rights of Corporations Revisited: Social and Political Expression and the Corporation after First National Bank v. Bellotti, 67 Geo. L.J. 1347 1369 (1979). Nor has the Court in any subsequent case elaborated on its rationale for protecting corporate expression or carefully examined the nature of corporations. See, *e.g.*, Pacific Gas & Elec. Co. v. Public Util. Comm'n., 106 S. Ct. 903, 907 (1986); Consolidated Edison Co. v. Public Serv. Comm'n, 447 U.S. 530, 534 n.1 (1980). See text accompanying notes 225–27 *infra*.

[138]435 U.S. at 807.

[139]*Ibid.*

[140]*Ibid.*

[141]*Id.* at 807–08.

corporate presentation of an idea, rather than a generalized interest in receiving that idea from non-corporate speakers. Justice Powell concluded that the "inherent worth of the speech in terms of its capacity for informing the public does not depend upon the identity of its source, whether corporation, association, union, or individual."[142] By relying on the audience's interest in receiving an idea from a variety of speakers, the Court also avoided the intractable line-drawing problems presented by the self-realization argument. Clearly perceiving the danger the self-realization argument would pose to newspaper editorials,[143] a form of corporate speech that is strongly protected,[144] the Court rejected Justice White's attempt to confine the First Amendment's protection to a single purpose.[145]

But according to Justice White, corporate wealth posed the danger of unfair political campaigns; restrictions on corporate expression were necessary to prevent corporations from dominating the debate on issues.[146] The majority first offered a false start in addressing this issue, stating that if there were a record showing that corporate advocacy threatened to undermine the democratic process, the argument would merit consideration.[147] This was followed by a reference to *Red Lion Broadcasting Co. v. FCC*,[148] where the Court found that restrictions designed to prevent broadcasters from "snuffing out" the expression of others were constitutional. But the *Bellotti* Court then indicated that even a showing of undue influence would not justify a restriction such as the Massachusetts statute. Justice Powell stated:[149]

> To be sure, corporate advertising may influence the outcome of the vote; this would be its purpose. But the fact that advocacy

---

[142]*Id.* at 777. Professor Schneider states that the *Bellotti* reasoning is circular: "whether the corporation has a right to speak depends on the listener's right to receive; but a listener presumably has a right to receive only what the speaker has a right to say." Schneider, note 74 *supra*, at 1235.

[143]435 U.S. at 783 n.19.

[144]See, *e.g.*, Mills v. Alabama, 384 U.S. 214 (1966) (ban on election day newspaper editorials held unconstitutional).

[145]435 U.S. at 777 n.12. See also FEC v. Massachusetts Citizens for Life, Inc., 107 S. Ct. 616, 627 n. 10 (1987) (stating that the First Amendment serves many purposes).

[146]*Id.* at 809–10.

[147]435 U.S. at 789.

[148]395 U.S. 367 (1969). See text accompanying notes 158–73 *infra*.

[149]435 U.S. at 791–92.

> may persuade the electorate is hardly reason to suppress it . . . .
> [T]he people in our democracy are entrusted with the respon-
> sibility for judging and evaluating the relative merits of con-
> flicting arguments. They may consider, in making their judg-
> ment, the source and credibility of the advocate. But if there
> be any danger that the people cannot evaluate the information
> and arguments advanced by appellants, it is a danger contem-
> plated by the Framers of the First Amendment.

Two important concepts strengthen this passage and diminish the
importance of the Court's earlier reference to *Red Lion*. Justice Powell said first that the First Amendment rejects paternalism,[150] that
is, the fear that the public will be unable to resist the pressures of
corporate advocacy, as a basis for regulating expression; and second,
Justice Powell noted that only in the special context of broadcasting
do Justice White's concerns for unfair advantages have vitality.[151]

Bellotti rests on the Court's belief that self-government, a paramount First Amendment value, suffers when government officials
decide who speaks on political questions.[152] Some commentators,
though, claim that self-government suffers when wealthy corporations are advocates in candidate elections,[153] an issue not addressed
in *Bellotti*.[154] But even assuming that the Court accepts undue influence in the abstract as a rationale for restricting corporate advocacy in candidate elections, defining and proving that influence
to the Court will be exceedingly difficult.[155] Moreover, confining
the undue influence rationale to business corporations may be ex-

---

[150]*Id.* at 791 n.31.

[151]*Id.* at 788 n.26. Professor Powe also found *Bellotti*'s reference to *Red Lion* to have little
substance. Powe, Mass Speech and the Newer First Amendment, 1982 Supreme Court
Review 243, 257.

[152]See 435 U.S. at 785 & 791 n.31.

[153]See, *e.g.*, Baldwin & Karpay, Corporate Political Free Speech: 2 U.S.C. §44lb and the
Superior Rights of Natural Persons, 14 Pac. L.J. 209, 237 (1983) (stating that unlimited
corporate advocacy may lead to corporate domination of the political process and the consequential decline in governmental effectiveness and legitimacy). One commentator, though,
claims that nonprofit, ideological corporations facilitate citizen involvement in politics. Note,
72 Cornell L. Rev. 159 (1986).

[154]435 U.S. at 788 n.26. In FEC v. Massachusetts Citizens for Life, Inc., 107 S.Ct. 616
(1986), though, the Court held that a federal law restricting direct corporate involvement in
candidate elections was unconstitutional as applied to a nonprofit, ideological corporation.

[155]See, *e.g.*, FEC v. Massachusetts Citizens for Life, Inc., 107 S.Ct. 616, 627–31 (1986)
(distinguishing the effects of a nonprofit, ideological corporation's advocacy in a candidate
election from the effects of a business corporation's advocacy); FEC v. National Conservative
Political Action Comm., 470 U.S. 480, 498 (1985) (restriction on campaign expenditures of

ceedingly difficult.[156] If the Court does sustain restrictions on corporate speech in candidate elections, most likely it will base its decision on rationales other than excessive influence.[157]

II. GOVERNMENT EFFORTS TO ENHANCE THE FREE FLOW OF EXPRESSION

A. BROADCASTING

1. Red Lion: *The uniqueness of spectrum scarcity?* Unique application of the right to receive expression came in *Red Lion Broadcasting Co. v. FCC*,[158] in which the Court upheld the constitutionality of the fairness doctrine.[159] While reciting the familiar and simplistic adage that the purpose of the First Amendment is to preserve an uninhibited marketplace,[160] the *Red Lion* Court added a new element to

---

independent political committees is not supported by proof that those expenditures "corrupt" the political process); Citizens Against Rent Control/Coalition for Fair Housing v. City of Berkeley, 454 U.S. 290, 299 (1981) (the record does not show that a restriction on donations to committees that support or oppose ballot measures is needed to preserve voter confidence in the ballot process). Professor Shiffrin comments that if the *Bellotti* Court intended to open the way "for case by case determinations of excessive power in particular campaigns, difficult questions of motive, concomitant institutional stress, and substantial risks of unfairness in the democratic process lie ahead." Shiffrin, Government Speech, 27 UCLA L. Rev. 565, 600 (1980).

[156]See *Bellotti*, 435 U.S. at 791 n.30 (stating that the potential impact of the undue influence argument, especially on the news media, is unsettling); *id.* at 796–97 (Burger, C.J., concurring) (noting that it could be argued that media conglomerates have an unfair advantage in the political process). For an attempt to distinguish the constitutional rights of press corporations from those of corporations involved in other lines of business, see O'Kelley, note 137 *supra*, at 1359–62.

[157]For example, a restriction on corporate advocacy in candidate elections might be justified as a method of preventing corruption of those legislators who are aided by such advocacy. FEC v. National Right to Work Comm., 459 U.S. 197, 207 (1982). A second justification would be that the restriction protects individuals who have paid money to a corporation for purposes other than the support of candidates from having that money used to support candidates to whom they may be opposed. *Id.* at 208.

[158]395 U.S. 367 (1969).

[159]See note 10 *supra*.

[160]*Id.* at 390. The description of an uninhibited marketplace as the purpose of the First Amendment neglects the other purposes of the First Amendment that the Court acknowledges. See, *e.g.*, FEC v. Massachusetts Citizens for Life, Inc., 107 S.Ct. 616, 627 n.10 (1987) (stating that First Amendment speech is not necessarily limited to an instrumental or marketplace purpose); First Nat'l Bank v. Bellotti, 435 U.S. 765, 777 n.12 (1978) (stating that an individual's interest in self-expression is a concern of the First Amendment separate from the concern for open and informed discussion). For criticism of the marketplace perspective, see Ingber, The Marketplace of Ideas: A Legitimizing Myth, 1984 Duke L.J. 1.

First Amendment analysis: the collective right of the people to receive expression justifies government action intended to broaden the views presented on radio and television. The Court concluded, "It is the right of the viewers and listeners, not the right of the broadcasters, which is paramount."[161] Stated in these terms, government restrictions of broadcaster speech are permissible because listeners benefit from those restrictions. But this new approach to regulating the speech of some speakers cannot be limited to broadcasting on a principled basis.

At issue in *Red Lion* were two radically different views of the First Amendment. The United States and various *amici* argued that the government had an affirmative obligation to preserve the public's right to be informed and to assure that the airwaves do not become monopolized by one point of view.[162] Broadcasters argued that the government was distorting traditional press freedom concepts. The First Amendment contemplated that the press would be free and independent of the government, not that the government would regulate access to it.[163] The Court rejected the broadcasters' arguments, predicating its opinion on the fallacious notion of spectrum scarcity.

[161]395 U.S. at 390.

[162]Brief for the United States and FCC in Opposition at 10. See also Brief of the Office of Communication of the United Church of Christ, et al., as *amici curiae* at 24 (stating that the government must regulate private censors to assure they grant access to all views); Brief for the American Federation of Labor and Congress of Industrial Organization as *amicus curiae* at 7 (stating that the government has a duty to promote variegated speech on the airwaves by assuring non-licensees an opportunity to exercise their right of free speech). The intellectual antecedents of these views are many, but a primary source is Learned Hand. In National Broadcasting Co. v. United States, 47 F. Supp. 940 (S.D.N.Y. 1942), aff'd, 319 U.S. 190 (1943), Hand upheld FCC regulations of network broadcasting, stating that the regulations protected "the very interests which the First Amendment itself protects, i.e., the interests, first, of the 'listeners,' next, of any licensees who may prefer to be freer of the 'networks' than they are, and last, of any future competing 'networks.' " *Id.* at 946. In United States v. Associated Press, 52 F. Supp. 362 (S.D.N.Y. 1943), aff'd, 326 U.S. 1 (1945), Hand applied the antitrust laws to the newspaper industry, stating that the interests of that industry were not conclusive because the public's general interest in receiving news from many different sources was involved. *Id.* at 372.

[163]Brief for Respondent NBC at 30. See also Brief for Petitioners at 13 (stating that the fundamental purpose of the First Amendment is to prevent prior restraints and legal devices which have the effect of chilling expression); Brief for Respondent NBC at 37 (the First Amendment recognizes that it is in the public interest that the press be free); *id.* at 38 (stating that the First Amendment will be served if there is a free and independent press active as a force in our society).

To the Court, broadcasting's unique attribute was the scarcity of broadcast frequencies.[164] But many commentators have observed that all economic goods are scarce,[165] and as Judge Bork recently observed, "The attempt to use a universal fact as a distinguishing principle necessarily leads to analytical confusion."[166] In addition to scarcity, the *Red Lion* Court stated that broadcasting required government regulation to prevent frequency interference.[167] Judge Bork again perceptively remarked that this is "another instance of a universal fact that does not offer an explanatory principle" for distinguishing broadcasting from other media.[168]

Red Lion's treatment of scarcity and interference draws from earlier cases that did not address content regulation.[169] To explain why these attributes justified content regulation, the *Red Lion* Court offered the fear of private censorship and harm to the public's right to receive expression. The Court stated, "There is no sanctuary in the First Amendment for unlimited private censorship in a medium

---

[164]395 U.S. at 376.

[165]Professor Ronald Coase has been a leading exponent of the view that the scarcity of broadcast frequencies is not unique. See, *e.g.*, Coase, The Federal Communications Commission, 2 J.L. & Econ. 1 (1959). For more recent criticisms of spectrum scarcity, see Diamond, Sandler & Mueller, Telecommunications in Crisis 65–72 (1983); Spitzer, Seven Dirty Words and Six Other Stories 9–27 (1986).

[166]Telecommunications Research and Action Center v. FCC, 801 F.2d 501, 508 (D.C. Cir. 1986), cert. denied, 107 S.Ct 3196 (1987). Judge Bork elaborated: "It is certainly true that broadcast frequencies are scarce but it is unclear why that fact justifies content regulation of broadcasting in a way that would be intolerable if applied to the editorial process of the print media. All economic goods are scarce, not the least newsprint, ink, delivery trucks, computers, and other resources that go into the production and dissemination of print journalism. Not everyone who wishes to publish a newspaper, or even a pamphlet, may do so. Since scarcity is a universal fact, it can hardly explain regulation in one context and not another." *Ibid.*

[167]395 U.S. at 388–89.

[168]801 F.2d at 509. Judge Bork explained the government's role in preventing interference in the delivery of newspapers: "A publisher can deliver his newspapers only because government provides streets and regulates traffic on the streets by allocating rights of way. Yet no one would contend that the necessity for these governmental functions, which are certainly analogous to the government's function in allocating broadcast frequencies, could justify regulation of the content of a newspaper to ensure that it serves the needs of the citizens." *Ibid.*

[169]For a discussion of those cases, see Lee, Antitrust Enforcement, Freedom of the Press, and the "Open Market": The Supreme Court on the Structure and Conduct of the Mass Media, 32 Vand. L. Rev. 1249, 1309–22 (1979).

not open to all."[170] It is difficult to take seriously the Court's fear that unrestrained broadcasters will "snuff out" the free speech of others.[171] More importantly, any danger of private censorship, a term which is a First Amendment oxymoron,[172] is not unique to broadcasting. And implicit in the Court's approach is a naive belief in the benefits of government supervision of broadcast speech, a belief the FCC recently found to be unfounded.[173]

Because *Red Lion* is based on concepts that apply to all media, it would seem that similar audience rights exist with nonbroadcast media. That is, inequalities in wealth and communicative opportunity in all media can be regarded as inhibitions on the marketplace of ideas and therefore a threat to audience rights. Shortly after *Red Lion* the literature exploded with proposals to promote the public's rights in other media.[174] But in *Miami Herald Publishing Co. v. Tornillo*,[175] the Court firmly rejected the claim that the government has an obligation to insure that newspapers present a variety of views

---

[170]395 U.S. at 392. The Court added that broadcasters have special obligations as fiduciaries. *Id.* at 394.

[171]*Id.* at 387. The Court's concern for broadcaster action "snuffing out" the free speech of others is a radical departure from the text of the First Amendment which addresses only governmental restraints on speech. Moreover, if broadcaster speech snuffs out the speech of others, then "an uninhibited marketplace of ideas can be attained only by total silence." Krattenmaker & Powe, The Fairness Doctrine Today: A Constitutional Curiosity and an Impossible Dream, 1985 Duke L.J. 151, 156. In addition to its concern for broadcaster action which snuffs out the speech of others, the Court feared that without the fairness doctrine, broadcasters might treat candidates unfairly, 395 U.S. at 382–83, or provide air time only to those with whom they agreed. *Id.* at 392. This concern for journalistic ethics is a novel source for First Amendment doctrine.

[172]As Justice Rehnquist observed during the oral argument of Miami Herald Publishing Co. v. Tornillo, 418 U.S. 241 (1974), "the only entity that the First Amendment is directed against is the Government. I take it the Miami Herald can chill anybody's rights to their heart's content and they are not violating the Constitution." 78 Landmark Briefs and Arguments of the Supreme Court of the United States 893 (Kurland & Casper eds. 1975). The basis for recognition of the public's right to receive in broadcasting is not that broadcaster action is state action. See CBS, Inc. v. Democratic Nat'l Comm., 412 U.S. 94, 114–21 (1973) (holding that the action of broadcasters is not state action for First Amendment purposes). Rather, since broadcasters use a scarce resource, the Court recognizes the audience's rights.

[173]102 F.C.C.2d 143, 158–96 (1985) (finding that the fairness doctrine chills broadcaster coverage of controversial issues).

[174]The literature is listed in Lange, The Role of the Access Doctrine in the Regulation of the Mass Media: A Critical Review and Assessment, 52 N.C. L. Rev. 1, 2 n.5 (1974).

[175]418 U.S. 241 (1974).

to their readers.[176] *Red Lion's* limited scope is especially clear from Justice White's concurring opinion in *Miami Herald*. The author of *Red Lion* stated that the balance struck by the First Amendment "is that society must take the risk that occasionally debate on vital matters will not be comprehensive and that all viewpoints may not be expressed."[177] Consequently, the rights of the public articulated in *Red Lion* derive solely from the Court's faulty perception of the uniqueness of broadcasting.

2. *CBS, Inc. v. FCC.* The Court reiterated its approach to broadcasting in *CBS, Inc. v. FCC,*[178] holding a statute assuring federal candidates reasonable access to broadcasting to be constitutional. Like *Red Lion*, *CBS* presented questions concerning the government's power to promote the rights of listeners. For example, the government argued that the purposes of the First Amendment would be frustrated if broadcasters could "censor" the expression of candidates.[179] In the hierarchy of First Amendment rights, the government claimed, the public's right to receive political expression was supreme.[180]

The Court held that the statute represented an effort by Congress to assure that an important resource, the electromagnetic spectrum, is used in the public interest.[181] This position resembled *Buckley v. Valeo,*[182] where the Court concluded that public financing of elections furthers, rather than abridges, First Amendment values. But

---

[176]*Id.* at 258. Noticeably missing from *Miami Herald* is any concern for the danger of private censorship and the benefits of government regulation. The Court stated, "A responsible press is an undoubtedly desirable goal, but press responsibility is not mandated by the Constitution and like many other virtues it cannot be legislated." *Id.* at 256. This opinion was foreshadowed during oral argument when Justice Blackmun stated the following to appellee's counsel: "Your eloquence prompts me to ask just one question. Perhaps you can help me over the hurdle. For better or worse, we have opted for a free press, not for a free debate." 78 Landmark Briefs and Arguments of the Supreme Court of the United States 892–93 (Kurland & Casper eds. 1975). In his comparison of *Red Lion* and *Miami Herald*, Professor Van Alstyne states that the former was a "first amendment misfortune" while the latter represents a "more confident view of the first amendment." Van Alstyne, The Mobius Strip of the First Amendment: Perspectives on Red Lion, 29 S.C. L. Rev. 539, 574 (1978).

[177]418 U.S. at 260.

[178]453 U.S. 367 (1981).

[179]Brief for the FCC and the United States at 59 n.50.

[180]*Id.* at 60.

[181]453 U.S. at 397.

[182]424 U.S. 1, 92–93 (1976).

unlike *Buckley*, where journalistic discretion was not impaired, *CBS* involved a restriction on broadcaster discretion. The *CBS* Court minimized that discretion by referring to the trustee concept[183] and iterating the phrase that listener's rights are paramount.[184]

Chief Justice Burger's opinion for the Court in *CBS* has an extremely cursory analysis of the First Amendment issues. The Court did not analyze whether the statute actually enhanced opportunities for candidates to advance their candidacies or whether any increase in access justified the accompanying governmental scrutiny of broadcasters.[185] Nor does *CBS* consider whether less intrusive measures should be employed.[186] And, though the statute provided access only to a narrow group of speakers, the Court did not consider the statute's impact on the government's obligation to be neutral in its regulation of expression. By favoring candidates, *CBS* departs from an important principle stated in *Bellotti*: the inherent capacity of speech to inform the public does not depend upon the identity of its source.[187] Finally, the looseness of *CBS* is captured by Chief Justice Burger's statement that the statute properly balanced the First Amendment rights of federal candidates, the public, and broadcasters.[188] But the candidate's rights came from a statute enacted through the Commerce Clause, not the First Amendment.[189] Any serious claim that the candidates' right of access was a First Amendment right would have to follow a finding of state action, but the *CBS* Court did not address the state action issue.

---

[183]453 U.S. at 395.

[184]*Ibid.*

[185]Lee, The Problems of "Reasonable Access" to Broadcasting for Noncommercial Expression: Content Discrimination, Appellate Review, and Separation of Commercial and Noncommercial Expression, 34 Fla. L. Rev. 348, 365 (1982).

[186]The Court merely stated that the statute lacked a chilling effect and did not impair the discretion of broadcasters to present their views on any issue. 453 U.S. at 367. Consequently, the Court treated the burden on broadcaster discretion as minimal and accepted the statute, without examination, as being sufficiently narrow. For a discussion of the manner in which journalistic discretion was defined in this case, see Lee, note 185 *supra*, at 358–61.

[187]See text accompanying note 142 *supra*. Although unarticulated, the Court may have sustained the statute because it did not facially discriminate among candidates on the basis of viewpoint. For a discussion of the statute's potential for discriminatory effects, see Lee, note 185 *supra*, at 365–68.

[188]453 U.S. at 397. Elsewhere the opinion refers to the First Amendment interests of candidates, voters, and broadcasters. *Id.* at 396.

[189]Professor Nimmer also reached a similar conclusion. Nimmer, note 14 *supra*, at §4.09 [D] (b), at 4–127.

3. League of Women Voters: *The end of scarcity? FCC v. League of Women Voters*,[190] where the Court declared a statute prohibiting public broadcasters from editorializing to be unconstitutional,[191] is more notable for what was said about broadcasting than for what was said about the issues in the case. *League of Women Voters* reiterates that within certain limits, the government may treat broadcasting differently from other media.[192] This distinction is based upon broadcaster use of a scarce and valuable national resource,[193] and the accompanying fiduciary responsibility. Also, the decision shows that regulations of broadcast content are entitled to a low level of judicial scrutiny.[194]

League of Women Voters is also notable because the Court reiterated the need for content regulation to protect audience rights. It stated that Congress may seek to assure that the public receives a balanced presentation on issues that "otherwise might not be addressed if control of the medium were left entirely in the hands of those who own and operate broadcasting stations."[195] Further, the Court described *Red Lion* and *CBS* as examples of permissible government regulations because those cases "secure the public's First Amendment interest in receiving a balanced presentation of views on diverse matters of public concern."[196]

Despite the Court's recitation of the standard broadcasting phrases, *League of Women Voters* arguably provides a faint indication that the Court is willing to modify the system of broadcast regulation.[197] The Court noted, without commentary, that others have criticized the spectrum-scarcity rationale.[198] But it stated, "We are not pre-

---

[190]468 U.S. 364 (1984).

[191]*Id.* at 386–99 (holding that the editorializing ban did not directly and narrowly advance the asserted governmental interests). In dissent, Justice Rehnquist, joined by Chief Justice Burger and Justice White, said the statute was rationally related to Congress' desire to avoid the appearance of government sponsorship of a particular view. *Id.* at 407. Justice Stevens's dissent found the statute to be content neutral and posing a minor burden on expression. *Id.* at 412–13.

[192]468 U.S. at 376–77; *id.* at 380; *id.* at 402.

[193]*Id.* at 376.

[194]*Id.* at 374–76.

[195]*Id.* at 377.

[196]*Id.* at 380.

[197]For competing views on the meaning of *League of Women Voters, compare* Note, 12 Pepperdine L. Rev. 699, 721–22 (1985), *with* Note, 39 Vand L. Rev. 323, 349, 357 (1986).

[198]468 U.S. at 376 n.11.

pared, however, to reconsider our long-standing approach without some signal from Congress or the FCC that technological developments have advanced so far that some revision of the system of broadcast regulation may be required."[199] Even if presented with findings showing a lack of scarcity, or more accurately a showing that scarcity is not confined to the electromagnetic spectrum, the Court conceivably could rely upon other characteristics of broadcasting as rationales for unique regulation. For example, in *FCC v. Pacifica Foundation*,[200] the Court did not rely on spectrum scarcity as the rationale for its distinct treatment of broadcast indecency. Instead, the Court cited broadcasting's pervasive presence and unique accessibility to children as justifications for the regulation.[201] Given the illogical approach the Court has taken with the so-called unique scarcity of broadcast frequencies, there is no reason the Court could not discard scarcity as a regulatory rationale and still distinguish broadcasting from other media because of its pervasive presence. Such an effort, though, would be propping up a house of cards. The attributes of broadcasting, and the accompanying rights of the audience, are unique only because the Court says so.

B. UTILITY BILLING ENVELOPES

The type of government intervention allowed by the Court under *Red Lion* and its progeny does not apply to non-broadcast means of communication, as *Pacific Gas & Electric Corp. v. Public Utilities Commission*[202] demonstrates. *PG & E* entailed a requirement that a utility periodically carry the expression of a consumer group in its billing envelopes.[203] During those months when the consumer group used the billing envelopes, the utility's newsletter could be included only if the utility paid additional postage.[204] The regulatory com-

---

[199]*Id.* at 377 n.11.

[200]438 U.S. 726 (1978).

[201]*Id.* at 748–49.

[202]106 S.Ct. 903 (1986).

[203] The utility commission ruled that the ratepayers owned the space remaining in the billing envelope after the inclusion of the monthly bill and any required notices. *Id.* at 906. TURN, a consumer group which had opposed the utility in rate increase actions, was given access to the extra space in the billing envelopes four times a year. *Ibid.*

[204]*Ibid.* The utility commission acknowledged that the practical effect of this requirement was to deter dissemination of the utility's newsletter four times per year. *Id.* at 908.

mission's action was premised on the assumption that consumers would benefit from a variety of views.[205]

At the Supreme Court, the consumer group which was granted access to the billing envelopes claimed that government action increasing the variety of sources of information consumers receive through billing envelopes promotes the core First Amendment value of an informed citizenry.[206] *Amici* in support of the consumer group stated that the space in billing envelopes resembles the broadcast spectrum[207] and that the government's proper role was to promote a free-flowing marketplace of ideas.[208] The utility, in contrast, argued that its speech could not be restricted to enhance the relative voice of the consumer group.[209]

Justice Powell's plurality opinion, joined by Chief Justice Burger and Justices Brennan and O'Connor, blends the views of his opinion for the Court in *Bellotti*[210] and his concurring opinion in *Pruneyard Shopping Center v. Robins.*[211] As in *Bellotti*, Justice Powell found that the utility's expression, a newsletter included in billing envelopes, was protected by the First Amendment.[212] Then, in a statement that set the tone of the opinion, he stated, "By protecting those who wish to enter the marketplace of ideas from governmental attack, the First Amendment protects the public's interest in receiving information."[213] This simple statement emphasizes governmental, rather than private restraints on the marketplace of ideas. And although the opinion recounted the regulation's burden on the utility's First Amendment rights,[214] a major theme of *PG & E* is that the government's authority to foster a variety of views is sharply limited.

---

[205]*Ibid.*

[206]Brief for Appellees TURN, *et al.*, at 39.

[207]Amicus Curiae Brief of Telecommunications Research and Action Center, et al., at 31–34.

[208]*Id.* at 13.

[209]Appellant's Reply Brief at 18–19; see also Amicus Brief of Edison Electric Institute at 11.

[210]435 U.S. 765 (1978); see text and notes accompanying notes 129–57 *supra*.

[211]447 U.S. 74 (1980).

[212]106 S.Ct. at 907. See also Consolidated Edison Co. v. Public Serv. Comm'n, 447 U.S. 530, 534 n.1 (1980); First Nat'l Bank v. Bellotti, 435 U.S. 765, 783 (1978).

[213]106 S.Ct. at 907.

[214]The plurality described the burdens as follows. First, faced with the task of disseminating views that are hostile to its own, the utility may avoid controversial subjects. *Id.* at 910. Second, the utility may be pressured to respond to arguments made by those using its

The State defended the order on the ground that it had a valid interest in making a variety of views available to the utility's customers.[215] The Court, though, having concluded that the order was viewpoint-based in that access to the envelopes was granted only to those who disagreed with the utility's views, held that the government's interest in promoting speech was not furthered by a content-based order.[216] Further, the order inhibited the expression of the utility while promoting the expression of the consumer group. This type of governmental action was contrasted with the permissible subsidies of expression in *Buckley v. Valeo*[217] and *Regan v. Taxation With Representation*[218] thus:[219]

> Unlike these permissible government subsidies of speech, the commission's order identifies the favored speaker "based on the identity of the interests that [the speaker] may represent," . . . and forces the speaker's opponent—not the taxpaying public—to assist in disseminating the speaker's message.

---

envelopes. *Id*. at 911–12. Third, the utility is forced to disseminate views that it would prefer not to associate with. *Id*. at 912–13. Justice Powell's discussion of these effects partially defines both a First Amendment right of corporations to be free from certain burdens on expression, and a First Amendment right of corporations to control use of their property. At several points in *PG & E*, Justice Powell referred to a corporation's First Amendment rights. See *id*. at 911; *id*. at 911 n.10; *id*. at 914. This contrasts with *Bellotti* where Justice Powell avoided discussing corporate rights and instead described speech as protected by the First Amendment. See text and notes accompanying notes 132–37 *supra*.

Justice Rehnquist's dissent, joined by Justice White and partly by Justice Stevens, disagreed that the order would cause the utility to avoid discussing certain topics. *Id*. at 920. As to the forced-association issue, Justice Rehnquist claimed that this harm was tied to freedom of conscience, a freedom corporations do not possess. *Id*. at 920–21. Newspapers, though, were entitled to such freedom, although Justice Rehnquist did not explain the reasoning for this except through a cryptic reference to the historic role of newspapers as conveyers of expression. *Id*. at 921.

[215]106 S.Ct. at 914.

[216]*Ibid*. It is important to note that the problem of compelled response and forced association that the plurality found unacceptable, see note 214 *supra*, will not be eliminated with a content neutral access requirement. As Justice Powell stated in his concurring opinion in *Pruneyard*, "even when no particular message is mandated by the State, First Amendment interests are affected by state action that forces a property owner to admit third-party speakers." 447 U.S. 74, 98 (1980). Justice Powell relied upon his *Pruneyard* concurring opinion in *PG & E*. 106 S.Ct. at 911. Thus, *PG & E* does not mean that a content neutral access requirement would necessarily be constitutional.

[217]424 U.S. 1, 92–93 (1976) (federal funding of elections furthers, rather than abridges, First Amendment values).

[218]461 U.S. 540, 548, (1983) (veteran's organizations are entitled to receive tax-deductible contributions regardless of the content of any speech they may use).

[219]106 S.Ct. at 911.

The plurality concluded that the government cannot advance some points of view by burdening the expression of others.[220]

The central point of *Red Lion* was that broadcasters have a privilege conferred upon them by government, and to avoid abuse of that privilege, broadcasters must comply with certain obligations. If a federally issued broadcast license confers privileges and obligations upon a broadcaster, does not a utility given the privileged status of monopolist also have to comply with certain obligations, such as disseminating the expression of others? Conversely, if a licensed utility does not have to disseminate the views of others, why should a similar requirement be permissible for broadcasters? In defining the First Amendment rights of the utility, the *PG & E* plurality went in two directions. The first distinguished broadcasters from utilities, presumably preserving the government's unique authority in broadcasting. The second defined the utility's power to control its property in a way that calls into question the validity of *Red Lion*.

Justice Powell distinguished broadcasting from the method of communication used by PG & E, but his reasoning was flawed. He stated that billing envelopes are not comparable to the broadcast spectrum. " '[A] broadcaster communicates through use of a scarce, publicly owned resource. No person can broadcast without a license, whereas all persons are free to send correspondence to private homes through the mails.' "[221] But broadcasters are not unique in their use of a scarce resource. PG & E used scarce resources such as ink, paper, and money for postage to disseminate its monthly newsletter. Moreover, the extra space in the billing envelopes used to disseminate the newsletter did not belong to the utility. Rather, it belonged to the rate payers. While anyone in theory may use the mail system, only those with large financial resources are "free" to purchase the materials and postage necessary to communicate through the mails with PG & E's millions of customers. And only a few entities control access to envelopes that are opened by nearly all of the residents of a large area.

---

[220]*Id.* at 914. See also First Nat'l Bank v. Bellotti, 435 U.S. 765, 785 (1978); Buckley v. Valeo, 424 U.S. 1, 48–49 (1976). See note 216 *supra*.

[221]106 S.Ct. at 908 n.6, quoting *Consolidated Edison*, 447 U.S. at 543. Professor Emerson, however, claims that government creation of a monopoly, such as a public utility, poses problems that are similar to those created by the scarcity of broadcast frequencies. Emerson, The Affirmative Side of the First Amendment, 15 Ga. L. Rev. 795, 827 (1981).

The plurality may have unwittingly signaled the end of *Red Lion* when it stated that the key issue was that the utility was forced to use its property to disseminate views it disagreed with.[222] Justice Powell recognized that this issue of forced dissemination applied to other properties owned by the utility as well as properties owned by "any other kind of regulated business. . . ."[223] Thus, the utility's status as a licensed monopolist and rate payer (public) ownership of the extra space in billing envelopes did not minimize this burden on expression.[224] If the forced use of PG & E's property was impermissible, how can a similar burden on broadcasters be permissible? Broadcasters must use their private property, such as cameras, microphones, amplifiers, and transmitters, to disseminate views they disagree with. Furthermore, parts of *PG & E* read as though Justice Powell were discussing a natural person. For example, he stated that there can be little doubt that the appellant "will feel compelled to respond to arguments and allegations made by TURN in its messages to appellant's customers."[225] This was followed by a citation to a religious freedom case in which the Court discussed freedom of the mind.[226] As Justice Rehnquist argued in dissent, to ascribe to corporations an intellect or mind is to confuse metaphor with reality.[227] Nonetheless, Justice Rehnquist recognized that the plurality's description of the utility casts doubt on the continuing validity of *Red Lion*.[228]

III. CONCLUSION

In the short period the Court has recognized the right to receive expression, the concept has been used for disparate purposes. A summary of those applications leads to dizzying observations such as the following: the audience's rights render distinc-

---

[222] 106 S.Ct. at 913.

[223] *Id.* at n.15. See also *id.* at 906 n.4.

[224] *Id.* at 912 n.14 (appellant's status as a regulated utility does not lessen its First Amendment rights); *id.* at 913 (the burden on the utility's rights did not depend upon ownership of the "extra space" in the billing envelopes).

[225] *Id.* at 912.

[226] Wooley v. Maynard, 430 U.S. 705, 714 (1977).

[227] 106 S.Ct. at 921.

[228] *Id.* at 922 n.3.

tions among speakers meaningless in *Bellotti* while the audience's rights render distinctions among speakers meaningful in *Red Lion*. Contradictions such as this reflect both the richness of problems posed by free expression, and the Court's failure to develop a cohesive theory of free speech. The contradictions also show that the right to receive consists of a bundle of concepts, each of which has vitality in a narrow context.

The primary utility and novelty of the right to receive expression is that it restricts the government's power to interfere with the recipient of communication. This aspect of the right to receive provides a powerful statement about freedom from government and adds life and substance to freedom of speech. Simply stated, speakers are only as free to speak as audiences are to listen, and the choices as to what is voiced and heard are largely in "the hands of each of us . . . ."[229]

The right to receive also serves as the basis for a marked expansion of First Amendment protection in the commercial and corporate speech contexts. But in *Virginia Pharmacy* and *Bellotti* the right to receive was advanced in the absence of analysis of why such speech is important to the speaker. If strongly grounded in a theory of autonomy, an emphasis on the audience's need for an uninhibited flow of expression may be sufficient to withstand attempts to suppress certain speakers. But the Court has not explicitly tied the right to receive to a theory of autonomy. Consequently, it can vary the strength of the right as it sees fit. For example, the right to receive can be defined in terms that do not strongly protect speakers. When defined in terms of the audience's generalized interest in receiving messages, the right to receive will be insufficient to prevent restrictions on certain speakers where the audience can obtain the same message from another speaker.

When viewed as a predicate to informed speech, the right to receive threatens to strip away all of the government's control over the content of its facilities such as museums, magazines, and public broadcasting stations, or to engulf the managers of these facilities in litigation challenging their decisions. But courts should not exercise close supervision over the content of these facilities, and as *Pico* illustrates, the Court's awkward effort to protect both the government's control over the library and the right to receive led to

---

[229]Cohen v. California, 403 U.S. 15, 24 (1971).

an arbitrarily confined right to receive expression. A more sensible approach in this context is to recognize the right to receive only where a speaker has a right to speak. This preserves the government's ability to make content choices for its non-forum facilities[230] and allows judges to be guided by the rich and carefully developed doctrine of the right to speak.

The right to receive also serves as part of the Court's justification for the unjustifiable—a spurious distinction between broadcasting and other media. While the Court has thus far confined *Red Lion* to broadcasting, the doctrine of that case threatens other media. For example, federal cable law, based on *Red Lion*, seeks to promote the rights of the audience by restricting the freedom of cable companies.[231] But policymakers and the Court should recognize that free speech and the accompanying right to receive are abridged only by government, not by private censorship. The right to receive is best served when speakers are free to speak and listeners are free to listen, not when government restricts some speakers to protect listeners.

---

[230] This approach does not mean that the government would have unlimited control over such facilities or that content decisions would be unreviewable. As Justice Blackmun recognized in *Pico*, see text accompanying note 118 *supra*, the government cannot suppress ideas solely for the purpose of suppressing ideas. This concern is separate from the issues raised by the definition of the right to receive as a predicate to informed expression.

[231] Cable Communications Policy Act of 1984, 98 Stat. 2779, 2782–85 (1984). For a discussion of this aspect of the Cable Act, see Lee, Cable Leased Access and the Conflict among First Amendments Rights and First Amendment Values, 35 Emory L.J. 563 (1986).

L. A. POWE, JR.

TORNILLO

I. Introduction

The Progressive Era impulse in Florida, as elsewhere, sought to make electoral politics safe for the return of the "honest and high minded."[1] The Trammell Corrupt Practices Act of 1913[2] required over two weeks advance notification of an intended attack by one candidate on his opponent and, more significantly, another part offered candidates a right of reply to newspaper attacks on them. Over a half century later this latter provision was resurrected in aid of Pat Tornillo, a feisty teachers' union leader, who was on the wrong side of *The Miami Herald*'s editorial position. Tornillo subsequently joined forces with Jerome Barron, the intellectual godfather of compulsory access to the press,[3] to produce one of the century's major press cases: *Miami Herald v. Tornillo.*[4]

L. A. Powe, Jr., is Bernard J. Ward Centennial Professor of Law at The University of Texas.

Author's Note: Tornillo is pronounced tor-nil-lo (not tor-nee-yo). Writing this article was greatly assisted by the generous cooperation of the principals in the case. Pat Tornillo answered all my questions, granted me unlimited access to his attorneys' files on the case, and authorized them to answer my questions. Donald Shoemaker, the former Editor of The Miami Herald, and Jim Hampton, the current Editor, were equally generous in granting me interviews and providing the Herald's microfiche file on Tornillo. The conclusions reached are, of course, mine. To Jerome Barron, Elizabeth duFresne, Jim Hampton, Dan Paul, Donald Shoemaker, Roberta Simon, and Pat Tornillo, many, many thanks. I would also like to thank David Anderson, Tom Krattenmaker, Doug Laycock, Sandy Levinson, and Richard Markovits for helpful comments on earlier drafts of this article.

[1] Keen, Brief History of the Corrupt Practice Acts of Florida, 9 Fla. L.J. 297, 299 (1935).

[2] Act of 1913, Ch. 6470.

[3] Barron, Access to the Press—A New First Amendment Right, 80 Harv. L. Rev. 1641 (1967).

[4] 418 U.S. 241 (1974).

The Miami Herald had not forgiven Tornillo for the illegal 1968 Florida teachers' strike which he had led, and consequently it savaged his candidacy for state representative four years later in a pair of pre-election editorials. Tornillo demanded a right of reply under the 1913 Florida statute, the *Herald* refused, and the litigation began. When Tornillo prevailed in the Florida Supreme Court, the nation's press gulped. The United States Supreme Court had sustained the fairness doctrine for broadcasting only four years earlier in *Red Lion*.[5] Might the Florida decision—a "devastating inroad" in the words of the American Newspaper Publishers Association[6]—begin a process leading to a similar rule for newspapers? Less than two years after the editorials, the Supreme Court unanimously answered "no" in an opinion by Chief Justice Burger.

Tornillo wished to speak and have his speech enhanced. Both his interest in speaking and the public's in having a well functioning marketplace of ideas supported his claim to reply. The *Herald*, quite naturally, wished to retain its autonomy to publish only what it selected. Yet instead of balancing, the Court held the press interests absolute. That absolutism is out of harmony with modern legal scholarship, and Melville Nimmer predicted Tornillo would not sit well with law professors: "those who doubt the efficacy of [Tornillo's] result are hardly persuaded by an approach that apparently fails to recognize that any balancing of speech and press rights is required."[7] Vincent Blasi,[8] Kenneth Karst,[9] and Benno Schmidt[10] quickly concurred.

The unease is understandable. When a major metropolitan newspaper goes on a rampage in an otherwise poorly covered race for state representative, denying the injured party—and the voting public—an opportunity to place the information in context, it is not the decision that many of the nation's law professors would

---

[5]Red Lion Broadcasting v. FCC, 395 U.S. 367 (1969).

[6]ANPA Amicus Brief, Miami Herald v. Tornillo No. 73-797 at 5.

[7]Nimmer, Is Freedom of the Press a Redundancy? 26 Hastings L.J. 639, 658 (1975).

[8]Blasi, The Checking Value in First Amendment Theory, 1977 Am. B. Found. Res. J. 521, 621–28.

[9]Karst, Equality as a Central Principle in the First Amendment, 43 U. Chi. L. Rev. 20, 49–51 (1975).

[10]Schmidt, Freedom of the Press vs. Public Access 219–35 (1976) [hereinafter cited as Schmidt, Freedom of the Press].

make. Yet Anthony Lewis,[11] Floyd Abrams,[12] and media representatives generally are equally sure that *Tornillo*'s recognition of rights
the press has always claimed and enjoyed is correct. While the press
rests on its traditional rights, the seemingly egregious behavior of
the *Herald* brings into question whether the local marketplaces of
ideas can properly function. Against this background, the Court's
solution has appeared unfortunate. The division of First Amendment interests is the key to why *Tornillo* is a very hard case. Briefly,
my position is that the Court reached the appropriate result because
editorial autonomy is embedded in the text, purpose, history, and
tradition of the First Amendment. Had the right of reply been
sustained, the psychological barrier of no interference with newspapers would have been broken. Legislators and judges would deal
more frequently with appropriate limits on the press. The outcome
of this process is unknowable, as is whether, at its end, we would
still associate freedom of the press with a fierce independence from
government. But what we do know, I will suggest, cautions strongly
against taking the first step.

Readers of *Tornillo* get but bare bones facts—because those were
all that were available to the Court. There was neither legislative
history of the Florida statute nor discussion of Tornillo's primary
race. These omissions can be cured and context provided. The in-
troductory parts of this article will provide the historical setting of
the Trammell Corrupt Practices Act, the 1968 teachers' strike, and
Tornillo's campaign for the Florida House. The following parts of
the article will examine the proceedings in Florida and the Supreme
Court. The final sections will discuss at length why the Court's decision, even if it seems a second-best solution, was exactly right.

II. THE TRAMMELL CORRUPT PRACTICES ACT

At the turn of the century, Florida was a state without meaningful elections. The Republican Party effectively died in the 1880s
and the Populist Party was stillborn when Farmers' Alliance leaders
were co-opted into the Democratic Party councils.[13] There were no

---

[11]Lewis, A Preferred Position for Journalism? 7 Hofstra L. Rev. 595, 603 (1979).

[12]Abrams, In Defense of Tornillo, 86 Yale L. J. 361 (1976) (reviewing Schmidt).

[13]Cash, History of the Democratic Party in Florida 85 (1936); Goodwyn, Democratic
Promise 215, 339–40 (1976).

primaries; instead candidates were selected by convention, and those selected by the Democratic conventions automatically won the pro forma November election. Many Floridians concluded that the convention system had become a way for those with power to perpetuate themselves in office and that primary elections were the appropriate means of correcting this. Furthermore, primaries would be a way to exclude blacks from voting, a goal on which there was no debate among the factions of the Democratic Party.[14] In 1901 the Florida legislature acceded to these demands and authorized selection of party candidates through primary elections.[15] The shift may have solved one problem, but it produced others, one of which was distorted news reporting. Southern newspapers, both the rural weeklies and city dailies, existed for politics.[16] Florida's new primary elections provided grist for a mill that treated voters to a barrage of distortion and outright lies. Rightly or wrongly, it was assumed that the distorted information adversely affected the voters.[17] Irresponsible reporting by the Florida press was not limited to any particular segment of the state. The urban press was conservative and slanted stories accordingly. The more numerous rural papers, for their part, found Southern demagogues especially seductive. Additionally, "allegiance between publishers and politicians was enhanced with printing contracts for session laws, sheriff's sales, county court calendars and campaign literature, which always went to a party publisher even though an independent shop might do it cheaper."[18] With the demise of the Republican Party went the need for unhesitating support for any Democrat. Newspapers could thus "appraise[ ] the chief executives on a factional basis."[19]

This Southern pattern held in Florida, where the dominant figure of the period, Florida's best-known governor,[20] Napoleon Bonaparte Broward, had "no greater foes" than the conservative urban press, but had ample support in its rural counterpart.[21] In his seminal

---

[14]Proctor, Napolean Bonaparte Broward 173–74 (1950).

[15]Keen, 9 Fla. L.J. at 298.

[16]Clark, The Southern Country Editor 283 (1948).

[17]Keen, 9 Fla. L.J. at 299.

[18]Hoffer & Butterfield, The Right to Reply, 53 Journalism Quarterly 111, 112–13 (1976).

[19]Clark, The Southern Country Editor at 295–96.

[20]2 Tebeau & Carson, Florida 19 (1965).

[21]Proctor, Broward at 187; see also Tebeau, A History of Florida 330 (1971).

work, *Southern Politics*, V. O. Key noted that Broward's "progressive program and personal qualities generated loyalties and antipathies so intense that even after his death in 1910 political divisions were for several years along pro- and anti-Broward lines."[22] Broward is best known for taking on Florida's big corporations, especially its railroads, in the battle to fund the drainage of the millions of acres of swampland south of Lake Okeechobee. At issue was whether the Everglades would be developed for profit and at the convenience of major corporations or by government instead.[23] Broward's proposal, to drain the Everglades as a public project, the cornerstone of his governorship, precipitated vitriolic attacks from segments of the press.[24]

These attacks, in turn, led Broward to devote 10 percent of his 1907 message to the legislature to the need for criminalizing newspaper lies.[25] The proposed statute may be what Key had in mind when he wrote that Broward "urged with great courage and persuasiveness all the tenets of progressivism of the day and added a few planks of his own."[26] Broward's proposed statute would "mak[e] public mendacity a misdemeanor and punish[ ] any newspaper writer or editor or publisher who deliberately and intentionally writes or publishes an article that is untrue, and mak[e] the public printing of an untruth prima facie evidence of the misdemeanor."[27] His message singled out the (Jacksonville) *Florida Times-Union* for special criticism. The *Times Union* then helped prove Broward's point by printing what it claimed to be the entire text of his message while deleting all the pejorative references to itself.[28] The legislature, however, took no action on Broward's newspaper proposal although it modified the electoral process further by requiring that those who supervised primaries themselves be elected at primaries.[29]

---

[22]Key, Southern Politics 103–04 (1949).

[23]Colburn & Scher, Florida's Gubernatorial Politics in the 20th Century 64, 213–14 (1980).

[24]2 Dovell, Florida 711 (1952); Proctor, Broward at 199, 249.

[25]The section immediately preceding this asked the legislature to pass a resolution memorializing Congress to purchase territory, "either domestic or foreign," for the purpose of resettling all black Americans. *Id.* at 252.

[26]Key, Southern Politics at 104 (1949).

[27]2 Dovell, Florida at 711–12 (1952), quoting 1907 Message to the Legislature from the House Journal at 70.

[28]Hoffer & Butterfield, 53 Journalism Quarterly at 112.

[29]Act of 1907, Ch. 5613.

The period after Broward's administration was one of consolidation[30] in Florida, and further primary election reforms reflect this. Under his immediate successor, Albert Gilchrist, the 1909 legislature enacted Florida's first corrupt practices statute dealing with primaries.[31] The act made no explicit reference to newspapers. It did, however, attempt to reach some speech by prohibiting the distribution near polling places on primary day of "any pictures, cards, literature, or other writing against any candidate."[32] Passage of the Corrupt Practices Act did not cause the problems that Broward addressed to go away, and in 1913 Governor Park Trammell returned to the issue. Public funding of highways and cleaning up Florida's primary elections constituted the two best-known actions of Trammell's term as governor.[33] His election reforms added sections to the Corrupt Practices Act to bring newspapers under its coverage. Rather than embracing Broward's suggestion to criminalize the publication of falsehood, Trammell tried to ensure that voters had the opportunity of seeing a bigger picture than just one-sided accusations. The act gave those candidates whose character or conduct were assailed in newspaper columns a right to reply, in space equally conspicuous, to the charges.[34] The Trammell Act also placed a limit on campaign spending, prohibited bribing newspapers to support a candidate, and forbade attacks on candidates in the last eighteen days of a campaign unless the candidate was first personally served with the charges.[35] Given the hostility the press displayed when Tornillo attempted to use this law fifty-nine years later, it is ironic that at its adoption, the Trammell Corrupt Practices Act had solid backing from newsmen-legislators. Trammell's proposals were sponsored and managed in the Florida House by an editor for the (Plant City) *Courier.* In passing the House all five newsmen-members voted yes. (The vote was fifty-eight to four.) The three newsmen-senators split two to one in favor as the Senate passed the law by a twenty-one to six

---

[30]Colburn & Scher, Florida's Gubernatorial Politics at 279; Cash's influential History of the Democratic Party in Florida 112 (1936) states, "All outstanding legislation during the period under discussion [1905–17] showed the Broward influence. . . ."

[31]Keen, 9 Fla. L.J. at 299–300.

[32]Act of 1909, Ch. 5928 §11.

[33]2 Dovell, Florida at 733.

[34]Act of 1913, Ch. 6470, §12.

[35]Act of 1913, Ch. 6470, §§10–11.

vote.[36] The right-of-reply statute thus entered the Florida statute books. Given the partisan nature of the Florida press, it is indeed surprising that there is no reported case indicating its use until the 1970s.[37] But when *The Miami Herald* twice editorialized against Tornillo's candidacy, its actions were exactly what the Act was meant to cover.

III. THE STRIKE

The strike was no small matter, not to the teachers, Tornillo, the *Herald*, the Florida Legislature, or Governor Claude Kirk. In fact it was no small matter nationally. It was the first statewide teachers strike in American history. Surprisingly, the traditionally non-militant National Education Association (NEA) was the sponsoring union. And Pat Tornillo was one of the Florida teachers' field commanders. A transplanted New Jersey teacher, Tornillo had abandoned Dade County classrooms for the executive offices of the Dade County Classroom Teachers' Association (CTA). By the time of the strike Tornillo was well known in Florida. Everything he said or advocated seemed to generate controversy. As early as 1965, Tornillo led the battle for higher teacher salaries.[38] Yet he also pushed for other causes—aid for Cuban refugees' children,[39] the headstart program for blacks,[40] and faster desegregation of the schools.[41]

Sometimes he did the bizarre. In July 1967 Tornillo sent telegrams to both the Republican and Democratic National Committees urging them to stay away from Miami in 1968 for their conventions. Apparently his belief that education was in a pathetic state in Dade County supplied sufficient reason for the conventions to go else-

---

[36]53 Journalism Qu. at 113–14.

[37]Tornillo, 418 U.S. at 247. *Id.* at n.7 cited State v. News Journal Corp., 36 Fla. Supp. 164 (Volusia County Judge's Court, 1972) as the first recorded case. The judge in the case held the statute unconstitutional.

[38]Miami Herald, August 17, 1965; February 1, 1966. All citations to The Miami Herald are from their microfiche file on Tornillo. As recorded on the microfiche, the articles carry a date, but not the page number.

[39]Miami Herald, October 22, 1965; November 22, 1965.

[40]Miami Herald, March 2, 1966.

[41]Miami Herald, June 28, 1966.

where.[42] Needless to say Dade County merchants were extremely upset. The chance to host one of the national conventions meant a shot at more tourism and money for the local economy.[43] No one could blame the merchants—and others—for thinking Tornillo was mostly interested in furthering the welfare of one group and one group only: teachers. He was aggressive, controversial, and militant. His opponents undoubtedly accused him of many things but never of wavering on his path. By 1967, he was Executive Secretary of the CTA and also a part of the statewide hierarchy of the Florida Education Association (FEA), an NEA affiliate.[44] When the threat of a statewide teacher strike first began to surface in the late summer of 1967 it was hard not to have an opinion about Pat Tornillo.

The strike might not have occurred had Florida not, in 1966, elected Kirk its first Republican governor since Reconstruction. He complicated the Florida education picture in two distinct ways. First, he had campaigned on a pledge of no new taxes.[45] Second, despite no obvious qualifications beyond being a Southern Republican Governor, Kirk had caught the presidential—or at least vice-presidential—bug. In an interview with Tom Wicker of *The New York Times*, Kirk "recoiled as if he had been confronted with a California orange" at the mention of the speculation he might be selected as the Republican Vice-President. "That offends me. It's discrimination. Why talk about a governor from a Southern state just for the vice presidency. Why not Kirk for president?"[46]

While it is arbitrary to select any specific time to begin a chronology, 1967 is a useful starting point to discuss the strike of February 19–March 11, 1968. Although the FEA had been criticizing the poor quality of the state's schools throughout the decade, it locked horns with Kirk during the 1967 session. It called for increased taxes for education; Kirk instead called for a cut in educational expenditures. The FEA censured him, and in June the NEA invoked sanctions against Florida, urging teachers to boycott the state's schools.[47]

---

[42]Miami Herald, July 14–17, 1967.

[43]Miami Herald, July 16, 1967.

[44]Tornillo Interview, March 24, 1986.

[45]New York Times, January 30, 1968 at 30.

[46]New York Times, January 23, 1968 at 38.

[47]Colburn & Scher, Florida's Gubernatorial Politics at 201–02.

In the summer of 1967 the FEA started gearing up for a strike. Although Dade schools did not have the problems of the schools elsewhere in the state, Tornillo began implementing what was to be the key aspect of the strike plan: resignations. Because a public employee strike would be illegal, the chosen tactic was mass resignations so that teachers could deny they were engaged in an illegal strike. Tornillo threatened such action in early September, but tempered it by stating the Dade teachers would not resign en masse except as part of a statewide effort. The strike talk was in fact aimed at forcing the governor to call a special session of the legislature to appropriate substantial new funds.[48]

Over the next six weeks FEA negotiators, including Tornillo, met with the governor; both sides engaged in considerable public bluster, but the crisis seemingly ended with the governor and teachers calling a truce. The *Herald* announced a "dramatic compromise which ended threats of mass resignation:" Kirk agreed to call a special session by January and the FEA called off a scheduled mass meeting to push for statewide teacher resignations.[49] But December waned and there was neither a special session nor even a call for one. The teachers gave the FEA carte blanche to call a walkout. Tornillo noted, "We're through with meetings. We are through with polls."[50] With threats mounting, Kirk indicated he would call the legislature into session on January 29. Kirk had thus far been all talk and no action, so his continued statement that he would call the session did not lessen the strike talk. The special session did begin January 29, however, and by call was limited to ten days.[51] Yet Kirk did not submit proposals for the first five days. Then, he tied the funding increases for education to a voter referendum. This was wholly unacceptable to the teachers, and they protested loudly and immediately.[52] After Kirk extended the session until February 16,[53] a compromise package was enacted that included a series of

[48]Miami Herald, September 9, 1967.

[49]Miami Herald, October 19, 1967.

[50]Miami Herald, December 30, 1967.

[51]Governor's Proclamation, January 13, 1968, Laws of Florida, Extraordinary Sessions 1967–68 at 150.

[52]New York Times, February 4, 1968 at 41.

[53]Governor's Proclamation, February 8, 1968, Laws of Florida, Extraordinary Sessions 1967–68 at 152.

laws so complex that they proved almost impossible for the press to report. Cutting to the basics, the teachers would get less than they had stated they would settle for, but with no referendum attached to the package.

The day the session ended the FEA called for a statewide walk-out, using the resignations previously turned over to union leaders.[54] The facts of the strike are simply stated. Kirk left the state immediately after the session to continue his national campaign.[55] The strike began Monday, February 19. The FEA submitted some 34,000 resignations, although only about 26,000 of the state's 60,000 teachers failed to show for work that day.[56] Kirk flew home quickly, denounced the strike and the Democrats, and left again.[57] A state court judge enjoined the strike, summarily rejecting the union contention that there was no strike, just a lot of resignations. Also enjoined were actions to persuade nonstrikers to join.[58] Tornillo was personally served with a copy of the injunction. Undeterred, he violated it and was served with a show cause order.[59] (Fourteen months later he took responsibility for the walkout and was found guilty of criminal contempt, sentenced to forty-eight hours in jail and a $1,000 fine. The sentence was subsequently suspended.[60]) The number of strikers increased, with an additional 9,000 joining within the next two days.[61] Hiring substitutes and moving quickly to accredit additional teachers were unsuccessful moves to break the strike; so was the injunction. Approximately 60 percent of the Dade teachers followed the union. During the strike they held pep rallies at Marine Stadium where Tornillo and the president of the CTA made wonderful grandstand arrivals by renting a hydrofoil and landing by sea. By all accounts morale was high, and pictures

---

[54]Miami Herald, February 16, 1968.

[55]New York Times, February 16, 1968 at 16.

[56]New York Times, February 18, 1968 at 29; February 20, 1968 at 1; February 21, 1968 at 31.

[57]New York Times, February 18, 1968 at 21.

[58]Miami Herald, February 24, 1968.

[59]Miami Herald, February 27, 1968.

[60]Miami Herald, April 18, 1969; April 19, 1969; April 24, 1969; Tornillo to Author, June 10, 1986.

[61]New York Times, February 26, 1968 at 31.

of the strikers at Marine Stadium show a festive atmosphere.[62] Sensing that all the powers in Florida were against them, the teachers nevertheless thought they could prevail.[63]

From California, Kirk stated that it was un-American to turn education over to the unions and he would not even negotiate with them.[64] He then returned home to negotiate. Negotiations occurred with appropriate denials—on a single day Tornillo told the *Herald* that the doors were closed to the teachers, while telling the teachers that negotiations were going better than reported[65]—and a settlement was reached. On March 6, Kirk told county school board members that he had "broken" the FEA and would let the education package become law without his signature.[66] On March 8 it became law. The teachers went back to work Monday, March 11.

The above description cries out with questions of why: why did it happen? Why were the teachers striking? The FEA publicly and clearly stated that the legislative compromise provided inadequate funding.[67] Kirk said the same thing in a different way, blaming the Democrats for not voting higher taxes, while adding he would not call another special session.[68] Was the strike to protest the failure of the special session to provide enough funding? Or to force the governor to call a second special session? In fact, it was neither. Although it may be a subsequent rationalization, Tornillo told me that the teachers walked because they feared Kirk would veto the package that they had labeled inadequate. The strike was to pressure him to sign.[69]

During the strike, Tornillo blasted the media for not presenting the facts to the public.[70] But, given the convoluted position of the union, the blame for any media failures belongs elsewhere. The

---

[62]Miami Herald, February 20, 1968; February 26, 1968.

[63]Miami Herald, February 22, 1968.

[64]New York Times, February 21, 1968 at 31.

[65]Miami Herald, March 6, 1968.

[66]New York Times, March 6, 1968 at 20. Kirk had flipped on the issue a couple of times during the week. New York Times, March 1, 1968 at 25; March 5, 1968 at 25.

[67]New York Times, February 16, 1968 at 16; February 17, 1968 at 13.

[68]New York Times, February 18, 1968 at 29.

[69]Tornillo Interview.

[70]Miami Herald, February 26, 1968.

timing of the strike simply made no sense. If Kirk vetoed the bill, then the union's position would have been clear to everyone and might well have had substantial public support. If Kirk signed the bill, then the strike threat could be saved for a later date and another issue. But striking before Kirk did anything left the public bewildered, the union friendless in the press, and the classrooms empty.

Kirk easily could have aborted or at least shortened the strike by signing the bill. That he waited and waited and then let it become law without a signature supports the assessment of the Commissioner of Education, a Democrat, that Kirk was more interested in his "national image" than Florida schools.[71] Still, the momentum to strike appears to have gotten out of hand. In my interview with Tornillo, he told me that in the FEA counsels he had opposed the timing, arguing to strike only if Kirk used his veto.[72] If this is accurate—and it is flatly contradictory to his public positions at the time—it showed judgment.

The intense opposition of the press, including the *Herald*, was understandable. Few newspapers like labor unions. Fewer still like public employee unions, and there are almost none who support illegal strikes by public employees, especially when the strike appears wholly unnecessary. Don Shoemaker, who ran the *Herald* during these events, told me that while the paper was not anti-worker, it unquestionably was anti-union.[73]

If the strike made no newspaper friends, it cost the CTA nothing with respect to future relations with the school board. Dade County recognized the CTA as the exclusive bargaining agent for the county's teachers in December 1968.[74] Although the Florida Supreme Court eventually set that recognition aside, the court held that teachers had the right to bargain collectively.[75] In the two-year period following the strike, Tornillo was in the pages of the *Herald* at least monthly, and twice the *Herald* devoted editorial attacks to him. One of these, in March 1969, coined the name "Boss Tornillo," a name that would change to "Czar" in one of the two 1972 election

[71]New York Times, March 11, 1968 at 18.

[72]Tornillo Interview.

[73]Shoemaker Interview, March 25, 1986.

[74]Miami Herald, December 12, 1968.

[75]Dade County Classroom Teachers' Ass'n v. Ryan, 225 So.2d 903 (Fla. 1969).

editorials.[76] The *Herald*'s attorney, Dan Paul, believes that the *Herald*'s contempt for Tornillo, which was apparent from the way the paper treated him, turned him from just another union leader to an important public figure. The *Herald* "made him."[77]

IV. RUNNING FOR OFFICE

If it had not been for the strike, few would know or care what happened in Tornillo's 1972 bid for the state legislature. But if it were not for *Reynolds v. Sims*,[78] there probably would have been no bid in the first place. While Florida's population had been growing explosively in the south, the legislature reflected the fact that, for most of its existence, Florida's citizens lived in the northern sections of the state. Prior to reapportionment by a federal district court, Dade County had a single senator and three representatives. Following the plan adopted by the court, Dade jumped to nine senators and twenty-two representatives.[79] Reapportionment opened new offices and allowed individuals like Tornillo a chance. Subsequent reapportionment after the 1970 census added four additional representatives.[80]

Tornillo ran in 1970 as well as in his famous 1972 campaign. In the earlier race, Tornillo was one of three challengers to a four-term incumbent. The incumbent got 34,562 votes in the primary, and Tornillo ran second with 20,359.[81] The other two received enough votes to force a run-off in which Tornillo was slaughtered 70,009 to 44,364.[82] The *Herald* did not editorialize; indeed it scarcely covered the race. Although Shoemaker, who made the decision to oppose Tornillo in 1972, states he cannot remember the 1970 race, both he and Tornillo speculate that no one thought Tornillo had a chance and so the *Herald* ignored him.[83]

---

[76]Miami Herald, March 7, 1969.

[77]Paul Interview, January 12, 1987.

[78]377 U.S. 533 (1964).

[79]Tebeau, A History of Florida 449 (1971).

[80]Shoemaker Interview.

[81]Miami Herald, September 9, 1970.

[82]Miami Herald, September 30, 1970.

[83]Shoemaker to Author, July 3, 1986; Tornillo to Author, June 10, 1986.

Tornillo stayed active in both the union and politics. Indeed, he thought it important that the two converge. When the 1972 Democratic Convention arrived, he was selected as a Humphrey delegate but on the eve of the convention shifted to McGovern.[84] Then, in late July he announced his candidacy for Florida House District 103.

There were two other candidates, Alan Becker and Hugh Duval. Coverage of the campaign was sparse, but with thirty-five races for the legislature plus numerous judicial and law enforcement races, coverage necessarily had to be minimal. According to Tornillo, he was the least liberal of the three.[85] This could not be inferred from the *Herald*'s pre-election edition on Sunday, September 10, which reflected an anti-Tornillo bias. While all three were discussed, Tornillo was last and received the least space. Neither alphabetical order—Duval was first—nor age—Becker was twenty-seven—can explain this.[86] When I brought this to Shoemaker's attention, he agreed it was "unfair" to Tornillo.[87] Maybe to the *Herald*'s surprise, Tornillo ran a strong second. Becker received 13,113 votes, Tornillo 11,967, and Duval 8,206.[88] In three weeks Tornillo and Becker would meet in the run-off with the winner assured of a seat in the statehouse.

There were few substantive differences between the two. Each had his own constituency, Tornillo had the teachers, and Becker, an aggressive tenants' rights attorney, had the renters.[89] In fact, the only "genuine issue" between the two was whether Becker lived in the 103rd. Becker and his wife had an apartment elsewhere, but for the race they moved into the district with his wife's grandparents, and he assured voters that he would soon find his own residence there.[90] Of course, where Becker lived and would live was not the issue; Tornillo was. The *Herald* made Tornillo the issue in a now-famous pair of editorials.

Tornillo had attacked Becker for failure to make a timely filing of campaign contributors as required by Florida law. The *Herald*

---

[84]Miami Herald, July 12, 1972.

[85]Tornillo Interview.

[86]Miami Herald, September 10, 1972.

[87]Shoemaker Interview.

[88]Miami Herald, September 13, 1972.

[89]Miami Herald, September 29, 1972; Tornillo Interview.

[90]Miami Herald, September 23, 1972.

did not, however, report this in a news story. Instead, on September 20 the *Herald* editorialized under the title "The State's Laws and Pat Tornillo." The editorial was fairly short and offered what was, for the *Herald*, a simple truism that a man who had led an "illegal" strike "against the public interest" was hardly in a position to refer, as Tornillo had, to an opponent as lacking "the knowledge to be a legislator." The editorial ended by stating: "We cannot say it would be illegal but certainly it would be inexcusable of the voters if they sent Pat Tornillo to Tallahassee."[91]

Tornillo was outraged. On reading the editorial he called Elizabeth duFresne, the partner of his then-vacationing lawyer, Tobias Simon, at home. She recalls Tornillo being so mad that she had to hold the phone at arms' length to protect her ear. As soon as duFresne reached her office, Tornillo was on the phone again blasting the *Herald*. She then began to research. Turning to Florida's libel statutes, she found a cross-reference to "right of reply." In less than an hour she turned up the long-neglected provision of the 1913 Trammell Corrupt Practices Act.[92]

Tornillo did nothing about the *Herald* editorial for a week. Why did he wait? He has no recollection. Dan Paul, the *Herald*'s lawyer, thought that Tornillo and Simon did not expect the *Herald* to publish the reply and that the delay was to get the best timing for publicity from the lawsuit they were sure to file to assist Tornillo's campaign

---

[91]Miami Herald, September 20, 1972 reprinted 418 U.S. at 243 n.1:

The State's Laws and Pat Tornillo

LOOK who's upholding the law!

Pat Tornillo, boss of the Classroom Teachers Association and candidate for the State Legislature in the Oct. 3 runoff election, has denounced his opponent as lacking "the knowledge to be a legislator, as evidenced by his failure to file a list of contributions to and expenditures of his campaign as required by law."

Czar Tornillo calls "violation of this law inexcusable."

This is the same Pat Tornillo who led the CTA strike from February 19 to March 11, 1968, against the school children and taxpayers of Dade County. Call it whatever you will, it was an illegal act against the public interest and clearly prohibited by the statutes.

We cannot say it would be illegal but certainly it would be inexcusable of the voters if they sent Pat Tornillo to Tallahassee to occupy the seat for District 103 in the House of Representatives.

[92]duFresne Interview, March 24, 1986.

(which Paul felt was going nowhere). Paul, however, was unaware that Simon had not been in town. It is possible that the delay stemmed from the decision to wait for Simon to return and offer his evaluation of the right-of-reply law.[93]

On Thursday, September 28, Tornillo called Fred Sherman, the *Herald*'s editorial writer, and said that he and Simon would be coming over just before noon and Shoemaker should also be present to meet with them. Shoemaker, however, had other appointments, and it was Sherman who met with Tornillo and Simon. Simon informed Sherman of the right-of-reply law, Tornillo gave him a typed response in the same number of words as the editorial, and they demanded that the *Herald* run it. They pointed out that the right-of-reply law carried criminal penalties.[94]

After Tornillo and Simon left, Paul was consulted, and there were internal discussions between Sherman and Shoemaker. All came out the same way. Paul told Shoemaker the law was unconstitutional, and Shoemaker likened the situation to having a gun pointed at his head. The *Herald* concluded not to run the reply. The discussions also foreclosed the possibility of running the reply as a letter to the editor.[95]

At the time of the meeting between Tornillo and Sherman, the *Herald*'s second editorial on Tornillo was already written. It ran the next day. Entitled "See Pat Run" it begins with a large picture of an empty classroom with chairs neatly stacked on top of desks. The editorial begins, "From the people who brought you this—the teacher strike of '68—come now instructions on how to vote for responsible government" and continues blasting Tornillo and the CTA on issue after issue.[96] No one could miss the point.

---

[93]Paul interview. duFresne agrees. duFresne to author, June 18, 1987.

[94]Jim Dance (Associate Editor Miami Herald) to Gilbert Cranberg (Editorial Writer Des Moines Register) Jan 17, 1974 at 1.

[95]Dance to Cranberg at 2.

[96]Miami Herald, September 29, 1972, reprinted without picture 418 U.S. at 243–44 n.1:

FROM the people who brought you this—the teacher strike of '68—come now instructions on how to vote for responsible government, i.e., against Crutcher Harrison and Ethel Beckham, for Pat Tornillo. The tracts and blurbs and bumper stickers pile up daily in teachers' school mailboxes amidst continuing pouts that the School Board should be delivering all this at your expense. The screeds say the strike is not an issue. We say maybe it wouldn't be were it not a part of a continuation of disregard of any and all laws the CTA might find aggravating. Whether in defiance of zoning laws at CTA Towers, contracts and laws during

With the election just four days away, the right-of-reply statute on the books, and the *Herald* refusing to comply, the only hope was a quick judicial order. Tornillo wrote and delivered a response to the second editorial, knowing that only a judge could get it in the *Herald*. Simon and duFresne, meanwhile, prepared for just that: papers for an immediate hearing on Monday morning to consider a request for injunctive relief.[97]

They got the hearing but not the injunction.[98] Because the constitutionality of a state statute would be at issue in the hearing, the trial judge, Francis Christie, informed the Florida Attorney General, Robert Shevin.[99] Seven months earlier, in the first reported case involving the right-of-reply statute, a Daytona trial judge had held the statute unconstitutional,[100] and Shevin, believing the decision correct, elected not to appeal. He adhered to that position, and Judge Christie adopted it also. Paul won without even having to answer Tornillo's complaint.[101]

A day later, Tornillo lost in the more significant forum 21,135 to 13,444.[102] He believed the *Herald* had "done him in."[103] Yet several factors point to the contrary. The first is that, despite an increase in voter turnout, Tornillo was barely able to add to his primary total. Almost all of Duval's votes went to Becker. Second, Tornillo's assessment of the *Herald*'s influence seems dubious. A percentage

---

the strike, or more recently state prohibitions against soliciting campaign funds amongst teachers, CTA says fie and try and sue us—what's good for CTA is good for CTA and that is natural law. Tornillo's law, maybe. For years now he has been kicking the public shin to call attention to his shakedown statesmanship. He and whichever acerbic prexy is in alleged office have always felt their private ventures so chock-full of public weal that we should leap at the chance to nab the tab, be it half the Glorious Leader's salary or the dues checkoff or anything else except perhaps mileage on the staff hydrofoil. Give him public office, says Pat, and he will no doubt live by the Golden Rule. Our translation reads that as more gold and more rule.

[97]duFresne Interview.

[98]38 Fla. Supp. 80, 81 (Cir. Ct. Dade County 1972). Chief Justice Burger's opinion is ambiguous about whether the suit was about one or both editorials. Schmidt states that Tornillo litigated to get his second reply published. Freedom of the Press 224. He is mistaken. The injunctive relief sought was a requirement to publish both replies.

[99]*Ibid.*

[100]State v. News-Journal Corp., 36 Fla. Supp. 164 (Cir. Ct. Volusia County 1972).

[101]Simon to Barron, August 17, 1973.

[102]Miami Herald, October 4, 1972.

[103]Tornillo Interview.

split of fifty-seven to forty-three hardly seems close enough to have been influenced by a pair of editorials, no matter how compelling. This is especially the case where a person, like Tornillo, has been so much a part of the local news for years that his positions, even if distorted, must be known to those willing to take the trouble to vote. Furthermore, the evening *Miami News*, albeit with a circulation only one-fifth of the *Herald*,[104] endorsed Tornillo.[105]

Nevertheless, whatever the real facts, Tornillo believed the *Herald* was to blame, and at a minimum he was correct in his conclusion that the paper had treated him very unfairly. The paper wrote a self-satisfied editorial about the election results, specifically jabbing Tornillo's post-mortem—"I think people believe what they read in the newspaper." "We appreciate the endorsement, Mr. Tornillo, and are pleased that now we have found an opportunity to compliment your judgment."[106] Tornillo again wrote a reply. This time, the election and the right-of-reply law behind, the *Herald* printed it in full.[107]

The election may have been over, but the hard feelings were not. An important principle—power in the democratic process—was at stake; at least Tornillo so believed. The *Herald*, too, thought an important principle—the freedom of the press from governmental coercion—was involved. Neither party liked the other, and there was still the lawsuit. Because only principle was at stake, the suit could not be settled.[108] It would go on until a winner emerged.

V. THE FLORIDA LITIGATION

Three weeks after the election, Judge Christie held a hearing and reaffirmed his earlier conclusions.[109] Tornillo had now lost the emergency hearing, the election, and the final judgment. But he had also decided to appeal, and the hurried posture of the case

---

[104]The Herald's circulation was 354,408, while the News was only 78,119. Editor and Publisher Yearbook 61, 62 (1973).

[105]The Miami News, September 11, 1972 at 30A; October 2, 1972 at 30A.

[106]Miami Herald, October 5, 1972.

[107]Miami Herald, October 7, 1972. Tornillo signed the letter: "Pat 'Boss' Tornillo."

[108]In addition to injunctive relief, Tornillo requested a declaratory judgment and punitive damages. Although no court mentioned mootness, the latter request solved the problem.

[109]38 Fla. Supp. 80 (Cir. Ct. Dade County 1972).

meant that it would involve the simple legal issue of whether a legislature could authorize a right of reply for a candidate for public office who had been attacked by a paper.

If the Attorney General would not defend the statute, Simon was able to find even better support in Jerome Barron, who had left the George Washington Law Center for what turned out to be a brief tenure as dean of the Syracuse Law School. Barron thus joined, and presented to the United States Supreme Court the major test of the First Amendment theory that he had been elaborating for the prior half-dozen years.[110]

Barron's *Harvard Law Review* article had argued, contrary to the prevailing wisdom, that *New York Times v. Sullivan*[111] had not been a landmark for freedom of expression but was rather a missed opportunity. It had simply perpetuated the romantic myth of a smoothly functioning, self-correcting marketplace of ideas. Instead, Barron argued that the concentration of ownership, canned editorials, and syndicated columnists had both diminished the "robust" debate called for by Justice Brennan's majority opinion[112] and effectively excluded most members of the public from participation in the debate.

Barron's thesis was a radical attack on both the Supreme Court's jurisprudence and the best of the academic writing on freedom of expression. From the end of the 1940s until 1961, loyalty-security problems dominated the Court's First Amendment docket. Even before they eased, obscenity and civil rights demonstrations moved in. Academic writing, beginning with the Meiklejohn-Chafee[113] debate of the late 1940s, argued a variety of theories, but all the leading authors concurred that if only the government would cease interference in the marketplace of ideas, the system of freedom of expression would be a lot better. This reached its fulfillment with Harry Kalven's majestic *The New York Times Case: A Note on "The Central*

---

[110]Barron, Freedom of the Press for Whom? (1973); Access to the Press—A New First Amendment Right, 80 Harv. L. Rev. 1641 (1967); An Emerging First Amendment Right of Access to the Media? 37 Geo. Wash. L. Rev. 487 (1969); Access—The Only Choice for the Media? 48 Tex. L. Rev. 766 (1970).

[111]376 U.S. 254 (1964).

[112]*Id.* at 270.

[113]Meiklejohn, Freedom of Speech and Its Relationship to Self-Government (1948); Chafee, Book Review, 62 Harv. L. Rev. 891 (1949).

Meaning of the First Amendment,"[114] merging the theories of Court and academy into a compelling thesis of an uninhibited marketplace. Then comes Barron to say everyone got it wrong and the refined doctrine should be junked for an active role of the government to remedy the defects of a concentrated market.

Barron had not been a part of the earlier writing. His specialty was broadcasting, and his scholarship vigorously supported regulation.[115] Furthermore, as a citizen he was concerned with the one-sided pro-war position of the media.[116] For Barron the issue was the quality of debate in the marketplace. Citizens could not hope to own presses and were excluded from the pages of papers. Yet *New York Times* took a powerful institution and gave it yet another right. As Mark Tushnet would later (and perhaps excessively) put it, "[T]he First Amendment, usually thought of as a vehicle by which otherwise powerless people can gain power, became another one of the assets held by the powerful."[117] Barron believed that the opportunity in *New York Times* had been to advance debate by fashioning a right to reply. That is, even without a legislative finding that such a right was desirable, Barron would have had the Court create one. How much more defensible, then, was a legislatively enacted statute.

Indeed, the next major case after *New York Times* did involve a statute, or at least an administrative agency's construction of a legislative mandate. *Red Lion v. Federal Communications Commission*,[118] sustaining the FCC's fairness doctrine against a First Amendment challenge, was decided two years after Barron's article. The Court's constitutional conclusion was that because the fairness doctrine provided responses to underbalanced programming it enhanced rather than abridged freedom of expression. For Barron, *Red Lion*, with its emphasis on a positive rather than a negative approach to the First Amendment, was the central case. Furthermore, *Red Lion*

---

[114]1964 Supreme Court Review 191.

[115]In Defense of Fairness: A First Amendment Rationale for Broadcasting's "Fairness" Doctrine, 37 U. Colo. L. Rev. 31 (1964); The Federal Communications Commission's Fairness Doctrine, 30 Geo. Wash. L. Rev. 1 (1961).

[116]Barron Interview, Jan. 6, 1986.

[117]Tushnet, Corporations and Free Speech, in Kairys, ed., The Politics of Law 253, 256–57 (1982).

[118]395 U.S. 367 (1969).

was an important first step. If a requirement for access, such as the fairness doctrine, was constitutionally permissible, might it not even be constitutionally required?

That argument would be made in the future. Tornillo's case in the present was as good as the current state of American law would provide. Florida's right-of-reply law might be seen as more limited than the fairness doctrine since the right of reply looked analogous to the FCC's more limited personal attack rules.[119] Thus, if Tornillo could prevail, then Barron would have achieved a necessary first step in moving his compulsory access idea from the pages of law reviews and the lacunae of broadcast regulation into the fabric of freedom of the press.

The Florida Supreme Court would not have been the first—or even close to the first—choice of venue for the *Herald* if it could have had its way. There was bad blood between the two institutions, and a major scandal was about to break. Three of the justices would be confronted with possible impeachment; a fourth was being asked to justify the court's unusual intervention in a parole board matter on behalf of a robber with good connections to the crime underworld; and a fifth was having a bout with the bottle. The *Herald*, as messengers are wont to learn, was seen as part of the problem. A written and initialed notation on a court document was discovered that "indicated a strong personal bias" against the *Herald*.[120] The *Herald* could be forgiven for not believing the denial that followed.

But the *Herald* got no choice of forum; it was off to the Florida Supreme Court. When the case was decided, Barron and Simon prevailed.[121] The decision tracked the arguments of Barron and other contributors to the access literature and added a touch of the press's own arguments just a year earlier in the losing effort to secure a constitutionally protected reporter's privilege.[122] Although the opinion did not cite the secondary literature, it fairly reflected it.

---

[119]Whether Florida's right of reply was in fact more limited than the fairness doctrine depended on future constructions. If construed to cover only editorials attacking candidates, then it would be more limited.

[120]Fisher, "And Who Will Take Care of the Damrons?" in The Trial of the First Amendment 16 (1975).

[121]287 So.2d 78 (1973).

[122]Branzburg v. Hayes, 408 U.S. 668 (1972).

The opinion coalesced around two basic ideas. First, information is necessary in a democracy. As Madison argued, "A popular government without popular information or the means of acquiring it is but a prologue to a farce or tragedy; or perhaps both."[123] The public's need for information is greatest during an election and the situation where a newspaper attacks a candidate not only hurts the candidate, it hurts the electorate by denying it both sides of the controversy. After all, the First Amendment's guarantee of a free press is "not for the benefit of the press so much as for the benefit of us all."[124]

Second, drawing heavily on, but not citing, the access literature, the court painted a picture of media concentration:[125]

> The right of the public to know all sides of a controversy and from such information to be able to make an enlightened choice is being jeopardized by the growing concentration of the ownership of the mass media into fewer and fewer hands, resulting ultimately in a form of private censorship. Through consolidation, syndication, acquisition of radio and television stations and the demise of vast numbers of newspapers, competition is rapidly vanishing and news corporations are acquiring monopolistic influence over huge areas of the country.

"Freedom of expression was retained by the people through the First Amendment for all the people and not merely for a select few."[126] When newspapers may attack candidates with impunity, "the public interest in free expression suffers."[127] The right-of-reply statute is an appropriate market corrective and is "consistent with the First Amendment."[128]

The *Herald* petitioned for a rehearing. Simon, confident of maintaining the victory, did not even respond. He was rewarded again when the court denied the petition "in an unusual way" by writing an opinion affirming the prior decision.[129] The concluding sentence in the opinion denying the petition hit hard: "In conclusion, it must be remembered that the First Amendment Freedom of the Press is

---

[123]287 So.2d at 80.

[124]*Id.* at 81.

[125]*Id.* at 82–83.

[126]*Id.* at 83.

[127]*Id.* at 84.

[128]*Ibid.*

[129]Simon to Louis Trager, March 25, 1974.

for the benefit of all the people and not just those who have invested money in the publishing business."[130]

Tornillo and Simon had picked up one ally when Barron joined the legal team. What they did not know was that they had picked up a second, J. S. Rawls, an intermediate appellate judge sitting by designation (and therefore untainted) in the absence of one of the seven members of the Supreme Court. Rawls was still "smarting"[131] from a reversal by the United States Supreme Court in his first major press case, *Ocala Star-Banner v. Damron*,[132] decided four years earlier.

Leonard Damron was the mayor of little Crystal City (population 1,423) and running for county tax assessor. Two weeks prior to the election his brother, James, was indicted for perjury by a federal grand jury. A rewriteman at the *Star-Banner* assumed the story was about Leonard and accordingly changed James's name. The story of the perjury indictment ran under a three-column headline on page one. Despite two subsequent corrections by the *Star-Banner*, Damron was defeated in his election bid. Justice Rawls served on a panel that unanimously affirmed a jury award of $22,000 against the paper after the trial judge directed a verdict on the issue of liability.[133]

Rawls's panel concluded that *New York Times v. Sullivan* was limited to falsehoods about public officials relating to official conduct. Since the perjury had nothing to do with Damron's official conduct, *New York Times* was inapplicable. After the Florida Supreme Court refused to hear the case, the paper successfully sought certiorari at the Supreme Court which unanimously—and very succinctly— reversed.[134]

Rawls saw *Tornillo* as another facet of *Damron*. When Paul was making his opening remarks, Rawls interrupted with the question: "Mr. Paul, what is the *Herald* doing about the Damrons of this world?"[135]

---

[130]287 So.2d at 91.

[131]Fisher, "And Who Will Take Care of the Damrons?" at 18.

[132]221 So.2d 459 (1st Dist. Fla. 1969).

[133]Fisher, "And Who Will Take Care of the Damrons?" at 18.

[134]401 U.S. 295 (1971). Fewer than two of the opinion's six pages state the rationale for reversal.

[135]Fisher, "And Who Will Take Care of the Damrons?" at 17.

According to Dean Roy Fisher's research, which included interviews with all of the members of the Florida Supreme Court, "[i]n the opinion of some persons most familiar" with the case, "including" Simon, "Justice Rawls swung the court to his view."[136] Paul, too, believes it was not the bad blood between the *Herald* and the court that cost him the case. Despite his client, he believed he would prevail in Florida. But judges are politicians, and Paul believes they reacted to a right of reply as politicians.[137] Maybe the United States Supreme Court would not allow damages for negligent falsehood, but a right of reply might well do service for a politician attacked during a reelection campaign.

VI. THE SUPREME COURT

Now it was the *Herald*'s turn. The *Herald* had new allies: virtually the entire media establishment. They decided to battle on two fronts, the Supreme Court and the media. If the nine to zero trouncing Tornillo, Barron, and Simon got in the Supreme Court seems one-sided, the media trouncing they received while the case was pending is in the same league.

The Florida Supreme Court decision shocked the press. Never reticent about using their own pages to assert their own interests, newspaper after newspaper editorialized about the threat to press freedom in the Florida decision. The *Herald* then printed these as guest editorials on its own pages. Simon, attempting to present the other side, wrote a letter to the editor explaining the decision, but it was not printed. Friends at the *Herald* told him that a decision had been made "upstairs" to print nothing he wrote.[138] (Once during the pendency of the case at the Supreme Court, the *Herald* ran an op-ed piece by Tornillo at the same time as it ran a piece by a Deputy Attorney General of Florida on the unconstitutionality of the right of reply.[139])

Simon then had Barron write a letter which was sent to one hundred major newspapers.[140] About six weeks later Simon sent a

---

[136]*Id.* at 15, 17.

[137]Paul interview.

[138]Simon to Cranberg, Jan. 8, 1974 at 2.

[139]Dance to Cranberg, Jan. 17, 1974 at 3.

[140]Undated, but sent approximately August 1, 1973 according to the undated letter in note 141 *infra.*

follow-up letter asking whether Barron's piece had been run.[141] Naturally not everyone replied, but Simon knew of only one newspaper that ran the Barron letter.[142] With that paper could be included *The South Dade News-Leader* of Homestead, which stood alone in editorializing in favor of the Florida Supreme Court.[143]

When the editorial writer of *The Des Moines Register* wrote Simon asking about the case, Simon responded with passion about his inability to present his side to the public. After noting he had been a cooperating lawyer with the ACLU since its Florida chapter opened, he hit on the refusal of newspapers to recognize two sides of the issue:[144]

> There seems to be something terribly wrong with all of this if "freedom of the press" means that our side will never even be published because it is critical of a position near and dear to the hearts of newspaper publishers. . . . In other words, if I had some mental reservations about the necessity for a right to reply, the treatment I have been accorded during the past twelve months has completely erased all doubts from my mind.

At least the Supreme Court would hear Simon's side. Winning in the media may well be satisfying, but winning in court is preferable.

Paul immediately filed an appeal to the Supreme Court and had an easy time making out a substantial federal question. A possible sticking point, unmentioned in the Jurisdictional Statement, was whether the judgment of the Florida Supreme Court was final for purposes of Supreme Court review under §1257.[145] All the Florida Supreme Court had done was overturn a trial court decision that the statute could have no constitutional applications. When the case went back to trial it would be open to argument that an editorial was not a "column" within the meaning of the statute and the *Herald* might also contend, although on the facts the argument is unpersuasive, that Tornillo's replies were not responsive to the editorials in question. If the *Herald* prevailed on either of these issues, the Court would lack jurisdiction; accordingly, the interim judgment would not be "final" under the prevailing interpretations of §1257.

---

[141]Undated, but the dates on responses from newspapers lead me to estimate six weeks.

[142]Simon to Cranberg, Jan. 8, 1974 at 1.

[143]Editorial July 25, 1973; Simon to Paul Brookshire (Editor The South Dade News-Leader), August 9, 1973.

[144]Simon to Cranberg, Jan. 8, 1974 at 3.

[145]28 U.S.C. §1257 (Supp. 1986).

In responding to the *Herald's* Jurisdictional Statement, Barron took this position, and the Court postponed the issue of its jurisdiction until briefing and argument on the merits.

The *Herald's* job of briefing the merits was the easier of the two, for its argument was clear, and there were no serious tactical choices to be made. Quite simply the statute was an intrusion on newspaper autonomy. It is censorship to forbid a newspaper to publish something, and it is no less censorship to order a newspaper to publish something.

Beyond the basic censorship argument, the *Herald*, and the numerous *amici* that flocked to file, all raised the specter of broadcast regulation and their concern that an affirmance would signal the beginnings of experiments in regulating the contents of newspapers. No matter how constitutional the fairness doctrine seemed in *Red Lion*, the briefs all were certain that such a regime was unthinkable and unconstitutional for newspapers. Although *Red Lion* had specifically rejected finding a chilling effect from the fairness doctrine, the newspaper position was that the fairness doctrine did in fact chill and thus would result in less rather than greater debate. Finally, because the access argument relies on market failure, the *Herald* stated that if a problem of market domination really existed, then the antitrust laws were the appropriate remedy.

Barron was faced with two tactical choices: the final judgment issue, and how broadly to state the case on the merits. He switched on the final judgment issue, believing he had as good a case as he was likely to get and that the Court was unlikely to be bothered by the issue anyway. His more interesting choice was to leave his creative work in the law reviews, by taking a narrow tack, attempting to sustain the opinion below largely by a refutation of the *Herald's* arguments. The only censorship involved, he argued, was that of the *Herald* in refusing to print Tornillo's replies as state law required. In context the right of reply would enhance rather than abridge speech both because it added voices and because the *Herald* dominates its market. Barron also argued that the loosening of the bounds of libel law by *New York Times* showed the wisdom of adding to that robust debate the additional voices of those that are on the receiving end of a paper's attacks. Justice Brennan's plurality opinion in *Rosenbloom*[146] had made just such a point, and Barron em-

---

[146]Rosenbloom v. Metromedia, 403 U.S. 29 (1971).

braced it wholeheartedly.[147] All of this was supported by a compelling state interest in free and fair elections.

Barron's argument was part defense, part offense. The few available facts allowed a strong showing for the *Herald*'s market domination. But here, as distinguished from his law review writings,
Barron wanted the fairness doctrine, with whatever scarce value it
carried, taken out of consideration. To make this essential point,
Barron used the writing of Thomas Emerson, who, in *The System
of Freedom of Expression*, had supported a limited right of reply for
newspapers.[148] Invoking Emerson carried the implicit argument that
a limited right to reply had to be constitutional since Emerson would
never support even a marginal restriction on First Amendment
rights. This also added needed credibility to the argument that
broadcast regulation and the fairness doctrine had nothing to do
with the case.

Setting up his market domination argument, Barron noted Tornillo's status:[149]

> Absent the Florida right of reply statute, Tornillo would be
> effectively muzzled in Dade County, Florida. The facts of this
> case illustrate the loneliness of someone in a position like Tor-
> nillo's. When Tornillo sought to enforce his right of reply rem-
> edy in court, the Attorney General of the state of Florida an-
> nounced his intention not to defend the statute. On appeal to
> the Supreme Court of Florida, the local ACLU chapter allied
> itself with the Herald. In this court, the amici on behalf of the
> Herald are almost impossible to count. Newspaper and broad-
> caster trade associations, newspaper chains, and other mass me-
> dia ownership groups have all joined to protest Tornillo's at-
> tempt to enforce the Florida right of reply statute.

Finally, in what may have been Barron's strongest argument, he
noted that the *Herald* was offering a perfect "Catch 22" with its
invocation of the antitrust laws. In 1970 Congress had passed the
Newspaper Preservation Act,[150] which created potential antitrust
exemptions for local newspapers which needed to operate jointly
to continue in existence. The *Miami Herald* and the weaker *Miami*

---

[147]Brief of Appellee at 31–40.
[148]Emerson, The System of Freedom of Expression 671 (1970).
[149]Appellee's Brief at 29–30.
[150]15 U.S.C. §1801.

News had formed such an agreement even prior to the Act. "Thus, appellant tells us soothingly that right of reply legislation is unnecessary to deal with problems of concentration of ownership in the media since that is the task of the antitrust laws. The only difficulty with this proffered solace is that appellant discreetly fails to mention that it has secured immunity from the antitrust laws."[151]

But these were debating points useful only if the Court were undecided. Oral argument showed it was not. Barron was buffetted by hostile questions from both the right and left. Justice Rehnquist wanted to know whether Barron "was suggesting that the First Amendment intended that one man could commandeer another man's printing press for his own use."[152] Justice Marshall, at the end of a couple of questions to Barron, announced: "So, anyone could silence the press by simply becoming a candidate!"[153] Although Barron retained a small hope of garnering five votes,[154] it was just that, a hope. The opinion, handed down three months later, was unanimous.

Chief Justice Burger's opinion for the Court is but sixteen pages divided into two brief sections and two longer sections. The two brief sections simply describe the statute and state the facts and dispose of the jurisdictional issue surrounding the question of whether there was a final judgment.

Since no brief contained more than two pages of facts, the Court's treatment would necessarily be perfunctory. The jurisdictional point might have proven more interesting since, in Benno Schmidt's phrase, the case was "in a state of semi-ripeness."[155] But, as I noted above, Barron had abandoned this issue, and there is little reason to believe arguing the point would have mattered. The Court needed less than a page to agree that the judgment was final enough for §1257.[156] Although the Court did not elaborate, its citations indicated it thought any further proceedings at the trial level would be simple formalities leaving the underlying result unchanged. On the facts of the case that conclusion was clearly correct.

---

[151]Appellee's Brief at 7.

[152]Fisher, "And Who Will Take Care of the Damrons?" at 13.

[153]*Ibid.*

[154]*Ibid.*

[155]Schmidt, Freedom of the Press at 225.

[156]418 U.S. at 246–47.

With the preliminaries out of the way, the Court turned to the First Amendment issue. But it did so in an interesting way. In the longest section of the opinion, the Court presented the argument for access in such a manner that, were it not for the Court's use of phrases like "access advocates,"[157] a person reading it and stopping there would assume that Barron, Simon, and Tornillo had won.

The forceful case presented reflected almost perfectly the arguments developed in the legal literature commencing with Barron's initial article.[158] At the time of ratification of the Bill of Rights there was a broadly representative, albeit highly partisan, press. "A true marketplace of ideas existed in which there was relatively easy access to the channels of communication."[159] But in the past half century vast changes had occurred. Newspapers became big business. Newspaper chains swallowed formerly independent papers, and economics caused the competing daily almost to vanish and prohibited the creation of new papers.

If these changes resulted in concentration in fewer hands, other simultaneous changes were cutting further into diversity. The rise of syndicated commentary adds another homogenizing note. The combination of the processes results in the public having lost its "ability to respond or to contribute in a meaningful way to the debate on issues."[160] As Robert Hutchins wrote in 1947: "The right of free public expression has . . . lost its earlier reality."[161] Media concentration has created a situation fundamentally inconsistent with our "profound national commitment to the principle that debate on public issues should be uninhibited, robust, and wide-open."[162]

What is striking about the Court's recitation of the argument for access is not only its force, but the fact that it is not the narrower

---

[157]*Id.* at 248, 253.

[158]As the Court stated, 418 U.S. at 248 n.9, "a good overview of the position of access advocates" was presented in Lange, The Role of the Access Doctrine in the Regulation of the Mass Media, 52 N.C. L. Rev. 1 (1973) and this section of the opinion clearly relied on Lange's summation.

[159]418 U.S. at 248.

[160]*Id.* at 250.

[161]Report of the Task Force, in Twentieth Century Fund Task Force Report for a National News Council, A Free and Responsible Press 4 (1947), quoted at 418 U.S. at 250.

[162]New York Times v. Sullivan, 376 U.S. 254, 270 (1964), quoted at 418 U.S. at 252.

argument Barron made in his brief. The Court intended to deal
with access in one shot only. Thus the absence of facts about the
case was far from a hindrance; it was perfect. The argument for
access could be set out in the general form as it existed in the
literature and bluntly rejected once and for all. The Court's next
section did just that in a shade over four pages, relying on almost
no relevant authority.[163]

The Court stated two separate reasons why a right of access was
inconsistent with the First Amendment. First, it accepted the argument offered by the *Herald* and *amici* that, instead of promoting
controversy, the effect of an access statute would be to chill debate.[164] The Court immediately moved to its second reason in the
next paragraph (the opinion's last): "Even if a newspaper would
face no additional costs . . . and would not be forced to forgo
publication of news or opinion . . . the Florida statute fails to clear
the barriers of the First Amendment because of its intrusion into
the function of editors."[165] The choice of what is and is not printed
is exclusively within the control of the editors, and government
may not intrude.

Period. It was not explained; it was not wordy; and it was not
ambiguous. It is not surprising that such an opinion did not sit well
with academics. Yet there is much to be said for both the outcome
and even the opinion.

VII. A CHILL?

That "much to be said" does not, however, encompass the
two paragraphs devoted to the chilling effect. The first stated the
right of reply "exacts a penalty" in the form of costs imposed:
"printing and composing time and materials."[166] The second stated
that these penalties "might well" cause editors to "conclude the safe
course is to avoid controversy."[167] "Might well" immediately became

---

[163]Schmidt, Freedom of the Press at 229–31.

[164]418 U.S. at 257.

[165]*Id.* at 258.

[166]418 U.S. at 256.

[167]*Id.* at 257.

"would." "Therefore under operation of the Florida statute, political and editoral coverage would be blunted or reduced."[168] One wonders.

As the Court's contemporaneous jurisprudence shows, chilling effect arguments were not high on credibility.[169] They appear to have too much of Chicken Little warning about the sky. But, it is worth remembering, Chicken Little got it right once. The Court's terse conclusion that a right of reply chills is hardly convincing, but that ought not foreclose the possibility that a chilling effect exists.

Is there a chill? How much? Could it be minimized? And, finally, is whatever chill outweighed by the benefits the right of reply provides?

The quickest argument for the existence of a chill is the broadcast analogy. The *Herald* and its *amici* understood the potential presented by the broadcast analogy and argued that to sustain the law would be the entering wedge for broadcast-like regulation. The Court might have myopically concluded that there is no chilling effect in broadcasting, but the Court offered no evidence for that view, and the evidence to the contrary is overwhelming.[170] Barron knew that even the Court was unlikely to rely on its five-year old *Red Lion* conclusion, and thus he argued that broadcasting and the fairness doctrine were irrelevant.

For chilling effect purposes, broadcasting is anything but irrelevant unless there is some reason to believe that the cause of the chilling effect in broadcasting might not occur with regard to newspapers. Is there? Initially, many newspapers might well avoid a chill because newspapers have a history of being willing to stand up to government: serving what Vincent Blasi describes as the

---

[168]*Ibid.*

[169]Laird v. Tatum, 408 U.S. 1 (1972); Younger v. Harris, 401 U.S. 37 (1971).

[170]Powe, American Broadcasting and the First Amendment (1987); Rowan, Broadcast Fairness (1984); Simmons, The Fairness Doctrine and the Media (1978); Krattenmaker & Powe, The Fairness Doctrine Today, 1985 Duke L.J. 151, which partially concludes: "An assessment of the effects and costs of the Fairness Doctrine paints a gloomy portrait indeed. For control by market forces the doctrine substitutes governmental control over programming, largely to attain the end of avoiding the appearance of one-sided presentations. The principal effect of the regulation is to reduce stations' incentives to broadcast controversy over public issues. This effect, ironically and thankfully, is mitigated by the FCC's apparent inability, given its limited resources, to enforce the doctrine except randomly or against the most visible broadcasters." *Id.* at 165–66.

checking value.[171] But if access claims were made and sustained (by whatever mechanism) it would be otherworldly to assert or expect that newspapers would not at least think about the possibility and consequences of having to print a reply to any particular story they were contemplating running.

Thinking is the first step toward getting cooler. There can be no chilling effect without an actor's understanding how a given law might affect his speech activities. What happens after that thought will be the test of whether there is a chilling effect. If the stories are always run the way they would have been, then the pause to think does not represent a chill. If stories are watered down or killed, then there is a chill. Would that happen?

It should, although I do not know how often. For example, suppose a federal right of reply had been on the books in 1972. What would the *Washington Post*'s Watergate coverage have looked like between July and November? Even assuming the *Post* could not be deterred, there would have been some difference in the paper. On those days that the *Post* did not choose to run the White House disclaimer as a separate story, instead of Ron Ziegler's routine denial being placed in the fifth paragraph of the principal story, the denial itself would run as a (front page) story. Even if that would not deter the *Post*, it might well convince other newspapers that the effort was not worth it.

Still, the *Post*, like the *Herald*, is a major, profitable newspaper with a sizable institutional ego. Although its resources (including pages) are not infinite, they are substantial. It may be possible for a large, powerful metropolitan paper to ignore the effect of a right of reply and continue business as usual by simply acknowledging that op-ed page stories would from time to time appear on page one.

Smaller newspapers have less space, profits, and ego. And it has always been the case that the weaker are likely to cool down more quickly than the strong. While smaller papers may not be significant in the larger scheme of things, whatever freedom of the press means, it applies just as much to *The Citrus County Chronicle* as to the *Washington Post*. Furthermore, larger papers are likely to be in areas where there are abundant media outlets and greater opportunity

---

[171]Blasi, 1977 Am. B. Found. Res. J. 521.

for alternative views to be presented (heard is a bit speculative). Smaller papers quite naturally will serve areas with fewer alternative media outlets although possibly areas where word of mouth may still have some viability.

After the Florida Supreme Court's initial decision, a number of smaller newspapers sent *amicus* affidavit-briefs to the court relating how the law might affect them. Their concerns reflected the problems that exist for smaller newspapers. *The (Brooksville) Sun-Journal* asked, "who decides whether I leave out the Church column or Miss Perch's women's news."[172] *The (Anna Maria) Islander* wondered about vagueness in the context of politicians' well-known thinskin: "any story or editorial that doesn't make him appear to be in favor of God and motherhood is [likely] reason enough to demand rebuttal space."[173] Demand, yes; receive, no. A right of reply may well chill, but it should not force editors to seek parkas every time some politician is not portrayed as his mother would have him seen.

Kenneth Karst, although assuming a chill and thus supporting *Tornillo*'s result, wondered if access statutes might minimize governmental supervision in order to limit any chill. If so, they should be viewed "sympathetically" in their attempts "to overcome the impact of private censorship."[174] Although Karst did not deal with how this would work, there would appear to be two ways to try to minimize any chill: first, have as limited and mechanical a rule as possible; second, have the best decision maker possible.

On *Tornillo*'s facts, the Florida right of reply could have been turned into a fairly mechanical statute. With some judicial surgery by Florida judges, the statute might have been held to apply solely to editorials (or material on the editorial page) urging a vote against a candidate. With such a narrowing, issues of vagueness ought to be eliminated, thereby reducing the potential of a chill to the question of whether editorializing against a candidate would be omitted because the attacked candidate would then get to present her side.

If my hypothetical narrowing were expanded to include endorsements, then any chill would be greater in two respects. It would automatically double the coverage of the statute in a typical two-

---

[172]Brief of The Citrus County Chronicle as Amicus Curiae at 2.

[173]Brief of The Islander as Amicus Curiae at 2.

[174]Karst, Equality as a Central Principle in the First Amendment, 43 U. Chi. L. Rev. 20, 51 (1975).

party race. But, it might have the consequence—like §315 of the Communications Act—in a multicandidate race of reducing endorsements because of the number of mandated replies.[175]

A very narrow statute, such as my first suggested surgery, would be close to self-executing, but the more coverage, the more important the identity of the decision maker. We know it is not going to be Bill Moyers or George Will, but knowing who it is not does not tell you who it is. I doubt if someone is going to jump around a Georgetown cocktail party pointing with pride to a recent appointment as right-of-reply czar. In a world where an appointment to the FCC is a fairly low-level political payoff (useful largely for the private sector career it will create subsequent to leaving), how much lower would be a person who makes right-of-reply determinations, especially on the state (or local) level? Yet this person would be on the front line of what are likely to be frequent First Amendment determinations. The FCC experience demonstrates that the regulations to be applied will favor incumbents, and that even when this is not necessarily true, the commission will construe them to have such an effect.[176] It is inconceivable that a similar experience would not occur under a right-of-reply or an access scheme.

Maybe these problems of decision-maker biases could be minimized, as in *Tornillo*, by applying to a judge for the order. But even with a judge, I share the concern expressed by both Lee Bollinger[177] and Laurence Tribe[178] that there will always be a danger of manipulation by the decision-maker. Some judges will lack the necessary knowledge, others the independence. The only way to reduce this potential chill would be to reduce the scope of discretion.

There is one further aspect to the chilling effect argument: regardless of how the chill is measured, it might be outweighed by the good the right of reply accomplishes. This argument may or may not be affected by the statute's range of discretion. While a narrow statute may minimize the chill, it also may provide fewer benefits. Conversely, the broader the statute (and it would not be difficult to write one that would generate replies to Doonesbury

---

[175]Powe, American Broadcasting and the First Amendment at 155, 158.

[176]*Id*. at ch. 7–9.

[177]Bollinger, Freedom of the Press and Public Access, 75 Mich. L. Rev. 1, 31 (1976).

[178]Tribe, American Constitutional Law 697 (1978).

with frequency) the more the likely chill, but also the more information that might reach the public. To use broadcasting as an
example, even though the fairness doctrine necessarily chills, one
might (erroneously) argue that when controversial issues are discussed, the discussion is so good it outweighs the chill.

It is important to remember that even if a chill exists, a law will
be constitutional if the countervailing benefits are sufficient. Whatever one may think of the law of libel, it illustrates this point well.[179]
With two decades of *New York Times v. Sullivan* behind us, we can
see that the law of libel chills in at least two important ways. First,
jury awards can seem so astronomical that publications will balk at
a story rather than run it.[180] Second, publishers realize that juries
may determine that non-negligent error is negligence or negligence
is reckless disregard. While all of this can be, and to a fair extent
is, minimized by judicial policing, the relevant point is what the
press thinks and how it behaves; and the press, with reason, believes
it is exposed to real legal risks.[181]

Yet despite this chill, it is constitutional to impose significant
liability for libel. If the chill is insufficient there, it could easily be
argued that it is *a fortiori* insignificant with a right of reply because
the astronomical jury awards would not be in the picture.

This extended discussion reveals that the chilling effect argument
has several problems: how much of a chill, whether a narrow statute
might minimize the chill, whether the Florida statute was narrow
enough, and whether the chill was offset by sufficient benefits so
that the statute should have been sustained. These problems could
not be disposed of in two paragraphs as Chief Justice Burger tried
to do. Indeed, attempting to do so in two paragraphs may have
served to demonstrate to skeptics how weak the chilling effect argument really is.

I believe that even a narrow right of reply would cause some
chill to smaller papers, and as a statute became broader the chill
would begin to show in the larger papers. Nevertheless, it is hard
to win a speculative chilling effect argument. I say "cool" and am

---

[179]Smolla, Suing the Press (1986).

[180]*Id.* at ch. 1; Lewis, "Silence by Libel," New York Times, April 17, 1987 at 24; Kup-
ferberg, Libel Fever, 20 Colum. J. Rev. 36 (1981).

[181]Forer, A Chilling Effect (1987); Lewis, New York Times v. Sullivan Reconsidered, 83
Colum. L. Rev. 603 (1983); Massing, The Libel Chill: How Cold is it Out There? 24 Colum.
J. Rev. 31 (1985).

met with the response "warm." I can substantially bolster my argument by noting that Bollinger,[182] Karst,[183] and Tribe,[184] too, believe there is a chill. But a response of "warm enough" remains possible. A neutral person may be able to determine who has the better of the debate, but chilling effect arguments, because they require predictions about an unknown future, are much more likely to persuade the already committed than bring others into the fold. This being the case, it may be that asserting a chilling effect, and especially offering it as the primary reason, weakened rather than strengthened *Tornillo*.

VIII. A CORE ABSOLUTE

Chief Justice Burger's conclusion that the Constitution locates all authority of inclusion and exclusion with editors both recognized the necessity of choice in the composition of a newspaper and found that the First Amendment placed that choice with a paper's editors. Newspapers are not put together by natural selection, but by decisions on what to include, with how much space, and where the story should be placed.

The principal argument for a right of reply is that under a certain defined set of circumstances editorial discretion can be improved upon because a reply will enhance public debate by placing more information in the wider public domain. Yet this assertion is incorrect and misleading. A reply does not make more information available to the newspaper's readers; rather, it makes different information available. Consequently, the argument for a right of reply must be down-sized a bit. At its strongest, it would be that a right of reply provides a fairer, more complete picture of one significant issue, and that whatever is cut from the paper will be the most trivial of all possible alternative inclusions. This may turn out to be true, but it need not, nor in fact is it likely to be true.

If we are to speculate on what will be cut, it is most realistic to expect that a reply to an editorial will displace material that would otherwise appear on the editorial pages and therefore will not displace material in the newspaper's "lifestyle" section. Under the

---

[182]Bollinger, 75 Mich. L. Rev. at 29.

[183]Karst, 43 U. Chi. L. Rev. at 49, 51.

[184]Tribe, American Constitutional Law at 700.

Florida statute, and most likely proposals, a reply must be as prominent as the original story. To allow otherwise would risk trivialization by the newspaper burying the reply in the most inconspicuous place possible. Furthermore, since readers of newspapers are drawn to the paper for varieties of reasons, the mix already created by the paper is the one it has concluded best serves its readers. It is therefore unrealistic to conclude that political news will displace "soft" news.

Under these, the most likely, circumstances, a reply will add information about a subject already discussed, with the result that some other subject, otherwise fit for the editorial pages, will receive less attention or none at all. Thus a right of reply will necessarily displace choices that an editor would otherwise have made and is likely to do so dealing with other current affairs topics.

A legislature has concluded that we are better served by more information about a person already discussed in the news than knowing whatever information is displaced. We also know that the author of the reply will be of the same view. It is not clear, however, whether this is accurate or whether any readers of the newspaper will believe they are better served by this substitution. It does not seem unreasonable to assume that if a newspaper carries a certain amount of church news, and that news is cut to carry a reply, those who value church news will not believe they were well served. The same can be said for any given subject including anything otherwise fit for the editorial pages. What makes the legislative choice appear attractive is that it deals with the paramountcy of political debate and is coupled with the unexplored (and probably inaccurate) assumption that "soft" news is the likely target for deletion.

Of course a newspaper could print the information the reply displaces and not print something else, or it could just add pages to the paper and print everything.[185] But newspapers do not print "everything." Each day choices are made; vastly more is excluded than printed, and there is no a priori reason why the reply material

---

[185]Hynds, American Newspapers in the 1970s 17 (1975) states that advertising constitutes 40%–75% of a paper. I have never heard anyone previously place the figure below 60%. According to the standard media text, Emery & Emery, The Press and America 233 (4th ed. 1978), advertising space reached 50% by World War I. Regardless of the exact amount of advertising space, a newspaper cannot print everything. The amount of advertising sets a limit on the amount of news that will be printed.

is more important than information already deemed of insufficient importance to be included in a given day's paper.

Is editorial autonomy a principle, consistent with our traditions, that we find in the First Amendment? If we revert to the framing, then the answer is easy. Editorial autonomy was absolutely protected because the federal government "had no legitimate power to pass any law respecting the press."[186] Such were the assurances given at the Constitutional Convention and repeated by James Wilson at the Pennsylvania convention. In fact, there was no dispute between the Federalists and the Anti-Federalists that Congress wholly lacked power to pass laws respecting the press. The difference was the well-founded Anti-Federalist belief that Congress would usurp the power.

While we are not prone to find denials of legislative power as part of any continuing tradition, the blunt denial by all sides of any power to pass any law respecting the press, when coupled with immediate adoption of the First Amendment, is powerful support for the conclusion that laws singling out the press are forbidden. General laws treating the press like all other members of society may or may not raise constitutional problems depending on how they may impinge on freedom of the press, but press laws are invalid.[187]

This is bolstered by the one further aspect of freedom of the press that everyone agrees is part of the First Amendment tradition both past and present: no prior restraints. Government is forbidden to order nonpublication (except, now, in very compelling circumstances). The principle that holds that government cannot tell people what they may not say is broad enough to prevent government from telling people what they must say. Were it not, government would be able to indirectly prevent publication by excessive demands to publish information. The principle that covers these circumstances is editorial autonomy. Within its scope it is indivisible. Someone has the final say: either the editor, the would-be replier, or the government.

---

[186]Anderson, The Origins of the Press Clause, 30 UCLA L. Rev. 455, 522 (1983). The rest of this paragraph is taken from Anderson.

[187]This explains Arkansas Writers' Project v. Ragland, 107 S.Ct. 1722 (1987) and Minneapolis Star and Tribune Co. v. Minnesota Commissioner of Revenue, 460 U.S. 575 (1983) far better than the Court's opinions do.

Because editorial autonomy is indivisible, it must be absolute. It is either there or it is not. Schmidt found *Tornillo* "a stark and unexplained deviation" from the Court's avoidance of absolutism in First Amendment adjudication.[188] Floyd Abrams responded that *Tornillo* "is hardly absolutist; rather it is representative of the vast freedom afforded the press at the apex of its first amendment protection."[189] Abrams is right that *Tornillo* represents the First Amendment at its apex, but there is no need to shy away from recognition of absolutism. When decisions must be made there must be a decision-maker. Someone must say what is printed and what is not. The principle of editorial autonomy cannot be divided between editor and judge. In a disputed case someone must prevail, and if it is not the editor, then we are discussing a different principle.

For some, complete recognition of editorial autonomy will be seen as so important that its recognition smothers any seeming "injustices" in given cases. A right of reply can, however, be seen as a simple and appropriate statement of ethics. If you savage someone, you owe it to that person and your readers to present the other side. Thus while the principle of editorial autonomy has its claims, so, too, may other competing principles such as fairness. An access proponent could concede that autonomy is absolute within its proper sphere, but hold that that sphere ends where fairness issues begin.

The problem here, assuming, as I do, that text, purpose, history, and tradition are valid sources of constitutional interpretation, is figuring out how fairness became a First Amendment value. The First Amendment, after all, does not refer to press "responsibility" even in the limited sense of the "abuse" clause found in most state constitutions.[190] Nor can we look to the Bill of Rights generally or the press of the late eighteenth century or even to evolving traditions to import fairness into the First Amendment. Some parts of the Bill of Rights, such as the fair trial provisions, promote fairness; others, such as the right against self-incrimination, do not. The First Amendment, to the extent that the framers would have thought

---

[188]Schmidt, Freedom of the Press at 233.

[189]Abrams, In Defense of Tornillo, 86 Yale L. J. 361 (1976).

[190]The standard clause reads as follows: "No law shall be passed to curtail, or restrain the liberty of speech, or of the press, and any person may speak, write and publish his sentiments, on all subjects, being responsible for the abuse of that liberty." Ga. Const., art. 1 §1 para. 5. Forty-two states have similar provisions. Collins, Reliance on State Constitutions, in McGraw, Developments in State Constitutional Law 1, 42–43 n.134 (1985).

about it, is a provision that would not promote fairness. The framers knew a partisan and scurrilous press, not a fair one. While two hundred subsequent years may have toned the press down, even since the advent of so-called objective journalism, it is still debatable whether fairness has become even a journalistic norm.

Indeed, our traditions are clear. A fair press, as determined by a government mechanism, is not a free press. A free press may be fair; we hope it will not be irresponsible; but, as Blasi so powerfully demonstrates, for the press to serve as a check on the government it must be free to gather and report information about government and those who do or would govern. A government official deciding which stories necessitate replies is both historically and theoretically inconsistent with this.[191]

That fairness would not have a First Amendment pedigree is not surprising. It really would not be much of a Constitution if the restraints did not occasionally block what is thought good legislation. Indeed it would trivialize the idea of a Constitution if it only prohibited bad legislation. To be sure, one way around trivialization is to view the Constitution as holding that it not only prohibits all that is wrong, but that it mandates all that is good and just as well. For the past decade and a half a not insignificant amount of constitutional literature has advocated the idea of a perfect Constitution. But even here there are troubles with considering fairness a First Amendment principle. Beyond the chilling effect and the necessary infringement of autonomy, the idea of enforced fairness requires placing an amazing amount of faith in government decision-makers to implement fairness.

The vast academic literature on the First Amendment, working explicitly or implicitly with Thomas Emerson's "Dynamics of Limitation,"[192] is a powerful testament to the belief that the government

---

[191] With a caveat to be noted immediately, I disagree with the suggestion of Justices Brennan and Rehnquist, in their *Tornillo* concurring opinion, 418 U.S. at 258, that "retraction" statutes, requiring the printing of a jury finding that a newspaper story untruthfully libeled the plaintiff, would be constitutional. The caveat is simple. The law of libel as it has developed in the last fifteen years protects neither reputations nor the press. Since the Court is unlikely to discard its own creation even if that creation can easily be seen to have a genuine chill, a "retraction" solution that minimized the chill of damages would be preferable as less unconstitutional. An optional retraction statute, left to the discretion of editors, would not raise any of these problems.

[192] Emerson, Toward a General Theory of the First Amendment ch. 2 (1966).

is inherently incapable of unbiased enforcement of fairness.[193]
Thomas P. Scanlan has observed that "where political issues are
involved governments are notoriously partisan and unreliable."[194]
My own history of broadcast regulation offers example after example of actual political interference.[195] And Mark Yudof's work
persuasively argued that with all its resources and prestige, government has a powerful incentive to influence public debate in ways
that favor those currently holding power.[196] Given its absence of
any pedigree and the substantial and traditional First Amendment
concerns on the other side, the case for fairness as a First Amendment principle seems impossible to sustain.

IX. A DIFFERENT FUTURE

Suppose, however, that the allure of a better world proves
irresistible: a right of reply being so ethically compelling that, despite chilling effect and autonomy arguments, it is found consistent
with the Constitution. Suppose, therefore, that Pat Tornillo prevailed. What would have happened?

Whether it reflected political power of the press ready to prevent
any legislative ox-goring or simply a respect for the long tradition
of press automony, in 1974 Florida stood alone with a right-of-reply
statute on its books.[197] In some states the status quo would doubtless
continue based on either of the two suggested reasons, albeit with
a little more emphasis on the former. But could anyone believe that
the status quo would remain? Are legislators such a selfless breed
that a judicial validation of their right, in the name of all good First
Amendment values, to protect their interests in the public debate

---

[193]Only one article, Fiss, Why the State?, 100 Harv. L. Rev. 781 (1987), dissents. See
generally, Powe, Scholarship and Markets, 56 Geo. Wash. L. Rev. 172 (1987).

[194]Scanlan, Freedom of Expression and Categories of Expression, 40 U. Pitt. L. Rev. 519,
534 (1979).

[195]Powe, American Broadcasting and the First Amendment ch. 5–9.

[196]Yudof, When Government Speaks (1983).

[197]Mississippi and Nevada once had similar statutes. Miss. Code Ann. §3175 (1942); Nev.
Rev. Stat. 200.570 (1963). In Manasco v. Walley, 63 So.2d 91 (Miss. 1953) Mississippi's
statute was turned into right of reply for defamatory statements. Nevada repealed its right
of reply statute in 1969 and replaced it with a libel retraction statute. Chapter 310, Laws
of Nevada, Fifty-fifth Session (Act of April 14, 1969).

would not result in some states passing new laws? Certainly not the ones I look at.

In 1971 the House of Representatives passed a measure that would have granted candidates for federal office the right to purchase newspaper space at bargain basement rates.[198] This is about as minimally intrusive as a reply (or more accurately in this case, access) statute could get. The House bill thus brought newspapers and broadcasters under a new §312(a)(7) of the Communications Act. The Senate version took the standard view that broadcasting was entitled to less First Amendment protections than print and accordingly that candidate access could be constitutionally applied to broadcasters. In conference the Senate prevailed.[199] If *Tornillo* had gone the other way the House version would be a highly likely candidate for the United States Code Annotated.

More intrusive measures would also be constitutional if Tornillo had prevailed; they therefore too become possible. After argument at the Supreme Court both President Nixon and Senator McClellan warmly supported the idea of a federal reply law, with the former noting it would both "enhance" debate and encourage "good and decent people" to run for office without fear of scurrilous attacks.[200] In 1974—and indeed today—that type of support might well be sufficient to carry the day for the other side. Barron's retrospective address to the Association for Education, less than two months after *Tornillo*, has a perfect summation: "With such friends, the cause of right to reply had less to fear from its enemies."[201] That Nixon was the kiss of death in 1974—and Barron believes it was the most important factor in his defeat[202]—would not have foreclosed the possibility of a federal statute at a later date.

Even if no federal statute were forthcoming, what about the states? Probably there would be a variety of measures, with most

---

[198]117 Cong. Rec. 43163–64 (92nd Cong. 1st Sess. 1971).

[199]S. Conf. Rep. 92-580. The statute was sustained in CBS v. FCC (Carter-Mondale), 453 U.S. 367 (1981).

[200]New York Times, March 12, 1974 at 17; Washington Post, March 13, 1974 at 26 (editorial).

[201]Reflections on the Tornillo Case, printed in Barron, Public Rights and the Private Press 1, 2 (1981).

[202]Barron Interview.

tracking whatever the Supreme Court said was okay. But here and there the little laboratories of experimentation would go farther, providing an interesting array. I would assume that the farthest reaches of legislation would be a "Politicians' Day-in-the-Paper Act," tracking the concerns of the editor of *The Islander* mentioned earlier: anything not pleasing to the incumbent would merit a right of reply.

The legislative process would have broken a barrier. For good or ill, newspapers would be even more a part of the political process and would find it necessary to attempt to protect themselves against adverse legislation (rather than the current position of trying to push favorable legislation). And legislation that can affect the content of a newspaper would have a more routine quality about it. Tribe rightly warns that access regulation in the print media would be seen as a "profound break" with tradition, transforming "the boundaries of the legally thinkable and [creating] a corresponding increase in pressure to regulate still more deeply."[203]

Given its resources, the press may do all right in the legislative process, but since the legislation in question is likely to pit politicians' interests against those of the press, I would suspect that the press will do less well than if the legislators were neutral arbitrators between competing interests. But press resources do guarantee that as night the day, litigation will follow legislation.

Here we all know the outcome. After about a decade of decisions the Supreme Court will "finally" settle the area. Some wonderful four-part test will be announced to determine when a right of reply is appropriate.[204] A not implausible choice would be that access may be granted (1) if the person attacked does not have access to an alternative equivalent media outlet;[205] (2) if the other side of the story is not generally available to the reading public; (3) if the mechanism for determining when a reply shall be granted is plain, efficient, and speedy; and (4) the statute as applied in the case enhances rather than abridges the quality of debate.

---

[203]Tribe, American Constitutional Law at 700; see also Bollinger, 75 Mich. L. Rev. at 31.

[204]See generally, Nagel, The Formulaic Constitution, 84 Mich. L. Rev. 165 (1985).

[205]This prong is consistent with Blasi's belief that incumbents, but presumably not challengers, "typically have ample opportunities to disseminate their views." 1977 Am B. Found. Res. J. at 628.

I am less interested in the content of the rule[206] than in the fact that there is a rule. Not only will the legislatures of the nation have had practice passing legislation for newspapers, the judges, too, will have gained practice and, in the process, acquired confidence in the ascertainment of appropriate limits. The Supreme Court's "rule" will allow them to weigh the needs of the local marketplace of ideas and the merits of the newspaper's and would-be replier's claims. It would be a different world.

There is every reason to wonder about the effect of judicial decisions in the real world. But sometimes we know. In the forty years between June 1931 and June 1971 courts did not issue injunctions against the press.[207] There was agreement that the historical meaning of freedom of the press encompassed "no prior restraints." *Near v. Minnesota*[208] incorporated that historic tradition into First Amendment doctrine, with the most limited exceptions, the key one, which grew quainter and quainter with each passing year, being that publishing sailing dates for troop ships was a terrible no-no and could be enjoined.

Then the *New York Times* began publishing "The Pentagon Papers." At the Executive's request, Judge Murry Gurfein immediately issued an injunction; he then held a quick hearing and ruled

---

[206]While my colleagues understood that my four part test was facetious, several told me they thought it was sound. Therefore, let me briefly explain its flaws: (1) It is probably impossible to find an equivalent to a daily newspaper given their scarcity and probable market dominance. Thus the first part of the test is either likely to be always satisfied or provide an interesting discussion of how many radio stations equal a newspaper. (2) What does "reading public" mean? How is it different from the public? Does "generally available" have any difference in content than "alternative equivalent media outlet"? (3) Sounds nice, but still it is a mechanism that could be abused. (4) Is conclusory and assumes, as discussed, that presenting the reply side is superior to any story that would be omitted.

[207]The best evidence for this statement is the fact that Thomas Emerson says so. Emerson, Where We Stand: A Legal View, 10 Colum. J. Rev. 34, 35 (1971). No one would have been more likely to be aware of prior restraints against the press during the era than this perceptive observer. The Court certainly believed there had been no newspaper prior restraints since *Near*, a point driven home by the Solicitor General's argument that in FTC v. Texaco, 393 U.S. 223 (1968) the Court had sustained one in affirming an FTC order that arrangements between an oil company and a tire manufacturer constituted unfair trade practices. Brief of the United States at 10–11. Thus even assuming there may have been a few subterranean prior restraints escaping notice, no one in authority, including the Supreme Court, knew of them, and it was that perception that guided the argument and decision in the *Pentagon Papers Case*.

[208]283 U.S. 697 (1931).

he could not continue enjoining publication. The Second Circuit acted immediately and preserved the injunction. The Supreme Court refused to lift the injunction on a Friday, listened to oral argument on Saturday, and ruled for the *Times* (and *Washington Post*) on Wednesday. It reaffirmed that a prior restraint comes to the "Court bearing a heavy presumption against its constitutional validity."[209]

If the most massive security leak in American history—which the government asserted would cost lives and imperil negotiations for peace in Southeast Asia—could not be enjoined, *Near* was a secure barrier to prior restraints. Yet in the real world of judicial operations something quite different has happened. Prior restraints, for so long unheard of, are now relatively common.[210] I do not wish to say they are an everyday occurrence or even necessarily routine; what I mean is that we are all familiar with judges enjoining publication of an article (or broadcast story) for some period of time. The legal barrier against prior restraints is just as tough as ever on paper. The psychological barrier is gone.

Instead of stating that the First Amendment prohibits prior restraints, judges now go through a more complex, and some might argue sensitive, calculus attuned to the possibilities of action: true, there is a very high burden, but what harms will occur if there is no temporary (or permanent) injunction? Are these harms sufficient to overcome the presumption? How serious would a little delay, for proper consideration of the issue, really be?

I do not wish to argue the law of prior restraints.[211] My point is a different one. *The Pentagon Papers Case* broke a major barrier. In so doing it turned the virtually impossible into the legally permissible. The signs that once said "no, never," now read a cautious "well, hardly ever." This is not surprising. No area of law worth the costs of litigation is static. When an area produces litigation it is moving. This is why it is so essential in civil liberties litigation to win the first case testing an area of settled rights. To lose that

---

[209]New York Times v. United States, 403 U.S. 713, 714 (1971).

[210]The Reporters Committee for Freedom of the Press Magazine, The News Media and the Law, has a regular section on prior restraints which—after correcting for mislabeling—invariably has at least one real prior restraint per quarterly issue although typically the prior restraint did not withstand the slightest challenge.

[211]*Compare* Blasi, Toward a Theory of Prior Restraint, 66 Minn. L. Rev. 11 (1981), *with* Jeffries, Rethinking Prior Restraint, 92 Yale L. J. 409 (1983).

initial case (and the Pentagon Papers serves as a reminder there is more than one way to lose a case) is to open up a whole new area for exploration.[212]

Fortunately, *Tornillo* reaffirmed our ninth-grade civics understanding of freedom of the press: that old South Carolina flag with its rattlesnake and motto "Don't Tread on Me." *Tornillo* left the old rights where it found them and preserved the status quo. Chief Justice Burger's opinion meshed perfectly with the defensive nature of the *Herald's* claim. After fully stating the arguments in favor of a right of reply, he just said no.

Schmidt was so outraged by the lack of engagement that he concluded "the Court's skimpy justification is certain to create doubts about the constitutional rule announced."[213] His certainty arose from his Bickelian analysis of the opinion.[214] Because the opinion did not meet the appropriate standards of craft, it was suspect—even though it reaffirmed a right thought part of the First Amendment for decades upon decades. As "a stark and unexplained deviation"[215] from the Court's avoidance of absolutism, *Tornillo* was out of place in a world of First Amendment relativism. Accordingly, he thought it appropriate for future unspecified narrowing.

Chief Justice Burger's failure to engage, so annoying to Schmidt and other commentators, is in fact a great strength of the opinion. Nice debates about our traditional rights are fine in the legal journals, but in the public forum there is no need to reason about old rights. We have them. Why legitimate the inquiry by engaging in the debate?[216] We can debate some other issue instead of the taking away of traditional rights Americans have long enjoyed.

---

[212]A useful contrast can be made with Branzburg v. Hayes, 408 U.S. 665 (1972). There the press tried and failed to create a new First Amendment right. The result was a "loss" and one that had adverse implications for other attempts to create new rights, but left untouched all the press's traditional liberties.

[213]Schmidt, Freedom of the Press at 231.

[214]The book is dedicated to Alexander Bickel, whose influence is apparent.

[215]*Id.* at 233.

[216]Alexander Bickel decried a story of faculty members debating with students over whether to burn an ROTC building. "The matter was ultimately voted upon, and the affirmative lost—narrowly. But the negative taken by the faculty was only one side of a debate which the faculty rendered legitimate by engaging in it. Where nothing is unspeakable, nothing is undoable." Bickel, The Morality of Consent 73 (1975).

I should not be misunderstood. I am not making the ironic point that the First Amendment, while facilitating debate, cannot itself be debated. My conclusion that Chief Justice Burger's failure to debate is praise-worthy is not an assertion that some principles, especially those of the First Amendment, cannot hold their own in an open debate. The points I am driving at are the place of the debate and the effects of the debate on our rights as citizens. I believe that we must debate our fundamental values when differences appear. But the arena of the debate may well affect the perception of the values. Quite frankly I do not believe that a twenty-page Supreme Court opinion meeting all the standards of craft (all considerations are ventilated fully and the opinion be of publishable quality for a good legal journal) can as effectively protect the right of press autonomy as the blunt rejection in *Tornillo*.

Given the principle of press autonomy, what was essential in *Tornillo* was an immediate halt to the notion that newspapers have enjoyed too many rights and should be placed under some legal duties to the reading public. If this movement were not halted in one shot, then the traditional barrier would be down and the legislative experimentation might begin. Where the process would then stop would be anyone's guess. Whether we would still think of freedom of the press in terms of the fierce independence from government would also be open.

We have few of our traditional liberties left. Over a half century ago Justice Brandeis wrote that *Boyd v. United States*[217] was "a case that will be remembered as long as civil liberty lives in the United States."[218] Now *Boyd* is both gone and forgotten. Since civil liberties still live in the United States, Brandeis got his prediction wrong. The same may be said for my concerns: even with an opposite result in *Tornillo* there still will be civil liberties and freedom of the press in the United States. They will just be different, and we cannot know if they will be better (or worse), for it is impossible to know futures we cannot live.

The complexities of modern life apparently made *Boyd*'s protections too costly. And faced with near panic over the issues relating

---

[217]116 U.S. 616 (1886).
[218]Olmstead v. United States, 277 U.S. 438, 474 (1927) (dissenting).

to drugs, more and more searches and seizures are constitutionally reasonable.[219] A retrenchment on the rights we traditionally have enjoyed is deemed necessary to keep the Constitution up with the times. Barron's scholarship presented similar claims. Abandon the romantic myth of the First Amendment and face modern press realities.

I am not a Fourth Amendment scholar and therefore need not speculate on whether the Court's keeping it abreast of the times is good constitutional law. But I am sure about the First Amendment. The synergy of text, purpose, history, and on-going tradition have combined to validate an absolute right of press autonomy from government in decisions about what and what not to publish. A break in that right, even for the best of reasons, would begin what I suspect would be an irresistible movement toward a government umpire.[220]

It has long been assumed that civil liberties are not lost wholesale but rather retail, at quite good prices and therefore, initially at least, for the best of reasons. I do not know how to put this to an empirical test, and naturally I would not want to do so even if I could. No one wishes to accidently begin on a path that, if uncorrected, would make a prediction like Brandeis's come true. Thus I am unwilling to start.

Pat Tornillo challenged a part of the traditional core of freedom of the press, albeit for very good reasons. Barron has consistently and persuasively expressed those reasons. Subsequently, Blasi added another point when, after demonstrating in detail the consistency between the checking value and the traditional hands-off rule, he switched to argue that some access statutes should be sustained because of the checking value. He concluded that the Florida statute was overbroad because it gave a reply to officeholders, but a narrower statute giving "a right of reply only to nonincumbents like Mr. Tornillo should be upheld."[221] Had the Florida Supreme Court given the right of reply a narrowing construction to exclude officeholders, a not inconceivable possibility, Blasi would have found in

---

[219]Maryland v. Garrison, 107 S.Ct. 1013 (1987); United States v. Sharpe, 470 U.S. 675 (1985); New Jersey v. T.L.O., 469 U.S. 325 (1985).

[220]*Compare* Powe, Scholarship and Markets, 56 Geo. Wash. L. Rev. 172 (1987). *with* Fiss, Why the State? 100 Harv. L. Rev. 781 (1987).

[221]Blasi, Am. B. Found. Res. J. at 628.

favor of Tornillo on the ground that a local news organization "may actually form a part of an abusive local oligarchy" and that incumbents, but presumably not challengers, "typically have ample opportunities to disseminate their views."[222]

Nevertheless, acceding to the arguments for a right of reply, even a bit, breaks the barrier and starts the legal momentum going. I predicted earlier a not unlikely resting spot, but I have no confidence that I can read events depending on so many interacting variables. Nor can the proponents of access know what the ultimate outcome would be. Will it provide a useful check—maybe even a modest but appropriate chill—on papers like the *Manchester Union Leader* and thus provide better service for the citizens of New Hampshire and other places in need of diversity? Or will it result, as Blasi could not have known, in people like Pat Tornillo, exceptionally well known in their communities, being given a legal basis for additional publicity while leaving the vast bulk of the population in the same position as they are now? We are being asked to partially abandon the constitutional rights we have known for a speculative balance that may or may not work. About the only thing that would be certain is that it would be unlikely for our system to start on the road and then turn back. The force needed to break the existing barriers would probably be too great to permit a full return even if, to many, it seemed wise.

Thus for me, *Tornillo* got it just right: a perfect tone for the correct result, preserving our pre-existing rights. Barron's argument, despite its persuasive power, did not merit a full judicial response. A succinct rejection was the best way to demonstrate that the old constitutional rights were still valid. Further discussion would just have opened the door to further litigation, and the point of the Court's opinion was that no matter how compelling a right of reply might seem, further litigation was not needed because, as Justice Jackson noted in a different context, the First Amendment "was designed to avoid these ends by avoiding these beginnings."[223]

The content of freedom of the press has a traditional core in editorial autonomy from government: one part is no prior restraints; the other is the inability of government to dictate coverage. We can

---

[222]*Ibid.*

[223]West Virginia v. Barnette, 319 U.S. 624, 641 (1943).

and do impute various values to explain why freedom of the press (or, as we more typically say it, "the First Amendment") has this content. The tough issues quite naturally arise when the content and the values point in differing directions (as they did for Barron). My own view is that civil liberties will always be better protected by holding to the traditional views that have come to us over the years. Holding to a fixed irreducible core rather than a value in whose name content will change, as an elite minority believes society needs changes, is more likely to preserve civil liberties to bequeath our grandchildren. *Tornillo* understands this, and if Chief Justice Burger did not say it with the eloquence of a Brandeis or Jackson, well, no one else does either; what he did was say it just right. For that he deserves a lot more credit than he typically receives.

X. Conclusion

Legality is not synonymous with right, nor is unconstitutionality with wrong. Descriptively, Barron was on target. A concentrated, homogenized press will overreport some stories and underreport (or ignore) others to the detriment of us all. While there are no easy solutions, the press has not been its normal complacent self in dealing with these problems.

During Tornillo's unnoticed 1970 campaign, the *New York Times* editorially announced a new policy. Henceforth, the *Times* would open its op-ed page several times a week to contributions from outside the industry. The *Times* hoped "to afford greater opportunity for exploration of issues and presentation of new insights and new ideas by writers and thinkers who have no institutional connection with the *Times* and whose views will very frequently be completely divergent from our own."[224] Other papers, including the *Miami Herald*,[225] have followed suit with one or more of the following responses: opening the op-ed pages, allocating more space

---

[224]New York Times, September 21, 1970 at 42.

[225]Jim Hampton to author, June 15, 1987: "I've opened our Op-Ed Page far more than in Shoemaker's day. Nothing to do with Tornillo; just my own recognition that, as the only real game in town, we have an obligation to provide an accessible soapbox for those of opposing views. We give priority in our Reader's Forum to letters opposing us, for the same reason." The Herald does not have an ombudsman.

to the letters to the editor column,[226] and, as with the *Washington Post*, creation of an ombudsman.[227]

These new approaches still leave the discretion of what to print with an editor of the paper. This does not mean, however, that the changes are cosmetic only. While Tornillo still would not get his two replies published under the circumstances prevailing in 1972, would-be contributors are only incidental beneficiaries of the new approaches. Instead these changes are designed to serve the readers of the paper. Sometimes the editorial choices will seem capricious; other times perfect. Inevitably that is the nature of editorial choice.

Although Barron lost his legal war, the concerns he articulated motivated others voluntarily to take steps in the direction he pointed. The new approaches deal with his prime concern: that different voices be heard and different issues addressed. The solutions are not perfect, but with such an intractable problem they could not be. Furthermore, as voluntary responses to a widely perceived problem, changes can be made as experience dictates.[228] These attempts, even if imperfect, beat the potential errors of legislation, a possibility always lurking within *Tornillo*.

XI. EPILOGUE

Political events in Florida moved swiftly in the period immediately following the Florida and the Supreme Court opinions in *Tornillo*. The looming scandal at the Florida Supreme Court resulted in a rapid transfusion of personnel. Within two years of

---

[226]Hynds, American Newspapers in the 1980s 294–95 (1980); Shaw, Journalism Today ch. 6 (1977).

[227]Tate, What Do Ombudsmen Do? 23 Colum. J. Rev. 37 (1984).

[228]One ambitious project, announced with much fanfare in the Columbia Journalism Review, was a National News Council. It was proposed by the Twentieth Century Fund as "an independent forum for public and press discussion of important issues affecting the flow of information." 11 Colum. J. Rev. at 44 (1973). With foundation funding its goal was "to receive, to examine, and to report on complaints concerning the accuracy and fairness of news reporting" thereby increasing public trust in journalism by assessing complaints about the work of major news organizations. *Id.* at 43. While the Columbia Journalism Review reported its decisions, many newspapers refused to cooperate, others cooperated tepidly, and the New York Times was vigorously opposed to the Council. New York Times, March 21, 1984 at 19. The Council eventually wound up so moribund that its death went unnoticed in the Columbia Journalism Review. See generally Brogan, Spiked: The Short Life and Death of the National News Council (1985).

Tornillo four of the seven justices had been replaced. Politics was working at the legislature, too. Following Chief Justice Burger's opinion, the legislature took up repeal of the unconstitutional right to reply. In the Florida House an amendment was proposed to let the public vote on the hiring and firing of managing editors of newspapers. It was defeated by seven votes.[229]

Tornillo never tried elective politics again. Now in his early sixties, he remains firmly in control of the union. The old CTA has both changed its name and its affiliation. The United Teachers of Dade has dropped the NEA and joined the American Federation of Teachers. UTD's lawyer is Elizabeth duFresne, who kept Tornillo as a client following Toby Simon's death. She is now a senior partner in the Miami firm that currently represents the *Herald!*[230]

Shoemaker has retired, but the *Herald* remains one of the outstanding newspapers in the United States. Time does heal: Tornillo's relations with the *Herald* are quite good, and he finds his way into the paper—including letters to the editor—with frequency.

Both Tornillo and Shoemaker look back on the events and see their positions as ones of principle which left no alternatives. Tornillo, at least, believes that some time in the future his position on the right of reply will prevail. Shoemaker still believes the *Herald* had no choice but not to print Tornillo's replies. John Knight, president of the chain owning the *Herald*, was unhappy about the suit but fully backed it. Nevertheless, Knight had a simple message for Shoemaker: "Don't do it again."[231]

---

[229]Editor & Publisher, May 3, 1975 at 40.

[230]duFresne to author, June 18, 1987.

[231]Shoemaker Interview.

GEOFFREY P. MILLER

THE TRUE STORY OF
CAROLENE PRODUCTS

United States v. Carolene Products Corporation,[1] as any second year law student knows, contains perhaps the most renowned footnote in constitutional history.[2] In famous footnote four Justice Stone, writing for himself and three others, suggested that the Court apply relatively strict scrutiny to legislation interfering with the political processes or affecting the rights of "discrete and insular minorities."[3] Because the Court had but recently abandoned strict scrutiny of economic regulation, the footnote is seen as paving the way for a two-tiered system of constitutional review in which individual rights are afforded greater protection than so-called economic liberties.

Geoffrey P. Miller is Professor of Law and Associate Dean, The University of Chicago Law School.

AUTHOR'S NOTE: The Brena D. and Lee A. Freeman Faculty Research Fund and Kirkland and Ellis Professorship provided financial support for this project. Albert W. Alschuler, David P. Currie, David D. Haddock, John H. Langbein, M. Harisingh Maskay, Fred S. McChesney, Richard A. Posner, Alan O. Sykes, and Cass R. Sunstein all made valuable comments on an earlier draft, as did participants in workshops at Stanford, Berkeley, and Chicago law schools. Catherine Torgerson, Brian Hedlund, and Leon Greenfield provided excellent research assistance. This article is part of work in progress, which traces the history of the dairy industry's campaign against butterfat substitutes between 1870 and 1950.

[1] 304 U.S. 144 (1938).

[2] *Cf.* Brown v. Board of Education, 343 U.S. 483, 494 n.11 (1954). See Mason, Harlan Fiske Stone: Pillar of Law 513–14 (1956); Hutchinson, Unanimity and Desegregation: Decision-Making in the Supreme Court 1948–1958, 68 Georgetown L. J. 1, 43 & n.349 (1979).

[3] 304 U.S. at 152 n.4. Justices Cardozo and Reed did not participate; Justice McReynolds dissented; Justice Butler concurred only in the result; and Justice Black did not concur in the part of the opinion containing the footnote.

Today, a half-century later, the footnote is widely honored as a cornerstone of constitutional law,[4] a "great and modern charter for ordering the relations between judges and other agencies of government."[5] The footnote has spawned noteworthy scholarship;[6] and its seminal ideas have been expanded in works by John Hart Ely[7] and others.[8]

The plaudits accorded the footnote are matched by the disregard of the case itself. The facts were not the stuff of great decisions. At issue was the constitutionality of the 1923 federal "Filled Milk Act,"[9] a statute that prohibited the shipment in interstate commerce of skimmed milk laced with vegetable oil.[10] The case appeared to be a routine challenge to an unimportant economic regulation, with the outcome foreordained by recent opinions sustaining other forms of economic regulation.[11] Commentators have denigrated its significance, finding it "unremarkable,"[12] "straightforward,"[13] even "easy."[14]

The lack of attention to the case itself is unfortunate, because it is interesting in its own right, and because its facts shed light on the meaning of the footnote. The statute upheld in the case was an utterly unprincipled example of special interest legislation. The

---

[4]See Lusky, Footnote Redux: A Carolene Products Reminiscence, 82 Colum. L. Rev. 1093 (1982); Lusky, Minority Rights and the Public Interest, 52 Yale L. J. 1 (1942); Gunther, Cases and Materials on Constitutional Law 542 (10th ed. 1980).

[5]Fiss, The Supreme Court, 1978 Term—Foreword: The Forms of Justice, 93 Harv. L. Rev. 1, 6 (1979).

[6]See Ackerman, Beyond Carolene Products, 98 Harv. L. Rev. 713 (1985); Ball, Judicial Protection of Powerless Minorities, 59 Iowa L. Rev. 1059, 1060–64 (1974); Brilmayer, Carolene, Conflicts, and the Fate of the "Inside-Outsider," 134 U. Pa. L. Rev. 1291 (1986); Erler, Equal Protection and Personal Rights: The Regime of the "Discrete and Insular Minority," 16 Ga. L. Rev. 407 (1982); Powell, Carolene Products Revisited, 82 Colum. L. Rev. 1087 (1982).

[7]Ely, Democracy and Distrust (1980).

[8]E.g., Cover, The Origins of Judicial Activism in the Protection of Minorities, 91 Yale L. J. 1287 (1982).

[9]21 U.S.C. § §61–63 (1982).

[10]The term "filled milk" was a dairy industry pejorative; manufacturers of the substance preferred "compound milk."

[11]E.g., West Coast Hotel Co. v. Parrish, 300 U.S. 379 (1937).

[12]Brilmayer, note 6 supra, at 1294.

[13]Lusky, note 4 supra, at 1095.

[14]Powell, note 6 supra, at 1987.

purported "public interest" justifications so credulously reported by Justice Stone were patently bogus. If the preference embodied by this statute was not "naked,"[15] it was clothed only in gossamer rationalizations. The consequence of the decision was to expropriate the property of a lawful and beneficial industry; to deprive working and poor people of a healthful, nutritious, and low-cost food; and to impair the health of the nation's children by encouraging the use as baby food of a sweetened condensed milk product that was 42 percent sugar.

It is difficult to believe that members of the Court were unaware of the true motivation behind this legislation. That they should nonetheless vote to uphold the statute strongly suggested that all bets were off as far as economic regulation was concerned. Footnote four, in this light, can be seen as indicating that the Court intended to keep its hands off economic regulation, no matter how egregious the discrimination or patent the special interest motivation. Rational basis scrutiny of the sort suggested in *West Coast Hotel*[16] could not be taken seriously if it precluded judicial protection of individual liberties. By separating economic and personal liberties, Justice Stone suggested that the Court might really mean what it said about deference to the legislative will in economic cases. Two-tiered scrutiny did much more than facilitate the creation of preferred constitutional categories entitled to exacting judicial review. It also freed the forces of interest group politics from the stumbling block of the federal courts. *Carolene's* legacy is not only *Brown v. Board of Education;*[17] it is also the unrivaled primacy of interest groups in American politics of the last half-century.

Fortunately for the nation's consumers, the *Carolene Products* case itself is no longer the law. Go to any supermarket and you will find filled milk for sale under trade names such as "Milnot" or "Melloream." Some firms, including the aptly-named Defiance Milk Products Company of Defiance, Ohio, are boldly marketing the product under its original colors.[18] The Supreme Court's decision in *Carolene Products* has been overruled, and the statute declared to

---

[15]Sunstein, Naked Preferences and the Constitution, 84 Colum. L. Rev. 1689 (1984).

[16]*West Coast Hotel*, note 11 *supra*.

[17]Brown v. Board of Education, note 2 *supra*.

[18]This manufacturer describes its products as "Evaporated Filled Milk—Vitamin A & D Added," and states that the contents are "a substitute for, but not evaporated milk or cream."

violate substantive due process.[19] Yet while the injustice of the case itself has been remedied, the footnote remains.

I. Politics, Technology, Markets, and Law: The Filled Milk Act of 1923

The Filled Milk Act arose out of complex interactions among the politics, technology, and markets of the canned milk industry. Technological innovations shaped milk markets; those markets, in turn, stimulated research and development of new technology. Markets powerfully influenced dairy politics; politics shaped the development of legal regulations.[20] Legal changes, in turn, altered market dynamics and created new incentives for technological innovation. These complex actions and reactions were at all times subtle, pervasive, and deeply reciprocal.

A. TECHNOLOGY

Filled milk was a technological innovation in the canned milk industry, an industry that was itself a response to the technological difficulties of bringing fluid milk to markets. The problem of dairy marketing has always been the perishability of fluid milk. In the nineteenth century, when refrigeration was in its infancy and transportation systems still relatively primitive, there was essentially no market for fluid milk outside of farming areas and major cities. Dairy products were consumed as butter or cheese, products less subject to spoilage than fluid milk. The early decades of the twentieth century saw rapid development of transportation, refrigeration, and pasteurization, facilitating the creation of home delivery systems of bottled milk. Even so, there remained a demand for fluid milk that resisted spoilage. Many homes, especially in poorer areas, did not have refrigerators; and it was useful for all households to have some extra fluid milk on hand for emergencies. Canned milk filled these needs. It resisted spoilage for years, came in a convenient condensed form suitable for easy storage, and required virtually no preparation. The flavor was not particularly palatable

---

[19]See text accompanying notes 87–90 *infra*.

[20]See, *e.g.*, Peltzman, Towards a More General Theory of Regulation, 19 J. Law & Econ. 211 (1976); Becker, A Theory of Competition among Pressure Groups for Political Influence, 98 Q. J. Econ. 371 (1983).

for use as a beverage, but it was extremely serviceable in cooking and for use as a whitener in coffee or tea.

There were then, as now, two principal forms of canned milks. Condensed milk is produced by heating raw fresh milk almost to the boiling point to destroy bacteria, adding sugar as a preservative, then boiling in a vacuum at about 150° F until the volume is reduced by about half. The mixture, now 40 percent sugar, is then drawn off, cooled, and packed in cans for sale to the public. Borden's "Eagle," first sold in 1857, was in 1923 (and still is) the industry leader in condensed milk. Evaporated milk, the other principal canned milk product, is produced by boiling raw fresh milk at low temperature in a vacuum, homogenizing it, packing it in hermetically sealed cans, and then sterilizing it in the cans by heating above the boiling point. The principal difference between condensed and evaporated milk is that the former is preserved with sugar while the latter is preserved through heat sterilization.[21]

Filled milk is evaporated skimmed milk to which vegetable oils have been added in place of the butterfat. It is indistinguishable from ordinary evaporated whole milk in taste, odor, color, consistency, specific gravity, and cooking qualities. In 1923, at the time of the federal statute, filled milk was made almost exclusively with coconut oil, which was the only vegetable oil then available at reasonable price that had a sufficiently neutral taste. All the coconut oil in filled milk was imported, principally from the Philippine Islands. Some of this oil was refined in the Philippines and imported under a tariff exemption that the islands enjoyed due to their status as American possessions after the Spanish-American War. The remainder was imported in the form of copra—dried coconut meat—and refined in the United States. Copra was on the free list and could be imported duty-free from any country.

B. MARKETS

Canned milk was produced by commercial milk dealers and distributors. There were apparently significant economies of scale in the production and distribution of the product. By the late teens the canned milk industry had become relatively concentrated as a result of merger and internal expansion. The top four companies

---

[21]Federal Trade Commission, Report on Milk and Milk Products 1914–18 34 (1921).

in 1918 controlled 54.2 percent of the market and the top ten firms controlled 76.7 percent.[22] These figures actually underestimated the amount of concentration because the bigger firms purchased and marketed the output of the smaller ones and because the two top firms, Borden and Nestle, operated under an agreement to divide markets.[23] It is probable that Borden and Nestle together controlled about half the total U.S. market through their own output or via long-term contracts with other companies.

Filled milk appeared on the scene in the early teens. It was produced by a few of the bigger milk dealers incident to their manufacture of condensed and evaporated milk. By 1923 there were seven or eight brands on the market, going under trade names such as "Enzo," "Nutro," "Nyko," "Silver Key," and "Carolene." The industry leader was "Hebe," produced by a subsidiary of the Carnation Company, one of the industry's top ten firms.

The great selling point of filled milk was price. Skimmed milk was virtually worthless at the time. Produced in the billions of pounds a year, its principal cash market was in the manufacture of paint. Mostly it was fed to hogs or calves on the farm. The only element of real value in milk was butterfat. Because the coconut oil in filled milk was much cheaper than butterfat, filled milk could be sold for considerably less than canned whole milk. The wholesale cost of a case of filled milk was about $3.50 for forty-eight cans, while the cost of a case of canned whole milk was $5.00.[24] At retail, filled milk typically sold for about 7½¢ a can, as compared with 10¢ for canned whole milk.[25]

The canned milk market was for many years a relatively unimportant part of the dairy industry. Beginning in 1915, however, European countries began demanding American dairy products as a result of the First World War. American exports of condensed and evaporated milk totaled only 16 million pounds in 1914; by 1917 they were 259 million pounds; and by 1919 they reached a peak of 729 million pounds.[26] The trade in filled milk expanded

---

[22]*Id.* at 21.

[23]*Ibid.*

[24]Filled Milk, Hearings on H.R. 6215 before the House Committee on Agriculture, 67th Cong., 1st Sess. 12; 87; 127 (1921) (hereinafter "House Hearings").

[25]*Id.* at 12–16; 127–28.

[26]The Agricultural Crisis and Its Causes, Report of the Joint Commission on Agriculture Inquiry, H. Rep. No. 408, 64th Cong., 1st Sess. 149 (1921).

along with the demand for canned milk generally: it was estimated
that in 1916 12,000 pounds of filled milk were produced; in 1917
19,000 pounds; in 1918 41 million pounds; in 1919 62 million pounds;
and in 1920 84 million pounds.[27] The explosion in the demand for
canned milk of all sorts was probably the most important single
development in dairy markets during the period.

In 1920–21, following the conclusion of the First World War, the
American economy suffered a serious decline. Farmers were particularly hard hit.[28] Prices for farm products plummeted in late
1920; and by 1921 the industry was in a depression that continued
until 1923. Meanwhile, the prices of farm supplies and of com-
modities generally were either increasing or decreasing at a much
slower rate than farm output prices.[29] Caught in a price squeeze,
many farmers were forced into distress sales or even bankruptcy.[30]
The "grim reality" of the agricultural economy in 1922, in the words
of President Harding, was one of "crisis . . . depression and
discouragements."[31]

The agricultural depression of 1920–23 was keenly felt in the
dairy industry, even if the level of distress was somewhat less for
this sector than for other agricultural products. Milk dropped from
$3.22 per hundredweight in 1920 to $2.30 in 1921; butter suffered
a similar loss from 54.3¢ a pound in 1920 to 37¢ in 1921.[32] Despite
the price drop, consumption of dairy products remained nearly
constant, reflecting the relatively inelastic demand for most farm
products.[33] The situation did not improve until 1923 when milk
and butter prices showed a small but significant increase.[34]

Conditions in the canned milk market were especially disrupted
because of the collapse in European demand. Exports dropped from

[27]Filled Milk, Hearings on H.R. 8086 before a Subcommittee of the Senate Committee
on Agriculture and Forestry, 77th Cong., 2d Sess. 45 (1922) (hereinafter "Senate Hearings").

[28]Report of the Joint Commission on Agricultural Inquiry, Part I, H. Rep. No. 408, 67th
Cong., 1st Sess. 35–36 (1921).

[29]U.S. Department of Justice, Milk Marketing, A Report to the Task Group on Antitrust
Immunities 33–34 (1977).

[30] Report of the Joint Commission on Agricultural Inquiry, *supra*, Part II, pp. 86–89.

[31]Report of the National Agricultural Conference, H. Doc. No. 115, 67th Cong., 2d Sess.
6–7 (1922).

[32]The Statistical History of the United States 522 (1976).

[33]*Id.* at 329–31; 522–23.

[34]*Id.* at 522.

711 million pounds in 1920 to 267 million pounds in 1921.[35] Total production fell from 2.03 billion pounds in 1919 to 1.58 billion pounds in 1920, and to 1.46 billion pounds in 1921.[36] In October 1920, many condenseries were closed for the first time in history; by December production by all the larger companies had practically ceased.[37] Plants did not begin to reopen until February 1921, and the industry did not reopen all its plants until the following spring.[38] Borden's net income dropped from $4.28 million in 1919 to $2.81 million in 1920 and $2.92 million in 1921.[39]

The downturn was felt in the filled milk industry as well: filled milk production continued to increase through 1920, but in 1921 fell to about 65 million pounds, a loss of approximately 20 million pounds over the previous year.[40]

C. POLITICS

The politics of filled milk was a predictable expression of the self-interest of the various affected parties. The opponents of the product can appropriately be referred to as the "dairy industry," although the term is not completely accurate because limited segments of the industry were aligned on the other side. Pressing for prohibition were various farmer associations: breed groups; county, state, and national political organizations; dairy newspapers; agricultural colleges and universities; granges; and dairy promotional organizations. Farmers understood, correctly, that the imported coconut oil in filled milk undercut the domestic butterfat market. Although filled milk was mostly skimmed milk, a dairy product, the net impact on dairy farmers was negative. The demand for skimmed milk created by Hebe and similar products was largely a replacement for skimmed milk that would otherwise have been used in whole evaporated milk. Worse, filled milk displaced millions of pounds of butter into the market, driving down the price of that commodity. The loss in profits from the reduction in butter prices

---

[35]The Agricultural Crisis and Its Causes, note 26 *supra*, at 149.

[36]See 62 Cong. Rec. 7591 (1922) (remarks of Rep. Knutson).

[37]Annual Report, The Borden Company 8 (1920).

[38]*Id.* at 10.

[39]1920 and 1921 Annual Reports, The Borden Company.

[40]New York Produce Review and American Creamery, May 10, 1922, at 104.

outweighed any gain from an enhanced skimmed milk market.[41] In this respect the impact of filled milk was similar to that of margarine, dairying's longtime bugaboo.

In addition to farmers, the other important member of this coalition was the Borden Company. Borden enjoyed substantial brand-name capital in its various kinds of canned milk, especially its "Eagle" condensed milk. Perhaps because of its dominant position, Borden failed to introduce its own brand of filled milk. By 1920 the various other proprietary brand names had gained consumer acceptance; if Borden were to enter the market at this point it would have to struggle to do as well in filled milk as it was doing in other segments of the canned milk industry. Thus by 1920 Borden apparently calculated that it had more to gain by suppressing the trade in filled milk than by entering into competition with its rivals. Much of the opposition to filled milk appears to have been instigated and actively supported by Borden throughout.[42] Borden cooperated amicably with the producer groups in the filled milk battle even though their relations were keenly adversarial on other issues such as milk prices.

The principal supporters of filled milk were the small group of producers who wanted to protect a source of profits and their investments in brand names. Their interests were informally represented in the Carnation Company, which had the most to lose because its Hebe brand was the industry leader. Other opponents of the measure were importers and refiners of copra and retail and wholesale grocers. The cotton interests of the South also opposed the bill, out of hope that filled milk might someday be made with cottonseed oil; their interest, however, was discounted because the amount of cottonseed oil in filled milk was negligible, and future prospects depended on an uncertain technology of taste neutralization.[43]

Sitting ostentatiously on the sidelines were the big Chicago packing houses. As leading producers of margarine, they might have

---

[41]Industry leaders recognized the threat posed by filled milk from the start. See, *e.g.*, "Hebe" Milk Likened to Oleo, Hoard's Dairyman, Jan. 10, 1919, at 846.

[42]House Hearings at 171; Senate Hearings at 81–83.

[43]While the bill was pending in Congress, filled milk manufacturers tried desperately to neutralize the taste of cottonseed and peanut oils. Their efforts met with mixed success at best, although opponents of the bill did display samples of milk filled with domestic oils during floor debate. See 62 Cong. Rec. 7583–84 (1922) (remarks of Rep. Aswell).

been expected to oppose discrimination against butterfat substitutes. The packinghouse interests, however, were interested principally in meat margarine, made from beef and hog fat, and secondarily in margarine made from cottonseed and other domestic oils, a business into which they had recently diversified. They had no interest in a product made from coconut oil. Indeed, they had reason to be antagonistic to coconut oil products because their margarine business was suffering competition from so-called "nut margarines" made from imported oils.[44] There is reason to suspect that the packing houses covertly supported the dairy industry in the filled milk battle, although their support could not be publicly expressed because of the longstanding hostility between the dairying and meatpacking industries over the margarine issue.[45]

D. THE 1923 STATUTE

Despite the threat posed by filled milk, the dairy industry made few efforts to combat the product prior to the onset of the farm depression in 1920. In part this was because there was no basis for challenging the product under existing law. The federal pure food and drug act required that the product not be adulterated or misbranded, but a proviso stated that an article would not be considered adulterated or misbranded if it was a compound of ingredients offered for sale under its own name and not an imitation of another article.[46] There was no question that filled milk, taken by itself, was a healthful product, since it was simply a compound of skimmed milk and vegetable oil, two substances universally recognized as healthful. Nor was there any basis to challenge the labeling of the various filled milks, under either state or federal law, since they correctly disclosed their ingredients and did not include "milk" in their names. Thus the executive branches of the state and federal

---

[44] In 1917, 145 million pounds of packing house fats were used in margarine as compared with only 19 million pounds of coconut oil; by 1921 packing house fats used in margarine had fallen to 86 million pounds and coconut oil had increased to 103 million pounds. Snodgrass, Margarine as a Butter Substitute 316 (1930).

[45] A decade later the packing houses and the dairy industry publicly made common cause in a successful effort to place legal restrictions on nut margarine. See President Hoover Signs the Cooking Compound Bill, Jersey Bulletin and Dairy World, July 30, 1930, at 1469.

[46] 34 Stat. 768, 771 (1906).

governments, which might have been the first resort for the dairy industry, were not initially available in its campaign.

In Ohio, however, an existing statute prohibited the manufacture or sale of condensed skimmed milk. Ohio authorities threatened prosecution against the manufacturer of Hebe for violation of the statute. The case reached the Supreme Court of the United States in 1919, where, despite an argument for Hebe by Charles Evans Hughes, Justice Holmes upheld the statute. Holmes deferred to the legislature to a degree rarely matched even in the Court's pro–New Deal decisions after 1937. Even assuming that Hebe was wholesome, said Holmes, the legislative power "is not to be denied simply because some innocent articles or transactions may be found within the proscribed class. The inquiry must be whether, considering the end in view, the statute passes the bounds of reason and assumes the character of a merely arbitrary fiat."[47] Holmes had no difficulty concluding that the statute represented a valid exercise of the police power.[48]

The result in *Hebe Co.*, coupled with the weakening in dairy prices that began in 1919, galvanized the industry into action. Prominent dairy journals sounded the alarm. Hoard's Dairyman accused Hebe of being oleo wearing "a tin jacket . . . instead of annatto paint and oil paper."[49] The *Jersey Bulletin and Dairy World*, a national journal for the Jersey breed, disparaged the product as "milk business a la sausage grinder" and noted pointedly that the skimmed milk in Hebe was supplied by a Holstein herd.[50] The equation of filled milk with margarine was well-calculated to capture the attention of farmers long conditioned to consider oleo the worst of all possible evils (except when served at their own dinner tables).[51]

---

[47]Hebe Co. v. Shaw, 248 U.S. 297, 303 (1919), quoting Purity Extract & Tonic Co. v. Lynch, 226 U.S. 192, 204 (1912).

[48]The *Hebe* case illustrates that the *Lochner* era was anything but monolithic. See Currie, The Constitution in the Supreme Court: The Protection of Economic Interests 1889–1910, 52 U. Chi. L. Rev. 324 (1985); Currie, The Constitution in the Supreme Court 1910–1921, 1985 Duke L. J. 1111, 1129–31.

[49]"Hebe" Milk Likened to Oleo, Hoard's Dairyman, Jan. 10, 1919, at 846.

[50]Milk Business a la Sausage Grinder, Jersey Bulletin and Dairy World, May 11, 1921, at 1683.

[51]Dairy industry journals of the period frequently condemn the habit of dairy farmers to use margarine for their own cooking needs.

Industry leaders charged that filled milk was unhealthy because it lacked vitamins, and that it induced fraud because it could so easily be confused with evaporated milk. These arguments formed the basis for a sustained campaign by the industry against filled milk at both the state and federal levels.[52]

Around 1920 bills to outlaw or severely restrict filled milk were introduced in various state legislatures. California and Washington passed the first such laws in 1919, followed by seventeen more states within the next four years.[53] The campaign for state legislation received a boost in 1922 when the Wisconsin Supreme Court upheld that state's filled milk statute against a challenge brought by the Hebe Company.[54]

Beneficial as these statutes were for the opponents of filled milk, they did not provide complete protection. The product could still be manufactured where it was not prohibited, and could, under the original package doctrine, be freely transported into states that had enacted prohibitory legislation.[55] As long as filled milk undersold canned whole milk by a significant amount, merchants, grocers, and peddlers could be found willing to risk prosecution for selling the product. To enforce the statute effectively prosecutors would have to go after these small-time operators, a strategy certain to prove both time-consuming and ineffective. Even if retailers could be apprehended, their defense costs would be paid by the filled milk manufacturers; and sympathy for defendants would often result in jury nullification or unfavorable judicial interpretations. Prosecutors were unlikely to enforce these statutes enthusiastically given the many other demands on their resources. The dairy industry had experienced all this and more in its frustrating campaign against margarine, and it was well aware of the difficulties it would face in a similar attack on filled milk.

---

[52]As shown below, the arguments were bogus. See text accompanying notes 92–112 *infra*.

[53]The states were Colorado (1921), Utah (1921), Oregon (1921), Wisconsin (1921), New Jersey (1922), New York (1922), New Hampshire (1923), Missouri (1923), Minnesota (1923), Michigan (1923), Massachusetts (1923), Iowa (1923), Illinois (1923), Connecticut (1923), Tennessee (1923), South Dakota (1923), and Pennsylvania (1923). See Brief for the United States in United States v. Carolene Products Co., Oct. Term 1937, at 60–68 (hereinafter cited as "United States Brief"). The early adoption of filled milk statutes by western states was probably due to the fact that Carnation, the manufacturer of Hebe, was a West Coast distributor.

[54]State v. Emery, 178 Wisc. 147, 189 N.W. 564 (1922).

[55]*E.g.*, Leisy v. Hardin, 135 U.S. 100 (1890).

This is not to say that the state prohibitions on filled milk were useless. By increasing the cost of the product, the statutes raised the price and reduced the quantity sold. Further, and perhaps equally important, the statutes provided a model for federal legislation. In the state legislative contests the dairy industry was able to hone and refine its arguments while at the same time organizing effective state- wide lobbies that could be unified in the subsequent national campaign.

Federal legislation therefore remained an attractive goal for the dairy industry despite its success in obtaining prohibitory legislation in many states. The question was what form the legislation should take. The choice was between taxing and regulating, with the decision turning on practical and legal considerations.

Existing federal legislation provided the model of a prohibitive tax. Yellow margarine had been subject to a prohibitive federal tax since 1902[56] and "filled cheese" (skimmed milk cheese with non-dairy fat) had been taxed out of existence since 1896.[57] There was reason to hope that a prohibitory tax would be sustained in court.[58] Moreover, a federal tax could reach the product at the point of manufacture. Because there were relatively few producers in the canned milk business, enforcement of a tax on manufacturers would be simple and effective.

State prohibitory statutes provided the other model. Such legislation would prohibit the transport of filled milk in interstate commerce; if effectively enforced it would balkanize the filled milk market along state lines and restrict the product to states where it was not prohibited. The disadvantage of legislation under the commerce power was that under existing jurisprudence it could not reach within a state to regulate manufacture.[59] In addition, commerce power regulation was subject to potential attack under the Due Process Clause. While the hands-off attitude of the *Hebe Co.* case suggested that a federal prohibition would be upheld, the Supreme Court had not always been deferential to economic reg-

---

[56]32 Stat. 197 (1902).

[57]29 Stat. 253 (1896).

[58]See McCray v. United States, 195 U.S. 27 (1904) (upholding federal margarine tax). See also Veazie Bank v. Fenno, 8 Wall. 533 (1869) (sustaining prohibitive tax on state bank notes).

[59]United States v. E.C. Knight Co., 156 U.S. 1 (1895).

ulation.[60] Accordingly, some sort of police power justification was necessary to guard against judicial invalidation. Under existing jurisprudence a prohibition of interstate commerce was likely to survive constitutional scrutiny if the product in question were shown to be dangerous to health, safety, or morals,[61] or if it worked some sort of fraud on the public.[62]

By 1921 the dairy industry as a whole had determined to support a direct federal prohibition of filled milk rather than a punitive tax, although segments of the industry worried about the constitutional difficulties.[63] The leading congressional supporters of the bill were congressmen from dairy states such as Wisconsin, Minnesota, New York, and Iowa. The opponents were largely from the South, especially cotton states such as Arkansas, Mississippi, and Louisiana. The bill passed the House 250 to 40,[64] passed the Senate by a voice vote,[65] and was signed into law on March 4, 1923.

The federal statute removed some of the pressure for prohibitory legislation in states that had not yet acted, but state legislation was still needed to prevent intrastate manufacture and sale of the product. Filled milk was banned or stringently regulated in Arkansas (1925), Indiana (1925), North Dakota (1925), Vermont (1925), Alabama (1927), New Mexico (1927), Montana (1929), Georgia (1929), Connecticut (1930), Arizona (1931), Delaware (1935), Texas (1935), and Kentucky (1940).[66] By 1937 thirty-one states had enacted laws prohibiting the manufacture or sale of filled milk; three had prescribed standards for condensed milk that effectively outlawed filled milk, and three had imposed conditions and regulations on the manufacture and sale of filled milk.[67]

The effect of the federal statute, coupled with prohibitory state legislation, was to drive most producers out of business. A small

---

[60]E.g., Hammer v. Dagenhart, 247 U.S. 251 (1918).

[61]E.g., Champion v. Ames, 188 U.S. 321 (1903).

[62]E.g., McDermott v. Wisconsin, 288 U.S. 115 (1913).

[63]See Senate Hearings at 87; Why Filled Milk Should Be Taxed, The Milk Dealer, Oct. 1921, at 93.

[64]62 Cong. Rec. 7669–70 (1922).

[65]64 Cong. Rec. 4986 (1923).

[66]United States Brief at 60–68; Carolene Products Co. v. Hanrahan, 291 Ky. 597, 164 S.W.2d 597, 598 (1942).

[67]United States Brief at 60–68.

trade in the product did continue, however, where permitted by law or where a producer was willing to risk prosecution in order to test a statute in court. The leading (perhaps the only) manufacturer of filled milk after 1923 was the Carolene Products Corporation. This firm continued to manufacture and sell the substance in a number of states, including several that had enacted prohibitory legislation.

Despite what appeared to be the unfavorable precedent in *Hebe Co.*, Carolene Products had some remarkable successes in its lonely legal odyssey. In 1931 the Supreme Court of Illinois—Carolene's home state—invalidated its filled milk statute on due process grounds.[68] When an organization of evaporated milk producers caused the legislature to enact a new statute complete with suitable recitations of "fact," the Illinois Supreme Court again struck it down, holding that the purported fact finding intruded on the judicial function and denied due process and equal protection of the laws.[69] These decisions established a safe harbor in which the company could operate its manufacturing plant and serve the large intrastate market, including the Chicago metropolitan area.

In 1934 the company won an even bigger victory when a judge in the Southern District of Illinois, in a sweeping if confused opinion, invalidated the federal statute.[70] The act, said the court, "strikes down a well-known lawful industry, one which theretofore was entitled to and had the protection of the Constitution and laws of the United States. It amounts to a taking of private property ostensibly for the public good without compensation, and deprives the defendant and others similarly situated of liberty and property, without due process of law."[71]

Carolene Products' situation improved still more in 1936 with decisions by the Supreme Courts of Michigan and Nebraska striking down their respective filled milk statutes.[72] Although prohibitory legislation was still being enacted in a number of states, it began

---

[68]People v. Carolene Products Co., 345 Ill. 166, 177 N.E. 698 (1931).

[69]Carolene Products Co. v. McLaughlin, 365 Ill. 62, 5 N.E.2d 447, 451 (1936).

[70]United States v. Carolene Products Co., 7 F.Supp. 500 (S.D. Ill. 1934).

[71]*Id.* at 507.

[72]Carolene Products Company v. Thompson, 276 Mich. 172, 267 N.W. 608 (1936) (state and federal constitutions); Carolene Products Company v. Banning, 131 Neb. 429, 268 N.W. 313 (1936) (state and federal constitutions).

to appear as if the dairy industry's campaign of 1920–23 would founder completely upon the rocks of the Due Process Clause.

In fact, however, it was Carolene Products that was on a headlong course for disaster. In 1937 it attempted to eliminate interference from its archenemy, the Evaporated Milk Association, by bringing a bill of complaint alleging that the Association's activities violated the antitrust law. The strategy backfired when the Seventh Circuit upheld the federal statute, overruling the prior decision by the Southern District of Illinois.[73]

The following year catastrophe struck. The Supreme Courts of Missouri and Pennsylvania upheld their states' prohibitory statutes.[74] Worse, the United States Supreme Court upheld the federal statute in *United States v. Carolene Products Co.*[75] Justice Stone's opinion for the Court deferred totally to congressional committee "findings" that filled milk threatened the public health (because it lacked vitamins) and encouraged consumer fraud (because it could be confused with evaporated milk).

Despite the Court's apparent renunciation of any meaningful role in economic cases, Carolene Products refused to abandon the fight. It added a little cod liver oil and marketed the product as "New Vitamin A Carolene."[76] The scheme failed. State supreme courts in Kentucky[77] and Kansas[78] sustained filled milk statutes as applied to the new formula. A renewed federal prosecution came to the United States Supreme Court in 1944.[79] The Court rejected the company's arguments out of hand, holding that congressional concerns about consumer fraud were sufficient to sustain the statute even if the product were assumed to be completely wholesome and nutritionally equivalent to milk. In a companion case, *Sage Stores*

---

[73]Carolene Products Co. v. Evaporated Milk Association, 93 F.2d 202 (7th Cir. 1938).

[74]Carolene Products Co. v. Harter, 329 Pa. 49, 197 A.627 (1938); Poole & C. Market Co. v. Breshears, 343 Mo. 1133, 125 S.W.2d 23 (1938) (prosecution of retailer for distributing Carolene).

[75]304 U.S. 144 (1938).

[76]See Carolene Products Co. v. Hanrahan, 291 Ky. 417, 164 S.W. 2d 597, 699 (Ky. 1942).

[77]*Ibid.*

[78]Carolene Products Co. v. Mohler, 152 Kan. 2, 102 P.2d 1044 (1940); State v. Sage Stores Co., 157 Kan. 622, 143 P.2d 652 (1943), aff'd, 323 U.S. 32 (1944) (proceeding against retailer for distributing Carolene).

[79]Carolene Products Co. v. United States, 323 U.S. 18 (1944).

v. Kansas,[80] the Court sustained the Kansas filled milk statute as applied to the new product.

By the end of 1944 Carolene Products appeared to have run out of options. The Supreme Court had made it abundantly clear that it was not about to overturn filled milk statutes no matter what proof the company might offer. Filled milk had been banned in more than thirty states and heavily regulated in others. Carolene was relegated to a marginal legal existence, able to survive by serving a few intrastate markets but without serious prospects for expansion. At this point the record falls almost silent on the fate of an organization known as the Carolene Products Corporation.

The controversy over butterfat substitutes, however, continued to simmer on the back burner of constitutional law. After the Second World War, markets, politics, and technology combined to create a more favorable environment for filled dairy products. The technology of taste neutralization advanced to the point where soybean, peanut, and cottonseed oils could be used in substitute milk products. This development, coupled with the imposition of tariff duties on copra and coconut oils incident to Philippine independence, meant that filled milks would be formulated from domestic oils if the product were legalized. Meanwhile the relative importance of canned milk ebbed as improvements in transportation, refrigeration, and pasteurization made fresh milk available nationwide. Increasing knowledge of nutrition established that fortified filled milk contained the same vitamins as canned whole milk; and scientific awareness of linkages between food cholesterol and heart disease impeached the healthfulness of butterfat. Consumer groups appeared and began to press for elimination of legal restrictions on margarine. With the repeal of the federal tax on colored margarine in 1950 the argument for prohibiting filled milk appeared increasingly preposterous. Meanwhile diversified food products companies began to experiment with new forms of imitation dairy products that promised big profits if the legal barriers against filled milk could be surmounted.

Filled milk litigation surfaced again in 1959, with a decision by the Arizona Supreme Court invalidating a prohibitory statute as

---

[80]323 U.S. 32 (1944).

applied to imitation ice cream made with vegetable oil.[81] The Massachusetts Supreme Judicial Court held in 1965 that its food and drug statute could not constitutionally prohibit the sale of a frozen non-dairy creamer.[82] The Colorado Supreme Court followed suit in 1971 by invalidating a filled milk statute as applied to sour cream substitutes made with vegetable oil.[83] Although the trend toward striking down filled milk statutes was not unwavering,[84] it was unmistakable. Moreover, the paucity of decisions almost certainly indicates that state statutes had fallen into desuetude. Some states repealed their statutes.[85]

The federal statute remained. By the 1950s, however, it was evident that the federal government had lost all enthusiasm for prosecuting violations. The Agriculture Department determined that many new filled dairy products were not made "in imitation or semblance of milk," hence not within the statute.[86] Interpretation had its limits, however. No amount of bureaucratic legerdemain could twist the statute so as not to apply to its original intended victim, evaporated skimmed milk with vegetable oil. At some point the issue that had apparently been conclusively settled in the *Carolene Products* cases was bound to arise again.

It did so in 1972 in a suit brought by the Milnot Company, a manufacturer of filled milk. A federal district court struck the statute down as a violation of substantive due process, thus overruling the Supreme Court's decisions in *Carolene Products*.[87] The statute was arbitrary and capricious, according to the court, because prod-

---

[81]State v. A.J. Bayless Markets, Inc., 86 Ariz. 193, 342 P.2d 1088 (1959) (state and federal Due Process Clauses). Three years earlier the New York Court of Appeals had struck down a statute prohibiting the sale of evaporated or condensed skimmed milk in containers of less than ten pounds. Defiance Milk Products Co. v. Du Mond, 309 N.Y. 537, 132 N.E.2d 829 (1956).

[82]Coffee-Rich, Inc. v. Commissioner of Public Health, 348 Mass. 414, 204 N.E.2d 281 (1965) (state constitution).

[83]People ex rel. Orcutt v. Instantwhip Denver, Inc., 176 Colo. 396, 490 P.2d 940 (1971) (en banc) (state constitution).

[84]A fresh filled milk product called "Farmer's Daughter" fell victim to several state statutes. See Reesman v. State, 74 Wash. 2d 646, 445 P.2d 1004 (1968)(en banc); Martin v. Wholesome Dairy, Inc., 437 S.W.2d 586 (Tex. Civ. App. 1969).

[85]See Milnot Co. v. Richardson, 350 F.Supp. 221, 224 n.1 (S.D. Ill. 1972).

[86]See *id*. at 224.

[87]*Ibid*. A district court obviously cannot "overrule" a Supreme Court opinion in the technical sense. The term "overrule," however, accurately describes the practical consequences of the *Milnot* decision, at least within the Southern District of Illinois.

ucts virtually identical to Milnot were circulating in interstate commerce free of statutory infirmity. Moreover, the market conditions and dangers of confusion that led to the passage and judicial upholding of the statute "have long since ceased."[88] Accordingly, Milnot had the right to market its product in interstate and foreign commerce free from federal interference under the Filled Milk Act.[89]

The *Milnot* decision has once again re-opened the channels of national commerce to trade in filled milk. Today, as noted, filled milk can be found on the canned milk shelves of any supermarket. Borden's "Eagle," meanwhile, is often ignominiously relegated to the bakery department, it having been recognized that a product comprised 42 percent of sugar is not a particularly appropriate beverage, especially for infants. And in one sense filled milk has gained the sweetest revenge of all: concerns about dietary cholesterol have made filled milk appear the more healthful product, since the vegetable oils (principally soybean oil) now contained in filled milk are cholesterol free, a virtue notoriously lacking in butterfat.

A final footnote is in order. The Milnot Company, which managed to overturn the Supreme Court's opinions in *Carolene Products*, was not always known by that title. Years ago it had a different, more familiar name—the Carolene Products Corporation.[90]

II. Constitutionality of the Federal Statute

The campaign against filled milk was grounded on three arguments: (1) filled milk is a threat to the public health because it does not contain the vitamins that exist in butterfat; (2) filled milk is a threat to the public welfare because it can be confused with evaporated milk; (3) filled milk is a threat to the public interest because it undermines the dairy industry, an essential national institution.[91] The first two arguments were designed to bring the

---

[88]*Ibid.*

[89]In 1983 a federal district court held the Kansas filled milk statute unconstitutional under the federal Due Process and Equal Protection Clauses, overruling the Supreme Court's decision in *Sage Stores*. General Foods Corp. v. Priddle, 569 F.Supp. 1378 (D.Kan. 1983).

[90]See Milnot v. Richardson, 350 F.Supp. at 222.

[91]See Filled Milk Legislation, The Milk Dealer, Oct. 1921, at 68; Brief on Voigt Bill, New York Produce Review and American Creamery, July 5, 1922, at 575; Oiled Milk is a Blow to Dairying, The Milk Dealer, August, 1922, at 72; About Filled Milk, The Milk Dealer, January, 1923, at 219; Filled Milk Catechism, The Milk Dealer, April, 1922, at 28; Why Filled Milk Should be Taxed, The Milk Dealer, Oct., 1921, at 93.

proposed statute within the police power. They were credulously accepted by the Supreme Court in *Carolene Products*. Yet even on the legislative record compiled in 1923 they were a tissue of insubstantial rationalizations covering the real motivation of the statute, namely, the desire to suppress trade in one article of commerce in order to eliminate competition with another.

A. VITAMINS

The dairy industry's campaign against filled milk was based on one indisputable proposition: butterfat was a rich source of vitamin A while coconut oil was almost devoid of the vitamin. This proposition did not, however, justify legislative prohibition of filled milk.

The history of vitamin research demonstrates that subtle but significant positive effects can often accompany the unambiguously wealth-reducing consequences of economic regulation. In the early years of the struggle against margarine the dairy industry had high hopes that butter's superiority could be demonstrated by chemical analysis. To the industry's chagrin, however, the two substances proved chemically indistinguishable. By the turn of the century the industry had given up on chemists and begun to focus on dietary studies. At the Wisconsin Agricultural Experiment Station a young research scientist, E. V. McCollum, began giving simplified diets to animals.[92] By 1913 McCollum and a colleague had demonstrated that young rats on restricted diets would grow when butterfat was added but did not grow when olive oil or lard was added. They interpreted these results to mean that butterfat contained a previously unrecognized dietary essential.[93] This mysterious substance, verified by Osborne and Mendel the same year,[94] was quickly iden-

---

[92]McCollum's mentor was S. A. Babcock, the titan of dairy scientists, whose butterfat test revolutionized the industry in the late nineteenth century. McCollum, The Newer Knowledge of Nutrition 6 (2d ed. 1922).

[93]McCollum & Davis, The Necessity of Certain Lipids in the Diet During Growth, 15 J. Bio. Chem. 167 (1913). McCollum's work was presaged in Hopkins, Feeding Experiments Ilustrating the Importance of Accessory Factors in Normal Dietaries, 44 J. Physiology 485 (1912).

[94]Osborne & Mendel, The Influence of Butter Fat on Growth, 16 J. Bio. Chem. 423 (1913).

tified as one of the "vitamines" postulated by an earlier researcher, C. Funk, as necessary to prevent certain dietary deficiency diseases.[95]

McCollum's work, needless to say, was music to the dairy industry's ears, for it confirmed the dogma of butter's superiority to margarine.[96] The industry was even more delighted when McCollum became a charismatic milk apostle, proclaiming the gospel "a quart a day" as the key to the kingdom of health.[97] The industry considered him its "best friend . . . in the world."[98]

The case against filled milk had the appearance of scientific rigor. McCollum, a researcher of undoubted stature, was ready at a moment's notice to testify to the many virtues of milk and to inadequacies of vegetable oils. He came equipped with gruesome photographs of young animals fed on vegetable oil, showing them to be scraggly, undernourished, and afflicted by eye disorders.[99] Young animals fed on butterfat, on the other hand, were shown with glossy coats, bright eyes, and healthy constitutions.

In spite of appearances, the case for prohibiting filled milk was utterly unproved. Filled milk was undoubtedly a wholesome food. No one would be harmed by drinking it. The entire argument against the product was based on the proposition that it would somehow crowd out consumption of other foods necessary to a well-balanced diet.

In the case of adult nutrition, this argument was patently preposterous. McCollum's studies had failed to document adverse consequences for adult animals fed on butterfat-poor diets. Although adults needed some vitamin A, the amount was obviously not large.

---

[95]Funk & Cooper, Experiments on the Causation of Beri-Beri, 11 Lancet 1266 (1911). See generally Pike & Brown, Nutrition: An Integrated Approach (3d ed. 1984) 11–13; McCollum, A History of Nutrition (1957).

[96]See Is Oleomargarine Healthful?, Hoard's Dairyman, April 2, 1915, at 396 ("The oleomargarine manufacturer and his chemist can no longer tell us that 'fat is fat.' We know differently and know that oleomargarine cannot ever be properly called a substitute for butter."); Nutritious Oleo (?), Hoard's Dairyman, May 21, 1915, at 648; Butter and Cottonseed Oil, Hoard's Dairyman, March 15, 1918, at 333; The Truth Goes Marching On, Hoard's Dairyman, June 7, 1918, at 848; Concerning Butterfat Substitutes, Jersey Bulletin and Dairy World, March 6, 1918, at 343; Some Butter History, Jersey Bulletin and Dairy World, Dec. 14, 1918, at 2056.

[97]E.g., House Hearings at 26; Senate Hearings at 21.

[98]The Milk Dealer, Sept., 1921, at 2.

[99]See House Hearings at 21–23; Senate Hearings at 23–24.

McCollum's own research had suggested that skimmed milk, the principal ingredient in filled milk, contained some vitamin A.[100] Moreover, the proposition that filled milk in an adult diet would crowd out other sources of vitamin A was absurd. The American diet was rich in many foods containing vitamin A, including butterfat products (whole milk, cheese, and butter), fish, eggs, greens, and yellow vegetables.[101] There was no evidence that any adult would ever drink so much filled milk as to cause vitamin A deficiency. The argument for banning filled milk, in the case of adults, was no more substantial than that for banning the use of rice or flour because these substances were deficient in vitamin A.

If the argument had any merit, it was in the case of infant nutrition. Everyone agreed that infants needed a certain amount of vitamin A for growth. Although occasional or even frequent use of filled milk in infant diet was harmless, it was possible that if filled milk were used as formula and fed to infants exclusively of other foods for an extended period, the babies would experience the sort of vitamin A deficiency McCollum had induced in baby rats. But there was no evidence in the legislative record that filled milk was fed to children at all, much less on an exclusive basis. The labels clearly warned against use as an infant food,[102] a statement that was probably unnecessary because mothers were not inclined to give filled milk to their babies in any event. Most filled milk consumers were working-class and immigrant families in which the mothers breast-fed their babies.[103] Even mothers who did not breast feed were unlikely to use filled milk as infant formula. The proponents of the bill commissioned the Visiting Nurses' Associations of several large cities to survey homes they visited in order to document instances of filled milk being fed to babies. Of 1,000 homes surveyed in Philadelphia and 1,500 surveyed in Milwaukee not a single instance was discovered of filled milk being fed to babies.[104] Inquiries of nineteen child care field nurses from the Boston Health De-

---

[100]See House Hearings at 54.

[101]See *ibid*; McCollum, The Newer Knowledge of Nutrition 123–56 (2d ed. 1922).

[102]House Hearings at 58; State v. Emery, 178 Wisc. 147, 189 N.W. 564, 566 (1922).

[103]House Hearings at 84.

[104]*Id*. at 103–04.

partment were equally unavailing.[105] No instance of filled milk being fed to babies was documented in the entire legislative record.

The fact was that filled milk undoubtedly improved the national health. Its lower price increased consumption of skimmed milk and vegetable fats, both wholesome and nutritious foods. And to the extent that it displaced other dairy products, the result was far from undesirable. The sugar content of condensed milk (including Borden's "Eagle") was high enough to raise questions about its desirability as a baby food.[106] Fresh whole milk was often positively dangerous. Milk was known to transmit typhoid fever, diphtheria, diarrhea, septic sore throat, and scarlet fever.[107] It was suspected in the transmission of poliomyelitis.[108] Most tragically, it was a leading cause of tuberculosis, a disease that carried away thousands of adults and tens of thousands of children annually.[109] These dangers were largely absent in the case of filled milk, which was manufactured in modern plants under hygenic conditions and sterilized at high temperature.

In the words of Lafayette Mendel, co-discoverer of vitamins with McCollum:[110]

> The opponents of "filled" milks (representing a special industry) have tried to exclude them on the plea of "menace to public health". No public health question is involved. The claim is a specious one. The House bill represents a fight between industrial "interests," and I am confident that the medical profession would not admit that any wholesome food is a menace. Life and health are not endangered: on the contrary, . . . our national nutrition would be benefited if, instead of discarding the milk separated from cream in the butter industry—instead of converting a unique food into roof paint, etc.—we encouraged

---

[105]*Id.* at 104.

[106]See Senate Hearings at 106. Eagle's label, unlike the labels of filled milks, expressly encouraged its use as baby food.

[107]Haslam, Recent Advances in Preventive Medicine 142 (1930).

[108]*Ibid.*

[109]See *id.* at 166–71. Dairy farmers contributed to the spread of the disease by resisting efforts to cull their herds or to pasteurize milk. *E.g.*, Some Problems in Our Milk Supply, Jersey Bulletin and Dairy World, June 24, 1914, at 950; Tuberculosis Must be Eradicated, Jersey Bulletin and Dairy World, May 14, 1919, at 858; Bovine Tuberculosis—Pasteurization, Jersey Bulletin and Dairy World, May 21, 1913, at 809.

[110]House Hearings at 54.

the greater use of the nonfat part of the milk in the preparation
of food. . . . Are you ready to sanction economic waste of food
by a new form of prohibition on the invalid plea of harmfulness
to children, who do not make use of the product?

The scientific case against filled milk, in short, was entirely bogus
from the start.

B. FRAUD

Whatever the merits of the vitamin argument, it is clear that these
contentions had no force as against filled milks to which vitamins
had been added. The second *Carolene Products* case presented that
fact situation. The filled milk in that case had been fortified with
cod liver oil, a rich source of vitamins A and D. Although the new
ingredient could not have enhanced the taste of the product, it did
supply at least as many vitamins as were in evaporated whole milk.
Accordingly, the second *Carolene Products* case isolated the fraud
argument for separate analysis and consideration.

This argument was even more whimsical than the health contentions. To begin with, there was a certain irony in the idea that
consumers would object to a product indistinguishable from evaporated whole milk in every practical way including vitamin content.
Ironies aside, it was evident that filled milk simply did not present
any dangers of fraud, or even serious dangers of confusion. It was
sold in cans clearly marked with proprietary brand names and
unequivocally stating that the products were not milk. The ingredients were listed for anyone to read. The product was in full
compliance with the labeling requirements of the federal food and
drug act and with virtually all state legislation. Filled milk producers
were willing to accept any further labeling requirements that Congress might impose.[111]

The forces pressing for prohibition fell back on the contention
that labeling would be ineffective at preventing confusion or fraud
in the case of non-English speaking consumers. Yet they failed to
produce a single documented instance of fraud or confusion. Those
who knew this market best testified that immigrants were more,
not less, aware of the food content of their diet because they needed
to stretch a dollar.[112] It was evident, moreover, that the confusion

[111]*Id.* at 70.

[112]*Id.* at 72.

argument would apply to all sorts of products in addition to filled milk, including, notoriously, evaporated skimmed milk, which contained the word "milk" in its label and was marketed by all the major producers, including Borden and Nestle, but which was not prohibited by the proposed statute.

As with the health argument, the argument from consumer welfare cut in exactly the wrong direction. The interests of consumers would have been much better served by permitting and encouraging trade in filled milk than by outlawing a healthful, nutritious, and low-cost item of food.

C. THE "NATIONAL INTEREST"

The final argument for the statute was the contention that filled milk posed a threat to the dairy industry, a vital institution essential to the national welfare. At bottom the argument was a thinly disguised expression of self-interest. So interpreted, it was no doubt valid: filled milk did threaten the dairy industry. Yet the argument at least purported to consider the broader public interest as well.

One oft-repeated assertion was that dairying preserved the "fertility of American soil."[113] The connection between dairying and the fertility of the soil was never spelled out, but it was obvious to anyone who had ever walked across a cow pasture. So understood, the argument is easily seen to be made of the same substance that gave such fertility to the soil. While the by-product of the dairy cow was undoubtedly good fertilizer, it was no better, and considerably less convenient, than other commercially available fertilizers. There was no evidence that the fertility of the soil would suffer a whit by a marginal decrease in the number of dairy cows due to competition from the "coconut cow" of the South Seas.

The "national interest" argument also incorporated disquieting ideas about the alleged superiority of milk-consuming cultures. McCollum, who was an odd blend of hard scientist, dairy huckster, and muddleheaded racist, epitomized these attitudes. His grand scheme divided humanity into milk-drinking and vegetable-eating peoples. With breathtaking disregard of history he asserted that milk drinkers had always enjoyed cultural and physical superiority over their leaf-chewing cousins. Not a single plant-eating culture,

---

[113]*E.g.*, *id.* at 32–33.

he claimed, "has ever come to the front in a matter of human achievement in any field of activity."[114] Take the Japanese. "These people . . . are the subjects or vassals; they are the peoples who multiply in considerable numbers, but whose life is short, who are inefficient, of low mentality, warped by peculiar religious prejudices which ruined them . . . They are a failure from the standpoint of living a normal human life." Milk-drinking peoples, on the other hand, "become large, strong, vigorous people, who . . . have the best trades in the world, who have an appreciation for art and literature and music, who are progressive in science and in every activity of the human intellect."[115] Unpleasant as it may now seem, this racial stereotype had considerable currency in the dairy districts of the country and in the Congress.[116] Farmers of the "coconut cow" were portrayed as lazy, ignorant, dark-skinned natives who had nothing to do all day but run up a tree and shake down a few nuts. A milk industry cartoon showed Congress, as a large white American, booting filled milk, personified as a small dark-skinned savage, back to the South Sea islands from which he came, while an American dairy cow watched with evident satisfaction.[117]

Aside from its crass appeal to self-interest, the various appeals to the "national interest" had even less to recommend them than the vitamin or fraud contentions. The arguments in support of the statute, in short, were entirely implausible under any reasonable view of the evidence.

III. THE STATUTE AS AN INTEREST GROUP MEASURE

The history recounted above suggests several thoughts about the dynamics of American politics as expressed in the filled milk controversy. The analysis is based on the interest group theory of regulation developed by (among others) Stigler,[118] Peltzman,[119] Pos-

---

[114]McCollum, Milk, The Necessity of Life, Jersey Bulletin and Dairy World, June 19, 1918, at 973.

[115]*Ibid.*

[116]*E.g.*, 62 Cong. Rec. 7583 (remarks of Rep. Voigt: "[T]he superiority of the white race is due at least to some extent to the fact that it is a milk-consuming race. Natives of tropical countries who use the products of the coconut are stunted in body and mind.").

[117]The Milk Dealer, May, 1922.

[118]Stigler, The Theory of Economic Regulation, 2 Bell J. Econ. & Man. Sci. 3 (1971).

[119]Peltzman, Toward a More General Theory of Regulation, 19 J. Law & Econ. 211 (1976); Peltzman, Constituent Interest and Congressional Voting, 27 J. Law & Econ. 181 (1984).

ner,[120] and Becker.[121] The familiar claim of this theory is that regulations are principally determined by the influence of political pressure groups rather than by ideology or rational debate. As currently constructed, the theory posits the existence of a political equilibrium in which interest groups "maximize their incomes by spending their optimal amount on political pressure, given the productivity of their expenditures and the behavior of other groups."[122] The theory recognizes that the outcome of the political struggle is rarely an absolute victory or defeat for any group, but rather reflects a balancing of interests in which each of the affected groups exerts equal pressure at the margin.

The battle over filled milk seems well-described by interest group theory. The most plausible inference is that the statute was enacted at the behest of a coalition of groups intent on advancing their own economic welfare at the expense of less powerful groups. An impressionistic view of the events surrounding the statute's enactment supports this inference: the sponsors were from big dairy states, while the chief opponents were from cotton states.

To test this hypothesis, I performed an OLS regression of the form:

$V = A + aM + bC + cH + u$, where
$V =$ House vote, a dummy variable equaling 1 if the vote was for the bill and 0 if the vote was against
$A =$ the constant term
$M =$ gallons of milk produced in the state divided by population of the state[123]
$C =$ acres planted in cotton in the state divided by population of the state[124]
$H =$ population of congressman's home town[125]
$u =$ residual error

For a response, see Goldberg, Peltzman on Regulation and Politics, 39 Public Choice 291 (1982).

[120]Posner, Theories of Economic Regulation, 5 Bell J. Econ. & Man. Sci. 335 (1974).

[121]Becker, A Theory of Competition among Pressure Groups for Political Influence, 98 Q. J. Econ. 371 (1983); Becker, Public Policies, Pressure Groups, and Dead Weight Costs, 28 J. Pol. Econ. 329 (1985).

[122]Becker, 98 Q. J. Econ., at 372.

[123]Sources: U.S. Census of Agriculture 1925 at 28–39; U.S. Census, 1920.

[124]Sources: U.S. Census of Agriculture 1925, at 38–47; U.S. Census 1920.

[125]Sources: Congressional Directory 1923; U.S. Census 1920.

The regression equation (*t*-statistics in parentheses) was:

$$V = .828 + .000825M - .000101C + .0000H$$
$$(23.32)\ (3.04) \qquad\qquad (-4.52)\ (.73)$$
$$R^2 = .126, \qquad\qquad N = 290$$

In this equation the effect of milk and cotton production is significant at well above the 99 percent confidence level, a strong result for voting studies of this type. The results suggest that a member was much more likely to vote for the bill if dairying was a major factor in the state's economy, and much more likely to vote against the bill if cotton was an important crop in the state.

The filled milk controversy also substantiates the proposition of interest group theory that regulations will be determined by an equilibrium of political forces. It is noteworthy that many of the arguments advanced against filled milk applied with even greater force to margarine. Margarine, like filled milk, lacked vitamin A, while butter was exceedingly rich in the substance. Margarine formed a much greater part of the American diet than did filled milk. And the "dangers" of consumer confusion and fraud were equally great in the case of margarine. Although federal law at the time effectively required that margarine be colored white,[126] there was plentiful evidence that margarine was being illegally colored and sold in yellow form.[127] Yet the dairy industry did not attempt to prohibit margarine.

The natural explanation is that the equilibrium of political forces was different for margarine than for filled milk. Most importantly, the beef and hog industries, including meat packers, western cattle ranchers, and midwestern hog farmers, would have vigorously contested any attempt to outlaw margarine, since animal fats were still among its principal ingredients. In addition, margarine had a much better base of public support, having been a staple in many family diets for nearly a half-century. Although disorganized masses of consumers are not usually viewed as exercising significant influence in interest group theory, the possibility that they will become organized probably should be included as one of the factors that

---

[126]The statute allowed the sale of yellow margarine, but imposed a prohibitive tax of 10 cents per pound.

[127]*E.g.*, Oleo Dealers Sentenced, Jersey Bulletin and Dairy World, Oct. 27, 1915, at 1525.

influence political outcomes, just as potential competition exercises a restraining influence on anticompetitive behavior in classical economic markets. In the case of margarine, there is little doubt that an attempt to prohibit the substance would have aroused popular resentment and might well have stimulated the creation of consumer groups. Because margarine supporters were stronger politically than filled milk supporters, margarine was allowed to exist, albeit subject to legal discrimination, while interstate commerce in filled milk was prohibited altogether at the federal level.

The filled milk controversy suggests some possible extensions of interest group analysis. First, the basic structural elements of the American constitutional system—federalism and separation of powers—mediated the process of interest group rivalry in quite different ways. A repeated phenomenon of dairy industry politics is that the interest groups would go first to the states before attempting federal legislation. This pattern held true in the case of filled milk, where the interest groups obtained discriminatory legislation in a number of states before presenting their case to Congress. The states acted as "laboratories," not in Brandeis's sense of experimental arenas for socially beneficial legislation,[128] but in the sense that they provided an ideal testing ground for special interest measures. State legislation gave the dairy industry an opportunity to develop its case against filled milk, to assess the feasibility, enforceability, and constitutionality of different legislative approaches, and to organize coalitions at the state level before attempting to develop a national campaign.

Although the existence of overlapping state and federal sovereigns provided opportunities for the dairy industry, it also posed problems. Under the limited interpretation of the Commerce Clause then in effect, Congress was powerless to prohibit the manufacture or intrastate sale of the substance. And the dairy industry was never able to obtain prohibitory legislation in all states. Thus federalism prevented the industry from achieving its goal of an absolute ban on filled milk. Filled milk continued to be produced and sold in states that had not banned the product. In a unitary system the dairy industry might have administered the coup de grace.[129]

---

[128]New State Ice Co. v. Liebmann, 285 U.S. 262, 310–11 (1932) (Brandeis, J., dissenting).

[129]The advantages to interest groups of obtaining overlapping state and federal legislation are significantly greater today under the Court's expansive interpretation of the Commerce Clause, although care must be taken to avoid loss of the overlap through federal preemption.

Separation of powers also played a powerful mediating role in the politics of filled milk. It was not enough for the dairy industry to obtain legislation; the legislation had to be enforced by the executive branches of the state or federal governments and upheld by the judicial branches. Although the campaign against filled milk was more successful in this regard than the industry's battles against margarine, it nevertheless ran into difficulties outside the legislative arenas. After a period of relatively vigorous enforcement the executive branches of the state and federal governments grew lax about prosecuting violations of the filled milk statutes. The Department of Agriculture eviscerated the federal statute through interpretation, and it is likely that state attorneys general were similarly disinclined to enforce their statutes. The judicial branches also proved nettlesome, at least at the state level where a substantial number of filled milk statutes were struck down. At the federal level, the *Carolene Products* cases suggested that the judiciary would no longer block economic regulation. That prophecy has apparently been disproved in the case of filled milk, but it remains generally true for economic legislation. There is, however, the possibility that the Court may someday tighten up its scrutiny in economic matters.[130]

On the other hand, separation of powers was not necessarily an unambiguous evil for the dairy industry. The system of divided powers allowed it to go first to the branch of government where it had the most influence—the legislature, where the votes of 5 million dairy farmers spoke loudly indeed. The industry was able to obtain some relief, even if the legislation was progressively weakened as it passed through the executive and judicial levels of the enforcement process. Moreover, it is not always the case that special interests will receive their most favorable reception in the legislature. Many groups find executive agencies to be the preferred forum from which to obtain protection. Others go first to the courts. In a unitary system, interest groups might have less, not more ability to obtain favorable action because they would have to present their petitions to the government as a whole.

Another noteworthy feature of filled milk legislation is that it was passed during a severe economic downturn. There was no

---

[130]For calls for a return to strict scrutiny of the *Lochner* variety, see Epstein, Takings: Private Property and the Power of Eminent Domain (1985); Siegen, Economic Liberties and the Constitution (1980). The Court would not have to go nearly as far as these authors recommend in order to strike down statutes like the Filled Milk Act.

significant effort to stamp out filled milk between 1917 and 1920, when production of the substance increased at an explosive rate. The battle over filled milk occurred between 1920 and 1923, years when filled milk production actually began to decrease. The likely cause of the increased political activity is the agricultural depression during those years.[131] The same pattern can be seen in the case of margarine, in which the dairy industry's major campaigns coincided with periods of low butter prices and low margarine production. The increased incidence of interest group activity may be due to the fact that there is no need to fear entry in times of depression when firms are leaving the industry. Gains from interest group activity will not be eroded by new entry in bad times as they will in good.[132] The heightened level of interest group activity may also be partially explained by the hypothesis that people will pay more to avoid losing an entitlement than they will pay to obtain one.

A final observation is that the dairy industry's campaign against filled milk may actually have benefited Carolene Products, the one surviving producer. In driving other firms from the business, these statutes eliminated competition for the firm that remained. Further, they probably created barriers to entry by making it impossible for a filled milk producer to survive unless it could assure retailers of protection in the event of prosecution. In addition, free rider effects in the disfavored industry were reduced or eliminated as firms were driven out. It is no accident that the initial challenges to filled milk legislation were all brought by the Carnation Company, which as the dominant firm had the most to gain from expenditures on litigation and lobbying. When Carnation abdicated as a result of the federal statute, the cause was taken up by Carolene Products, which was willing to litigate case after case because as the only remaining producer it could capture all the benefits of its litigation expenditures (in the short run). Thus, while the filled milk statutes increased Carolene Products' costs and limited its markets, they also eliminated its competition.

---

[131]This period was one of vigorous interest-group activity throughout the agricultural sector. The Farm Bloc was established within Congress as a de facto voting trust on agricultural issues in 1921, see McCune, The Farm Bloc (1943); and the Capper-Volstead Act (exempting agricultural cooperatives from the antitrust laws) was enacted in 1922, Act. of Feb. 18, 1922, 42 Stat. 388, codified at 7 U.S.C. § §291–92 (1983).

[132]This interesting thesis is suggested in Haddock, Basing Point Pricing: Competitive v. Collusive Theories, 72 Am. Econ. Rev. 289, 300–301 (1982).

These observations appear as if they may capture some general characteristics of American politics: (l) the contours of regulation reflect an equilibrium of political forces; (2) federalism and separation of powers mediate the expression of interest group forces in important ways; (3) pressure by industrial interests to obtain protection from competition is likely to be more intense in bad times than in good; and (4) protective measures may actually confer a benefit on those firms that are able to remain in the disfavored market. It is, however, dangerous to speculate beyond the evidence, and this study has examined only a narrow controversy within a single industry. Further study would be necessary in order to assess whether these hypotheses hold in other industrial and political contexts as well.

IV. CONCLUSION

In the *Carolene Products* footnote, Justice Stone suggested that special protections were needed for "discrete and insular minorities" because such groups would not be adequately served by the political process.[133] The statement, if meant as a general observation about American politics, is obviously misplaced. Public choice theory demonstrates that, in general, "discrete and insular minorities" are exactly the groups that are likely to obtain disproportionately large benefits from the political process.

The insights of public choice theory are amply demonstrated by the battle over filled milk, where one discrete minority—the nation's dairy farmers and their allies—obtained legislation harmful to consumers and the public at large. To be sure, the legislation discriminated against another discrete minority—the filled milk industry—but this fact simply reflects the complexity of the dairy industry. Filled milk producers, if they had not been trumped by a politically more powerful group, might themselves have been able to obtain special legislative favors to the detriment of the public interest.

The political theory underlying the *Carolene Products* footnote, now a half-century old, needs to be updated. The results of that process may call in question the Supreme Court's policy of blind deference to legislation favoring special industrial interests. Is it time to re-examine the wisdom of "see-no-evil, hear-no-evil" as the prevailing philosophy in economic regulation cases?

---

[133]United States v. Carolene Products Co., 304 U.S. at 152 n.4.